Hydroponic Food Production

*A Definitive Guidebook
Of Soilless Food Growing Methods*

By Howard M. Resh, Ph.D.

Formerly, Department of Plant Science
University of British Columbia, Vancouver
International Horticultural Consultant
President, International Aquaponics, Inc.*

*For the Professional and Commercial Grower
And the Advanced Home Hydroponics Gardener*

Published by

Woodbridge Press Publishing Company
Santa Barbara, California 93160

*See Next Page

*Spanish and Japanese
editions are available.*

1991

Fourth Edition

Published by

Woodbridge Press Publishing Company
Post Office Box 6189
Santa Barbara, California 93160

Copyright © 1989, 1987, 1985, 1981, 1978 by Howard M. Resh

Distributed simultaneously in the United States and Canada

Printed in the United States of America

Library of Congress Cataloging-in-Publication Data

Resh, Howard M.
  Hydroponic food production.

  "For the professional and commercial grower and the advanced home hydroponics gardener."
  Bibliography: p.
  Includes index.
  1. Hydroponics. 2. Food crops. I. Title.
SB126.5.R47 1988   635'.0485   88-33748
ISBN 0-88007-171-0

*International Aquaponics, Inc., are greenhouse and hydroponics specialists and may be contacted at 819-20th Avenue, Vancouver, B.C., Canada V5Z 1Y3, (604) 874-2605 or (604) 764-7756.

ACKNOWLEDGMENTS

This book, like all scientific books, is based on information acquired from many sources. Books, scientific journals and government extension bulletins have all contributed. Recognition of such sources is given in the references following each chapter and in the general bibliography.

In addition to these sources, personal experience and communication with other scientists over the past ten years have greatly added to the information presented. As a member of the International Society for Soilless Culture (ISOSC), I was fortunate to attend their 1976 congress in Las Palmas. This enabled me to renew friendships and make new acquaintances with many other members having significant contributions to present in the field of hydroponics. This experience gave me additional impetus to complete and update my book.

I wish to thank all of these members of the ISOSC and particularly the following people who provided me with photographs and additional information that was included in this writing: Bob Adamson; Michael Anselm of Soil-less Cultivation Systems Ltd; Carlos Arano; Andreas Bruppacher and Sheldon Pomer of Hydroculture Luwasa; Allen Cooper of The Glasshouse Crops Research Institute, Littlehampton, England; Mickey Fontes of the Environmental Research Laboratory, Tucson, Arizona; Herbert Corte; Franco Bernardi, Superior Farming Company; Ted Maas, O. Ruthner, E. Ruthner, P. A. Schippers, Michele Tropea, Alessandro Vincenzoni, and Bent Vestergaard.

Special thanks to Dr. Silvio Velandia of Hidroponias Venezolanas C.A. of Caracas, Venezuela, for the hospitality and inspiration given me during our association over the past years in developing his sand culture operation. He gave me the opportunity to gain experience in tropical hydroponics and encouraged me to write a section about it.

My sincere thanks to Arne McRadu for working patiently with me in doing the drawings which add greatly to the interest and understanding of the text.

My grateful thanks to all of these people and to my loving wife, Elvira, who has had the patience of waiting for me while I was writing, lecturing and traveling to numerous countries to acquire photographs and technical information on soilless culture.

In no way is the use of trade names intended to imply approval of any particular source or brand name over other similar ones not mentioned in this book.

The Author

CONTENTS

LIST OF TABLES

LIST OF FIGURES

Chapter 1

Introduction

1.1 The Past

Hydroponics, the growing of plants without soil, has developed from the findings of experiments carried out to determine what substances make plants grow and the composition of plants. Such work on plant constituents dates back as early as the 1600s. However, plants were being grown in a soilless culture far earlier than this. The hanging gardens of Babylon, the floating gardens of the Aztecs of Mexico and those of the Chinese are examples of "hydroponic" culture. Egyptian hieroglyphic records dating back to several hundred years B.C. describe the growing of plants in water.

Before the time of Aristotle, Theophrastus (372–287 B.C.) undertook various experiments in crop nutrition. Botanical studies by Dioscorides date back to the first century A.D.

The earliest recorded scientific approach to discover plant constituents was in 1600 when Belgian Jan van Helmont showed in his classical experiment that plants obtain substances from water. He planted a 5-pound willow shoot in a tube containing 200 pounds of dried soil that was covered to keep out dust. After 5 years of regular watering with rainwater he found the willow shoot increased in weight by 160 pounds, while the soil lost less than 2 ounces. His conclusion that plants obtain substances for growth from water was correct. However, he failed to realize that they also require carbon dioxide and oxygen from the air. In 1699, an Englishman, John Woodward, grew plants in water containing various types of soil, and found that the greatest growth occurred in water which contained the most soil. He thereby concluded that plant growth was a result of certain substances in the water, derived from soil, rather than simply from water itself.

21

Further progress in identifying these substances was slow until more sophisticated research techniques were developed and advances were made in the field of chemistry. In 1804, De Saussure proposed that plants are composed of chemical elements obtained from water, soil and air. This proposition was verified later by Boussingault (1851), a French chemist, in his experiments with plants grown in sand, quartz and charcoal to which were added solutions of known chemical composition. He concluded that water was essential for plant growth in providing hydrogen and that plant dry matter consisted of hydrogen plus carbon and oxygen which came from the air. He also stated that plants contain nitrogen and other mineral elements.

Various research workers had demonstrated by that time that plants could be grown in an inert medium moistened with a water solution containing minerals required by the plants. The next step was to eliminate the medium entirely and grow the plants in a water solution containing these minerals. This was accomplished by two German scientists, Sachs (1860) and Knop (1861). This was the origin of "nutriculture" and similar techniques are still used today in laboratory studies of plant physiology and plant nutrition. These early investigations in plant nutrition demonstrated that normal plant growth can be achieved by immersing the roots of a plant in a water solution containing salts of nitrogen (N), phosphorus (P), sulfur (S), potassium (K), calcium (Ca) and magnesium (Mg), which are now defined as the macroelements or macronutrients (elements required in relatively large amounts).

With further refinements in laboratory techniques and chemistry, scientists discovered seven elements required by plants in relatively small quantities—the microelements or trace elements. These include iron (Fe), chlorine (Cl), manganese (Mn), boron (B), zinc (Zn), copper (Cu) and molybdenum (Mo).

In following years, researchers developed many diverse basic formulas for the study of plant nutrition. Some of these workers were Tollens (1882), Tottingham (1914), Shive (1915), Hoagland (1919), Trelease (1933), Arnon (1938), and Robbins (1946). Many of their formulas are still used in laboratory research on plant nutrition and physiology.

Interest in practical application of this "nutriculture" did not develop until about 1925 when the greenhouse industry expressed interest in its use. Greenhouse soils had to be replaced frequently to overcome problems of soil structure, fertility and pests. As a result, research workers became aware of the potential use of nutriculture to replace conventional soil cultural methods. Between 1925 and 1935, extensive development took place in modifying the laboratory techniques of nutriculture to large-scale crop production.

In the early 1930s, W. F. Gericke of the University of California put laboratory experiments in plant nutrition on a commercial scale. In doing so he termed these nutriculture systems *hydroponics*. The word was derived from two Greek words *hydro* ("water") and *ponos* ("labor")—literally "water working."

Hydroponics can be defined as the science of growing plants without the use of soil, but by use of an inert medium, such as gravel, sand, peat, vermiculite, pumice or sawdust, to which is added a nutrient solution containing all the essential elements needed by the plant for its normal growth and development. Since many hydroponic methods employ some type of medium it is often termed "soilless culture," while water culture alone would be true hydroponics.

Gericke grew vegetables hydroponically, including root crops, such as beets, radishes, carrots and potatoes, and cereal crops, fruits, ornamentals and flowers. Using water culture in large tanks, he grew tomatoes to such heights that he had to harvest them with a ladder. The American press made many irrational claims, calling it the discovery of the century. After an unsettled period in which unscrupulous people tried to cash in on the idea by selling useless equipment, more practical research was done and hydroponics became established on a sound scientific basis in horticulture, with recognition of its two principal advantages, high crop yields and its special utility in nonarable regions of the world.

Gericke's application of hydroponics soon proved itself by providing food for troops stationed on nonarable islands in the Pacific in the early 1940s. In 1945 the U.S. Air Force solved its problem of providing its personnel with fresh vegetables by practicing hydroponics on a large scale on the rocky islands normally incapable of producing such crops.

After World War II the military command continued to use hydroponics. For example, the U.S. Army established a 22-hectare project at Chofu, Japan. The commercial use of hydroponics expanded throughout the world in the 1950s to such countries as Italy, Spain, France, England, Germany, Sweden, the USSR and Israel.

1.2 The Present

With the development of plastics, hydroponics took another large step forward. Plastics freed growers from the costly construction associated with the concrete beds and tanks previously used. Beds are scraped out of the underlying medium and simply lined with a heavy vinyl (20 mil), then filled with the growing medium. With the development of suitable pumps, time clocks, plastic plumbing, solenoid valves and other equipment, the entire hydroponic system can now be automated, reducing both capital and operational costs.

Hydroponics has become a reality for greenhouse growers in virtually all climate areas. Large hydroponic installations exist throughout the world for the growing of both flowers and vegetables. For example, large hydroponic greenhouse complexes are now in operation in Tucson, Arizona (11 acres); Phoenix, Arizona (about 15 acres); and Abu Dhabi (5 acres, presently expanding to 20 acres). In the Canary Islands, hundreds of acres of land are covered with polyethylene supported by posts to form a single continuous structure housing tomatoes grown hydroponically. The structure has open walls so that the prevailing wind blows through to cool the plants. The structure helps to reduce transpirational loss of water from the plants and to protect them from sudden rainstorms. Such structures can also be used in such areas as the Caribbean and Hawaii. Almost every state in the United States has a substantial hydroponic greenhouse industry. Canada also uses hydroponics extensively in the growing of greenhouse vegetable crops. About 90 percent of the greenhouse industry in British Columbia, Canada, uses sawdust culture to overcome soil structure and soil pest problems.

In arid regions of the world, such as Mexico and the Middle East, where the supply of fresh water is limited, hydroponic complexes combined with desalination units are being developed to use sea water as a source of fresh water. The complexes are located near the ocean and the plants are grown in the existing beach sand.

In the USSR large greenhouse, soilless farms exist at Moscow and Kiev, while in Armenia an Institute of Hydroponics has been established at Erevan in the Caucasus region. Other countries where hydroponics is used include Australia, New Zealand, South Africa, the Bahama Islands, Central and East Africa, Kuwait, Brazil, Poland, the Seychelles, Singapore, Malaysia and Iran.

1.3 The Future

Hydroponics is a very young science. It has been used on a commercial basis for only 40 years. However, even in this relatively short period of time it has been adapted to many situations, from outdoor field culture and indoor greenhouse culture to highly specialized culture in atomic submarines to grow fresh vegetables for crews. It is a space age science, but at the same time can be used in developing countries of the Third World to provide intensive food production in a limited area. Its only restraints are sources of fresh water and nutrients. In areas where fresh water is not available, hydroponics can use seawater through desalination. Therefore, it has potential application in providing food in areas having vast regions of nonarable land, such as deserts. Hydroponic complexes can be located along coastal regions in combination with petroleum-fueled or atomic desalination units, using the beach sand as the medium for growing the plants.

Hydroponics is a valuable means of growing fresh vegetables not only in countries having little arable land and in those which are very small in area yet have a large population. It could also be particularly useful in some smaller countries whose chief industry is tourism. In such countries tourist facilities, such as hotels, have often taken over most arable areas of the country, forcing local agriculture out of existence. Hydroponics could be used on the remaining nonarable land to provide sufficient fresh vegetables for the indigenous population as well as the tourists. Typical examples of such regions are the West Indies and Hawaii, which have a large tourist industry and very little farm land in vegetable production. To illustrate the potential use of hydroponics, tomatoes grown in this way could yield 150 tons per acre annually. A 10-acre site could produce 3 million pounds annually. In Canada the average per capita consumption of tomatoes is 20 pounds. Thus, with a population of 20 million, the total annual consumption of tomatoes is 400 million pounds· (200,000 tons). These tomatoes could be produced hydroponically on 1300 acres of land!

1.4 Suitable Site Characteristics

When considering a site location a grower should try to meet as many of the following requirements as possible to reduce any risks of failure:

1. Full, east, south and west exposure to sunlight with windbreak on north.

2. Level area or one that can be easily leveled.

3. Good internal drainage with minimum percolation rate of 1 inch per hour.

4. Have natural gas, three-phase electricity, telephone and good quality water capable of supplying at least one half gallon of water per plant per day.

5. On a good road close to a population center for wholesale market and retail market at greenhouses if you choose to sell retail.

6. Close to residence for ease of checking greenhouse during extremes of weather.

7. North-south oriented greenhouses with rows also north-south.

8. A region which has a maximum amount of sunlight.

9. Avoid areas having excessively strong winds.

1.5 Soil versus Soilless Culture

The large increases in yields under hydroponic culture over that of soil may be due to several factors. In some cases the soil may have been exceptionally poor; therefore soilless culture would be very beneficial. The presence of pests or diseases in the soils greatly reduces overall production. Under greenhouse conditions when environmental conditions other than the medium are similar for both soil and soilless culture, the increased production of tomatoes grown hydroponically is usually 20–25 percent. Such greenhouses practice soil sterilization and use heavy fertilizer applications; as a result, many of the problems encountered under field conditions in soil would be overcome. This would account for the smaller increases in yields using soilless culture under greenhouse conditions over the very striking 4 to 10 times increase in yields obtained by soilless culture outdoors over conventional soil-grown conditions.

The main disadvantages of hydroponics are the high initial capital cost, some diseases such as *Fusarium* and *Verticillium* which can spread rapidly through the system, and the encountering of complex nutritional problems. Most of these disadvantages can be overcome. Capital cost and complexity of operating the system can be reduced by use of new simplified hydroponic methods, such as the nutrient film technique. Many varieties resistant to the above diseases have been bred. Overall, the main

Table 1.1 Advantages of Soilless Culture versus Soil Culture

Cultural Practice	*Soil*	*Soilless*
1. Sterilization of growing medium	Steam, chemical fumigants; labor-intensive; time required is lengthy, minimum of 2–3 weeks	Steam, chemical fumigants with some systems; others can use simply bleach or HCl; short time needed to sterilize
2. Plant nutrition	Highly variable, localized deficiencies, often unavailable to plants due to poor soil structure or pH, unstable conditions, difficult to sample, test and adjust	Completely controlled, relatively stable, homogeneous to all plants, readily available in sufficient quantities, good control of pH, easily tested, sampled and adjusted
3. Plant spacing	Limited by soil nutrition and available light	Limited only by available light; therefore closer spacing is possible; increased number of plants per unit area, therefore more efficient use of space which results in greater yields per unit area
4. Weed control, cultivation	Weeds present, cultivate regularly	No weeds, no cultivation
5. Diseases and soil inhabitants	Many soil-borne diseases, nematodes, insects and animals which can attack crop, often use crop rotation to overcome buildup of infestation	No diseases, insects, animals in medium, no root diseases; no need for crop rotation
6. Water	Plants often subjected to water stress due to poor soil-water relations, soil structure and low water-holding capacity. Saline waters cannot be used. Inefficient use of water; much is lost as deep percolation past the plant root zone and also by evaporation from the soil surface.	No water stress. Complete automation by use of moisture-sensing devices and a feed-back control mechanism; reduces labor costs, can use relatively high saline waters, efficient water use, no loss of water to percolation beyond root zone or suface evaporation; if managed properly water loss should equal transpirational loss.

Cultural Practice	*Soil*	*Soilless*
7. Fruit quality	Often fruit is soft or puffy due to potassium and calcium deficiencies. This results in poor shelf life.	Fruit is firm with long shelf life. This enables growers to pick vine-ripened fruit and still be able to ship it relatively long distances. Also little, if any, spoilage occurs at the supermarket. Some tests have shown higher Vitamin A content in hydroponically grown tomatoes than those grown in soil.
8. Fertilizers	Broadcast large quantities over the soil, nonuniform distribution to plants, large amount leached past plant root zone (50-80%), inefficient use.	Use small quantities, uniformly distributed to all plants, no leaching beyond root zone, efficient use
9. Sanitation	Organic wastes used as fertilizers onto edible portions of plants causes many human diseases.	No biological agents added to nutrients; no human disease organisms present on plants
10. Trans- planting	Need to prepare soil, uproot plants which leads to transplanting shock. Difficult to control soil temperatures, disease organisms which may retard or kill transplants.	No preparation of medium required prior to transplanting; transplanting shock minimized, faster "take" and subsequent growth. Medium temperature can be maintained optimum by flooding with the nutrient solution. No diseases present
11. Plant maturity		With adequate light conditions, plant can mature faster under a soilless system than under soil.
12. Perma- nence of medium	Soil in a greenhouse must be changed regularly every several years since fertility and structure break down. Under field conditions must fallow	No need to change medium in gravel, sand or water cultures; no need to fallow. Sawdust, peat, vermiculite may last for several years between changes.
13. Yields	Greenhouse tomatoes 8-15 lb/yr/plt	18-20 lb/yr/plt

advantages of hydroponics over soil culture are more efficient nutrition regulation, availability in regions of the world having nonarable land, efficient use of water and fertilizers, ease and low cost of sterilization of the medium, and higher density planting, leading to increased yields per acre.

Table 1.2 Comparative Yields Per Acre in Soil and Soilless Culture

Crop	Soil	Soilless
Soya	600 lb	1550 lb
Beans	5 tons	21 tons
Peas	1 ton	9 tons
Wheat	600 lb	4100 lb
Rice	1000 lb	5000 lb
Oats	1000 lb	2500 lb
Beets	4 tons	12 tons
Potatoes	8 tons	70 tons
Cabbage	13,000 lb	18,000 lb
Lettuce	9000 lb	21,000 lb
Tomatoes	5-10 tons	60-300 tons
Cucumbers	7000 lb	28,000 lb

Chapter 2

Plant Nutrition

2.1 Plant Constituents

The composition of fresh plant matter includes about 80 to 95 percent water. The exact percentage of water will depend on the plant species and on the turgidity of the plant at the time of sampling, which will be a result of the time of day, the amount of available moisture in the soil, the temperature, wind velocity and other factors. Because of the variability in fresh weights chemical analyses of plant matter are usually based on the more stable dry matter. Fresh plant material is dried at 70°C. for 24 to 48 hours. The dry matter remaining will be roughly 10 to 20 percent of the initial fresh weight. Over 90 percent of the dry weight of most plant matter consists of the three elements, carbon (C), oxygen (O), and hydrogen (H). Water supplies hydrogen and oxygen, and oxygen also comes from carbon dioxide from the atmosphere, as does carbon.

If only 15 percent of the fresh weight of a plant is dry matter, and 90 percent of this is represented by carbon, oxygen, and hydrogen, then all the remaining elements in the plant account for roughly 1.5 percent of the fresh weight of the plant ($0.15 \times 0.10 = 0.015$).

2.2 Mineral and Essential Elements

While a total of 92 natural mineral elements are known, only 60 elements have been found in various plants. Although many of these elements are not considered essential for plant growth, plant roots probably absorb to some extent from the surrounding soil solution any element existing in a soluble form. However, plants do have some ability to select the rate at which they absorb various ions, so absorption is usually not in direct proportion to nutrient availability. Furthermore, different species vary in their ability to select particular ions.

An element must meet each of three criteria to be considered essential to plant growth (Arnon and Stout 1939; Arnon 1950; 1951). (1) The plant cannot complete its life cycle in the absence of the element. (2) Action of the element must be specific; no other element can wholly substitute for it. (3) The element must be directly involved in the nutrition of the plant, that is, be a constituent of an essential metabolite or, at least, required for the action of an essential enzyme and not simply causing some other element to be more readily available or antagonize a toxic effect of another element.

Only 16 elements are generally considered to be essential for growth of higher plants. They are arbitrarily divided into the macronutrients (macroelements), those required in relatively large quantities, and the micronutrients (trace or minor elements), those needed in considerably smaller quantities.

The macroelements include carbon (C), hydrogen (H), oxygen (O), nitrogen (N), phosphorus (P) potassium (K), calcium (Ca), sulfur (S) and magnesium (Mg). The microelements include iron (Fe), chlorine (Cl), manganese (Mn), boron (B), zinc (Zn), copper (Cu), and molybdenum (Mo). The relative concentrations of these elements found in most higher plants are given in table 2.1.

TABLE 2.1   Elements Essential for Most Higher Plants and Internal Concentrations Considered Adequate

Element	Symbol	Available Form	Atomic Weight	Concentration in Dry Tissue ppm	Concentration in Dry Tissue %	Relative No. of Atoms compared to Molybdenum
Hydrogen	H	H_2O	1.01	60,000	6	60,000,000
Carbon	C	CO_2	12.01	450,000	45	35,000,000
Oxygen	O	O_2, H_2O	16.00	450,000	45	30,000,000
Macronutrients						
Nitrogen	N	NO_3^-, NH_4^+	14.01	15,000	1.5	1,000,000
Potassium	K	K^+	39.10	10,000	1.0	250,000
Calcium	Ca	Ca^{++}	40.08	5,000	0.5	125,000
Magnesium	Mg	Mg^{++}	24.32	2,000	0.2	80,000
Phosphorus	P	$H_2PO_4^-, HPO_4=$	30.98	2,000	0.2	60,000
Sulfur	S	$SO_4 =$	32.07	1,000	0.1	30,000
Micronutrients						
Chlorine	Cl	Cl^-	35.46	100	0.01	3,000
Boron	B	$BO_3\equiv, B_4O_7^-$	10.82	20	0.002	2,000
Iron	Fe	Fe^{+++}, Fe^{++}	55.85	100	0.01	2,000
Manganese	Mn	Mn^{++}	54.94	50	0.005	1,000
Zinc	Zn	Zn^{++}	65.38	20	0.002	300
Copper	Cu	Cu^{++}, Cu^+	63.54	6	0.0006	100
Molybdenum	Mo	$MoO_4 =$	95.95	0.1	0.00001	1

Source: Salisbury, F. B., and C. Ross. 1969. *Plant Physiology*. Belmont, Calif.: Wadsworth, p. 194.

Although most higher plants require only those 16 essential elements, certain species may need others. They may, at least, accumulate these other elements even if they are not essential to their normal growth. Silicon, aluminum, cobalt, vanadium and selenium are a few of these elements absorbed by plants and used in their growth.

The roles of the essential elements are summarized in table 2.2. All of them play some role in the manufacture and breakdown of various metabolites required for plant growth. Many are found in enzymes and coenzymes which regulate the rate of biochemical reactions. Others are important in energy-carrying compounds and food storage.

TABLE 2.2   Functions of the Essential Elements within the Plant

1. *Nitrogen*

Part of a large number of necessary organic compounds, including amino acids, proteins, coenzymes, nucleic acids and chlorophyll

2. *Phosphorus*

Part of many important organic compounds including sugar phosphates, ATP, nucleic acids, phospholipids and certain coenzymes

3. *Potassium*

Acts as a coenzyme or activator for many enzymes (e.g., pyruvate kinase). Protein synthesis requires high potassium levels. Potassium does not form a stable structural part of any molecules inside plant cells.

4. *Sulfur*

Incorporated into several organic compounds including amino acids and proteins. Coenzyme A and the vitamins thiamine and biotin contain sulfur.

5. *Magnesium*

An essential part of the chlorophyll molecule and required for activation of many enzymes including steps involving ATP bond breakage. Essential to maintain ribosome structure

6. *Calcium*

Often precipitates as crystals of calcium oxalate in vacuoles. Found in cell walls as calcium pectate which cements together primary walls of adjacent cells. Required to maintain membrane integrity and is part of the enzyme α-amylase. Sometimes interferes with the ability of magnesium to activate enzymes

7. *Iron*

Required for chlorophyll synthesis and is an essential part of the cytochromes which act as electron carriers in photosynthesis and respiration. Is an essential part of ferredoxin and possibly nitrate reductase. Activates certain other enzymes

8. *Chlorine*

Required for photosynthesis where it acts as an enzyme activator during the production of oxygen from water. Additional functions are suggested by effects of deficiency on roots.

9. *Manganese*

Activates one or more enzymes in fatty acid synthesis, the enzymes responsible for DNA and RNA formation, and the enzyme isocitrate dehydrogenease in the Krebs cycle. Participates directly in the photosynthetic production of O_2 from H_2O and may be involved in chlorophyll formation

10. *Boron*

Role in plants not well understood. May be required for carbohydrate transport in the phloem

11. *Zinc*

Required for the formation of the hormone indoleacetic acid. Activates the enzymes alcohol dehydrogenase, lactic acid dehydrogenase, glutamic acid dehydrogenase and carboxypeptidase

12. *Copper*

Acts as an electron carrier and as part of certain enzymes. Part of plastocyanin which is involved in photosynthesis, and also of polyphenol oxidase and possible nitrate reductase. May be involved in N_2 fixation

13. *Molybdenum*

Acts as an electron carrier in conversion of nitrate to ammonium and is also essential for N_2 fixation

14. *Carbon*

Constituent of all organic compounds found in plants

15. *Hydrogen*

Constituent of all organic compounds of which carbon is a constituent. Important in cation exchange in plant-soil relations

16. *Oxygen*

Constituent of many organic compounds in plants. Only a few organic compounds, such as carotene, do not contain oxygen. Also involved in anion exchange between roots and the external medium. It is a terminal acceptor of H^+ in aerobic respiration.

2.3 Plant Mineral and Water Uptake

Plants normally obtain their water and mineral needs from the soil. In a soilless medium the plants must still be provided with water and minerals. Therefore, in order to understand the plant relations in a hydroponic system we must understand the soil-plant relations under which they normally grow.

2.3.1 The Soil

Soil provides four needs to the plant: (1) a supply of water, (2) a supply of essential nutrients, (3) a supply of oxygen and (4) support for the plant root system. Mineral soils consist of four major components: mineral elements, organic matter, water and air. For example, a volume composition of a representative silt loam soil in optimum condition for plant growth may consist of: 25 percent water space, 25 percent air space, 45 percent mineral matter and 5 percent organic matter. The mineral (inorganic) matter is made up of small rock fragments and of minerals of various kinds. The organic matter represents an accumulation of partially decayed plant and animal residues. The soil organic matter consists of two general groups: (1) original tissue and its partially decomposed equivalents; and (2) humus. The original tissue includes undecomposed plant and animal matter which is subject to attack by soil organisms, both plant and animal, which use it as a source of energy and as tissue-building material. Humus is the more resistant product of decomposition, both that synthesized by the microorganism and that modified from the original plant tissue.

The soil water is held within the soil pores and together with its dissolved salts makes up the soil solution which is so important as a medium for supplying nutrients to growing plants. The soil air located in the soil pores has a higher carbon dioxide and lower oxygen content than that found in the atmosphere. The soil air is important in providing oxygen and carbon dioxide to all the soil organisms and to plant roots.

The ability of the soil to provide adequate nutrition to the plant depends on four factors: (1) the amounts of the various essential elements present in the soil; (2) their forms of combination; (3) the processes by which these elements become available to plants; and (4) the soil solution and its pH. The amounts of the various elements present in the soil will depend on the nature of the soil and on its organic matter content since it is a source of several nutrient elements. Soil nutrients exist both as complex, insoluble compounds and as simple forms usually soluble in soil water and readily available to plants. The complex forms must be broken down through decomposition to the simpler and more available forms in order to benefit the plant. These available forms are summarized in table 2.1. The reaction of the soil solution (*p*H) will

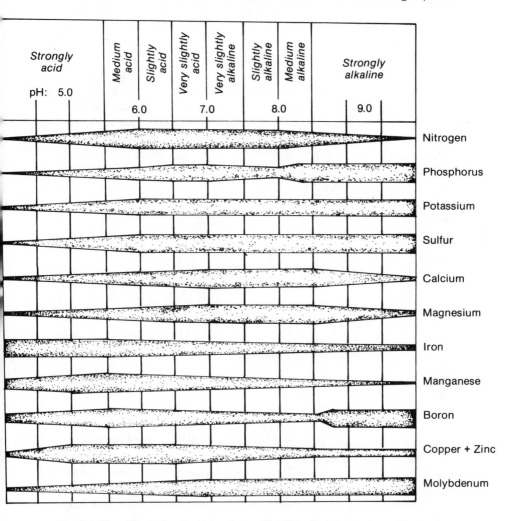

Fig. 2.1. The effect of soil *p*H on the availability of plant nutrients (From *Hunger Signs in Crops,* edited by H.B. Sprague, 1964, p.18.)

determine the availability of the various elements to the plant. The *p*H value is a measure of acidity or alkalinity. A soil is acid if the *p*H is less than 7, neutral if at 7 and alkaline if the *p*H is above 7. Most plants prefer a *p*H level between 6.0 and 7.0 for optimum nutrient uptake. The effect of *p*H on availability of essential elements is shown in figure 2.1. Iron, manganese, and zinc become less available as the *p*H is raised from 6.5 to 7.5 or 8.0. Molybdenum and phosphorus availability, on the other hand, is affected in the opposite way, being greater at the higher *p*H levels. At very high *p*H values the bicarbonate ion ($HCO_3\ -$) may be present in sufficient quantities to interfere with the normal uptake of other ions and thus is detrimental to optimum growth.

When inorganic salts are placed in a dilute solution they dissociate into electrically charged units called ions. These ions are available to the plant from the surface of the soil colloids and from salts in the soil solution. The positively charged ions (*cations*) such as potassium (K^+) and calcium (Ca^{++}) are mostly absorbed by the soil colloids, whereas the negatively charged ions (*anions,*) such as chloride (Cl^-) and sulfate ($SO_4\ ^=$) are found in the soil solution.

2.3.2 Soil and Plant Interrelations

Plant rootlets and root hairs are in very intimate contact with the soil colloidal surfaces. Nutrient uptake by the plants' roots takes place at the surface of the soil colloids and through the soil solution proper, as shown in figure 2.2. Ions are interchanged between the soil colloids and the soil solution. Movement of ions takes place between the plant root surfaces and soil colloids and between the plant root surfaces and soil solution in both directions.

2.3.3 Cation Exchange

The soil solution is the most important source of nutrients for absorption by plant roots. Since it is very dilute, as plants deplete the nutrients from the soil solution they must be replenished from the soil particles. The solid phase of the soil releases mineral elements into the soil solution partly by solubilization of soil minerals and organic matter, partly by solution of soluble salts,

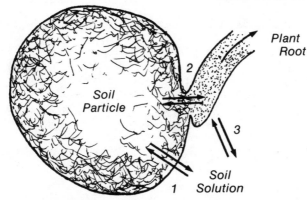

Fig. 2.2. The movement of nutrients between plant roots and soil particles. (1) Interchange between soil particles and the soil solution. (2) Movement of ions from the soil colloids (particles) to the plant root surface and vice versa. (3) Interchange between the soil solution and the absorbing surface of plant root systems. (Adapted from Buckman and Brady, *The Nature and Properties of Soils.*)

and partly by cation exchange. The negatively charged clay particles and solid organic matter of the soil hold cations, such as calcium (Ca^{++}), magnesium (Mg^{++}), potassium (K^+), sodium (Na^+) aluminium (Al^{+++}), and hydrogen ions (H^+). Anions, such as nitrate (NO_3^-), phosphate ($HPO_4^=$), sulfate ($SO_4^=$), chloride (Cl^-) and others are found almost exclusively in the soil solution. Cations are also found in the soil solution and their ability to exchange freely with cations adsorbed on the soil colloids enable cation exchange to take place.

2.3.4 Soil versus Hydroponics

There is no physiological difference between plants grown hydroponically and those grown in soil. In soil both the organic and inorganic components must be decomposed into inorganic elements, such as calcium, magnesium, nitrogen, potassium, phosphorus, iron and others before they are available to the plant (fig. 2.3). These elements adhere to the soil particles and are exchanged into the soil solution where they are absorbed by the plants. In hydroponics the plant roots are moistened with a nutrient solution containing the elements. The subsequent processes of mineral uptake by the plant are the same, as detailed in 2.3.5 and 2.3.6.

2.3.5 Transfer of Water and Solutes from Soil (or Nutrient Solution) to Root

The question of organic versus inorganic gardening can be clarified by a discussion of mineral uptake by the plant.

In 1932, E. Münch of Germany introduced the apoplast-symplast concept to describe water and mineral uptake by plants. He

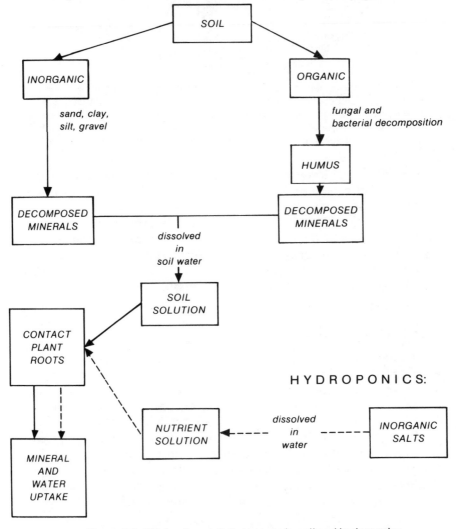

Figure 2.3. Origin of essential elements in soil and hydroponics.

suggested that water and mineral ions move into the plant root via the interconnecting cell walls and intercellular spaces, including the xylem elements, which he called the *apoplast,* or via the system of interconnected protoplasm (excluding the vacuoles) which he termed the *symplast*. However, whatever the movement may be, its uptake is regulated by the endodermal layer of cells around the stele which constitutes a barrier to free movement of water and solutes through the cell walls. There is a waxy strip, the Casparian strip, around each endodermal cell which isolates the inner portion of the root (stele) from the outer epidermal and cortex regions in which water and mineral movement is relatively free.

If the root is in contact with a soil (nutrient) solution, ions will diffuse into the root via the apoplast across the epidermis, through

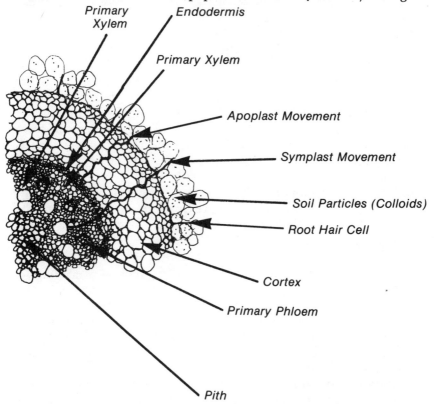

Fig. 2.4. A cross section of a root with movement of water and minerals from the soil (nutrient) solution into the plant vascular system.

the cortex and up to the endodermal layer. Some ions will pass from the apoplast into the symplast by an active respiration-requiring process. Since the symplast is continuous across the endodermal layer, ions can move freely into the pericycle and other living cells within the stele (fig. 2.4).

2.3.6 Movement of Water and Minerals Across Membranes

If a substance is moving across a cell membrane, the number of particles moving per unit of time through a given area of the membrane is termed the *flux*. The flux is equal to the permeability of the membrane multiplied by the driving force causing diffusion. The driving force is due to the difference in concentration (the chemical potential) of that ion on the two sides of the membrane. If the chemical potential of the solute is higher outside the membrane than inside, the transport inward is passive. That is, energy is not expended by the plant to take up the ion. If, however, a cell accumulates ions against a chemical potential gradient, it must provide energy sufficient to overcome the difference in chemical potential. Transport against a gradient is active since the cells must actively metabolize in order to carry out the solute uptake.

When ions are transported across membranes, the driving force is composed of both a chemical and electrical potential difference. That is, an electrochemical potential gradient exists across the membrane. The electrical potential difference arises from cations diffusing across more rapidly than their corresponding anions of a salt. Thus, the inside will become positive with respect to the outside. Whether the transport of an ion is active or passive depends upon the contribution of both the electrical potential difference and the chemical potential difference. Sometimes these two factors will act in the same direction, while in other cases they act oppositely. For example, a cation might have a higher concentration inside the cell and yet be transported inward passively with no energy expenditure on the part of the cell if the electrical potential is sufficiently negative. On the other hand, anion absorption against both a chemical potential gradient and a negative electrical potential would always be an active process.

There are a number of theories proposed to explain how respiration and active absorption are coupled, but most of them employ the mechanism of a carrier. For example, when an ion contacts the outside of a membrane of a cell, neutralization may occur as the ion is attached to some molecular entity that is a part of the membrane. The ion attached to this carrier might then diffuse readily across the membrane, being released on the opposite side. The attachment may require the expenditure of metabolic energy and can occur on only one side of the membrane, while release can occur only on the other side of the membrane. The ions separate and move into the cell and the carrier becomes available to move more ions (fig. 2.5). Selectivity in ion accumulation could be controlled by differences in ability of carriers to form specific combinations with various ions. For example, potassium absorption is inhibited competitively by rubidium, indicating that the two ions use the same carrier or the same site on the carrier.

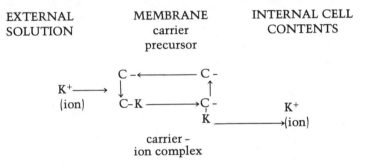

EXTERNAL SOLUTION   MEMBRANE carrier precursor   INTERNAL CELL CONTENTS

carrier – ion complex

Fig. 2.5. Movement of ions across cell membranes by a carrier. (Adapted from Salisbury, F.B. and C. Ross, 1969. *Plant Physiology*. Belmont, Calif.: Wadsworth, p. 158.)

As previously indicated, the foregoing explanation of mineral uptake by plant roots has been presented in an effort to clarify the question of organic versus inorganic gardening. The existence of specific relationships between ions and their carriers which enables their transport across cell membranes to enter the cell demonstrates that mineral uptake functions in the same manner whether the source of such minerals is from organic matter or fertilizers. Large organic compounds making up soil humus are not absorbed by the plant, but must first undergo decomposition into the basic inorganic elements. They can be accumulated by their contact with plant cell membranes only in their ionic form. Thus, organic gardening cannot provide any compounds to the plant which could not exist in a hydroponic system. The function of organic matter in soil is to supply inorganic elements for the plant and at the same time maintain the structure of the soil in optimum condition so that these minerals will be available to the plant.

Thus, the indiscriminate application of large amounts of fertilizers
to soil without addition of organic matter results in a breakdown of
the soil structure and subsequently makes the abundant supply of
minerals unavailable to the plant. This is not the fault of the
fertilizer but the misuse of it in soil management.

2.4 The Upward Movement of Water and Nutrients

Water with its dissolved minerals moves primarily upward in
the plant through xylem tissue. The xylem, composed of several
cell types, forms a conduit system within the plant. This vascular
tissue is commonly termed *veins*. The veins are actually composed
of xylem and phloem tissue. The phloem tissue is the main conduit
of manufactured food. The actual phloem translocation of photosynthates is still not fully understood. In general, water and minerals move upward in the xylem to the sites of photosynthesis, and
photosynthates move from this source of manufacture to other
parts of the plant.

The ascent of sap within a plant was suggested by Dixon (1914)
and Renner (1911) in their cohesion hypothesis. They claimed that
the force sucking up water and nutrients from the soil into the
plant root comes from water evaporation from cell walls in the
leaves. The binding force is in the inherent tensile strength of
water, a property arising from cohesion of the water molecules (the
forces of attraction between water molecules). This cohesion of
water in the xylem is due to the capillary dimensions of the xylem
elements. The water uptake from the soil comes from the negative
water potential which is transferred down the plant to the root
cells and soil by the upward driving force of evaporation.

The leaves of plants have a waxy cuticle cover on the outside
surface to prevent excessive water loss by evaporation (fig. 2.6).
Small pores (*stomates*) in the epidermis, particularly numerous in
the lower epidermis, regulate the passage of carbon dioxide and
oxygen in and out of the leaf. Water vapor also moves through these
openings. Therefore, water loss is regulated largely by the stomates. Water moves from the xylem vessels in the veins to the leaf
mesophyll cells, evaporates and diffuses through the stomates into
the atmosphere. This water lost in evapotranspiration must be
replaced by water entering the plant roots or water stress will
result, which, if continued, will lead to death of the plant. In the
process of water uptake minerals are transported to chlorophyll-
containing cells (palisade parenchyma, spongy mesophyll and

bundle sheath cells, if present), where they are used in the man-ufacture of foods through the process of photosynthesis.

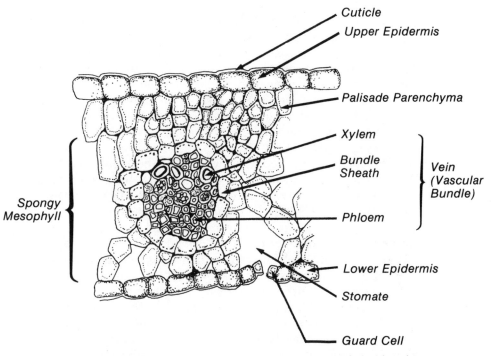

Fig. 2.6. A cross section of a typical broad-leaved plant leaf showing the pathway of water movement.

2.5 Plant Nutrition

As mentioned in chapter 1, hydroponics developed through studies of plant constituents, which led to the discovery of plant essential elements. Plant nutrition is therefore the basis of hydroponics. Anyone intending to employ hydroponic techniques must have a thorough knowledge of plant nutrition. The management of plant nutrition through management of the nutrient solution is the key to successful hydroponic growing.

The absorption and transport of plant nutrients within the plant has already been discussed. The next question is how to maintain the plant in optimum nutrient status. Hydroponics enables us to do this, but it also presents the risk of error which could result in rapid starvation or other adverse effects on the plant. A diagnostic program to determine the nutritional level of the plant at any time is extremely important to avoid nutritional stresses which limit plant growth.

The ideal method of diagnosing the nutritional status of plants is to take tissue analyses of plant leaves periodically (once or twice a week) and, in conjunction with these tests, nutrient solution analyses. The level of each essential element in the plant tissue and nutrient solution must be determined and correlated so that, if needed, adjustments can be made in the nutrient solution to avoid potential nutritional problems. Of course, such a program is costly in time and labor and is not always economically feasible. To do such tests requires a proper laboratory fully equipped with a muffle furnace, atomic absorption analyzer, glassware and other materials. The cost of such a laboratory would have been about $30,000 in 1977. Therefore, it could only be justified by a very large greenhouse complex having a minimum area of 4-5 acres. Often these analyses can be done by commercial laboratories on a contract basis, but sometimes results are slow and crop damage may occur before recommendations are received.

The alternative to such laboratory analyses is visual diagnosis of nutrient stress symptoms expressed by the plant. However, it must be emphasized that once the plant shows symptoms it has already undergone severe nutritional stress and will take some time to regain its health after remedial steps have been taken. Therefore, it is important to correctly identify the nutrient problem immediately in order to prevent the plant from losing vigor.

2.5.1 Nutritional Disorders

A nutritional disorder is a malfunction in the physiology of a plant resulting in abnormal growth caused by either a deficiency or excess of a mineral element(s). The disorder is expressed by the plant externally and/or internally in the form of symptoms. Diagnosis of a nutritional disorder involves accurate description and identification of the disorder. A deficiency or excess of each essential element causes distinct plant symptoms which can be used to identify the disorder.

Elements are grouped basically into those which are mobile and those which are immobile with some having gradations of mobility. Mobile elements are those which can be retranslocated. They will move from their original site of deposition (older leaves) to the actively growing region of the plant (younger leaves) when a deficiency occurs. As a result, the first symptoms will appear on the older leaves on the lower portion of the plant. The mobile elements are magnesium, phosphorus, potassium, zinc and nitrogen. When a shortage of the immobile elements occurs, they are not retranslocated to the growing region of the plant, but remain in the older leaves where they were originally deposited. Deficiency symptoms, therefore, first appear on the upper young leaves of the plant. The immobile elements include calcium, iron, sulfur, boron, copper, and manganese.

It is important to detect nutritional disorders early, since as they increase in severity the symptoms spread rapidly over the entire plant, resulting in the death of much of the plant tissue. Then symptom characteristics become very general, such as chlorosis (yellowing) and necrosis (browning) of the plant tissue. In addition, disorders of one element often upset the plant's ability to accumulate other elements, and shortly two or more essential elements are simultaneously deficient or in excess. This is particularly true of nutrient deficiencies. When two or more elements are deficient simultaneously, the composite picture or syndrome expressed by the symptoms may resemble no given deficiency. Under such conditions it is generally impossible to determine visually which elements are responsible for the symptoms.

Often a deficiency of one element leads to antagonism toward the uptake of another element. For instance, boron deficiency can also cause calcium deficiency. Calcium deficiency may lead to potassium deficiency and vice versa. The need for accurate and fast identification of a symptom expression cannot be overemphasized. It is often beneficial to grow an indicator plant along with the regular crop. The susceptibility of different plant species to various nutritional disorders varies greatly. For example, if a crop of tomatoes is being grown, plant a few cucumbers, lettuce or even a weed or two if it is known to be very sensitive to nutritional disorders. Cucumbers are very sensitive to boron and calcium deficiency. If such a deficiency occurs the cucumbers will express symptoms from several days to a week before they appear on the tomatoes. Such early warning enables the grower to adjust his nutrient solution to prevent a deficiency in the tomato crop. In addition, weaker plants of the same species will show symptoms prior to the more vigorous ones. Every possible tactic must be employed to avoid a nutritional disorder in the main crop, since once symptoms are expressed in the crop, some reduction in yield is inevitable.

Once a nutritional disorder has been identified, steps to remedy it can be taken. In a hydroponic system the first step is to change the nutrient solution. This should be done as soon as a nutritional disorder is suspected even before identifying it. If the disorder has been diagnosed as a deficiency a foliar spray can be applied for a rapid response. However, care must be taken not to use a concentration high enough to burn the plants. It is best to try the recommended foliar spray on a few plants and then observe the results for several days before treating the whole crop. The nutrient formulation probably will have to be adjusted (see chapter 3) to overcome the disorder. If a nutrient deficiency is present, the level of the deficient nutrient should be increased to an above-normal level (up to 25 to 30 percent). As the plants come out of the deficiency the increase in the identified nutrient could be lowered to about 10 to 15 percent above the level at which the deficiency occurred. Depending upon the severity of disorder, weather conditions and the element itself, the plant may take 7 to 10 days before response toward the control measure is evident.

If a toxicity has occurred, the soilless medium will have to be flushed with water alone to reduce residual levels in the medium. Flushing may have to be done over a period of a week or so depending again on the severity of the disorder. However, nutrient deficiencies are far more common than toxicities in hydroponics. For this reason, nutrient deficiencies will be emphasized in the following discussion on symptomatology.

2.5.2 Symptomatology

One of the first steps in identifying a nutritional disorder is to describe the symptoms in distinct, accurate terms. Table 2.3 summarizes terms commonly used in symptomatology. When observing a disorder determine what plant part or organ is affected. Does it occur on the lower older leaves or the younger upper leaves? Are the symptoms on the stem, fruit, flowers, and/or growing point of the plant? What is the appearance of the whole plant? Is it dwarfed, deformed, or branched excessively? What is the nature of the ailment? Is the tissue chlorotic (yellow), necrotic (brown) or deformed? Then describe the color pattern and location of this chlorosis, necrosis or deformation using the terms given in table 2.3.

TABLE 2.3   Terminology used in the Description of Symptoms on Plants

Term/Description

Localized: Symptoms limited to one area of plant or leaf

Generalized: Symptoms not limited to one area but spread generally over entire plant or leaf

Drying (firing): Necrosis—scorched, dry, papery appearance

Marginal: Chlorosis or necrosis—on margins of leaves initially; usually spreads inward as symptom progresses

Interveinal chlorosis: Chlorosis (yellowing) between veins of leaves only

Mottling: Irregular spotted surface—blotchy pattern of indistinct light and dark areas; often associated with virus diseases

Spots: Discolored area with distinct boundaries adjacent to normal tissue

Color of leaf undersides: Often a particular coloration occurs mostly or entirely on the lower surface of the leaves, e.g., phosphorus deficiency—purple coloration of leaf undersides

Cupping: Leaf margins or tips may cup or bend upward or downward, e.g., copper deficiency—margins of leaves curl into a tube; potassium deficiency—margins of leaves curl inward

Checkered (reticulate): Pattern of small veins of leaves remaining green while interveinal tissue yellows—manganese deficiency

Brittle tissue: Leaves, petioles, stems may lack flexibility, break off easily when touched—calcium or boron deficiency

Soft tissue: Leaves very soft, easily damaged—nitrogen excess

Dieback: May be leaves or growing point that dies rapidly and dries out—boron or calcium deficiencies

Stunting: Plant shorter than normal

Spindly: Growth of stem and leaf petioles very thin and succulent

After the symptoms have been observed closely and described, it should be determined whether the disorder may be caused by something other than a nutritional imbalance. The following list of other possible disorders should be checked: insect damage; parasitic diseases; pesticide damage; pollution damage; water stress; light and temperature injury. Pesticide damage may cause burning if greater than recommended dosages are used on the plants. Also, the use of herbicides such as 2,4-D near a greenhouse may cause deformation of plant leaves closely resembling the symptoms of tobacco mosaic virus (TMV). Pollution damage may cause burning or bleaching of leaf tissue or a stippled effect (pinpoint-sized chlorotic spots) on leaves. Water stress, either lack of or excess of, will cause wilting (loss of turgidity) of leaves. Excessive sunlight or temperature may burn and dry leaf tissue, particularly on the margins.

TABLE 2.4   A Key to Mineral Deficiency Symptoms

Symptoms	*Element Deficient*

A. Older or lower leaves of plant mostly affected; effects localized or generalized.
  B. Effects mostly *generalized* over whole plant: more or less drying or firing of lower leaves.
    C. Plant *light* green; lower leaves yellow, drying to light brown color; stalks short and slender if element is deficient in later stages of growth .... Nitrogen
    CC. Plant *dark* green, often developing red and purple colors; lower leaves sometimes yellow, drying to greenish brown or black color; stalks short and slender if element is deficient in later stages of growth .... Phosphorus
  BB. Effects mostly *localized*; mottling or chlorosis with or without spots of dead tissue on lower leaves; little or no drying up of lower leaves.
    C. Mottled or chlorotic leaves, typically may redden, as with cotton; sometimes with dead spots; tips and margins turned or cupped upward; stalks slender .... Magnesium
    CC. Mottled or chlorotic leaves with large or small spots of dead tissue
      D. Spots of dead tissue small, usually at tips and between veins, more marked at margins of leaves: stalks slender .... Potassium
      DD. Spots generalized, rapidly enlarging, generally involving areas between veins and eventually involving secondary and even primary veins; leaves thick; stalks with shortened internodes .... Zinc
AA. Newer or bud leaves affected; symptoms localized.
  B. Terminal bud *dies*, following appearance of distortions at tips or bases of young leaves.
    C. Young leaves of terminal bud at first typically hooked, finally dying back at tips and margins, so that later growth is characterized by a cut-out appearance at these points; stalk finally dies at terminal bud. Calcium

CC. Young leaves of terminal bud becoming
light green at bases, with final breakdown
here; in later growth, leaves become twisted,
stalk finally dies back at terminal bud ....Boron
BB. Terminal bud commonly *remains alive*; wilting
or chlorosis of younger or bud leaves with or
without spots of dead tissue, veins light or dark
green.
C. Young leaves permanently *wilted* (wither-tip
effect) without spotting or marked chlorosis;
twig or stalk just below tip and seedhead often
unable to stand erect in later stages
when shortage is acute ....Copper
CC. Young leaves *not wilted*; chlorosis present
with or without spots of dead tissue scattered over the leaf.
D. *Spots of dead tissue* scattered over the
leaf; smallest veins tend to remain green,
producing a checkered or reticulating effect ....Manganese
DD. *Dead spots not commonly present*;
chlorosis may or may not involve veins,
making them light or dark green in color.
E. Young leaves with veins and tissue between veins *light green* in color ....Sulfur
EE. Young leaves chlorotic, principal veins
typically green; stalks short and slen-
der ....Iron

Source: McMurtrey. 1950. *Diagnostic Techniques for Soil and Crops*, American
Potash Institute.

Once the above factors have been checked and eliminated as
potential causes, a nutritional disorder would be suspected. In
general, in hydroponics, nutritional disorders will show up on all
plants at the same time, whereas many of the nonnutritional
disorders would begin on a few plants and progress to neighboring
ones. The next step is to identify the nutrient disorder(s) by the use
of a "key" (table 2.4). Deficiency and toxicity symptoms for all the
essential elements are given in table 2.5. These descriptions can be
used in conjunction with the key to assist in identification of the
nutrient disorder(s). These two tables describe symptoms which
could be expected generally on most plants. As discussed earlier,

different plant species will express various symptoms to a lesser or greater degree than others. Therefore, in addition to the general table (table 2.5) information is included on specific symptoms and remedies for tomatoes and cucumbers (table 2.6).

2.5.3 Use of a Key

The key presented here is a dichotomous table. A decision must be made at each alternative route and finally a single explanation is given at the end. The key to nutritional disorders is based on symptoms observed on the plant, hence the importance of accurate symptom description. The key (table 2.4) is for use in determining mineral deficiencies only, not toxicities.

The first decision to make is effects on older leaves (A) versus effects on younger upper leaves (AA). Once this choice is made a series of choices follows. The next step is (B) versus (BB) under the previous choice of (A) or (AA). Then, (C) versus (CC), (D) versus (DD) and so on. For example, use the key to find the following symptoms: The young (upper) leaves of a plant are chlorotic, the veins green and no dead spots are visible. The terminal bud is alive and not wilted. The older (lower) leaves show no symptoms. The terminal growing area is somewhat spindly and there is some abortion of flowers. Since the upper leaves are affected the first choice is (AA). The terminal bud is alive, therefore the next choice is (BB). The next decision is (C) versus (CC). Since chlorosis is present, but no wilting, the correct choice would be (CC). The alternative of (D) or (DD) can be made on the basis of the lack of dead spots. The proper choice is (DD). The choice between sulfur (E) versus iron (EE) is a little difficult. In the case of sulfur the interveinal tissue is a light green, not the bright yellow that appears with iron deficiency. The spindly stalks and flower abortion also indicate iron over sulfur deficiency. As a result, the final choice is iron deficiency.

Table 2.5 Deficiency and Toxicity Symptoms for the Essential Elements

1. *Nitrogen*

Deficiency Symptoms: Growth is restricted and plants are generally yellow (chlorotic) from lack of chlorophyll, especially older leaves. Younger leaves remain green longer. Stems, petioles and lower leaf surfaces of corn and tomato can turn purple.

Toxicity Symptoms: Plants usually dark green in color with abundant foliage but usually with a restricted root system. Potatoes form only small tubers and flowering and seed production can be retarded.

2. *Phosphorus*

Deficiency Symptoms: Plants are stunted and often a dark green color. Anthocyanin pigments may accumulate. Deficiency symptoms occur first in more mature leaves. Plant maturity often delayed

Toxicity Symptoms: No primary symptoms yet noted. Sometimes copper and zinc deficiency occurs in the presence of excess phosphorus.

3. *Potassium*

Deficiency Symptoms: Symptoms first visible on older leaves. In dicots, these leaves are initially chlorotic but soon scattered dark necrotic lesions (dead areas) develop. In many monocots, the tips and margins of the leaves die first. Potassium-deficient corn develops weak stalks and is easily lodged.

Toxicity Symptoms: Usually not excessively absorbed by plants. Oranges develop coarse fruit at high potassium levels. Excess potassium may lead to magnesium deficiency and possible manganese, zinc or iron deficiency.

4. *Sulfur*

Deficiency Symptoms: Not often encountered. Generally yellowing of leaves, usually first visible in younger leaves

Toxicity Symptoms: Reduction in growth and leaf size. Leaf symptoms often absent or poorly defined. Sometimes interveinal yellowing or leaf burning

5. *Magnesium*
Deficiency Symptoms: Interveinal chlorosis which first develops on the older leaves. The chlorosis may start at leaf margins or tip and progress inward interveinally.
Toxicity Symptoms: Very little information available on visual symptoms

6. *Calcium*
Deficiency Symptoms: Bud development is inhibited and root tips often die. Young leaves are affected before old leaves and become distorted and small with irregular margins and spotted or necrotic areas.
Toxicity Symptoms: No consistent visible symptoms. Usually associated with excess carbonate

7. *Iron*
Deficiency Symptoms: Pronounced interveinal chlorosis similar to that caused by magnesium deficiency but on the younger leaves.
Toxicity Symptoms: Not often evident in natural conditions. Has been observed after the application of sprays where it appears as necrotic spots

8. *Chlorine*
Deficiency Symptoms: Wilted leaves which then become chlorotic and necrotic, eventually attaining a bronze color. Roots become stunted and thickened near tips.
Toxicity Symptoms: Burning or firing of leaf tip or margins. Bronzing, yellowing and leaf abscission and sometimes chlorosis. Reduced leaf size and lower growth rate

9. *Manganese*
Deficiency Symptoms: Initial symptoms are often interveinal chlorosis on younger or older leaves depending on species. Necrotic lesions and leaf shedding can develop later. Disorganization of chloroplast lamellae
Toxicity Symptoms: Sometimes chlorosis, uneven chlorophyll distribution and iron deficiency (pineapple). Reduction in growth

10. *Boron*
Deficiency Symptoms: Symptoms vary with species. Stem and root apical meristems often die. Root tips often become swollen and discolored. Internal tissues sometimes disintegrate (or discolor) (e.g. "heart rot" of beets). Leaves show various symptoms including thickening, brittleness, curling, wilting and chlorotic spotting.
Toxicity Symptoms: Yellowing of leaf tip followed by progressive necrosis of the leaf beginning at tip or margins and proceeding toward midrib.

11. *Zinc*
Deficiency Symptoms: Reduction in internode length and leaf size. Leaf margins are often distorted or puckered. Sometimes interveinal chlorosis
Toxicity Symptoms: Excess zinc commonly produces iron chlorosis in plants.

12. *Copper*
Deficiency Symptoms: Natural deficiency is rare. Young leaves often become dark green and twisted or misshapen, often with necrotic spots.
Toxicity Symptoms: Reduced growth followed by symptoms of iron chlorosis, stunting, reduced branching, thickening and abnormal darkening of rootlets

13. *Molybdenum*
Deficiency Symptoms: Often interveinal chlorosis developing first on older or midstem leaves, then progressing to the youngest (similar to nitrogen deficiency). Sometimes marginal scorching or cupping of leaves
Toxicity Symptoms: Rarely observed. Tomato leaves turn golden yellow, cauliflower seedlings turn bright purple.

TABLE 2.6   Summary of Mineral Deficiencies in Tomatoes and Cucumbers and their Controls

Mobile elements (first symptoms on older leaves):

1. Nitrogen:

Tomatoes	*Cucumbers*
spindly plant	stunted growth
lower leaves—yellowish green	lower leaves—yellowish green
severe cases—entire plant pale green	severe cases—entire plant pale green
major veins—purple color	younger leaves stop growing
small fruit	fruit—short, thick, light green, spiny

Remedies:

1. Use a foliar spray of 0.25 to 0.5 percent solution of urea.
2. Add calcium nitrate or potassium nitrate to nutrient solution.

2. Phosphorus:

Tomatoes	*Cucumbers*
shoot growth restricted	stunted
thin stem	
severe cases—leaves small, stiff, curved downward	severe cases—young leaves small, stiff, dark green
leaf upper sides—bluish green	older leaves and
leaf undersides—including veins—purple	cotyledons—large water-soaked spots including both veins and interveinal areas
older leaves—yellow with scattered purple dry spots —premature leaf drop	affected leaves fade, spots turn brown and desiccate, shrivel— except for petiole

Remedies:

1. Add monopotassium phosphate to nutrient solution.

3. Potassium:

Tomatoes	*Cucumbers*
older leaves—leaflets scorched, curled margins, interveinal chlorosis, small dry spots	older leaves—discolored yellowish green at margins, later turn brown and dry
middle leaves—interveinal chlorosis with small dead spots	
plant growth—restricted, leaves remain small	plant growth—stunted, short internodes, small leaves
later stages—chlorosis and necrosis spreads over large area of leaves, also up plant, leaflets dieback	later stages—interveinal and marginal chlorosis extends to center of leaf, also progresses up plant, leaf margins desiccate, extensive necrosis, larger veins remain green
fruit—blotchy, uneven ripening, greenish areas	

Remedies:

1. Foliar spray of 2 percent potassium sulfate
2. Add potassium sulfate or if no sodium chloride present in water, can add potassium chloride to nutrient solution.

4. **Magnesium:**

Tomatoes

older leaves—marginal chlorosis progressing inwards as interveinal chlorosis, necrotic spots in chlorotic areas

small veins—not green

severe starvation—older leaves die, whole plant turns yellow, fruit production reduced

Cucumbers

older leaves—interveinal chlorosis from leaf margins inward—necrotic spots develop

small veins—not green

severe starvation—
symptoms progress from older to younger leaves, entire plant yellows, older leaves shrivel and die

Remedies:

1. Foliar spray—high-volume spray with 2 percent magnesium sulfate or low-volume spray with 10 percent magnesium sulfate
2. Add magnesium sulfate to nutrient solution.

5. **Zinc:**

Tomatoes

older leaves and terminal leaves—smaller than normal

little chlorosis, but irregular shriveled brown spots develop, especially on petiolules (small petioles of leaflets) and on and between veins of leaflets

petioles—curl downward, complete leaves coil up

severe starvation—rapid necrosis, entire foliage withers

Cucumbers

older leaves—interveinal mottling, symptoms progress from older to younger leaves, no necrosis

internodes—at top of plant stop growing, leading to upper leaves closely spaced, giving bushy appearance

Remedies:

1. Foliar spray with 0.1 to 0.5 percent solution of zinc sulfate
2. Add zinc sulfate to nutrient solution.

Immobile elements (first symptoms on younger leaves):

1. Calcium:

Tomatoes
upper leaves—marginal yellowing,
   undersides turn purple-brown
   color especially on margins,
   leaflets remain tiny, deformed,
   margins curl up

progression to later stages—leaf tips and
   margins wither, curled petioles die back
growing point dies
older leaves—finally, chlorosis and
   necrotic spots form
fruit—blossom-end rot
   (leather-like decay at blossom ends of
   fruit)

Cucumbers
upper leaves—white spots
   near edges and between veins,
   marginal interveinal chlorosis
   progresses inward
youngest leaves (growing point region)
   —remain small, edges deeply incised,
   curl upwards, later shrivel from
   edges inwards and growing point dies
growth—stunted, short internodes,
   especially near apex
buds—abort, finally plant dies
   back from apex
older leaves—curve downwards

Remedies:

1. Foliar spray in acute cases with 0.75 to 1.0 percent calcium nitrate solution.
Can also use 0.4 percent calcium chloride
2. Add calcium nitrate to nutrient solution, or calcium chloride if do not want to
increase nitrogen level, but be sure there is little, if any, sodium chloride in the
nutrient solution if calcium chloride is used.

2. Sulfur:

Tomatoes
upper leaves—stiff, curl downward,
   eventually large irregular necrotic spots
   appear, leaves become yellow
stem, veins, petioles—purple
older leaves, leaflets—necrosis
   at tips and margins, small purple spots
   between veins

Cucumbers
upper leaves—remain small, bend
   downwards, pale green to yellow,
   margins markedly serrate
plant growth—restricted
older leaves—very little
   yellowing

Remedies:

1. Add any sulfates to the nutrient solution. Potassium sulfate would be safest
since the plants require high levels of potassium.
Note: Sulfate deficiency rarely occurs since sufficient amounts are added by use
of potassium, magnesium and other sulfate salts in the normal nutrient formulation.

3. Iron:

Tomatoes
terminal leaves—chlorosis starts at
   margins and spreads through entire leaf,
   initially smallest veins remain green,
   giving reticulate pattern of green veins on
   yellow leaf tissues; leaf eventually turns
   completely pale yellow, no necrosis
progression—symptoms start from terminal
   leaves and work down to older leaves

Cucumbers
young leaves—fine pattern of
   green veins with yellow interveinal
   tissue, later chlorosis spreads to
   veins and entire leaves turn lemon-
   yellow; some necrosis may develop
   on margins of leaves
progression—from top downward

growth—stunted, spindly, leaves smaller
  than normal
flowers—abortion

growth—stunted, spindly

axillary shoots and fruits—also
  turn lemon-yellow

Remedies:

1. Foliar spray with 0.02 to 0.05 percent solution of iron chelate (Fe-EDTA) every
3 to 4 days
2. Add iron chelate to nutrient solution.

4. **Boron:**

Tomatoes

growing point—shoot growth restricted,
  leads to withering and dying of
  growing point
upper leaves—interveinal chlorosis,
  mottling of leaflets, remain small,
  curl inward, deformed, smallest leaflets
  turn brown and die

middle leaves—yellow-orange tints,
  veins yellow or purple
older leaves—yellowish-green
lateral shoots—growing points die
petioles—very brittle, break off easily,
  clogged vascular tissue

Cucumbers

apex—growing point plus youngest
  unexpanded leaves curl up and die

axillary shoots—wither and die

older leaves—cupped upward beginning along margins, stiff, interveinal
  mottling

shoot tip—stops growing, leads to
  stunting

Remedies:

1. Apply a foliar spray as soon as detected of 0.1 to 0.25 percent solution of borax.
2. Add borax to nutrient solution.

5. **Copper:**

Tomatoes

middle and younger leaves—margins curl
  into a tube toward the midribs, no
  chlorosis or necrosis, bluish green color,
  terminal leaves small, stiff and folded up

petioles—bend downward, directing
  opposite tubular leaflets toward
  each other

stem—growth stunted

progression—later stages get necrotic spots
  adjacent to and on midribs and larger veins

Cucumbers

young leaves—remain small

plant growth—restricted, short
  internodes, bushy plant

older leaves—interveinal chlorosis
  in blotches

progression—leaves turn dull green
  to bronze, necrosis, entire leaf
  withers, chlorosis spreads from older
  to younger leaves

Remedies:

1. Foliar spray with 0.1 to 0.2 percent solution of copper sulfate to which 0.5
percent hydrated lime has been added.
2. Add copper sulfate to nutrient solution.

6. Manganese:

Tomatoes

middle and older leaves—turn pale, later younger leaves also, characteristic checkered pattern of green veins and yellowish interveinal areas, later stages get small necrotic spots in pale areas, chlorosis less severe than in iron deficiency, also chlorosis is not confined to younger leaves as is the case with iron

Cucumbers

terminal or young leaves—yellowish interveinal mottling, at first even the small veins remain green, giving a reticular green pattern on a yellow background

progression—later, all except main veins turn yellow with sunken necrotic spots between the veins

shoots—stunted, new leaves remain small

older leaves—turn palest and die first

Remedies:

1. Foliar spray using high-volume spray of 0.1 percent or low-volume spray of 1 percent solution of manganese sulfate

2. Add manganese sulfate to nutrient solution.

7. Molybdenum

Tomatoes

all leaves—leaflets show a pale green to yellowish interveinal mottling, margins curl upward to form a spout, smallest veins do not remain green, necrosis starts in the yellow areas, at the margins of the top leaflets and finally includes entire composite leaves which shrivel

progression—from the older to the younger leaves, but the cotyledons stay green for a long time

Cucumbers

older leaves—fade, particularly between veins, later leaves turn pale green, finally yellow and die

progression—from older leaves up to young leaves, youngest leaves remain green

plant growth—normal, but flowers are small

Remedies:

1. Foliar spray with 0.07 to 0.1 percent solution of ammonium or sodium molybdate

2. Add ammonium or sodium molybdate to nutrient solution.

References

Arnon, D. I. 1950. Inorganic micronutrient requirements of higher plants. *Proc. 7th Int. Bot. Cong.*, Stockholm.

————— 1951. Growth and function as criteria in determining the essential nature of inorganic nutrients. In *Mineral nutrition of plants*, ed. E. Truog, pp. 313–41. Madison: Univ. Wisconsin Press.

Arnon, D. I. and P. R. Stout. 1939. The essentiality of certain elements in minute quantity for plants with special reference to copper. *Plant Physiol*. 14:371–75.

Buckman, H. O., and N. C. Brady. 1966. *The nature and properties of soils*. 6th ed. New York: Macmillan.

Epstein, E. 1972. *Mineral nutrition of plants: principles and perspectives*. New York: Wiley.

Gauch, H. G. 1972. *Inorganic plant nutrition*. Stroudsburg, Pa.: Dowden, Hutchinson and Ross.

Kramer, P. J. 1969. *Plant and soil water relationships: a modern synthesis*. New York: McGraw-Hill.

Roorda van Eysinga, J. P. N. L., and K. W. Smilde. 1969. *Nutritional disorders in cucumbers and gherkins under glass*. Wageningen: Center for Agric. Publ. and Documentation.

——— 1971. *Nutritional disorders in glasshouse lettuce*. Wageningen: Center for Agric. Publ. and Documentation.

Salisbury, F. B., and C. Ross. 1969. *Plant physiology*. Belmont, Calif.: Wadsworth.

Smilde, K. W., and J. P. N. L. Roorda van Eysinga. 1968. *Nutritional diseases in glasshouse tomatoes*. Wageningen: Center for Agric. Publ. and Documentation.

Sprague, H. B., ed. 1964. *Hunger signs in crops: a symposium*. 3rd ed. New York: David McKay.

Chapter 3

The Nutrient Solution

3.1 Inorganic Salts (Fertilizers)

In hydroponics all the essential elements are supplied to the plants by dissolving fertilizer salts in water to make up the nutrient solution. The choice of salts to be used depends on a number of factors. The relative proportion of ions a compound will supply must be compared with that required in the nutrient formulation. For example, one molecule of potassium nitrate (KNO_3) will yield one ion of potassium (K^+) and one of nitrate (NO_3^-), whereas one molecule of calcium nitrate ($Ca(NO_3)_2$) will yield one ion of calcium (Ca^{++}) and two ions of nitrate $2(NO_3)^-$. Therefore, if a minimum number of cations is wanted while supplying sufficient nitrate (anions) then calcium nitrate should be used. That is, half as much calcium nitrate as potassium nitrate would be required to satisfy the needs of the nitrate anion.

The various fertilizer salts which can be used for the nutrient solution have different solubilities. Solubility is a measure of the concentration of the salt which will remain in solution when dissolved in water. If a salt has a low solubility, only small amounts of it will dissolve in water. In hydroponics, fertilizer salts having high solubility must be used since they must remain in solution to be available to the plants. For example, calcium may be supplied by either calcium nitrate or calcium sulfate. Calcium sulfate is cheaper but its solubility is very low. Therefore, calcium nitrate should be used to supply the entire calcium requirements.

The cost of a particular fertilizer must be considered in deciding on its use. In general, a greenhouse grade should be used. The cost is somewhat greater than a standard grade, but the purity and solubility will be greater. A poor grade will contain a large amount of inert carriers (clay, silt particles) which form a sludge upon settling. Such sludge can tie up other nutrients as well as plug feeder lines.

TABLE 3.1   Summary of Fertilizer Salts for Use in Hydroponics

Chemical Formula	Chemical Name	Mol. Wt.	Elements Supplied	Solubility Ratio of Solute to Water	Cost	Other Remarks
A. Macroelements						
•KNO_3	Potassium Nitrate (Saltpeter)	101.1	K^+, NO_3^-	1:4	Low	Highly soluble, high purity
•$Ca(NO_3)_2$	Calcium nitrate	164.1	Ca^{++}, $2(NO_3^-)$	1:1	Low-medium	Highly soluble, but is shipped with a greasy plasticizer coat—must be skimmed off nutrient solution
$(NH_4)_2SO_4$	Ammonium sulfate	132.2	$2(NH_4^+)$, $SO_4^=$	1:2	Medium	These compounds should be used only under very good light conditions or to correct N - deficiencies
$NH_4H_2PO_4$	Ammonium dihydrogen phosphate	115.0	NH_4^+,$H_2PO_4^-$	1:4	Medium	
NH_4NO_3	Ammonium nitrate	80.05	NH_4^+, NO_3^-	1:1	Medium	
$(NH_4)_2HPO_4$	Ammonium monohydrogen phosphate	132.1	$2(NH_4^+)$, $HPO_4^=$	1:2	Medium	
•KH_2PO_4	Monopotassium phosphate	136.1	K^+, $H_2PO_4^-$	1:3	Very expensive	An excellent salt, highly soluble and pure, but costly.
KCl	Potassium chloride (Muriate of potash)	74.55	K^+, Cl^-	1:3	Expensive	Should only be used for K deficiencies and when no sodium chloride is present in nutrient solution
•K_2SO_4	Potassium sulfate	174.3	$2K^+$, $SO_4^=$	1:15	Inexpensive	It has low solubility, must dissolve in hot water
$Ca(H_2PO_4)_2H_2O$	Monocalcium phosphate	252.1	Ca^{++}, $2(H_2PO_4^-)$	1:60	Inexpensive	Very difficult to obtain a soluble grade
$CaH_4(PO_4)_2$	Triple super phosphate	Variable	Ca^{++}, $2(PO_4^\equiv)$	1:300	Inexpensive	Very low solubility; good only for dry pre-mixes, not for nutrient solutions
•$MgSO_4 \cdot 7H_2O$	Magnesium sulfate (Epsom salts)	246.5	Mg^{++},$SO_4^=$	1:2	Inexpensive	Excellent cheap, highly soluble, pure salt
$CaCl_2 \cdot 6H_2O$	Calcium chloride	219.1	Ca^{++}, $2Cl^-$	1:1	Expensive	Highly soluble, good to overcome Ca deficiencies, but use only if no NaCl present in nutrient solution
$CaSO_4 \cdot 2H_2O$	Calcium sulfate (Gypsum)	172.2	Ca^{++}, $SO_4^=$	1:500	Inexpensive	Very insoluble, cannot be used for nutrient solutions
H_3PO_4	Phosphoric acid Orthophosphoric acid	98.0	$PO_4^=$	Concentrated acid solution	Expensive	Good use in correction of P-deficiencies

Chemical Formula	Chemical Name	Mol. Wt.	Elements Supplied	Solubility Ratio of Solute to Water	Cost	Other Remarks
B. Microelements						
$FeSO_4 \cdot 7H_2O$	Ferrous sulfate (Green vitriol)	278.0	Fe^{++}, SO_4^-	1:4		
$FeCl_3 \cdot 6H_2O$	Ferric chloride	270.3	Fe^{+++}, $3Cl^-$	1:2		
*FeEDTA	Iron chelate (Sequestrene) (10.5% iron)	382.1	Fe^{++}	Highly soluble	Expensive	Best source of iron; dissolve in hot water
*H_3BO_3	Boric acid	61.8	B^{+++}	1:20	Expensive	Best source of boron; dissolve in hot water
$Na_2B_4O_7 \cdot 10H_2O$	Sodium tetraborate (Borax)	381.4	B^{+++}	1:25		
*$CuSO_4 \cdot 5H_2O$	Copper sulfate (Bluestone)	249.7	Cu^{++}, SO_4^-	1:5	Inexpensive	
*$Mn\,SO_4 \cdot 4H_2O$	Manganese sulfate	223.1	Mn^{++}, SO_4^-	1:2	Inexpensive	
$MnCl_2 \cdot 4H_2O$	Manganese chloride	197.9	Mn^{++}, $2Cl^-$	1:2	Inexpensive	
*$ZnSO_4 \cdot 7H_2O$	Zinc sulfate	287.6	Zn^{++}, SO_4^-	1:3	Inexpensive	
$ZnCl_2$	Zinc chloride	136.3	Zn^{++}, $2Cl^-$	1:1.5	Inexpensive	
$(NH_4)_6Mo_7O_{24}$	Ammonium molybdate	1163.9	NH_4^+, Mo^{+6}	1:2.3 Highly soluble	Moderately expensive	
*ZnEDTA	Zinc chelate	431.6	Zn^{++}	Highly soluble	Expensive	
*MnEDTA	Manganese chelate	381.2	Mn^{++}	Highly soluble	Expensive	

*These more soluble compounds should be used for preparing nutrient solutions.

The availability of nitrate versus ammonium compounds to plants is important in promoting either vegetative or reproductive growth. Plants can absorb both the cationic ammonium ion (NH_4^+) and the anion nitrate (NO_3^-). Ammonium, once absorbed, can immediately serve in the synthesis of amino acids and other compounds containing reduced nitrogen. Absorption of ammonium can therefore cause excessive vegetative growth, particularly under poor light conditions. Nitrate nitrogen, on the other hand, must be reduced before it is assimilated; therefore, vegetative growth will be held back. Ammonium salts could be used under bright summer conditions when photosynthetic rates are high or if a nitrogen deficiency occurs and a rapid source of nitrogen is needed. In all other cases nitrate salts should be used.

A summary of some salts which could be used for a hydroponic nutrient solution is given in table 3.1. The particular choice of salt will depend on the above factors and market availability. If a dry premix is to be used, such as in sawdust, peat, or vermiculite media, some of the more insoluble salts could be used, while if a nutrient solution is to be made up in advance, the more soluble compounds should be used (those marked with an asterisk). Potassium chloride and calcium chloride should be used only to correct potassium and calcium deficiencies respectively. These, however, can be used only if insignificant amounts of sodium chloride (less than 50 ppm) are present in the nutrient solution. If chlorides are added in the presence of sodium, poisoning of the plants will result.

The use of chelates (of iron, manganese, and zinc) is highly recommended since they remain in solution and are readily available to plants even under pH shifts. A chelated salt is one having a soluble organic component to which the mineral element can adhere until uptake by the plant roots occurs. The organic component is EDTA (ethylene-diaminetetra acetic acid). EDTA has a high affinity for calcium ions and is thus a poor chelating agent for calcareous media (limestone, coral sand). In this case it should be replaced with EDDHA (ethylene-diamine dihydroxyphenyl acetic acid).

3.2 Recommended Compounds for Complete Nutrient Solutions

Calcium should be provided by calcium nitrate. Calcium nitrate will also provide nitrate nitrogen. Any additional nitrogen required should be provided by potassium nitrate, which also provides some potassium. All phosphorus may be obtained from monopotassium phosphate, which also provides some potassium. The remaining potassium requirement can be obtained from potassium sulfate, which also supplies some sulfur. Additional sulfur comes from other sulfates such as magnesium sulfate, which is used to supply the magnesium needs.

Micronutrients may be obtained from commercial pre-mixes. While these are relatively expensive, they save the substantial labor of weighing the individual compounds contained in the mix.

3.3 Fertilizer Chemical Analyses

The amounts of available nitrogen, phosphorus, and potassium are given on fertilizer bags as the percentage of nitrogen (N), phosphoric anhydride (P_2O_5) and potassium oxide (K_2O). It has traditionally been expressed in these terms, not in percentage of N, P, or K alone. For example, potassium nitrate is given as 13-0-44, indicating 13 percent N, 0 percent P_2O_5, and 44 percent K_2O.

Nutrient formulations for hydroponics express: nitrogen as N, NH^+_4, or NO_3^-; phosphorus as P or $PO_4\equiv$, not P_2O_5; and potassium as K^+, not K_2O. Therefore, it is necessary to convert N to NO_3^-, P_2O_5 as P or $PO_4\equiv$, and K_2O as K^+ or vice versa in each case. Conversions of this nature can be made by calculating the fraction of each element within its compound source. Table 3.2 lists conversion factors to determine the fraction of an element within a compound and vice versa. It was derived by the use of atomic and molecular weights as follows: The fraction of N in NO_3^- is the atomic weight of nitrogen (14) divided by the molecular weight of nitrate (62).

TABLE 3.2   Conversion Factors for Fertilizer Salts

Column A*	Column B*	Conversion factor	
		A to B	B to A
Nitrogen (N)	Ammonia (NH_3)	1.216	0.822
	Nitrate (NO_3)	4.429	0.226
	Potassium nitrate (KNO_3)	7.221	0.1385
	Calcium nitrate ($Ca(NO_3)_2$)	5.861	0.171
	Ammonium sulfate (($NH_4)_2SO_4$)	4.721	0.212
	Ammonium nitrate (NH_4NO_3)	2.857	0.350
	Diammonium phosphate (($NH_4)_2HPO_4$)	4.717	0.212
Phosphorus (P)	Phosphoric anhydride (P_2O_5)	2.292	0.436
	Phosphate (PO_4)	3.066	0.326
	Monopotassium phosphate (KH_2PO_4)	4.394	0.228
	Diammonium phosphate (($NH_4)_2HPO_4$)	4.255	0.235
	Phosphoric acid (H_3PO_4)	3.164	0.316
Potassium (K)	Potash (K_2O)	1.205	0.830
	Potassium nitrate (KNO_3)	2.586	0.387
	Monopotassium phosphate (KH_2PO_4)	3.481	0.287
	Potassium chloride (KCl)	1.907	0.524
	Potassium sulfate (K_2SO_4)	2.229	0.449
Calcium (Ca)	Calcium oxide (CaO)	1.399	0.715
	Calcium nitrate ($Ca(NO_3)_2$)	4.094	0.244
	Calcium chloride ($CaCl_2\cdot6H_2O$)	5.467	0.183
	Calcium sulfate ($CaSO_4\cdot2H_2O$)	4.296	0.233
Magnesium (Mg)	Magnesium oxide (MgO)	1.658	0.603
	Magnesium sulfate ($MgSO_4\cdot7H_2O$)	10.14	0.0986
Sulfur (S)	Sulfuric acid (H_2SO_4)	3.059	0.327
	Ammonium sulfate (($NH_4)_2SO_4$)	4.124	0.2425
	Potassium sulfate (K_2SO_4)	5.437	0.184
	Magnesium sulfate ($MgSO_4\cdot7H_2O$)	7.689	0.130
	Calcium sulfate ($CaSO_4\cdot2H_2O$)	5.371	0.186

Source: Adapted from Schwarz, M. 1968. *Guide to commercial hydroponics.* Jerusalem: Israel Univ. Press.

*In order to find the equivalents of items in column A in terms of those in column B, multiply the amount of A by factor in column A to B. For reverse procedure multiply amount of B by factor B to A.

3.4 Fertilizer Impurities

Most fertilizer salts are not 100 percent pure. They often contain inert "carriers" such as clay, silt, and sand particles which do not supply ions. Therefore, a percentage purity or a guaranteed analysis is often given on the fertilizer bag. Some of the percentage purities of common fertilizers are given in table 3.3. These impurities must be taken into consideration when calculating the fertilizer requirements for a particular nutrient formulation.

TABLE 3.3—Percentage Purities of Commercial Fertilizers

Salt	% Purity
Ammonium phosphate ($NH_4H_2PO_4$) (food grade)	98
Ammonium sulfate ((NH_4)$_2$ SO_4)	94
Ammonium nitrate, pure (NH_4NO_3)	98
Potassium nitrate (KNO_3)	95
Calcium nitrate ($Ca(NO_3)_2$)	90
Monocalcium phosphate ($Ca(H_2PO_4)_2$) (food grade)	92
Potassium sulfate (K_2SO_4)	90
Potassium chloride (KCl)	95
*Magnesium sulfate ($MgSo_4 \cdot 7H_2O$)	45
Calcium chloride ($CaCl_2$)	75
Calcium sulfate ($CaSO_4$) (Gypsum)	70
Monopotassium phosphate (KH_2PO_4)	98

*The purity is calculated on the basis of the designated formula. Water of crystallization (eg: $MgSO_4 \cdot 7H_2O$) is considered as impurity.

NOTE: When using Table 3.2, note that the water of crystallization has already been adjusted. Therefore, the percentage purity in Table 3.3 for $MgSo_4 \cdot 7H_2O$ should be 98%.

Many fertilizers have synonyms or common names. A list of these common names is given in table 3.4.

TABLE 3.4   Chemical Names and Synonyms of Compounds Generally Used in Nutrient Solutions

Chemical Name	Synonyms or Common Name
Potassium nitrate KNO_3	Saltpeter, niter (not to be confused with Chili niter or Chili saltpeter which is sodium nitrate, or with "niter cake" which is impure sodium sulfate)
Sodium nitrate $NaNO_3$	Chili saltpeter; niter; Chili niter (See item above)
Ammonium acid phosphate $NH_4H_2PO_4$	Primary ammonium phosphate; ammonium biphosphate; ammonium bihydrogenphosphate; monobasic ammonium phosphate; "Ammophos A"
Urea $CO(NH_2)_2$	Carbamide; carbonyldiamide
Potassium sulfate K_2SO_4	Sulfate of potash
Potassium acid phosphate KH_2PO_4	Potassium biphosphate; potassium dihydrogen phosphate; monobasic potassium phosphate
Potassium chloride KCl	Muriate of potash; chloride of potash (not chlorate of potash which is $KClO_3$); Sylvite (mineral form)
Monocalcium phosphate $Ca(H_2PO_4)_2H_2O$	Calcium "superphosphate" (usually 20 percent pure); calcium "treble superphosphate" (usually 75 percent pure); calcium biphosphate; calcium acid phosphate; primary calcium phosphate
Phosphoric acid H_3PO_4	Orthophosphoric acid (U.S.P. grade is 85-88 percent H_3PO_4, but commercial technical grade is 70-75 percent pure H_3PO_4)
Calcium sulfate $CaSO_4 \cdot 2H_2O$	Precipitated or native calcium sulfate; gypsum alabaster
Calcium chloride $CaCl_2 \cdot 2H_2O$	Calcium chloride dihydrate. This salt may sometimes be available as the hexa-hydrate or $CaCl_2 \cdot 6H_2O$
Magnesium sulfate $MgSO_4 \cdot 7H_2O$	Epsom salts. This salt is available as the anhydrous form without water.
Ferrous sulfate $FeSO_4 \cdot 7H_2O$	Green vitriol; iron vitriol; copperas (tech. grade)
Zinc sulfate $ZnSO_4 \cdot 7H_2O$	White or zinc vitriol
Boric acid H_3BO_3	Boracic acid; orthoboric acid
Copper sulfate $CuSO_4 \cdot 5H_2O$	Cupric sulfate; bluestone; blue copperas

Source: Adapted from Withrow, R. B. and A. P. Withrow, 1948. *Nutriculture.* Lafayette, Ind.: Purdue Univ. Agr. Expt. Stn. Publ. S.C. 328.

3.5 Nutrient Formulations

Nutrient formulations are usually given in parts per million (ppm) concentrations of each essential element. One part per million is one part of one item in 1 million parts of another. It may be a weight measure, for example, $1\mu g/g$ (one microgram per gram), a weight-volume measure, for example, 1 mg/l (one milligram per liter) or a volume-volume measure, for example $1\mu l/l$ (one microliter per liter). Proof for these are as follows:

$$(1)\ 1\mu g/g = \frac{\dfrac{1}{1,000,000}\,g}{1\ g} = \frac{1}{1,000,000}\,g$$

$$(2)\ 1\mu l/l = \frac{\dfrac{1}{1,000,000}\,l}{1\ l} = \frac{1}{1,000,000}\,l$$

(3) 1 mg/l:

$$1\ mg = \frac{1}{1000}\ g \quad 1\ l = 1000\ ml$$

Therefore:

$$1\ mg/l = \frac{\dfrac{1}{1000}\,g}{1000\ ml\ H_2O} = \frac{1}{1,000,000}\ g \quad \text{since 1 ml of } H_2O \text{ weighs 1 gram (g).}$$

3.5.1 Atomic and Molecular Weights

Atomic and molecular weights of elements and compounds respectively must be used in calculating nutrient formulation concentration requirements. Atomic weights indicate the relative weights of different atoms, that is, how the weight of one atom compares with that of another. Tables of atomic weights for every atom have been drawn up by establishing a relative scale of atomic weights. In doing so one element is chosen as a standard and all other elements are compared with it. Oxygen (O) has in the past been assigned the atomic weight of exactly 16, and all other elements are related to it. Table 3.5 lists the atomic weights of elements commonly used in hydroponics.

When a number of atoms combine they form a molecule. These are expressed as molecular formulae. For example water is H_2O,

TABLE 3.5 Atomic Weights of Elements Commonly Used in Hydroponics

Name	Symbol	Atomic Wt.
Aluminium	Al	26.98
Boron	B	10.81
Calcium	Ca	40.08
Carbon	C	12.01
Chlorine	Cl	35.45
Copper	Cu	63.54
Hydrogen	H	1.008
Iron	Fe	55.85
Magnesium	Mg	24.31
Manganese	Mn	54.94
Molybdenum	Mo	95.94
Nitrogen	N	14.01
Oxygen	O	16.00
Phosphorus	P	30.97
Potassium	K	39.10
Selenium	Se	78.96
Silicon	Si	28.09
Sodium	Na	22.99
Sulfur	S	32.06
Zinc	Zn	65.37

consisting of two atoms of hydrogen (H) and one atom of oxygen (O). The weight of any molecular formula is the molecular weight. It is simply the sum of the atomic weights within the molecule. The molecular weight of water is 18 (there are two atoms of hydrogen, each having atomic weight of 1.00, and one atom of oxygen having an atomic weight of 16.0). Molecular weights of commonly used fertilizers for hydroponics are given in Table 3.1. The atomic weights of all known elements are given in tables and periodic charts of chemistry texts.

The following examples will clarify the use of atomic and molecular weights in their use with nutrient formulation calculations:

Calcium nitrate - $Ca(NO_3)_2$

Atomic weight:

Ca = 40.08
N = 14.008
O = 16.000

Molecular weight:

Ca   =   40.08
2 N =   28.016
6 O =   96.0
_____
164.096

*Note: There are two nitrogen atoms and six oxygen atoms in calcium nitrate.

3.5.2 Calculations

If a nutrient formulation calls for 200 ppm of calcium (200 mg/l) we need 200 mg of calcium in every liter of water. In 164 mg. of $Ca(NO_3)_2$ we have 40 mg of Ca (using the atomic and molecular weights to determine the fraction of calcium in calcium nitrate— assuming 100 percent purity of $Ca(NO_3)_2$. The first step is to calculate how much Ca $(NO_3)_2$ is required to obtain 200 mg. of Ca. This is done by setting up a ratio as follows:

$$164 \text{ mg } Ca(NO_3)_2 \text{ yields } 40 \text{ mg Ca}$$
$$x \text{ mg } Ca(NO_3)_2 \text{ yields } 200 \text{ mg Ca}$$

$$\text{Ratio: } \frac{40}{164} = \frac{200}{x}$$

Solve for x:

$$40 \text{ x} = 200 \times 164 \text{ (cross multiply)}$$

$$x = \frac{200 \times 164}{40} \text{ (divide by 40)} = 820$$

Therefore, 820 mg of $Ca(NO_3)_2$ will yield 200 mg Ca. If the 820 mg of $Ca(NO_3)_2$ is dissolved in 1 liter of water the resultant solution will have a concentration of 200 ppm (200 mg/l) of Ca. This as- sumes, however, that the $Ca(NO_3)_2$ is 100 percent pure. If it is not—which is the usual case—it will be necessary to add more to compensate for the impurity. For example, if the $Ca(NO_3)$ is 90 percent pure it will be necessary to add:

$$\frac{100}{90} \times 820 = 911 \text{ mg } Ca(NO_3)_2$$

The 911 mg $Ca(NO_3)_2$ in 1 liter of water will give 200 ppm of Ca.

Of course, in most cases a larger volume of nutrient solution than 1 liter will be required. The second step, then, is to calculate the amount of fertilizer required for a given volume of nutrients. A conversion factor to change from mg/l to lbs/Imp. or U.S. gallons must be generated.

Conversion Factors:

(1) mg/l → lb/Imp. gal.

1 mg = 0.0000022046 lb.
1 l = 0.21998 Imp. gal.

$$\frac{1\,mg}{1\,l} \times \frac{0.0000022046\,lb}{1\,mg} \times \frac{1\,l}{0.21998\,Imp.\,gal.}$$

$$= 0.00001002182 \text{ lb./Imp. gal.}$$

In most cases, the concentration of a compound needed will be initially calculated in terms of mg/l and this will have to be converted to lbs/gal. To eliminate some of the decimal places in the above conversion factor its reciprocal can be used:

$$\frac{1}{99780} = 0.00001002182 \qquad K_{Imp} = \frac{1}{99780}$$

Therefore, the conversion constant (K) should be expressed as:

$$K = \frac{1}{99780}$$

(2) mg/l → lb/U.S. gal.

1 mg = 0.0000022046 lb.
1 l = 0.26417 U.S. gal.

$$\frac{1\,mg}{1\,l} \times \frac{0.0000022046\,lb.}{1\,mg} \times \frac{1\,l}{0.26417\,U.S.\,gal}$$

$$= 0.0000083453 \text{ lb./U.S. gal.}$$

Hence the reciprocal constant is: $K_{U.S.} = \dfrac{1}{119828}$

To continue now with the above example, the 911 mg of $Ca(NO_3)_2$ in 1 liter of water must be converted to pounds of $Ca(NO_3)_2$ in 1 Imp. gallon of water as follows:

$$911 \text{ mg/l} \times \frac{1}{99780} = 0.00913 \text{ lbs/Imp. gal.}$$

If a 100-Imperial gallon tank is to be used as a nutrient reservoir, the above figure must be multiplied by 100 as follows:

0.00913 × 100 = 0.913 lbs/100 Imp. gal. expressed as ounces:
0.913 × 16 = 14.608 oz/100 Imp. gal.

These steps can be combined into a general formula:

$$W = \frac{(CM)}{A}\frac{(100)}{P}K \quad \text{where:}$$

W = weight of compound needed expressed in lb/gal.
C = ppm concentration of desired element
M = molecular weight of salt used
A = atomic weight of element

P = percentage purity of salt

K = reciprocal conversion constant for either Imperial gallons (K_{IMP}) or U.S. gallons (K_{US})

For the previous example:

$$W = \frac{(200 \times 164)}{40} \frac{(100)}{90} \frac{(1)}{99780} = 0.00913 \text{ lb/Imp. gal.}$$

If the compound used contains more than one essential element—this is the usual case—the third step is to determine how much of each of the other elements was added when satisfying the needs of the first essential element. Calcium nitrate contains both calcium and nitrogen. Therefore, the third step is to calculate the amount of nitrogen added while satisfying the calcium needs. This is calculated by making use of the fraction of nitrogen in calcium nitrate and multiplying the amount of calcium nitrate used by this fraction:

$$\frac{2(14)}{164} \times 820 = 140 \text{ mg/l (ppm)}$$

This should be done using the ppm concepts so that adjustments can be made for this element. This calculation can be generalized as:

$$C_{E_2} = \frac{(A_{E_2})}{M} \cdot \frac{(C_{E_1}M)}{A_{E_1}} = \frac{A_{E_2} C_{E_1}}{A_{E_1}}$$

where:

C_{E2} = ppm concentration of second desired element

C_{E1} = ppm concentration of first desired element

A_{E2} = total atomic weight of second element

A_{E1} = total atomic weight of first element

M = molecular weight of compound

Since the molecular weight is common to both terms the equation simplifies to:

$$C_{E_2} = \frac{(A_{E_2})}{A_{E_1}} C_{E1}$$

The fourth step is to calculate the additional amount of the second element needed from another compound source. For example, if the nutrient formulation asked for 150 ppm of N then the additional requirement would be:

$$150 - 140 = 10 \text{ ppm of N}$$

This could be obtained from KNO_3. Then the amount of KNO_3 needed to supply 10 ppm of N would be:

$$W_{KNO_3} = \frac{(C_N M_{KNO_3})}{A_N} \frac{(100)}{P} K_{IMP}$$

$$W_{KNO_3} = \frac{(10 \times 101)}{14} \frac{(100)}{95} \frac{(1)}{99780}$$

$$= 0.000761 \text{ lb/Imp. gal.}$$

$C_N = 10$ ppm
$M_{KNO_3} = 101.1$
$A_N = 14$
$P_{KNO_3} = 95$
$K_{IMP} = \dfrac{1}{99780}$

These calculations may be continued for all the essential elements. The types and quantities of the various fertilizer salts must be manipulated until the desired formulation is achieved.

In some cases a problem may arise if the requirements of one element are satisfied by use of a compound which contains two or more essential elements, but the concentration of another element exceeds the level required.

For instance, if the nutrient formulation called for 300 ppm Ca and 150 ppm N, the calcium would be supplied by $Ca(NO_3)_2$ as follows:

(1) Weight of $Ca(NO_3)_2$ needed:

$$W = \frac{(C\ M)}{A} \frac{(100)}{P} K_{IMP}$$

$$\frac{(300 \times 164)}{40} \frac{(100)}{90} \frac{(1)}{99780}$$

$$= 0.0137 \text{ lb/Imp. gal.}$$

$C = 300$ ppm Ca
$M = 164$
$A = 40$
$P = 90$
$K_{IMP} \dfrac{1}{99780}$

(2) Amount of N added:

$$C_N = \frac{(A_N)C_{Ca}}{A_{Ca}} \cong \frac{(28)}{40}\ 300 = 210 \text{ ppm N}$$

$$A_N = 2(14) = 28 \quad A_{Ca} = 40 \quad C_{Ca} = 300 \text{ ppm}$$

This gives an excess of 60 ppm of N over the recommended 150 ppm N given in the formulation. Therefore, the level of N will govern how much $Ca(NO_3)_2$ can be used as a source of Ca. The previous steps must now be recalculated using the limit of 150 ppm N:

(1) Weight of $Ca(NO_3)_2$ needed:

$$W = \frac{(CM)}{A} \frac{(100)}{P} K_{IMP}$$

$$= \frac{(150 \times 164)}{28} \frac{(100)}{90} \frac{(1)}{99780}$$

$$= 0.0098 \text{ lb/Imp. gal.}$$

$C = 150$ ppm N
$M = 164$
$A = 2(14) = 28$
$P = 90$
$K_{IMP} = \dfrac{1}{99780}$

(2) Amount of Ca added:

$$C_{Ca} = \frac{(A_{Ca}) C_N}{A_N} = \frac{(40)}{28} \ 150 \ = 214.3 \ \text{ppm Ca}$$

$$A_{Ca} = 40 \quad A_N = 28 \quad C_N = 150 \ \text{ppm}$$

If the recommended level of Ca is 300 ppm, then $(300 - 214) = 86$ ppm Ca must be supplied from other sources than $Ca(NO_3)_2$. Since $CaSO_4$ is very insoluble the only alternative is to use $CaCl_2$:

$$(3) \ W_{CaCl_2} = \frac{(C_{Ca}M)}{A_{Ca}} \ \frac{(100)}{P} \ K_{IMP}$$

$$= \frac{(86 \times 111)}{40} \ \frac{(100)}{75} \ \frac{(1)}{99780}$$

$$= 0.0032 \ \text{lb/Imp. gal.}$$

$C_{Ca} = 86$ ppm
$M = 111$
$A_{Ca} = 40$
$P = 75$
$K_{IMP} = \dfrac{1}{99780}$

(4) Amount of Cl added:

$$C_{Cl} = \frac{(A_{Cl}) C_{Ca}}{A_{Ca}} = \frac{(71)}{40} \ (86) \ = 152.6 \ \text{ppm Cl}$$

$$A_{Cl} = 2(35.5) = 71 \quad A_{Ca} = 40 \quad C_{Ca} = 86 \ \text{ppm}$$

This level of chlorine is tolerable to the plants as long as the level of sodium in the water and other fertilizers used is negligible.

In some areas of the world a number of basic fertilizers required may not be available. In that case it becomes necessary to substitute other chemicals that are available to provide the needed amount of essential elements. Calculations for such substitutions are as follows:

1. Substitute potassium hydroxide (KOH) and phosphoric acid (H_3PO_4) for diammonium phosphate $((NH_4)_2HPO_4)$ or monopotassium phosphate (KH_2PO_4) to supply phosphorus (P) and some potassium (K).

Note that KOH must be used to neutralize the strong acid of H_3PO_4. The reaction is as follows:

$$H_3PO_4 + KOH \rightarrow K^+ + OH^- + 3H^+ + PO_4^{\equiv}$$
$$\rightarrow K^+ + PO_4^{\equiv} + H_2O + 2H^+$$

H_3PO_4: $\qquad M_{H_3PO_4} = 97.99$

Need: 60 ppm of P from H_3PO_4:

60×3.164 (from Table 3.2) $= 189.8$ mg/l

KOH: $M_{KOH}=56.108$

Need: 189.8   x
$\dfrac{}{H_3PO_4+KOH}$, therefore; $x=\dfrac{189.8\times56.108}{97.99}$
97.99   56.108

$$=108.7\ mg/l$$

Amount of K: $\dfrac{39.1}{56.108}\times108.7=0.6969\times108.7=75.7\,mg/l$

But, phosphoric acid is a liquid, therefore, the weight required must be converted to volume measure.

To do this the specific gravity or density (D) must be used. Density is the ratio of weight to volume $(D=\dfrac{W}{V})$. Density of phosphoric acid is 1.834 (see Appendix 4).

To find the volume: $D=\dfrac{W}{V}$ or $V=\dfrac{W}{D}$; that is, $V=\dfrac{189.8}{1.834}=103.5\ \mu l/l$

2. Substitute nitric acid (HNO_3) and calcium carbonate ($CaCO_3$) for calcium nitrate ($Ca(NO_3)_2\cdot4H_2O$) to supply calcium (Ca) and nitrogen (N). Note that $CaCO_3$ must be used to neutralize the strong acid of HNO_3. The reaction is as follows:

$$CaCO_3+HNO_3\rightarrow Ca^{++}+NO_3^-+H^++CO_3^=$$
$$\rightarrow Ca^{++}+NO_3^-+HCO_3^-$$

$CaCO_3$: $M_{CaCO_3}=100.1$

Need: 150 ppm of Ca from $CaCO_3$:
$$150\times\dfrac{100.1}{40.08}=374.6\ mg/l$$

HNO_3: $M_{HNO_3}=63.016$

374.6   x
$\dfrac{}{CaCO_3+HNO_3}$, therefore; $x=\dfrac{374.6\times63.016}{100.1}$
100.1   63.016

$$=235.8\ mg/l$$

Amount of N: $235.8\times\dfrac{14}{63.016}=52\ mg/l$

Since HNO_3 is a liquid it must be converted to volume:
D=1.5027

$$D=\dfrac{W}{V}\ \text{or:}\ V=\dfrac{W}{D}=\dfrac{235.8}{1.5027}=156.9\ \mu l/l$$

Often HNO_3 is not 100% pure, therefore, it must be adjusted by the percentage purity.

In summary, 375 mg/l of $CaCO_3$ and 157 $\mu l/l$ of HNO_3 will provide 150 ppm Ca and 52 ppm N.

3. Substitute nitric acid (HNO$_3$) and potassium hydroxide (KOH) for potassium nitrate (KNO$_3$). Note that KOH must be used to neutralize the strong acid of HNO$_3$. The reaction is as follows:

$$KOH + HNO_3 \rightarrow K^+ + NO_3^- + H_2O$$

Amount of K needed in formulation is 150 ppm. From KOH used with H$_3$PO$_4$ for P source there is 76 ppm of K, therefore, need: 150−76=74 ppm K.

$$KOH: 74 \times \frac{56.108}{39.1} = 106 \text{ mg/l}$$

HNO$_3$:

Need: $\dfrac{106}{KOH} + \dfrac{x}{HNO_3}$ therefore, $x = 106 \times \dfrac{63.016}{56.108}$
 56.108 63.016 $= 119$ mg/l

Amount of N: $119 \times \dfrac{14}{63.016} = 26.4$ mg/l

Since HNO$_3$ is a liquid, it must be converted to volume: D=1.5027

$$D = \frac{W}{V} \text{ or: } V = \frac{W}{D} = \frac{119}{1.5027} = 79.2 \text{ } \mu l/l$$

That is, 106 mg/l of KOH and 79.2 μl/l of HNO$_3$ will provide 74 ppm of K and 26 ppm of N.

4. To make Fe-EDTA chelate (ethylenediaminetetraacetatoferrate):

The objective is to make a 200 kg stock solution containing 10,000 mg/l (ppm) (1% iron) of chelated iron.

(1) Dissolve 10.4 kg EDTA (acid) in a solution of 16 kg of KOH in 114 l of water. Adjust the weight of KOH used acordingly if the KOH is not 100% pure. Do not add all of the KOH to the solution initially in order to maintain the pH at 5.5. Should the pH exceed 5.5 reduce it by addition of a 10% nitric acid (HNO$_3$) solution. If the pH is substantially less than 5.5, add KOH dissolved in water to the solution slowly stirring until the pH reaches 5.5

(2) Separately dissolve 10 kg of ferrous sulfate (FeSO$_4$) in 64 l of hot water. Slowly add the ferrous sulfate solution, while stirring, to the EDTA/KOH solution of pH 5.5. If the pH goes below 5.0, add some of the KOH solution while stirring vigorously. With each addition of KOH solution precipitation of ferrous hydroxide (Fe(OH)$_2$) will occur. As the pH adjusts itself this will redissolve, but the redissolution will become slower as the pH of the stock solution rises closer to pH 5.5.

(3) After all of the ferrous sulfate and KOH solutions have been added to the EDTA/KOH solution, weigh the final solution and adjust the volume with addition of water until a final solution weight of 200 kg is achieved.

Example:

In order to obtain 5 ppm of iron in 30,000 liters of water:

(1) The stock solution contains 10,000 mg/l of iron.

(2) We need 5 mg/l (ppm) of iron in the nutrient solution.

(3) In 30,000 liters of water we need: $30,000 \times 5 = 150,000$ mg or 150 g of iron.

(4) If the FeEDTA stock solution contains 10,000 mg/l or 10 g/l of iron, we need:

For 150 g of iron: $\frac{150}{10} = 15$ liters of FeEDTA stock solution.

Note: The density of a compound should be obtained from the manufacturer as variations will occur from one source to another. A general table of solubilities and densities is given in the Appendix.

3.5.3 Nutrient Formulation Adjustments

Since the nutrient formulation will have to be adjusted frequently during the growing of any crop, it is essential to understand the calculations and manipulations outlined in the previous section. Many claims have been made as to the derivation of "optimum formulations" for a particular crop. Too often, however, these claims are not substantiated and cannot be supported since the optimum formulation depends on too many variables which cannot be controlled. An optimum formulation would depend on the following variables:

1. plant species and variety
2. stage of plant growth
3. part of the plant representing the harvested crop (root, stem, leaf, fruit)
4. season of year—day length
5. weather—temperature, light intensity, sunshine hours

Different varieties and plant species have different nutrient requirements, particularly nitrogen, phosphorus and potassium. For example, lettuce and other leafy vegetables can be given higher rates of nitrogen than tomatoes or cucumbers. The latter two require higher rates of phosphorus, potassium and calcium than do leafy plants.

Ulises Durany (1982) states that the nitrogen (N) level should remain lower (N=80 to 90 ppm) for species that produce fruit than those species producing leaves (N=140 ppm). For species that are grown for roots, potassium (K) should be higher (K=300 ppm). For lettuce, on the other hand, relatively low levels of potassium (K=150 ppm) favor the closing of the heads and therefore result in greater weights.

The proportions among the various elements must vary according to the species of plant, the growth cycle and development of the plant, and climatic conditions, particularly light intensity and duration.

Nutrient formulations are often composed of several different levels to be used at the different stages of plant growth. Formulations specifically for tomatoes usually consist of three levels—A, B and C. These levels apply only to the macroelements; the microelements are kept the same for all three levels. The A formulation is approximately one-third of C and B is approximately two-thirds of C. Nonetheless, individual elements are often adjusted independently. The A formulation is used for seedlings from first true-leaf stage (10 to 14 days old) until they are 14 to 16 inches tall. The B formulation is used from 14 to 16 inches until the plants are 24 inches tall, when initial fruit is about ¼ to ½ inch in diameter. After that the C formulation is used.

Cucumbers use only A and B formulations, where A is approximately one-half of the B level. The A level is used until the first cucumbers have set. Similarly, leafy vegetables also use a two-level formulation. The first level (lower) is used until the plants are about 3 weeks old and the second level thereafter.

In general, plants harvested for their leaves can tolerate higher N levels since nitrogen promotes vegetative growth. However, plants grown for fruit production should have lower N and higher P, K, and Ca levels. Under high light conditions plants will use more nitrogen than under poor light. High potash (K) levels during the fall and early winter will improve fruit quality. This potassium/ nitrogen ratio is more important and should be varied with the

TABLE 3.6 Composition of Nutrient Solutions (ppm)

Reference	pH	Ca++	Mg++	Na+	K+	N as NH4+	N as NO3-	P as PO4≡	S as SO4=	Cl-	Fe	Mn	Cu	Zn	B	Mo
Knop (1865)		244	24		168		206	57	32		Trace					
Shive (1915)		208	484		562		148	448	640		Trace					
Hoagland (1919)	6.8	200	99	12	284		158	44	125	18	As required					
Jones & Shive (1921)		292	172		102	39	204	65	227		0.83					
*Rothamsted	6.2	116	48		593		139	117	157	17	8	0.25			0.2	
Hoagland & Snyder (1933, 1938)		200	48		234		210	31	64	~1	As required	0.1	0.014	0.01	0.1	0.016
Hoagland & Arnon (1938)		160	48		234	14	196	31	64		0.6 3× weekly	0.5	0.02	0.05	0.5	0.01
Long Ashton Soln	5.5–6.0	134–300	36	30	130–295		140–284	41	48	3.5	5.6 or 2.8	0.55	0.064	0.065	0.50	0.05
Eaton (1931)		240	72		117		168	93	96		0.8	0.5			1	
Shive & Robbins (1942)		60	53	92	117		56	46	70	107	As required	0.15	0.15	0.15	~0.1	
Robbins (1946)		200	48		195		196	31	64		0.5	0.25	0.02	0.25	0.25	0.01
White (1943)	4.8	50	72	70	65		47	4	140	31	1.0	1.67	0.005	0.59	0.26	0.001
Duclos (1957)	5–6	136	72		234		210	27	32		3	0.25	0.15	0.25	0.4	2.5
Tumanov (1960)	6–7	300–500	50		150		100–150	80–100	64	4	2	0.5	0.05	0.1	0.5	0.02

Source		pH															
A. J. Abbott		6.5	210	50		200		150	60	147		5.6	0.55	0.064	0.065	0.5	0.05
E. B. Kidson		5.5	340	54	35	234		208	57	114	75	2	0.25	0.05	0.05	0.5	0.1
Purdue A			200	96		390	28	70	63	607		20	0.3	0.02	0.05	0.5	
(1948) B			200	96		390	28	140	63	447		1.0	0.3	0.02	0.05	0.5	
C			120	96		390	14	224	63	64		1.0	0.3	0.02	0.05	0.5	
Schwartz [Israel]			124	43		312		*98	93	160			0.3	0.02	0.05	0.5	
California			160	48		234	15	196	31	64							
New Jersey			180	55		90	20.5	126	71	96							
South Africa			320	50		300		200	65								
CDA	A		131	22		209	33	93	36.7	29.5	188	1.7	0.8	0.035	0.094	0.46	0.027
Saanichton	B		146	22		209	33	135	36.7	29.5	108	1.7	0.8	0.035	0.094	0.46	0.027
B.C., Canada	C		146	22		209	33	177	36.7	29.5	—	1.7	0.8	0.035	0.094	0.46	0.027
Dr. Pilgrim	C		272	54.3	—	400	—	143.4	93.0	237.5	—		—	—	—	—	—
Elizabeth	B		204	40.7	—	300	—	107.6	69.75	178.1	—		—	—	—	—	—
N.C., USA	A		136	27.15	—	200	—	71.7	46.5	118.75	—		—	—	—	—	—
Dr. H. Resh	C		197	44	—	400	30	145	65	197.5	—	2	0.5	0.03	0.05	0.5	0.02
Univ. of B.C.	B		148	33	—	300	20	110	55	144.3	—	2	0.5	0.03	0.05	0.5	0.02
Vancouver B.C. Canada (1971)	A		98.5	22	—	200	10	80	40	83.2	—	2	0.5	0.03	0.05	0.5	0.02
Dr. H. M. Resh, Canada (1971) Tropical	Dry Season		250	36	—	200	53	177	60	129	—	5	0.5	0.03	0.05	0.5	0.02
Formulations (1984) [Lettuce]	Wet Season		150	50	—	150	32	115	50	52	—	5	0.5	0.03	0.05	0.5	0.02

*Add additional 1 m M (14 ppm) per week to a total of about 12 m M, (128 ppm), for the first 6-8 weeks.

79

climate. During the longer sunny summer days, the plant needs more nitrogen and less potassium than during the shorter, darker winter days. It is common practice therefore to double the ratio K/N during the winter. This will make for harder growth in winter than would take place on a summer formulation. Some typical nutrient formulations derived over the past by various researchers are given in table 3.6.

Ulises Durany (1982) recommends that for the development of tomatoes during the initial vegetative phase the N:K proportion should be 1:5 (eg: 80 ppm N:400 ppm K), the intermediate phase during blossoming and fruit set the N:K ratio should be 1:3 (eg: 110 ppm N:330 ppm K) and the mature stage with ripening fruit should have a N:K ratio of 1:1.5 (eg: 140 ppm N:210 ppm K). This can be achieved through the use of potassium nitrate and calcium nitrate with potassium sulfate.

Schwarz (1968) lists a number of ratios for N:P:K to be used during the summer and winter seasons for various crops grown in European, Mediterranean and subtropical climates (table 3.7).

TABLE 3.7   Ratios of N:P:K Recommended for Summer and Winter Seasons in Several Climatic Regions

Crop, Climate, Season		N	P	K
Carnation, rose, tomato, etc. mature stage of development Middle European climate				
	—summer	1	0.2-0.3	1-1.5
	—winter	1	0.3-0.5	2-4
Mediterranean and	—summer	1	0.2	1
subtropical climate	—winter	1	0.3	1.5-2
Lettuce and other leafy vegetables				
	—summer	1	0.2	1
	—winter	2	0.3	2
Ammonium:Nitrate ratio is: $(NH_4 : NO_3)$	—summer	1:3-4		
	—winter	1:4-8		

Adapted from Schwarz (1968) p. 32.

3.6 Preparing the Nutrient Solution

1. Weigh out fertilizer salts individually, arranging them in piles on polyethylene sheets so that there is no loss. This should be done accurately to within plus or minus 5 percent using a gram scale.

2. Fill the storage tank to within 10 percent of the final volume with water.

3. Dissolve each salt individually in a large bucket of water and pour off the solution into the storage tank. Repeat, stirring and adding water, until the entire salt has been dissolved. With salts that are hard to dissolve use hot water.

4. Dissolve the macronutrients first, then the micronutrients.

5. In small systems such as backyard greenhouses all the sulfates can be mixed together in dry form before dissolving; e.g.: K_2SO_4, $MgSO_4$. Then the nitrates and phosphates can be mixed in dry form before dissolving; e.g.: KNO_3, KH_2PO_4. Add $Ca(NO_3)_2$ last.

6. Check the pH of the nutrient solution and adjust it, if necessary, with either sulphuric acid (H_2SO_4) or potassium hydroxide (KOH). High pH (more than 7.0) causes precipitation of Fe^{++}, Mn^{++}, $PO_4^{\equiv}$, Ca^{++} and Mg^{++} to insoluble and unavailable salts.

7. Circulate the nutrient solution through the beds for 5–10 minutes, then check the pH again and adjust it to between 6.0 and 6.5. Finally, add the micronutrients.

3.7 Plant Relations and Cause of Nutrient Solution Changes

In a cyclic (closed) system in which the nutrient solution is drained back to the reservoir after use, the life of the nutrient solution is 2–3 weeks, depending upon the season of the year and the stage of plant growth. During the summer months, under mature high-yielding plants, the nutrient solution may have to be changed as often as every week. The reason for changing the solution is that plants differentially absorb the various elements. As a result, some elements become in short supply before others. Just how deficient they are at any point can be determined only by atomic absorption analyses of the nutrient solution. Such analyses can be done only in costly laboratory facilities. Consequently, many people are unable to carry out such analyses. The only safeguard against a nutrient disorder then is to change the solution periodically. In some cases it is possible to add partial formulations between changes, but this is only by trial and error and can result in excess salt buildup of nutrients which are taken up by the plant at relatively low rates.

The relative uptake of the various mineral elements by the plant is affected by:

a. environmental conditions—temperature, humidity, light intensity;

b. nature of the crop;

c. stage of plant development.

As a result of the differential uptake of the various elements, the composition of the nutrient solution is changing constantly. Some of the elements are being depleted more rapidly than others, and the concentration is being increased by the plants' relatively greater absorption of water than of salts. In addition to changes in salt composition, the pH is also changing as a result of reactions with the aggregate and the unbalanced absorption of the anions and cations from the solutions.

3.7.1 Nutrient Analysis

Before replacing mineral elements it is necessary to determine their concentration by chemical methods of analysis in order to determine the quantities absorbed by the plant. The difference in concentration of the mineral elements from the time of first mixing the nutrient solution to that at the time of analysis tells how much of each element must be added to bring the concentration to its original level.

Besides testing the solutions for depletions, it is necessary to test for the accumulation of unused ions such as sodium, sulfate or chloride, or for the presence of excesses of toxic elements as copper or zinc.

3.7.2 Plant Tissue Analysis

By conducting both plant tissue and nutrient solution analyses, we can compare and relate plant physiological upsets to imbalances of various mineral elements in the nutrient solution. It is possible to control the changes in the nutrient solution once a precise relationship is established between fluctuations in mineral elements in the plant tissue and those in the nutrient solution. Then the nutrient solution should be adjusted before visual symptoms appear in the plant tissue. This would prevent any mineral stress from occurring within the plant and thus increase yields by allowing the plant to grow under optimum mineral nutrition conditions.

An advantage of tissue analysis over nutrient analysis is that tissue analysis indicates what has been or is being absorbed from the nutrient solution by the plant, whereas nutrient analysis indicates only the relative availability of nutrients to the plant. Actual uptake of essential elements may be restricted by conditions of the medium, solution, environmental factors or the plant itself. For instance, if the medium is not inert and reacts with the nutrient solution, ions may be retained by the particles and unavailable to the plant. Imbalances within the nutrient solution or fluctuating pH levels will reduce uptake by the plants. Diseases or nematodes in the roots of plants would reduce their absorption capacity for nutrients. Environmental factors such as insufficient light, extremes in temperatures and insufficient carbon dioxide levels will prevent plants from efficiently utilizing the available nutrients in the solution. Plant tissue analysis measures the effects of these conditions on nutrient uptake.

The use of tissue analysis in relating the nutrient status of a plant is based upon the fact that normal, healthy growth is associated with specific levels of each nutrient in certain plant tissues. Since these normal levels are not the same for all tissues on any plant or for all species, it is necessary to select an indicator tissue which is representative of a definite stage of growth. Generally, a young, vigorous leaf near the growing point of the main stem of the plant is selected. It is more reliable to take samples at various stages of growth than to concentrate on a large number of samples at any one stage since the concentration of most nutrients decreases as the plants age and mature.

To accurately relate tissue analysis results to nutritional requirements of plants considerable data must be available on optimum levels of nutrients in specific plant species and tissues to be compared. This information is available for greenhouse lettuce, tomatoes and cucumbers (table 3.8). The indicator tissue for tomatoes is the fifth leaf down from the growing tip of the main stem and it includes both petiole and blade tissue. At least ten samples should be taken of only one variety under one fertilizer treatment. The indicator tissue for cucumbers is a young leaf, without petiole, about 10 cm (4 inches) in diameter, usually the third visible leaf from the top of the main stem. A representative sample should consist of ten uniform replicates. The leaves should be either oven dried (70°C for 48 hours) or delivered promptly in a fresh condition to a commercial laboratory. Before drying, separate the blades from the petioles. Analysis for NO_3-N, PO_4-P, K, Ca, and Mg are usually performed on the petioles; minor elements on the blades.

To examine the results, date of planting, stage of growth, and previous fertilizer treatment must be known. A weekly series of tests will indicate clearly the trends in any nutrient level. A combination of nutrient and tissue analysis will allow the grower to anticipate any problems before they occur and make the necessary adjustments in the nutrient solution formulation.

TABLE 3.8   Range of Nutrient Levels in Tissues of Apparently Healthy Plants

Element	Tomatoes	Cucumbers	Lettuce
N%	4.5	5.25	4.3
	4.5-5.5	5.0-6.0	3.0-6.0
P%	0.7	0.75	1.0
	0.6-1.0	0.7-1.0	0.8-1.3
K%	4.5	4.75	5.4
	4.0-5.5	4.5-5.5	5.0-10.8
Ca%	1.5	3.0	1.5
	1.5-2.5	2.0-4.0	1.1-2.1
Mg%	0.5	0.75	0.42
	0.4-0.6	0.5-1.0	0.3-0.9
Fe (ppm)	100	125	120
	80-150	100-150	130-600
B (ppm)	50	40	32
	35-60	35-60	25-40
Mn (ppm)	70	70	70
	70-150	60-150	20-150
Zn (ppm)	30	50	45
	30-45	40-80	60-120
Cu (ppm)	5	8	14
	4-6	5-10	7-17
Mo (ppm)	2	2	2-3
	1-3	1-3	1-4
N/K ratio	1.0	1.1	
	0.9-1.2	1.0-1.5	

3.7.3 Changing of Solutions

Work by Steiner (1980) on nutrient solutions indicates that if the ratios of nutrient uptake for a certain crop under given conditions are known, ions can be applied continuously to the solution in these mutual ratios, controlled only by a conductivity meter. While generally this is true, extended use of the same nutrient solution may result in accumulation of toxic quantities of minor elements such as zinc and copper from metals in the plumbing system, fertilizer impurities, or from the water itself.

The useful life of a nutrient solution depends principally on the rate of accumulation of extraneous ions which are not utilized by the plants at rapid rates. Such an accumulation results in a high osmotic concentration of the nutrient solution. An electrical conductivity device, commercially available, should be used to determine the rate at which the nutrient solution becomes concentrated. Determinations should be made on a new nutrient solution and then repeated after each makeup with nutrient salts. As the total salt level increases it will more readily conduct an electric current. The unit of measurement used to express conductance is a *mho*. For simplicity, conductivity is often expressed as millimhos/cm, with the desired range 2.00 to 4.00. Salt levels above 4 millimhos/cm may result in wilting, suppressed growth, and fruit cracking. One mMho/cm=1 Millisiemen/cm (mS/cm).

The total concentration of elements in a nutrient solution should be between 1000 and 1500 ppm so that osmotic pressure will facilitate the absorption processes by the roots. This should correspond to total salt conductivity readings between 1.5 and 3.5 millimhos (mMho). In general, the lower values (1.5-2.0 mMho) are preferred by crops such as cucumbers while higher values are better for tomatoes (2.5-3.5 mMho). One mMho/cm is approximately equal to 650 ppm of salt.

In general, no nutrient solution should be used for more than three months without complete replacement, together with a tap water flushing of the whole system, including the beds. Two months is probably the average economical life of a nutrient solution which has been adjusted by use of analyses on a regular weekly basis. Of course, without such analyses, as mentioned earlier, the life of the solution would be no more than 2 to 3 weeks.

3.7.4 Adjustment of Nutrient Solutions by Use of Electrical Conductivity

Total dissolved solutes (TDS) instruments which determine the dissolved solids in water are basically water conductivity measuring instruments. The quantity of dissolved solids in parts per million (ppm) or mg/l by weight is directly proportional to conductivity in millimhos (mMho) per unit volume. However, the electrical conductivity (EC) varies not only to the concentration of salts present, but also to the chemical composition of the nutrient solution. Some fertilizer salts conduct electric current better than others. For instance, ammonium sulfate conducts twice as much electricity as calcium nitrate and more than three times that of magnesium sulfate, whereas, urea does not conduct electricity at all. Nitrate ions do not produce as close a relationship with electrical conductivity as do potassium ions (Alt, D. 1980). The higher

TABLE 3.9   Relationship between Total Dissolved Solutes (TDS) and Electrical Conductivity (EC) for Sodium Chloride and Calcium Carbonate Solutions (Solution A)

Solution A TDS (ppm)	EC (mMho)	NaCl (ppm)	$CaCO_3$ (ppm)
10,000	15	8400	7250
6660	10	5500	4700
5000	7.5	4000	3450
4000	6	3200	2700
3000	4.5	2350	2000
2000	3	1550	1300
1000	1.5	750	640
750	1.125	560	475
666	1	490	420
500	0.75	365	315
400	0.6	285	250
250	0.375	175	150
100	0.15	71	60
66	0.10	47	40
50	0.075	35	30
40	0.06	28	24
25	0.0375	17.5	15
6.6	0.01	4.7	4

the nitrogen to potassium the lower will be the electrical conductivity values for the nutrient solution. Electrical conductivity measures total solutes, it does not differentiate among the various elements. For this reason, while a close theoretical relationship exists between TDS and EC, standard solutions of a nutrient formulation should be measured to determine their correlation in a given solution. For example, in table 3.9 a 666 ppm TDS is equivalent to 1.0 mMho which is the measurement of a solution containing 490 ppm of sodium chloride or 420 ppm of calcium carbonate. That is, a 490 ppm solution of sodium chloride or a 420 ppm solution of calcium carbonate each give an electrical conductivity reading of 1.0 mMho.

Table 3.9 relates concentration of sodium chloride and calcium carbonate with conductivity. A list of conductivities for 0.2% solutions (2 grams of fertilizer in 1 liter of distilled water) of various fertilizers are given in table 3.10. Conductivities for various concentrations of calcium nitrate are outlined in table 3.11. These conductivity standards should be used to derive a theoretical relationship between conductivity and TDS. Actual conductivity measurements for fertilizers may vary somewhat from those in tables 3.10 and 3.11 due to the solubility and purity of the particular fertilizer source.

If electrical conductivity readings are not taken at the standard temperature of 25°C, a correction factor must be used (table 3.12).

TABLE 3.10   Conductivity (EC) of 0.2% Solution in Distilled Water

Fertilizer Compound	EC (mMho)
$Ca(NO_3)_2$	2.0
KNO_3	2.5
NH_4NO_3	2.9
$(NH_4)_2SO_4$	3.4
K_2SO_4	2.4
$MgSO_4 \cdot 7H_2O$	1.2
$MnSO_4 \cdot 4H_2O$	1.55
NaH_2PO_4	0.9
KH_2PO_4	1.3
HNO_3	4.8
H_3PO_4	1.8

Some instruments such as the "Volmatic" conductivity meter, have a built-in temperature compensation which automatically makes the necessary adjustment.

Since most waters contain a number of dissolved solids and these solutes have different weights per ion, they will have a different concentration (ppm) for a given conductivity value. To adjust for these extraneous solids in a specific source of water to be used for a nutrient solution a series of standards of known fertilizer concentrations should be made up with the water in question and their conductivities measured.

These measurements should be plotted graphically to better represent the actual relationship. When actual values for electrical conductivity for given nutrient solutions are plotted against known total dissolved solutes, a straight line direct relationship is revealed (table 3.13, 3.14 and fig. 3.1). If the theoretical TDS and EC values from table 3.9 (solution A) are plotted on this graph, a large difference is apparent due to the different chemical compositions of the solutions (fig. 3.1). For example, the electrical conductivities of 1.0, 2.0, 3.0, 4.0, and 5.0 mMho are equivalent to actual TDS contents of 350 ppm, 720 ppm, 1100 ppm, 1460 ppm, and 1840 ppm respectively for Solution B (fig. 3.1) while the theoretical values from table 3.9 and figure 3.1 are 666 ppm, 1330 ppm, 2000 ppm, 2680 ppm, and 3340 ppm respectively. If nutrient solutions differ only slightly in their composition, the correlation between EC and TDS will be similar for both solutions (tables 3.13, 3.14 and fig. 3.1). While a substantial difference exists between the actual and theoretical values of TDS for a given conductivity reading due to solubility differences of fertilizers, the ratios and compositions of various ions in the solution, the data is useful to determine the overall changes which occur in a specific nutrient solution.

TABLE 3.11   Conductivity (EC) of Various Concentrations of Calcium Nitrate in Distilled Water

Concentration (%)	EC (mMho)
0.05	0.5
0.1	1.0
0.2	2.0
0.3	3.0
0.5	4.8
1.0	9.0

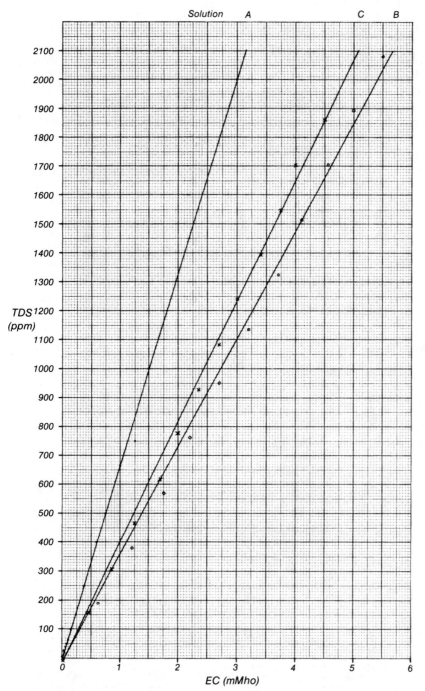

Fig. 3.1. Electrical Conductivity (EC) versus Total Dissolved Solutes (TDS) for a Number of Nutrient Solutions.

With sufficient data collected over time to verify the statistical significance of the relationship between EC and TDS a relatively inexpensive and simple method to monitor changes in the nutrient solution over time will indicate what adjustments should be made to keep the solution in balance for the crop being grown.

This principle can become more useful by determining for each crop the relationships among total dissolved solutes, electrical conductivity, concentration of each essential element and stage of

TABLE 3.12   Temperature Factors for Correcting Conductivity Data to Standard Temperature of 25°C*

°C	°F	Temperature Factor
5	41.0	1.613
10	50.0	1.411
15	59.0	1.247
16	60.8	1.211
17	62.6	1.189
18	64.4	1.163
19	66.2	1.136
20	68.0	1.112
21	69.8	1.087
22	71.6	1.064
23	73.4	1.043
24	75.2	1.020
25	**77.0**	**1.000**
26	78.8	0.979
27	80.6	0.960
28	82.4	0.943
29	84.2	0.925
30	86.0	0.907
31	87.8	0.890
32	89.6	0.873
33	91.4	0.858
34	93.2	0.843
35	95.0	0.829
40	104.0	0.763
45	113.0	0.705

* From "Saline and Alkali Soils," U.S. Salinity Laboratory Staff, Agricultural Handbook, No. 60, p. 90.

TABLE 3.13   Electrical Conductivity (EC) and Total Dissolved Solutes (TDS) of a Standard 30 Liter Nutrient Solution (Solution B)

g/30 l.				TDS	EC
K₂SO₄	Ca(NO₃)₂	(NH₄)₂HPO₄	MgSO₄·7H₂O	(ppm)	(mMho)
0	0	0	0	0	0.05
2.82	7.4	1.88	2.75	189.4	0.62
5.65	14.8	3.75	5.5	379	1.2
8.5	22.2	5.62	8.25	568	1.75
11.3	29.6	7.5	11.0	757.5	2.2
14.1	37.0	9.38	13.75	947	2.7
17.0	44.4	11.25	16.5	1136	3.2
19.8	51.8	13.12	19.25	1326	3.7
22.6	59.2	15.0	22.0	1515	4.1
25.4	66.6	16.88	24.75	1704	4.55
28.25	74.0	18.75	27.5	1894	5.0
31.1	81.4	20.62	30.25	2083	5.5
33.9	88.8	22.5	33.0	2272.5	6.3

TABLE 3.14   Electrical Conductivity (EC) and Total Dissolved Solutes (TDS) of a Standard 30 Liter Nutrient Solution (Solution C)

g/30 l.				TDS	EC
KNO₃	Ca(NO₃)₂	(NH₄)₂HPO₄	MgSO₄·7H₂O	(ppm)	(mMho)
0	0	0	0	0	0.05
3.08	5.75	1.88	2.75	154.9	0.45
6.15	11.5	3.75	5.5	309.8	0.86
9.22	17.25	5.62	8.25	464.6	1.25
12.3	23.0	7.5	11.0	619.5	1.7
15.38	28.75	9.38	13.75	774.4	2.0
18.45	34.5	11.25	16.5	929.2	2.35
21.52	40.25	13.12	19.25	1084.1	2.7
24.6	46.0	15.0	22.0	1239	3.0
27.68	51.75	16.88	24.75	1393.9	3.4
30.75	57.5	18.75	27.5	1548.8	3.75
33.82	63.25	20.62	30.25	1703.6	4.0
36.9	69.0	22.5	33.0	1858.5	4.5

plant growth under similar light conditions. Data can be obtained through a laboratory analysis of the nutrient solution each week. Samples should always be taken from the same nutrient tank having the same volume of solution, growing the same number of plants. If these factors change between sample periods, error will result in the interpretation, as variations would have occurred among samples and comparisons would not have the same basis.

If these tests are taken at the same stages of growth for each crop for a number of crops during the year, the only variable remaining would be sunlight hours. Adjustments could be made in the results of the analyses for changes in weekly total sunlight hours.

Head lettuce requires about 84 days (12 weeks) to maturity. The nutrient solution should be changed completely at 6 weeks. Analysis should be taken weekly, that is, days 0, 7, 14, 21, 28, 35, and 42 for the first solution make-up and days 42, 49, 56, 63, 70, 77, and 84 for the second solution make-up. By analyzing 12 of the essential elements (N, P, K, Ca, Mg, S, Fe, Mn, B, Cu, Zn, and Mo) weekly, changes in the levels of each element could be plotted against age of the plants.

Since data is not presently available to substantiate these relationships, a hypothetical situation is used to demonstrate the expected relationships of levels of essential elements, TDS and E C with plant stage of growth for head lettuce (fig. 3.2). When the plants are seedlings (0-21 days) little change in solution element levels would occur. As the plant leaf area increases, demand upon nutrients would increase, resulting in a depletion of existing elements within the nutrient solution to suboptimal levels. Due to differential uptake of elements by plants at various stages of their growth the rate of decrease would differ for each element. For example, the negative slope of the nitrogen (N) curve is greater than that of K and P indicating that nitrogen is used more rapidly by the plants than K or P. As the plants mature the overall demand upon nutrients increases and the demand for some elements will be greater than for others as shown by the greater negative slopes of the curves. This is more evident in the second set of curves (days 42-84) during the second nutrient solution make-up. All elements are decreasing in concentration at a faster rate, that is, the negative slope of the curves has increased.

The curves should be used to determine when to add those fertilizers whose elements are rapidly being depleted before a deficiency causes nutritional stress in the plants and a resultant sig-

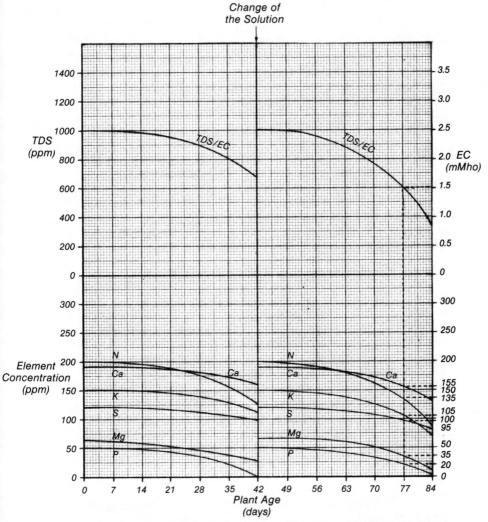

Fig. 3.2. Hypothetical Relationship among Macroelements, Total Dissolved Solutes (TDS), Electrical Conductivity (EC) of the Nutrient Solution and the Age of the Plants. (Solution C.)

nificant loss in crop productivity. In the hypothetical example above, nitrogen (N) should have been added after the 28-day period in the first solution and weekly after the 56-day period in the second solution. Phosphorus (P) and potassium (K) should have been added after the 28-day period in the first solution and weekly after the 63-day period in the second solution. Additions of fertilizers should be made to bring up the individual element to its original optimal level each time.

According to work by Steiner (1980) salts may be added to the nutrient solution during culture using electrical conductivity as a measure of the solution status. But he emphasizes that any additions of ions should be made as close as possible in the same mutual ratio as they are utilized by the plants. There is no evidence to support the idea that plants can be forced to consume ions in the ratio of the nutrient solution. Plants select their desired uptake ratio of nutrients from widely different ratios in the nutrient solution. Therefore, ions should be added in the same mutual ratio as the plants absorb them.

Based upon this knowledge a favorable nutrient solution for any given crop can be developed and its ratios of nutrients can be adjusted to optimum levels by use of electrical conductivity of the nutrient solution, provided the relationship among the stage of crop growth, sunlight hours and total dissolved solutes has been determined. As Steiner (1980) points out, even if small deviations in the chemical composition of the nutrient solution occur, the plants themselves can select the ions in a mutual ratio favorable for their growth and development.

The same type of curves and reasoning can be made for the micronutrients, the differences being that the changes and levels are much smaller. Nonetheless, adjustments are equally important in order to maintain an optimum nutrient status without encountering deficiencies.

With total dissolved solutes (TDS) and electrical conductivity (EC) included in the above graphs (fig.3.1, Solution C) the relationships to the age of plants and levels of individual elements are evident. An electrical conductivity reading would indicate the total dissolved solute level and the probable levels of each essential element at any given plant age. With this information supported by sufficient data for a given nutrient formulation, future EC readings on a nutrient solution sample having the same formulation but no laboratory analysis carried out on it, could be used to determine the levels of individual elements within the solution. Accurate adjustments could be made in the nutrient solution at any given season and stage of plant growth.

For example, if the EC was taken at day 56 and was found to be 1.5, follow the TDS/EC curve (fig. 3.2) along until the point of EC=1.5, then read directly below it the levels of each element. Since the plant age is within the second nutrient solution make-up, the second set of graphs should be used. As plants mature their uptake of specific elements changes. For instance, more K and Ca would be taken up by tomatoes as they produce fruit. That is, their ratio of uptake of K and Ca increases in comparison with the other elements. During early vegetative growth N would be more in demand. In this example it is assumed that no fertilizers had been added earlier to adjust for plant uptake. If some were added, the EC would have been higher and the intersection point on the TDS/EC curve would have been further to the left indicating the solution varied little from its original preparation at day 42.

The points of intersection of the individual elements corresponding to the TDS/EC curve at EC=1.5 would be: Ca=155 ppm, N=135 ppm, K=105 ppm, S=95 ppm, Mg=35 ppm, and P=20 ppm. If the original formulation had Ca=190 ppm, N=200 ppm, K=150 ppm, S=120 ppm, Mg=65 ppm, and P=50 ppm, the differences that have to be made up by addition of fertilizers are: Ca=35 ppm, N=65 ppm, K=45 ppm, S=25 ppm, Mg=30 ppm, and P=30 ppm. Generally, sulfur (S) need not be added specifically as it is included in several fertilizers such as potassium sulfate and magnesium sulfate which would be used to increase potassium (K) and magnesium (Mg) levels.

If the original nutrient solution volume was 30,000 liters (7925 U.S. gallons) and it had to be maintained, the solution level should be topped-up before recording the electrical conductivity. If the conductivity value was taken within several weeks of crop maturity and the solution volume was at 20,000 liters (5283 U.S. gallons) but that volume was sufficient to maintain the crop until harvest then the conductivity should be recorded on that solution volume without topping it up since less fertilizers would be required to adjust the solution. If water needs to be added to the solution, it should be done before recording conductivity. In general, as the volume of water decreases it concentrates the solution, unless the plants are taking up nutrients faster than utilizing water.

The amount of fertilizers needed to adjust the 30,000 liters (7925 U.S. gallons) of solution in the above example would be as follows (using conversion factors from table 3.2):

Ca: 35 ppm, source: $Ca(NO_3)_2$
        Need: $35\times4.094=143.3$ mg/l
        For 30,000 liters: $30,000 \times \dfrac{143.3}{1000} = 4299$ g. or 4.3 kg.
        Amount of N: $143.3\times0.171=24.5$ mg/l (ppm)

Mg: 30 ppm, source: $MgSO_4\cdot7H_2O$
        Need: $30\times10.14=304$ mg/l or 9.1 kg/30,000 l.
        Amount of S: $304\times0.130=39.5$ ppm

P: 30 ppm, source: KH_2PO_4
        Need: $30\times4.394=131.8$ mg/l or 3.95 kg/30,000 l.
        Amount of K: $131.8\times0.287=37.8$ ppm

K: 38 ppm, source: KH_2PO_4; 7 ppm, source KNO_3
        Need: $7\times2.586=18.1$ mg/l or 0.54 kg/30,000 l.
        Amount of N: $18.1\times0.1385=2.5$ ppm
S: 39.5 ppm, source: $MgSO_4\cdot7H_2O$
*N: 24.5 ppm, source: $Ca(NO_3)_2$
        2.5 ppm, source: KNO_3
        Total: 27 ppm

* Since the amount of N that can be obtained is limited by the amount of KNO_3 used as a source of K, either additional N could be added from $Ca(NO_3)_2, NH_4NO_3$ or alternatively, the N level should be left at 27 ppm from the present levels of $Ca(NO_3)_2$ and KNO_3 required to provide Ca and K respectively.

The amount of fertilizers to be added to 30,000 liters (7925 U.S. gallons) of solution are: 4.3 kg of calcium nitrate, 9.1 kg of magnesium sulfate, 3.95 kg of monopotassium phosphate, and 0.54 kg of potassium nitrate. The fertilizers add the following amounts of each element: N=27 ppm, P =30 ppm, K=45 ppm, Ca=35 ppm, Mg=30 ppm, and S=39.5 ppm. After adding the fertilizers the pH and electrical conductivity should be recorded. The conductivity value should approach that when the solution was first prepared.

Using EC to adjust a nutrient solution weekly instead of changing it every few weeks could extend its life to at least 6 weeks. In this way substantial savings in fertilizers, water and labour would be realized. These savings would be particularly beneficial in countries having a scarcity of water and/or a shortage of fertilizers. Such savings would more than compensate for the initial cost of solution analyses.

Several plant laboratories capable of analyzing nutrient solutions are listed in the Appendix. In addition, many universities are prepared to do such analyses.

The management of nutrient solutions through the use of electrical conductivity applies particularly to closed systems of NFT and subirrigation. However, it can be used to monitor open systems having large storage tanks of solution rather than those using proportioners.

3.7.5 Maintenance of the Solution Volume

The solution volume must be kept relatively constant in order to secure adequate plant growth. Plants take up much more water and at a much greater rate than the essential mineral elements. As water is removed from the nutrient solution, the volume of the solution naturally decreases. This effects an increase in the total solution concentration and in the concentration of the individual nutrient ions.

The average daily water loss can range from 5 to 30 percent, depending upon the volume of the unit and the number and type of plants. Water to compensate for this loss can be added daily as long as the solution is used. Using NFT systems, workers can more accurately determine the rate of water uptake by plants. In England, Spensley and co-workers (1978) found that on a clear summer's day fully grown tomatoes consumed 1.33 liters (⅓ gal) of water per plant. Winsor and associates (1980) determined that tomato plants lost through evapotranspiration 15 ml/plant/hr during the night, rising to a maximum of 134 ml/plant/hr at midday on a clear summer day. Adams (1980) calculated that cucumbers consumed water at approximately twice the rate for tomatoes due to their greater leaf area. Water uptake reached a maximum of 230 ml/plant/hr during maximum light intensity and temperatures of the afternoon. A rule-of-thumb estimate of water useage in a greenhouse is about 1 liter/sq ft/day for vine crops such as tomatoes and cucumbers. Experienced commercial growers can add water weekly or they can attach an automatic float valve assembly to the inlet valve to the nutrient tank which will fill it daily. When water is added weekly, water in excess of the original volume of the solution is introduced. The solution is then allowed to concentrate as the plants remove water to below the original solution level. Usually the best procedure is to allow the solution volume to fluctuate equally on both sides of the original level. It follows that a solution-testing technique must be used in conjunction with this method of regulation of the solution volume.

3.7.6 Injector or Proportioner System

A fertilizer injector or proportioner automatically makes up the nutrient solution by injecting preset amounts of concentrated stock solutions into the water feeding lines. In this way a new nutrient solution is made up with each watering cycle (fig. 3.3). Such a system is used as an "open" system in which the nutrient solution is not recycled. Therefore, changing of the nutrient solution is eliminated. Additional stock solutions are simply made up every week or so.

Plant tissue analysis can still be made on a regular basis so that appropriate adjustments in the formulation can be carried out. The injector can easily be set to alter the formulation. Imbalances of the nutrient solution do not occur since it is always made up fresh each time the watering cycle is activated.

Fig. 3.3. Injector system with two stock solution tanks (left & right) and acid tank in center using nitric acid to adjust pH. Injector sits behind acid tank. pH and EC monitors are downstream from injector to give constant read-out of nutrient solution pH and EC on its way to the greenhouse.

References

Adams, P. 1980. Nutrient uptake by cucumbers from recirculating solutions. *Acta Hort.* 98:119-126.

Alt, D. 1980. Changes in the composition of the nutrient solution during plant growth—an important factor in soilless culture. *Proc. 5th Int. Congress on Soilless Culture,* Wageningen, May 1980, pp. 97-109.

Butler, J. N. 1964. *Solubility and pH calculations.* Reading, Mass.: Addison-Wesley.

Schaum, D., Beckmann, C. O., and J. L. Rosenberg. 1962. *Schaum's outline of theory and problems of college chemistry.* 4th ed. New York: Schaum.

Schwarz, M. 1968. *Guide to commercial hydroponics.* Jerusalem: Israel Univ. Press.

Sienko, M. J. and R. A. Plane. 1961. *Chemistry,* 2d ed. New York: McGraw-Hill.

Spensley, K., G. W. Winsor, and A. J. Cooper, 1978. Nutrient film technique crop culture in flowing nutrient solution. *Outlook on Agriculture.* 9:299-305.

Steiner, A. A. 1980. The selective capacity of plants for ions and its importance for the composition and treatment of the nutrient solution. *Proc. 5th Int. Congress on Soilless Culture,* Wageningen, May 1980, pp. 83-95.

Ulises Durany, Carol. 1982. *Hidroponia—Cultivo de plantas sin tierra.* 4th ed. Editorial Sintes, S.A., Barcelona, Spain, 106 pp.

Winsor, G. W., P. Adams, and D. Massey. 1980. New light on nutrition. *Suppl. Grower.* 93(8):99, 103.

Withrow, R. B., and A. P. Withrow. 1948. *Nutriculture.* Lafayette, Ind.: Purdue Univ. Agr. Expt. Stn. Publ. S. C. 328.

Chapter 4

The Medium

A soilless medium, such as water, gravel, sand, sawdust, peat, pumice, vermiculite, or peanut hulls must provide oxygen, water, nutrients and support for plant roots just as does soil. The nutrient solution will provide water, nutrients and to some extent oxygen. How each of these soilless cultural methods satisfies plant needs will be discussed in detail in the chapters to follow.

4.1 Medium Characteristics

Moisture retention of a medium is determined by particle size, shape and porosity. Water is retained on the surface of the particles and within the pore space. The smaller the particles, the closer they will pack, the greater the surface area and pore space, and hence the greater the water retention. Irregular-shaped particles have a greater surface area and hence higher water retention than smooth, round, particles. Porous materials can store water within the particles themselves, therefore water retention is high. While the medium must be capable of good water retention it must also be capable of good drainage. Therefore, excessively fine materials must be avoided so as to prevent excessive water retention and lack of oxygen movement within the medium.

The choice of the medium will be determined by availability, cost, quality, and the type of hydroponic method to be employed. A gravel subirrigation system can use very coarse material, whereas a gravel trickle irrigation system must use a finer material (see Chapter 6).

The medium must not contain any toxic materials. Sawdust, for example, often contains a high sodium chloride content due to logs

100

having remained in salt water for a long period of time. The salt content must be tested and if any amount of sodium chloride is present, it will be necessary to leach it through with fresh water. Gravel and sand of calcareous (limestone) origin should be avoided. Such materials have a very high content of calcium carbonate ($CaCO_3$), which is released from the medium into the nutrient solution, resulting in high pH. This increased alkalinity ties up iron, causing iron deficiency in plants. Such materials can be pretreated with water-leaching, acid-leaching or soaking in a phosphate solution. This will buffer the release of carbonate ions. Nonetheless, this procedure is only a short-term solution and eventually nutritional problems will arise. This problem makes gravel and sand culture very difficult in some areas such as the Caribbean, where the materials are all of calcareous origin. The best gravel or sand is that of igneous (volcanic) origin.

The media must be of sufficient hardness in order to be durable for a long time. Soft aggregates which disintegrate easily should be avoided. They lose their structure and their particle size decreases, which results in compaction leading to poor root aeration. Again, aggregates of granitic origin are best, especially those high in quartz, calcite and feldspars. If a hydroponic system is to be set up out of doors, particles having sharp edges should be avoided, since wind can abrade the plant stem and crown against them, leading to injury and a port of entry for plant parasites. If a relatively sharp medium must be used, the top 2 inches should consist of smooth-edged medium so the area where most plant movement takes place will be protected from abrasion.

Igneous gravel and sand have little influence on the nutrient solution pH, whereas calcareous material will buffer the nutrient solution pH at about 7.5. Treatment with phosphate solutions can bring the pH down to 6.8 (see Chapter 6).

4.2 Water Characteristics

The water quality is of prime concern in hydroponic growing. Water with sodium chloride content of 50 ppm or greater is not suitable for optimum plant growth. As sodium chloride content is increased, plant growth is restricted; high levels result finally in death of the plant. Besides the sodium chloride content, the total dissolved solutes in the nutrient solution must be considered.

Hardness is a measure of the carbonate ion (HCO_3^-) content. As mentioned earlier, as hardness increases (pH increases) certain ions such as iron become unavailable. In particular, ground water which lies in calcareous and dolomitic limestone strata could contain high levels of calcium and magnesium carbonate which may be higher than or equal to the normal levels used in the nutrient solution.

Hard water contains salts of calcium and magnesium. Normally such waters are just as suitable as soft water for growing plants. Calcium and magnesium both are essential nutrient elements and ordinarily the amount present in hard waters is much less than that used in nutrient solutions. Most hard waters contain calcium and magnesium as carbonates or sulfates. While the sulfate ion is an essential nutrient, the carbonate is not. In low concentrations the carbonate is not injurious to plants. Before any water is used, an analysis should be made for at least calcium, magnesium, iron, carbonate, sulfate and chloride. If a commercial hydroponic complex is being planned, water should be analyzed for all major and minor elements. Once the level of each ion has been determined, correspondingly less of each of these elements should be added to make up the nutrient solution. For example, the magnesium concentration of some well waters is so high that it is not necessary to add any to the nutrient solution.

The naturally occurring dissolved salts in the water accumulate with the additions of makeup water. Over a period of time this buildup will exceed the optimum levels for plant growth and the nutrient solution will have to be changed to avoid injuring the plants.

The concentration of salts in a nutrient solution may be specified in terms of ppm, millimolar (mM), and milliequivalents per liter (me/l). Parts per million, as mentioned in Chapter 3, is based on a specified number of units by weight of salt for each million parts of solution. The millimolar unit of concentration involves the molecular weight of the substance. One mole of a substance is a weight in grams numerically equal to the molecular weight and commonly is called a *gram molecular weight*. A solution of one molar concentration is that which has one mole of the substance dissolved in one liter of solution. A millimolar concentration is 1/1000 as concentrated as a molar concentration and amounts to one mole in 1000 liters of solution.

Both solutions (KNO_3 and KCl) would have the same number of potassium ions, and the chloride ions in one solution would be the same in number as the nitrate ions of the other. In the absorption of nutrients, it is the concentration of ions and not the weight of the element or ion that is of significance.

Where there are bivalent ions present in a compound it is better to use milliequivalents per liter. Milliequivalents per liter is similar to the millimolar unit, but involves gram equivalents instead of the mole or gram molecular weight. The gram equivalent is the gram molecular weight divided by the valency (number of charges on the ion). The gram equivalent of a salt like KCl, which consists of singly valent ions (K^+, Cl^-), is numerically the same as the mole, but where there are bivalent ions ($SO_4^=$) as in potassium sulfate (K_2SO_4), a gram equivalent would contain numerically only half as much as a mole. Thus two solutions of K_2SO_4 and KCl, having the same millequivalent per liter concentration, would have in solution the same concentration of potassium ions, but half as many sulfate ions ($SO_4^=$) as chloride ions (Cl^-).

Milliequivalents per liter (me/l) is the most meaningful method of expressing the major constituents of water. This is a measure of the chemical equivalence of an ion.

The total concentration of a nutrient solution or water source occasionally is specified in terms of its potential osmotic pressure. It is a measure of the availability or activity of the water. The osmotic pressure difference between cells usually determines the direction in which water will diffuse. The osmotic pressure is proportional to the number of solute particles in solution and depends upon the number of ions per unit volume for inorganic materials. Osmotic pressure is usually given in atmosphere units, where 1 atmosphere (atm.) is 14.7 pounds per square inch.

In summary,

$$1 \text{ molar (M)} = \frac{\text{M.W.}}{1 \text{ l.}}$$

eg: KNO_3 M.W. = 101

$$1 \text{ M} = \frac{101 \text{ g.}}{1 \text{ l.}}$$

eg. KCl M.W. = 74.6

$$1 \text{ M} = \frac{74.6 \text{ g}}{1 \text{ l.}}$$

1 millimolar (mM) $= \dfrac{\text{M.W.}}{1000 \ \text{l.}}$

eg: KNO_3

$1 \text{ mM} = \dfrac{101 \text{ g.}}{1000 \ \text{l.}}$ $\qquad$ $10 \text{mM} = \dfrac{1010 \text{ g}}{1000 \text{l}}$

eg: KCl

$1 \text{mM} = \dfrac{74.6 \text{ g}}{1000 \text{l}}$ $\qquad$ $10 \text{mM} = \dfrac{746 \text{ g}}{1000 \text{l}}$

where: M.W. = molecular weight of the compound.

1 equivalent (Eq) $= \dfrac{\text{M.W.}}{\text{Valence}}$ eg: K_2SO_4; M.W.$=174.3$
$\qquad\qquad\qquad\qquad\qquad\qquad$ Valence $=2$

$\qquad$ 1 Eq. W.$= \dfrac{174.3}{2} = 87.15$

1 milliequivalent + (me) $= \dfrac{\text{Eq}}{1000}$ eg: K_2SO_4; $\dfrac{87.15}{1000} = 0.08715$

1 milliequivalent/l (me/l)$= \dfrac{\text{me}}{1\text{l}} = \dfrac{\text{Eq}}{1000\text{l}}$

1 me/l$= \dfrac{\text{ppm}}{\text{Eq}}$ eg: 100 ppm of $SO_4^{=}$

$\qquad\qquad\qquad$ me/l$= \dfrac{100}{48} = 2.08$ $\qquad$ Eq. of $SO_4^{=}$ is:$\dfrac{96}{2} = 48$

The use of saline waters for hydroponic growing of crops has been investigated by several workers (Victor 1973; Schwarz 1968). Possibilities of using saline water of 3000 ppm total salt were investigated by Schwarz (1968). Salt tolerance of varieties, stage of development, addition of nutrient absent in the raw water and frequency of irrigation are some factors to be considered in using saline water. The concentration expressed by 0.4 atm. osmotic pressure was recommended as best for good development of to-mato plants in tropical areas (Steiner 1968).

Saline waters are those containing sodium chloride. Highly saline water can be used for hydroponics, but a number of consid-erations are involved. The plants that can be grown are limited to salt-tolerant and moderately salt-tolerant species, such as carna-tion, tomato, cucumber, and lettuce. Even among salt-tolerant species, one variety may be more tolerant than another. A grower should conduct his own varietal trials to determine the most salt-tolerant varieties.

Salt tolerance is also dependent on plant growth stage. No mature cucumber plants have yet been shown to adapt gradually to saline conditions; however, Schwarz (1968) points out that cucumbers started in nonsaline conditions may be irrigated with solutions of gradually increasing salinity until the desired level is reached. The younger the plant, the easier it adapts to saline conditions. Schwarz (1968) reported that tomatoes and cucumbers generally take about 20 percent longer to germinate under saline than under nonsaline conditions.

Depending upon the species and variety and on the salinity of nutrient solutions, yields may be lowered by 10 to 25 percent in saline conditions. Schwarz (1968) reported yield reductions of 10 to 15 percent in tomatoes and lettuce and 20 to 25 percent in cucumbers grown with water containing 3000 ppm salts.

The total solute concentration (high osmotic pressure), by leading to a reduction in water uptake, is responsible for the inhibitory effect of saline solutions on plant growth. Schwarz (1968) found that extremely high osmotic pressures (over 10 atm.) for short periods are less damaging than long periods of moderately high pressures (4-5 atm.). Symptoms of salt toxicity are a general stunting of growth with smaller and darker green leaves, a marginal leaf burn and a blueing and bleaching of the plant tissues.

Salinity may inhibit uptake of certain ions. High sulfate concentrations promote the uptake of sodium (leading to sodium toxicity), decrease the uptake of calcium (leading to calcium deficiency, especially in lettuce), and interfere with potassium uptake. High calcium concentrations in nutrient solutions also affect potassium uptake. High total salt contents are thought to affect calcium uptake, leading to "blossom-end-rot" symptoms in tomatoes. Saline conditions reduce the availability of certain microelements, especially iron, so that additional iron must be added. In addition to chloride and sodium toxicity, boron toxicity is relatively common with some saline waters.

Schwarz (1968) reports that saline waters have some favorable effects on cucumbers and tomatoes in giving them a sweeter taste than those grown with freshwater solutions. Lettuce heads are generally more solid, and carnations are longer lasting. Plants grown in saline solutions apparently have a much higher tolerance to zinc and copper, so that zinc and copper levels previously considered toxic may be present without causing injury.

4.3 Irrigation

The minimum frequency of irrigation depends upon the surfaces of the aggregate, crop stage of growth and climatic factors. Smooth, regularly shaped, coarse aggregates must be irrigated more frequently than porous, irregularly shaped, fine aggregates having large surface areas. Large plants require more frequent irrigation than small plants. In outdoor installations, hot, dry weather accompanied by winds promotes rapid evaporation and makes it necessary to irrigate more often. Coarse aggregates may need watering as often as once every hour during the day, while fine media such as sand or sawdust could get by on one to two irrigations per day under similar conditions. More specific details on watering are presented for each type of hydroponic system in the following chapters.

4.4 Pumping of Nutrient Solution into Beds

As mentioned earlier, the nutrient solution must provide water, nutrients, and oxygen to the plants. The frequency of irrigations will depend on the nature of the medium, the size of the crop and the weather conditions. To provide these plant needs most efficiently during each irrigation cycle the solution must moisten the bed uniformly and drain completely and rapidly so that oxygen will be available to the plant roots.

Details of pumping frequency are discussed more thoroughly in the chapters on each soilless system. In all cases free water must not remain in the medium. The voids (air spaces between the particles) should be filled with moist air, not water, in order to maintain oxygen concentration around the roots at high levels. In most systems irrigation should be done only during the daylight hours, not at night.

Ideally, moisture levels in the medium can be maintained at optimum levels through a feedback system. Such a system has a moisture-sensing device, such as a tensiometer, placed in the medium. This apparatus is connected to an electrical circuit which activates a valve or pump which waters the plants when the moisture falls below a preset level. In this way, optimum moisture conditions are maintained within a fairly narrow range of variation.

In greenhouse culture, the temperature of the nutrient solution in contact with the roots should not fall below the high air temperature of the house. Immersion heaters can be placed in the sump to heat the nutrient solution, but care must be taken not to use heating elements such as lead which may react electrolytically with the nutrient solution to release toxic amounts of ions into the solution. Heat lamps could be used instead of immersion heaters. In general, the nutrient solution should be maintained between 60°-65° F. Recent experiments have demonstrated that by heating the nutrient solution, air temperatures can be decreased to conserve heat in the greenhouses. Some crops, such as tomatoes, grow better if the temperature of the root medium is maintained a few degrees above the average night air temperature during the winter season in the greenhouse.

In no case should heating lines or electric heating cables be placed in the bed itself. Such a placement causes localized high temperatures around the heating elements, which injure the roots and may cause lead toxicity if lead cables are used.

4.5 Sterilization of Medium

When crops are grown for extended periods in any aggregate, soil-borne pathogenic microorganisms accumulate in the medium and the chances of a disease occurring increase with each successive crop. It may be possible to grow several crops successively without sterilization between them; however, for best results the medium should be sterilized between each crop to prevent any possible disease carry-over. The most common methods of sterilization are steam and chemical.

If a greenhouse is being heated by a central hot water or steam boiler, sterilization by steam would be the most economical. A steam converter attachment would be installed on the boiler and steam pipes run to the greenhouse with outlet attachments at each bed. A steam line is run down the center of each bed and covered with canvas or some other heat-resistant material. Steam is then injected along the entire length of the bed at 180°F. for at least half an hour. This surface steaming is effective to a depth of 8 inches for sawdust beds but only to 4 inches deep for a 3:1 sand-sawdust mixture. Where surface steaming is not effective, install a permanent tile or perforated rigid pipe in the bottom of the bed through which steam can be injected.

Several chemicals may also be used in place of steam for sterilization, keeping in mind that some of these chemicals, particularly chloropicrin and methyl bromide, are toxic to humans and should be applied only by persons trained in their use. In all cases, precautions prescribed by the manufacturer should be observed.

Formaldehyde is a good fungicide but is not reliable for killing nematodes or insects. A mixture of 1 gallon of commercial formalin (40 percent strength) with 50 gallons of water is applied to the medium at the rate of 2 to 4 quarts per square foot. The treated area should be covered immediately with an airtight material for 24 hours or more. Following the treatment, about 2 weeks should be allowed for drying and airing before planting.

Chloropicrin is applied as a liquid by use of an injector, which should put 2 to 4 milliliters into holes 3 to 6 inches deep, spaced 9 to 12 inches apart, or it may be applied at the rate of 5 milliliters per cubic foot of medium. Chloropicrin changes to a gas which penetrates the medium. The gas should be confined by sprinkling the medium surface with water and then covering it with an airtight material for 3 days. Seven to 10 days is required for thorough aeration of the medium before it can be planted. Chloropicrin is effective against nematodes, insects, some weed seeds, *Verticillium*, and most other resistant fungi. Chloropicrin fumes are very toxic to living plant tissue.

Methyl bromide will kill most nematodes, insects, weed seeds, and some fungi, but it will not kill *Verticillium*. It is injected at 1 to 4 pounds per 100 square feet into an open vessel under a plastic cover placed over the medium to be treated. The cover must be kept sealed for 48 hours. Pressurized cannisters having an injection tube for dispersing into the plastic-covered bed are available. Penetration is very good, extending to a depth of 12 inches.

Materials are available which contain a mixture of methyl bromide and chloropicrin. These combinations are effective in controlling weeds, insects, nematodes and fungi. Aeration for 10 to 14 days is required following their application.

Vapam, a water-soluble fumigant, will kill weeds, most fungi and nematodes. It is applied as a spray to the surface of the medium through irrigation systems or with injection equipment at a rate of 1 quart of Vapam in 2 to 3 gallons of water sprinkled uniformly over 100 square feet of area. After application, the Vapam is sealed with additional water. Two weeks after application the area can be planted.

In gravel cultural systems, common bleach (calcium or sodium hypochlorite) or hydrochloric acid used for swimming pools can be used. A concentration of 10,000 ppm of available chlorine is made up in the sump tank and the beds are thoroughly moistened for one-half hour. The beds must then be thoroughly leached with fresh water to eliminate any chlorine before planting. Therefore, the entire sterilization process can be done in a very short time. After 4 to 5 years' use, it is advisable to remove all the gravel and clean all decayed roots from the beds.

References

Chapman, H. D., and P. F. Pratt. 1961. *Methods of analysis for soils, plants, and waters*. Univ. of Calif. Div. of Agr. Sc.

Schwarz, M. 1968. *Guide to commercial hydroponics*. Jerusalem: Israel Univ. Press.

Steiner, A. A. 1968. Soilless culture. *Proc. 6th Coll. Int. Potash Inst.,* Florence, pp. 324–41.

Victor, R. S. 1973. Growing tomatoes using calcareous gravel and neutral gravel with high saline water in the Bahamas. *Proc. 3rd Intern. Congr. on Soilless Culture*. Sassari, Italy, May 7–12, 1973, pp. 213–17.

Withrow, R. B., and A. P. Withrow. 1948. *Nutriculture*. Lafayette, Ind.: Purdue Univ. Agr. Expt. Stn. Publ. S.C. 328.

Chapter 5

Water Culture

5.1 Introduction

Of all the soilless methods, water culture, by definition, is true hydroponics. Water culture includes aeroponics. In aeroponic systems plant roots are suspended into a closed dark chamber in which jets of nutrient solution are periodically sprayed over them to maintain 100 percent relative humidity. In water culture plant roots are suspended in a liquid medium (nutrient solution) while their crowns are supported in a thin layer of inert medium.

For successful operation a number of plant requirements must be met:

(1) Root aeration:

This may be achieved in one of two ways. First, forced aeration (by a pump or compressor) is used to bubble air into the nutrient solution through a perforated pipe placed at the bottom of the bed or container. Second, the nutrient solution is circulated with a pump through the beds and back to a reservoir. A series of baffles placed at the end of the beds will aerate the water as it returns to the reservoir. A rate of about one to two complete changes per hour is required for a bed 100 feet long containing from 4 to 6 inches of nutrient solution. Best results can be achieved in a system in which the nutrient solution is pumped into the beds and allowed to flow past the plant roots continuously. In this way freshly aerated solution will be in constant contact with the plant roots.

(2) Root darkness:

Plants can function normally with their roots exposed to light during the daytime, provided they are always at 100 percent relative humidity. However, light will promote the growth of algae, which interferes with plant growth by competing for nutrients, reducing solution acidity, creating odors, competing for oxygen

110

from the nutrient solution at night, and producing toxic products through its decomposition which could interfere with plant growth. To eliminate algae growth construct beds of or cover containers with opaque materials.

(3) Plant Support:

Plants may be supported by the use of a litter tray which sits above the nutrient solution as part of the bed (see figure 5.1).

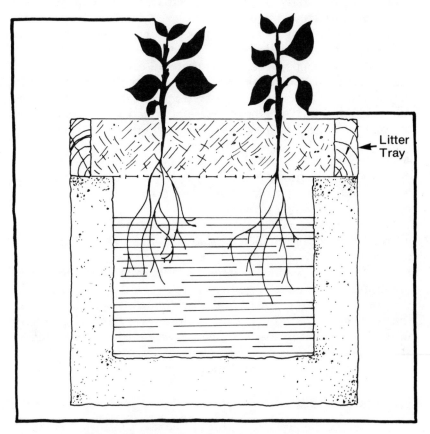

Litter Tray

Fig. 5.1. Cross section of a typical water culture bed.

5.1.1 Early Commercial Methods

Water culture was one of the earliest methods of hydroponics used both in laboratory experiments and in commercial crop production. Concrete beds coated with bituminous paint were used for commercial growing. Bed widths varied from 12 to 42 inches, lengths from 25 to 100 feet and depth from 6 to 9 inches. A solution depth of 4 to 6 inches with an air space from 2 to 3 inches was generally used. On top of the bed was a litter tray for support of the plant, as illustrated in figure 5.1.

The litter tray was a wooden framework which sat on top of the bed. The tray was usually 2 to 4 inches deep with wire mesh across the bottom to support the porous material contained in the tray. Early trays used 1-inch chicken wire coated with asphalt paint to prevent zinc from being released from the galvanized wire into the nutrient solution. The type of litter material used depended upon the nature of the plant root system and whether direct seeding or transplanting was followed. Materials used were excelsior, straw, wood shavings, coarse sawdust, chaff, peat moss, sphagnum moss, dried hay or rice hulls. A finer upper layer with a coarser lower layer could be used to facilitate seed germination when direct sowing into the tray was practiced.

Today, plastic screen could be used instead of galvanized wire to overcome any zinc problems. Also styrofoam and other plastic particles could be used for the litter.

Initially, upon seeding or transplanting, the solution level was maintained at a higher level than normal—within ½ to 1 inch of the bottom of the tray—but not close enough to wet the tray. As the roots elongated, the solution volume was reduced gradually until a 2- to 3-inch air space existed between the top of the solution and the bottom of the tray. An overflow pipe at the end of the bed allowed adjustment of the solution level.

5.2 Home Units

On a smaller scale water culture can be set up in an ordinary fruit jar. The jar should be fitted with a large cork or rubber stopper through which two holes are bored. Bore a smaller hole for placing an aeration tube into the solution and a larger hole through which the plant is placed. The plant is positioned in the large hole and then supported by pressing either cotton, glass wool, or foam plastic around the stem. Several inches of air space are left in the neck of the jar with the remainder being filled with nutrient solution (fig. 5.2). Air can be bubbled via the tube into the jar by means of a small fish-aquarium pump. A series of these containers can be set up to grow a number of plants, each container having one plant (fig. 5.3). The jar(s) must be covered with aluminum foil or other opaque material to prevent light from entering.

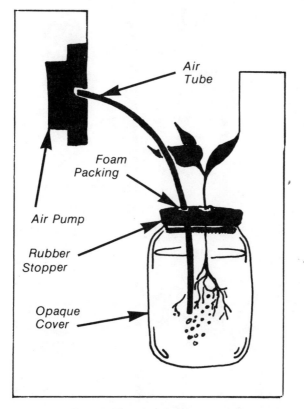

Fig. 5.2. The glass jar home unit.

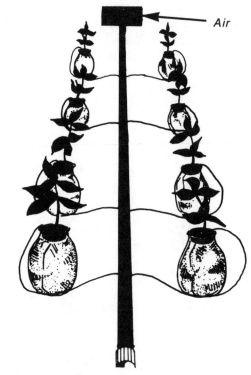

Fig. 5.3. A series of glass jar home units using water culture.

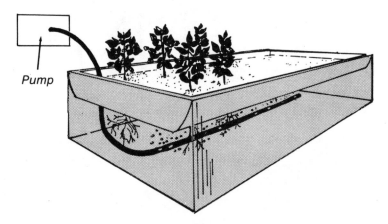

Fig. 5.4. A home unit using a plastic tub or fish aquarium.

A somewhat larger home unit based on the commercial units can be constructed using a fish aquarium, plastic dishpan, tub or wooden box lined with vinyl. A small, shallow plastic tray such as the commercial seed trays (see chapter 10) with holes punched in the bottom can be used as the litter tray. The litter tray can be filled with any porous material as mentioned earlier. The tray can nest into the tank by fitting the lip of the tray over the edge of the tank, as shown in figure 5.4. An aquarium pump can be used to aerate the nutrient solution. In a plastic tray, a fine medium such as vermiculite, perlite or peat could be used as the litter so that direct seeding into the tray can be accomplished.

Upon seeding, the litter should be thoroughly moistened and, in this case, the nutrient solution in the tank should be just touching the bottom of the tray. Daily watering just to keep the litter moist or covering of the litter with polyethylene until the seeds germinate is necessary. The nutrient solution level should be kept topped up to within ¼ inch of the bottom of the tray until plant roots have developed sufficiently to remain immersed in the nutrient solution.Then as the plants become established, the nutrient solution should be maintained to within 1 to 2 inches from the tray bottom.

5.3 Present Commercial Systems in Japan

When Japan's total greenhouse area was 27,079 hectares, in 1977, water cultural systems were installed in four percent of the glasshouse area and one percent of the plastic house area. At the time, the plastic house area accounted for 25,795 hectares, or 95 percent. Therefore, water cultural systems amounted to 51 hectares under glass and 258 hectares under plastic, a total of slightly over 300 hectares (309), or more than 750 acres. About 2000 greenhouses use water culture.

Typical water culture units are a series of troughs which are 80 cm (31.5 in.) wide and about 3m (9.8 ft.) long filled with nutrient solution to a depth of about 6-8 cm (2.4-3.2 in.) as shown in fig. 5.5. These troughs are made of rigid plastic and are available commercially at a cost of 20,000 Yen (in 1980), about $100, each.

Plants are inserted through holes in a styrofoam lid which caps the whole length (fig. 5.6, 5.7). The nutrient solution is pumped around the troughs for ten minutes every hour, mainly for aeration. The troughs are always full of nutrient solution in which roots are

Fig. 5.5 Japanese water culture system. Rigid plastic trough with styrofoam lid.

Fig. 5.6 Commercial water culture system in Japan using rigid plastic troughs and styrofoam lids.

Fig. 5.7. Position of plants (melons) in styrofoam lid of Japanese water culture system.

Fig. 5.8 Roots suspended into nutrient solution of underlying plastic trough—the roots supported by plastic mesh container.

Fig. 5.9 Pipe in trough for aeration of nutrient solution.

suspended (fig. 5.8). The cost of the total water culture system is about 3,000,000 Yen per 1000 sq.m. ($15,000 per 10,000 sq. ft.).

An aeration hose can be installed in the troughs to increase oxygenation. This hose has two 2 mm holes along its length every 4 cm (1.57 in.) (fig. 5.9). The Ninomiya Agricultural Research Station doing work on such a water culture system recommended an aeration cycle of 15-minute periods every two hours during the day and once at midnight.

Seedlings are started in perlite and transplanted into the styrofoam lids once they are large enough to support themselves, generally four to six weeks for cucumbers and tomatoes (fig. 5.8).

The principal crops produced in water culture are tomato, Japanese honewort (*Cryptotaenia japonica*), cucumber, and salad crops.

5.4 Ruthner Industrial Continuous Plant Cultivation System

A system developed by Othmar Ruthner of Vienna, Austria, uses a vertical conveyor belt system in large vertical greenhouses. Seeds are sown in trays at the beginning of the conveyor. The speed of the conveyor is set so that the plants are ready for harvesting when the end of the run is reached. For example, if lettuce takes 35 to 40 days from time of seeding to harvest, the time to complete the run would be set for 35 to 40 days. The conveyor carries the seed and resultant plants through a number of growing rooms (greenhouses) in which they are exposed to optimal environmental conditions for periods varying according to their particular stage of development (fig. 5.10). The life cycle is usually divided into four phases: germination, young plant, middle stage, and mature stage. A certain number of seeds are sown daily or weekly at the beginning of the conveyor run and the resulting plants are harvested daily or weekly at the same rate (35 to 40 days for lettuce). In this way continuous production is achieved. It facilitates the even programming of daily work loads so that a steady labor force can be utilized. No labor peaks of harvesting or planting are encountered as in normal greenhouse operations.

To ensure that older plants have adequate space, three conveyors traveling one after the other are used, each with its own growing

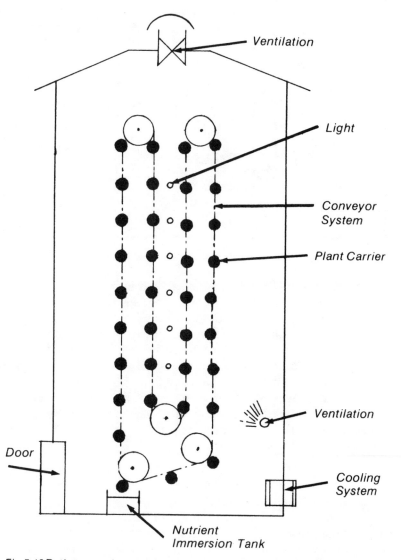

Fig.5.10 Ruthner continuous plant cultivation system in a vertical greenhouse.

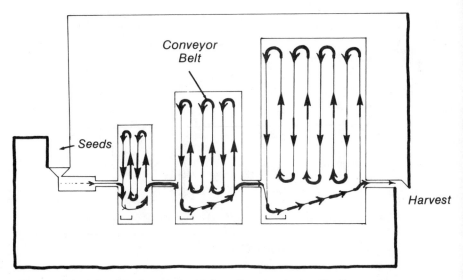

Fig.5.11. Principle of Ruthner industrial continuous plant cultivation system.

room (greenhouse). At the end of each growth phase the plants are placed on the next conveyor with wider spacing (fig. 5.11).

Seeds are sown in inert substrate cubes on a horizontal system. Later they are transplanted to tubular or similarly shaped sub-strates fixed horizontally or vertically on the vertically moving conveyors. The conveyors are constantly circulating the plants through the greenhouse, as shown in figure 5.10. At the completion of each cycle the bases of the plants with their substrate cubes are immersed in the nutrient supply tank. The entire operation can be mechanized so that labor costs are kept to a minimum. Some of the advantages of this system are:

1. The production lines can be erected close to consumer centers.

2. Close proximity to markets reduces costs of marketing, trans-porting, storage and packing.

3. Waste heat from refuse incinerators, thermal power plants and atomic reactors may be utilized.

4. The low ground area requirements make the system particu-larly suitable to congested centers such as Hong Kong or Tokyo where traditional systems of horticulture cannot economically be practiced.

5. The automated cropping system (combined with a processing

plant and laboratory on the same site) makes it very suitable to the growing of pharmaceutical crops.

5.5 Nutrient Film Technique (NFT)

The Nutrient Film Technique (NFT) is a water cultural technique in which plants are grown with their root systems contained in a plastic film (trough) through which nutrient solution is continuously circulated.

Work on NFT cropping was pioneered by Allen Cooper at the Glasshouse Crops Research Institute in Littlehampton, England, in 1965. The term *nutrient film technique* was coined at the Glasshouse Crops Research Institute to stress that the depth of liquid flowing past the roots of the plants should be very shallow in order to ensure that sufficient oxygen would be supplied to the plant roots. Other workers (Schippers, 1977) call it *nutrient flow technique* since the nutrient solution is continuously circulated.

5.5.1 Early NFT System

In the earliest NFT system a catchment trench was dug across the middle of the greenhouse floor and the ground sloped on either side toward this trench. The least acceptable slope was about 1 in 100. A steeper gradient, up to 1 in 25, was favored to reduce the effect of localized depressions. The trench was lined with an expanded polystyrene sheet and polyethylene film. The "layflat" polyethylene troughs were placed on strips of hardboard 8 inches wide at the normal spacing of plant rows sloping toward the central catchment trench from each side(fig. 5.12).

Fourteen-inch layflat was prepared by punching out holes along one edge at the within-row plant spacing, as shown in figure5.13a. The line of holes was then relocated centrally along the layflat as shown in plan view (fig.5.13b) and cross section (fig.5.13c). The edges of the layflat were then turned upward and into the center and secured together with a small piece of PVC tape at 10-foot intervals (fig.5.13d).

Small slits were cut in the upper surface of the upper folds to prevent possible ethylene buildup in the layflat which would cause premature root senescence. The lower end of each line of layflat hung down into the catchment trench while the upper end of each line was turned upward and over and sealed with PVC tape to prevent the loss of nutrient solution.

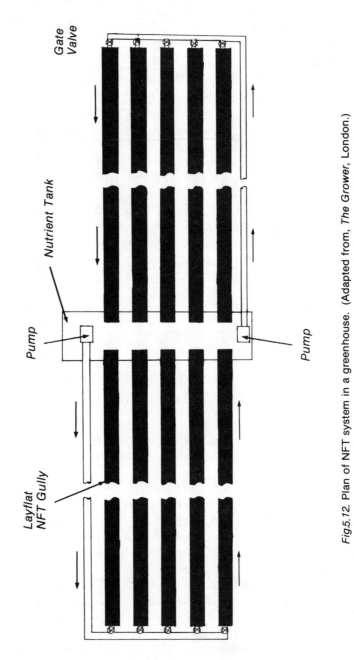

Fig.5.12. Plan of NFT system in a greenhouse. (Adapted from, *The Grower*, London.)

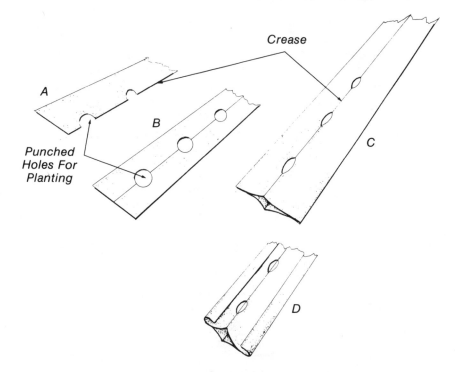

Fig.5.13. Details of preparation of layflat polyethylene into a NFT trough. (Adapted from, *The Grower*, London.)

Nutrient solution in the catchment trench was circulated to the upper ends of each layflat by two small submersible pumps and ABS plastic piping, as shown in fig.5.12. Gate valves installed at the inlets to each layflat line regulated the flow of nutrient solution evenly into each line. The roots of the plants were inserted into the layflat through the planting holes shown in figure 5.13. The upper part of the plants were supported in the normal way by tie strings suspended from support cables in the greenhouse.

5.5.2 Later NFT Systems

Although good crops were obtained from the earlier NFT system technique, experience showed that ethylene buildup inside the layflat caused root damage which led to blossom-end rot fruit in tomatoes and reduced yields. This buildup of ethylene necessitated a modification of the technique to improve ventilation.

The layflat was replaced by long narrow sheets of black polyethylene film laid on the ground, each corresponding to a row of plants. Peat pots, peat pellets, (Jiffy-7's) or stonewool cubes were placed on the polyethylene at each plant position in the row. The edges of the polyethylene were then turned up and around the sides of these growing pots or cubes and stapled between every other pot (or cube) to form a gully through which a thin stream of nutrient solution flowed, as shown in figure 5.14.

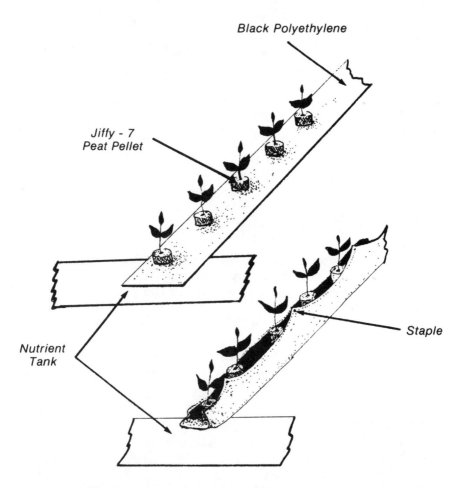

Fig.5.14. NFT gully using growing pots or cubes to support plants and the gully. (Adapted from *The Grower*, London.)

Plants were seeded directly into the pots or cubes, and once they had grown to several true leaves they, with their containers, were placed directly onto the polyethylene at which time the gully was formed as described above.

The use of pots or cubes serves a number of purposes. First, they support the polyethylene film so that when the edges of the film are stapled together a gully is formed. Second, support of the film by the pots or cubes keeps the film apart and therefore allows good ventilation of air within the gully, thus reducing ethylene buildup. Third, they support the young seedling or cutting in the early stages of growth.

The technique can be extended to pot plant production, enabling such plants to be automatically watered and fed in a very simple, inexpensive system.

In a greenhouse a series of gullies are laid out on a slope to a catchment tank as shown in figure 5.15. As in the early NFT system, a submersible pump is placed in the bottom of the tank and ABS piping is used to conduct the nutrient solution being con-

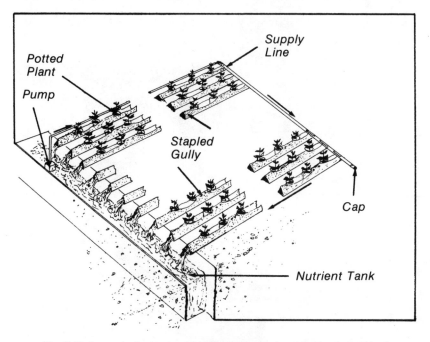

Fig. 5.15. Layout of a series of NFT gullies and nutrient solution tank. (Adapted from, *The Grower*, London.)

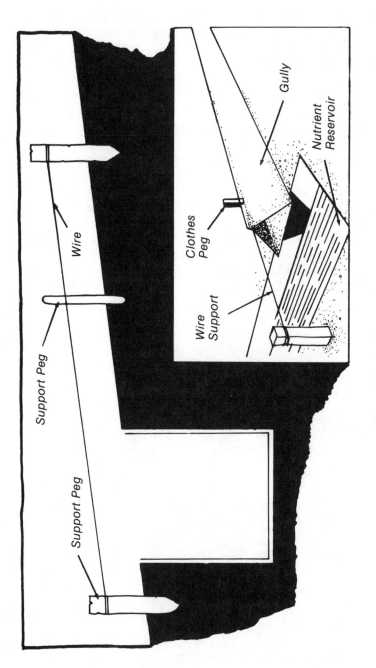

Fig. 5.16. Wire-supported NFT gully. (Adapted from, *The Grower*, London.)

stantly pumped to the upper ends of the gullies. By suspending the flow pipe several inches above the gullies and drilling small holes above each gully, the nutrient solution enters each gully. This facilitates checking for blocked outlets and aerates the solution as it falls through the air. The top end of each gully is sealed by rolling a few inches of the polyethylene up tightly and packing some soil under the roll.

The lower end of the gully is made into a chute which projects out over the trench by stapling the top edges of the polyethylene together every few inches for the last 18 inches. In this way, rapid discharge aerates the solution as it falls into the trench. A constant volume of water is maintained in the trench by a plastic float valve.

Roots quickly grow through the pots (or cubes) and spread out in the shallow stream of nutrient solution flowing down the gullies. They merge to form a single, thick, continuous mat in the bottom of the gullies which provides support for large plants.

A further modification of this NFT system is by use of a supporting wire to hold the gully. The ground must be prepared with a slope of 1 in 25 and be evenly smooth so that there are no localized depressions. At both ends of each plant row a wooden peg is driven into the ground until it is projecting approximately 4 inches. Between these two pegs two strands of fine wire are stretched along the length of the row. A 6-inch length of steel rod is inserted between two strands of wire in the center of the row to serve as a turn-buckle to adjust the wire until it is taut.

In long rows, intermediate pegs can be driven into the ground to provide extra support. An 18-inch wide strip of black polyethylene film is laid on the ground along the length of the row. The edges of the polyethylene are clipped to the wire with clothespins to form the gully down which the shallow stream of nutrient solution flows, as illustrated in figure 5.16.

To supply nutrient solution to the gullies a plastic pipe is supported just above the higher inlet ends of the gullies at right angles. In this pipe a 1/16-inch hole is drilled above each gully in such a position that the nutrient solution is discharged into each gully (fig. 5.17).

The outlet ends of the gullies hang down into a catchment gutter which conducts the solution back to the nutrient reservoir or directly into the reservoir, depending on the size of the operation. The catchment gutters and reservoir must be covered with an opaque material such as black polyethylene in order to exclude light and prevent the growth of algae. The outlet ends of the gullies are inserted through slits in the polyethylene cover.

By use of support wires and clothespins the gully walls can be kept closed at the top to prevent light from adversely affecting plant roots. At the same time there is adequate space above the plant roots to provide ventilation for the escape of ethylene and for gas exchange.

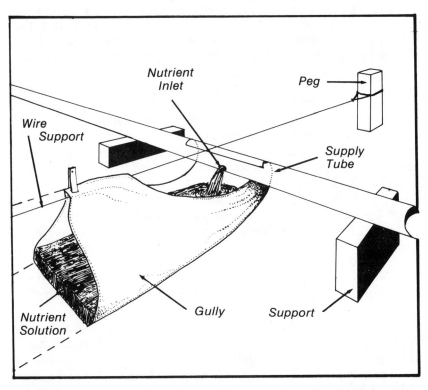

Fig. 5.17. Inlet supply of nutrient solution to each gully. (Courtesy of the Glasshouse Crops Research Institute, Littlehampton, England.)

5.5.3 Other NFT Modifications

Other workers (Resh 1976, Adamson*) have carried out experiments, independently, in studies attempting to solve the problem of inadequate root oxygenation. The greatest problem facing the NFT systems has been root dieback caused by inadequate oxygen in the nutrient solution immediately around the roots. This root dieback results in water stress within the plant which causes wilting and blossom-end rot (a sinking-in of the fruit at the blossom end with a resultant leathery depression) of fruit in crops such as tomatoes. The problem is associated with large root mats developing in the bottom of the NFT canal (gully) which impedes the flow of water, especially at the interface between the gully and plant roots. This is termed *puddling*. This stagnation of water allows plant roots to use up all the available oxygen in that area and with slow exchange of water a shortage of oxygen develops.

The solution to this poor root aeration was believed to be in providing a supporting medium in the gully through which roots could grow laterally without concentrating on the root-gully interface. A number of fibrous mats were tested with reasonable success (Resh 1976). However, the most suitable type of matting is difficult to obtain commercially. The matting material must satisfy a number of criteria. It must be readily available in large quantities and inexpensive. It must be dense and fairly rigid to give support to the plant roots and prevent their rapid growth downward. It must retain sufficient moisture to prevent root desiccation, yet not hold excessive gravitational water or puddling will occur. Several matting materials were tested, but none adequately satisfied the above criteria. Some of the materials were too porous and roots still grew along the bottom of the matting at the gully-mat interface. All of them were too expensive to justify their use commercially since they must be disposed of at the end of each crop. Also the cost of labor for installation was prohibitive. The aims of the NFT systems are low cost and simplicity. Matting materials do not conform with these aims.

Other trials using soaker hoses on the top of the matting for even water distribution and spaghetti feeders to each plant also make the NFT system too expensive and complicated for commercial use.

It is the present belief of the author that a NFT canal with a false bottom or collecting gully underneath may be the answer to the

*R. M. Adamson 1976: personal communication.

problem. In this way water would move vertically past the plant root instead of laterally, assuring good root aeration (fig. 5.18).

Such a system has been developed on an experimental scale in Denmark.* The Danish system is constructed of rigid ABS plastic having a molded nutrient feed line, CO_2 enrichment line, growing conveyor belt, collecting trough and solution heating tubes, as shown in fig. 5.19. This product is presently undergoing tests using crops such as lettuce, tomatoes and cucumbers. Once proven successful, it will be marketed commercially for greenhouse growers.

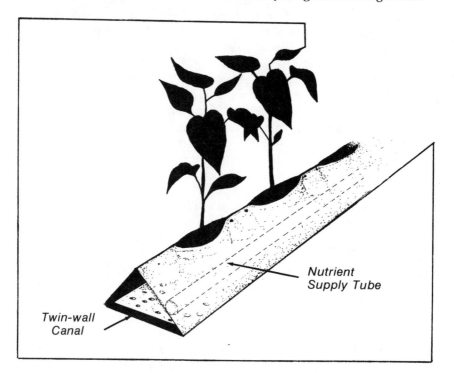

Nutrient Supply Tube

Twin-wall Canal

Fig. 5.18. A twin-wall NFT canal system.

5.5.4 Present Commercial NFT Systems

The manufacturing industry is currently engaged in designing, developing and manufacturing component items of NFT equipment in the United Kingdom, South Africa, Italy, France and the

*Bent Vestergaard 1976: personal communication.

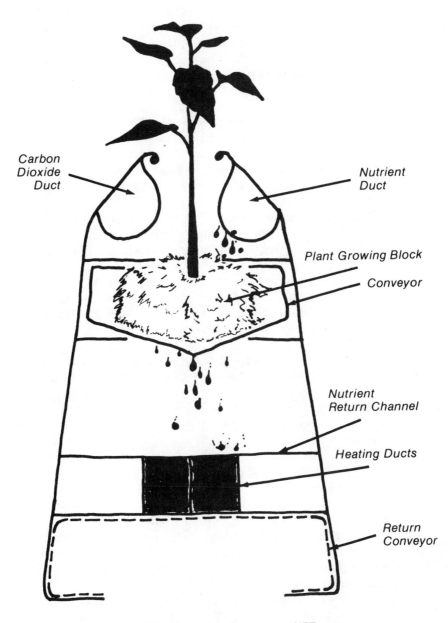

Fig. 5.19. Vestergaard's conveyor NFT system.
(Scale: 3×)

United States. In addition, NFT cropping is being tested, or is in large-scale commercial use, in at least 68 countries (Cooper 1976).

One of the leaders in the manufacturing of commercial NFT systems is Soil-less Cultivation Systems Ltd. of Aldershot, England. They have worked together with Allen Cooper in the design and development of their "Hydrocanal." Their Hydrocanal system is marketed as a complete package with all the growing requirements. The other components are the "Nutrient Feed System," comprised of pumps, valves, filters, tanks, a range of flexible ducting, monitoring and dosage equipment and prepackaged nutrients. All components are designed to form an integrated whole, balanced precisely to give optimum results and minimum operational difficulties.

The Hydrocanal is extruded polyethylene which when unreeled forms a self-supporting continuous growing canal. It is available in reel lengths of 25, 50, and 100 meters and widths of 7½ centimeters (3 inches), 15 centimeters (6 inches) and 22½ centimeters (9 inches). The life span of the Hydrocanal has been projected to 5 to 6 years under climatic conditions similar to those of England, while in warmer countries 3 to 4 years are expected. The Hydrocanal is supplied prepunched with small holes in its outer edges to facilitate fastening studs at 10-centimeter or 4-inch spacings. These fastening studs incorporate hook rings for attaching wire strings to plants. The Hydrocanal fastener studs ensure a continuous opening along the canal, thus enabling good air exchange to plant roots. Secondly, they protect young seedlings against abrasion from the top edge of the canal and they are used for attachment of plant support strings.

The site should be prepared similarly to that described in earlier NFT systems above. A long and narrow rectangular land area is ideally suited to the Hydrocanal system. Ideally there should be a two-way fall on the land with the greatest fall along the length of the rectangle and a slight fall across the width. In this way one corner of the rectangle will be lower than the other three. A hole one cubic meter in volume is excavated in the lowest corner. The size of the hole is not determined by the area of the rectangle on which the hydrocanal system is placed.

The slope along the length of the rectangle is graded so that there are no lengthwise localized depressions. The steeper the slope the less care is needed in grading. However, with a minimum gradient of 1 in 100 there must be virtually no localized depressions.

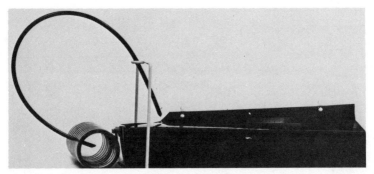

Fig. 5.20. Supply end of the Soil-less Cultivation System (SCS) Hydrocanal. (Courtesy of Soil-less Cultivation Systems Ltd., Aldershot, England.)

The Hydrocanals are laid on the ground along the length of the rectangle. A catchment tank is placed in the prepared hole. This is filled with nutrient solution which is pumped through flexible plastic pipe up to the top edge of the rectangle. Solution is discharged from this flow pipe into the gullies through small flexible discharge pipes (fig. 5.20). The solution flows down the gullies by gravity. At the ends of the gullies the solution is discharged into a large-diameter, flexible plastic catchment pipe (fig. 5.21), down which it flows by gravity back to the catchment tank. A complete Hydrocanal NFT system is shown in figure 5.22.

Fig. 5.21. Catchment end of the SCS Hydrocanal. (Courtesy of Soil-less Cultivation Systems Ltd., Aldershot, England.)

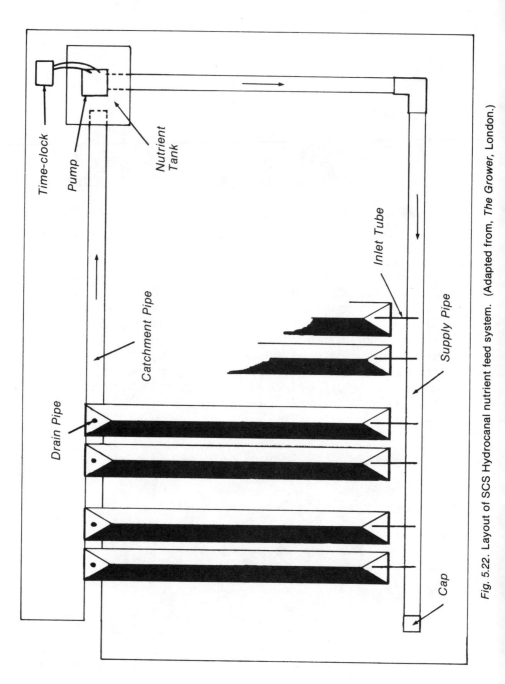

Fig. 5.22. Layout of SCS Hydrocanal nutrient feed system. (Adapted from, *The Grower*, London.)

Fig. 5.23. The Hydrocanal inlet end with a dense, healthy root mat receiving adequate oxygen. (Courtesy of the Glasshouse Crops Research Institute, Littlehampton, England.)

Fig. 5.24. The Hydrocanal capillary matting system.

The film of nutrient solution must not rise above the upper surface of the plant root mat. This ensures that all the roots are moist but that the upper surface of the root mat is in the air. Thus, no matter how long the gully is, there should be no shortage of oxygen supply to the roots even at the end of the row (fig. 5.23).

A capillary matting is placed along the bottom of the Hydro-canal, as shown in figure 5.24. It provides even distribution of the nutrient solution, encourages oxygenation by complete surface coverage of roots, secures roots as they grow out of the growing containers and ensures water retention for some time if a pump fails (fig. 5.25).

Fig. 5.25. Hydrocanal capillary matting with plant roots growing from Jiffy-7 peat pellet into matting. (Courtesy of the Glasshouse Crops Research Institute, Littlehampton, England.)

Various systems have been designed for ground level and elevated positions, with or without gradient support devices according to natural level, as shown in fig. 5.26. Sheet galvanized metal ducting supports the nutrient fluid canal and gradients can be adjusted to provide the 1 in 100 minimum operating slope.

Soil-less Cultivation Systems' Hydrocanal systems have been introduced to growers in many parts of the United Kingdom. Installations range from small-scale experimental systems to relatively large commercial schemes. So far in the United Kingdom and Channel Islands there are 4 hectares (about 10 acres) using this technique, mainly in trial units but there is one 0.3-hectare (about ¾ acre) unit and four of 0.2 hectares (about ½ acre), as shown in figures 5.27 to 5.30. Soil-less Cultivation Systems is presently supplying several acres of Hydrocanal equipment to the United

States, Australia, New Zealand and South Africa. They urge caution in adapting the NFT to the environmental conditions in these areas. A diversity of crops, foliage plants and shrubs may be grown with the Hydrocanal system (figs. 5.31 and 5.32).

The prices of Hydrocanal and Nutrient Feed Systems depend upon the type of Hydrocanal used (long-life or disposable) and the size of the system. In general the costs, especially for small areas, are relatively expensive.

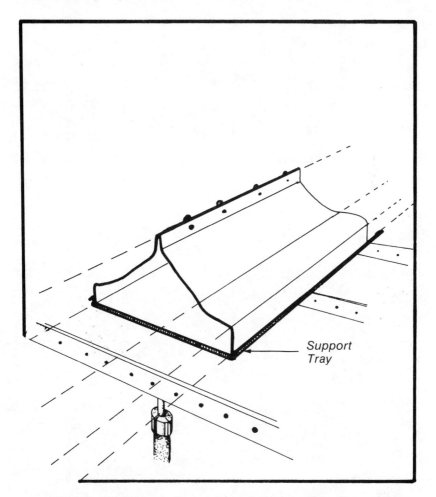

Fig. 5.26. The Hydrocanal elevated ground system which offers an auto-gradient support device.

Fig. 5.27 and Fig. 5.28. Hydrocanal Basic Ground System 100. (Courtesy of Soil-less Cultivation Systems Ltd., Aldershot, England.)

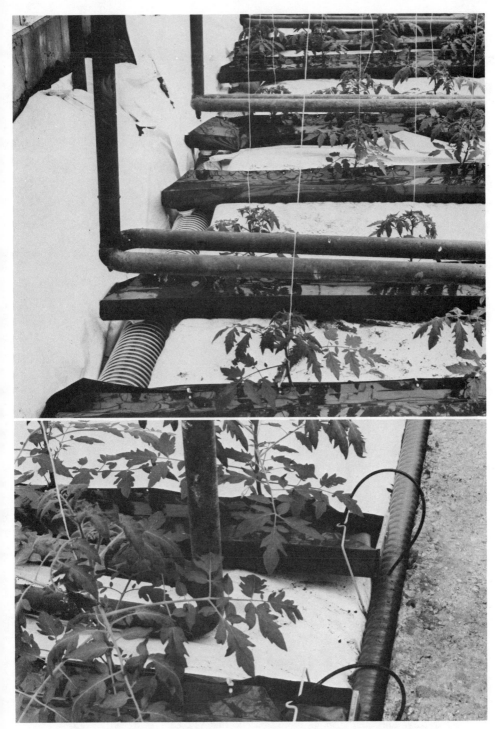

Fig. 5.29. Catchment end; *Fig. 5.30.* Supply end of the Hydrocanal with tomato plants. (Courtesy of the Glasshouse Crops Research Institute, Littlehampton, England.)

Fig. 5.31. A wide range of vegetable and ornamental crops may be grown in the NFT system. (Courtesy of the Glasshouse Crops Research Institute, Littlehampton, England.)

Fig. 5.32. Unrooted cuttings of shrubs and foliage plants have been rooted and grown successfully using the NFT. (Courtesy of the Glasshouse Crops Research Institute, Littlehampton, England.)

Conventional NFT channels are now generally formed by use of white-on-black polyethylene of 6- to 10-mil (0.15–0.25 mm) thickness. The thicker polyethylene gives a smoother, more even base for more uniform spreading of solution. The film is placed with the white side facing outwards to reflect light and reduce solar insolation. The sides are raised and supported by stapling together between the plants to form a gully as described for the Hydrocanal system. The width of the channel should be from 15 to 30 centimeters (6 to 12 in), depending on the crop grown. Generally, the narrower channels are suitable for smaller plants such as lettuce, while the wider channels are suitable for tomatoes and cucumbers, to avoid thick root mats developing in the channel, which may impede the flow of nutrient solution. The nutrient solution should flow at a rate of 1–2 liters (¼–½ gallon) per minute. Generally, with a slope of 1 in 50, the length of the channels should not exceed 20–25 meters (65–80 ft) or nutrient gradients may become evident and solution oxygenation reduced. While it is possible to introduce the solution into the channels at several points along their length with longer channels, risk of oxygen deficit and temperature build-up in the solution exists.

To prevent plants from drying out during transplanting a narrow strip of capillary matting 5 centimeters (2 in) wide should be placed across the width of the channel directly under the transplant. This ensures that the flow of nutrient solution does not bypass the plant as it flows down the channel.

5.5.5 Update on Nutrient Film Technique

Since 1978, rapid progress has been made with the commercial development of nutrient film technique (NFT). A recent text by Dr. Allen Cooper, *The ABC of NFT*, provides much technical information and speculation on the potential future uses of NFT. Independent of Dr. Cooper's work has been research by Dr. P. A. Schippers on what he terms the "Nutrient Flow Technique" at the Long Island Horticultural Research Laboratory of Cornell University at Riverhead, New York.

With the increasing cost of heating greenhouses in North America, Dr. Schippers has looked at modifications to the NFT system in an effort to save greenhouse space. By increasing the number of plants that can be grown in a given area of greenhouse the cost per plant can be reduced. Experimental work was performed with lettuce in vertical pipes, down through which the nutrient solution dripped, moistening and feeding the plants. The principle is similar to that of the sack culture system discussed in Chapter 9, but without a medium. Twenty-five to thirty plants were grown in each pipe, five feet in length. A similar system is shown in figures 5.33 and 5.34 of the Environmental Research Laboratory in Tucson, Arizona. A nutrient solution is sprayed into the vertical pipes traveling on a conveyor system. As the pipes carrying the plants pass the point where nutrients are sprayed onto their roots within the pipe, they travel above a nutrient collector reservoir, thus the immediate drainage flows back into the system.

Schippers (1977) speculated that while this system was technically feasible, commercial application did not seem imminent at the time, especially in lettuce production, since differences in light intensity caused differences in growth between top and bottom plants. But he suggested that other crops which are harvested over a longer period, such as strawberries, peas, beans, etc. might offer better prospects.

He pursued different ways to increase the use of vertical space in the greenhouse by use of the NFT, particularly for low growing crops such as lettuce. He built what he termed the "cascade" system. Growing troughs of 3 in. (7.6 cm) diameter PVC plastic pipe were cut open and suspended one above the other up to eight high. The nutrient solution entered the high end of the slightly sloping top pipe, exited at the low end of that pipe into the high end of the next one and so on to the reservoir from where it was pumped. The system was successful with lettuce, radish, peas and other crops. This system, shown in figure 5.35, is used for fairly small plants.

This system can be made more efficient in the utilization of greenhouse space by mounting the growing channels on A-frames. The A-frames must be oriented north-south so that shade from one side will not be cast upon the other. The system is suitable only for low-profile plants such as lettuce, strawberries, spinach, and some herbs.

Several factors must be considered in the design of the A-frame system. The base of the frame must be wide enough to eliminate any mutual shading of one tier over the next lower one. The tiers of growing channels must be separated from each other with adequate distance to allow for the mature height of the crop

Fig.5.33. Lettuce in vertical pipe showing nutrient mist nozzle at top.
Fig. 5.34. Vertical pipes pass above a collector reservoir for re-cycling excess nutrient solution.

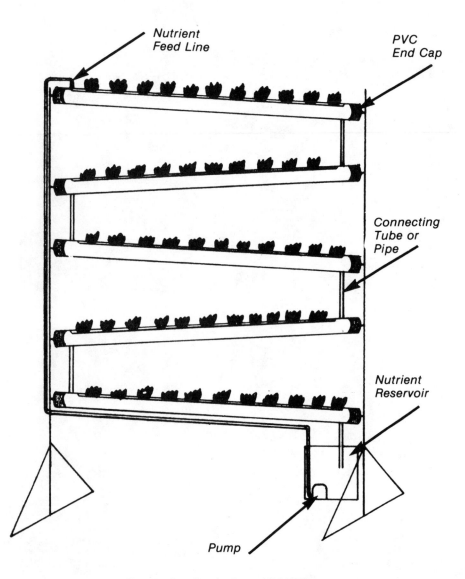

*Fig. 5.35.*Details of a "cascade" NFT system.

grown. That is, the plants of a lower tier must not grow into those of the above tier. Finally, since this is basically an NFT system, all principles of oxygenation, nutrition, and optimum solution temperature apply. The total channel length for any combination of tiers should not exceed 30 meters (100 ft) in order to provide sufficient oxygenation. A minimum slope of 2 percent is necessary to provide adequate solution flow. If the A-frame unit is 30 meters (100 ft) in length, solution must be pumped into an inlet end of each channel and returned from the outlet end into a central nutrient tank.

If the A-frame is less than 100 feet, a series of channels occupying several tiers may be connected to obtain 100 feet in length. The growing channels should be spirally arranged on the A-frame. They are parallel to each other with opposite slopes from one side to the other of the A-frame similar to an expanded coiled spring (fig. 5.36). Each subunit of approximately 100 feet in length will have an inlet and outlet to the nutrient tank. An inlet line from the main header to the pump connects to each subunit. Similarly, outlet lines from each subunit connect to a common return to the nutrient tank (fig. 5.37). The unit illustrated in figure 5.36 was 4 meters (13 ft) long. It used 2½-inch (6.35 cm) diameter PVC pipe as its growing channels mounted on a 1½-inch × ⅛-inch angle iron frame.

Plants may be seeded in rockwool cubes (1-inch × 1-inch × 1½-inch—200 per 1020 flat) or in mesh pots filled with a peat-lite medium. They are transplanted directly into the growing channels with the rockwool or pots suspended into the troughs so that the nutrient solution is touching the base of the pot or cube and will rise into the medium through capillary action (fig. 5.38).

The slope of the growing troughs should be about 1 in 30 so that a rapid flow of solution will maintain high oxygenation. These units may be used in hot desert or tropical regions if a chiller refrigeration unit is placed in the nutrient tank to cool the solution temperature to 21–23°C (70–75°F). Solution temperatures may also be reduced by insulating the growing channels. If the channels are constructed of PVC pipes, styrofoam insulation with a reflective aluminum foil cover could be wrapped around the channels to reflect solar radiation.

The unit illustrated in figure 5.36 was designed to grow lettuce at 20-centimeters (8-in) centers within the growing channels. Nine growing beds were placed on each side of the A-frame, giving

Fig. 5.36. "Cascade" NFT system mounted on A-frame supporting structure. PVC plastic pipes of 2½ inch diameter, arranged spirally and parallel to each other, with opposing slopes of one side from the other.

Fig. 5.37. Supply lines from pump on right, and return lines to tank on left, attached to each subunit of three coils of pipe.

Fig. 5.38. A-frame cascade system with lettuce seedlings growing in mesh pots supported by the pot rims, in PVC channels.

a total of 18 beds. Six beds were joined into a subunit with its own inlet and outlet. Each bed of 4 meters (13 ft) contained 20 plants, totalling 360 lettuce in an area of 4 meters by 1.8 meters or 7.2 square meters (77 sq ft). This is equivalent to 50 head per square meter (4.6 lettuce/sq ft). This compares to 32 lettuce per square meter (3 head/sq ft) using the floating or raft water culture system and 18 plants per square meter (1.67 plants/sq ft) using the double row NFT system.

These figures are based on available growing area without allowance for aisles. Considering a greenhouse of one acre, for example, 132 feet by 330 feet in dimensions, the useable growing area would be: length 132 feet–12 feet walkways = 120 feet; number of rows of A-frames is: 330 feet ÷ (6 feet frames + 2.5 feet aisles) = 38. Actual growing area is 120 feet × 6 feet × 38 = 27,360 square feet or 63 percent. Total number of plants per acre is:

$$360 \times \frac{27,360}{77} = 128,000 \text{ plants, which is 4.6 plants per square foot}$$

of growing area or 3 plants/square foot of greenhouse area. This compares to 2.6 head/square feet of greenhouse area using the raft system.

While the productivity is greater, the capital cost of such a cascade system and the additional time required to clean each channel between crops does not make it economically feasible when almost the same plant density can be achieved using the floating (raft) system.

A recent development by Schippers (1979) was the use of moveable gutters for lettuce. Normally the lettuce is transplanted into fixed beds in the greenhouse, with spacing sufficiently wide to allow room for growth. This means that at the early growth stages after transplanting, much of the area is wasted and will only later fill in as the plants reach maturity. The nutrient flow (film) technique offers an alternative in the fact that the beds need not be in a fixed position. By adapting the distances between the gutters to the space requirements of the plants at various stages of growth the plant population can be increased by about 50 percent. In this system a group of plants is moved, at intervals of one to two weeks, from one side of the greenhouse to the other at increased spacings and the abandoned section is occupied by the next lot which is seeded a week or ten days later. The final end section is harvested, making room always for the section immediately adjacent to it. This system, of course, can only work for crops which can be sown and harvested at regular time intervals. A sketch of this moveable system is given in figure 5.39.

The channels can be made of aluminum downspouts cut lengthwise along the narrow sides. Several can be riveted together to increase the length. They can be lined with black polyethylene or painted with bituminous paint. The channels can be filled with perlite or left empty and covered with black polyethylene punctured at the location of each plant. The catchment basin or nutrient reservoir may consist of a trench lined with vinyl or black polyethylene or it may be simply a 3-inch (7.6 cm) PVC pipe slit in half and used as a return channel to a nutrient tank at the end. The nutrient reservoir should be of sufficient volume to hold a litre of nutrient solution per plant for lettuce or other plants of comparable size.

It is generally better to have an automatic float valve attached to a water inlet line to keep the reservoir level topped-up rather than depend on the nutrient solution lasting for a number of days. In this way when plants become mature under high light days, their high water demand will not cause the level of the nutrient solution to fall drastically with changes in its concentration.

A pump placed in the nutrient reservoir circulates the solution via a manifold system constructed of a 1-inch (2.54 cm) PVC header line with small ¼-inch (0.6 cm) diameter feeder lines to each channel. The growing channels must be sloped at least three percent. The low ends of the growing channels protrude slightly over the edge of the catchment channel so that excess solution drains back for recycling.

The width of the growing channels for tomatoes and cucumbers need not exceed six inches (15 cm) while that for lettuce need be only three inches (7.5 cm). For the growing of lettuce on a small scale it is better to use two inches (5 cm) of perlite in the channels of a flat bed or cascade system. It gives better results and adds safety against any possible drying out due to pump failure or plugging of inlet tubes. For commercial growing it is more attractive to use beds without a substrate, since this would facilitate the removal of the old crop and sterilization of the beds before replanting.

Perlite is necessary for the growing of root crops. Fairly deep channels are needed with a thick layer of perlite. Eight-inch (20 cm) deep channels for potatoes, 6-inch (15 cm) for large carrots and 4-inch (10 cm) for smaller carrots.

A relatively simple method of constructing channels for small-

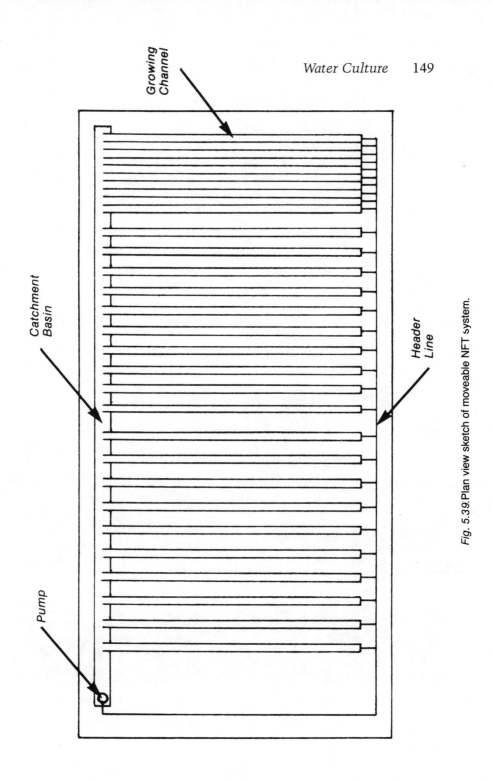

Fig. 5.39. Plan view sketch of moveable NFT system.

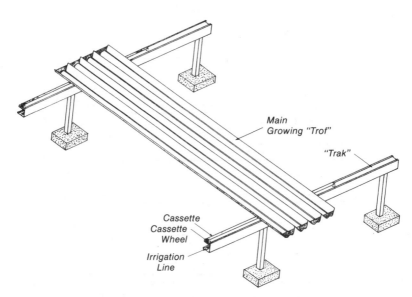

Main
Growing "Trof"

"Trak"

Cassette
Cassette
Wheel

Irrigation
Line

Fig. 5.40 The Trof-Trak Mobile Growing System.

Fig. 5.41 Trof-Trak aluminum troughs supported by wheeled carriers which run on steel tracks supported by stanchions. Irrigation lines run from mains carried inside the support tracks. (Courtesy of TTS - Baggaley Ltd., Gloucestershire, England).

scale purposes was suggested by Schippers (1979). He constructed channels by nailing at the proper distances, 1-inch by 2-inch (2.5 by 5 cm) wood strips with their narrow sides on a sheet of plywood. Channels are formed by pushing a sheet of black polyethylene down between the strips.

He made a further suggestion to use a flat bed system for small plants which are seeded directly in place, such as radish, peas, beans, spinach, chives, etc. It consisted of a sheet of plywood or masonite with a rim on three sides, lined with plastic and filled with several inches of perlite. The perlite is prevented from falling into the catchment trench at the low end by use of a nylon screen. An inlet tube should be used for each foot width of the bed.

5.5.6 Moveable NFT

A moveable growing system (Trof-Track System) designed for pot plant and NFT production is manufactured by a British company, Trough Track Systems Ltd. It is based upon the moveable canal system developed by Schippers (1979). It consists of extruded aluminum troughs supported by wheeled carriers, which in turn, run on steel tracks. Parallel steel tracks run the entire length of the greenhouse and are supported on steel stanchions (figs. 5.40, 5.41).

Troughs are 5.5 m (18 ft.) long and wide enough to accommodate 14 cm (5½-inch) wide pots. The troughs have a "W" with a flattened middle cross sectional form on which the pots rest. The side gullies thus formed give strength and act as water channels. Each trough is fed a nutrient solution through a single drip irrigation line. The irrigation line runs the entire length of the greenhouse inside the track channel (fig. 5.41).

As plants increase in size from the seedling stage, the carriers are moved along the greenhouse and the distance between troughs increased to allow proper spacing of the plants as they reach maturity. Spacing may be done a number of times throughout the entire crop schedule. Such a system is especially suitable to low growing crops such as lettuce. With increased spacing of the troughs aeration of the crop is improved. Mobility of the troughs allows free movement of workers among the plants. Such a moveable system is particularly useful in reducing energy costs of greenhouses during the early winter months. Plants can be spaced close together in a seedling area of the greenhouse with supplementary artificial lighting. The remainder of the greenhouse can be shut down. As the plants grow and require additional space, the troughs merely need to be spaced further apart and transplanting can be eliminated. The manufacturer claims that the system can increase production for a given area by 35 per cent.

5.5.7 Agri-Systems NFT

A very efficient system of NFT is that of Whittaker Corporation's Agri-Systems Division in Somis, California. Special plastic trays filled with vermiculite by a flat filler machine are sown with European bibb lettuce using an automatic seeder. The seedlings are ready for transplanting into NFT channels in a growing house within three weeks. While Agri-Systems tested lettuce production with two to five tiers of troughs, they found the two-tier system was most productive by utilizing all available light (figs. 5.42, 5.43). The small cells containing the seedlings in the plastic trays are punched out of the trays and the small lettuce plant with its cell is planted directly into a moveable tape within the troughs (figs. 5.44, 5.45). Slits in the bottom of the cells allow roots to grow through into the nutrient solution.　Hundreds of nutrient troughs stacked in two tiers extend the width of the greenhouse.

A planting-harvesting machine feeds a coiled heavy plastic tape into grooves of the nutrient solution trough. Holes have been punched in the tape at the correct spacing for the lettuce. The operator of the planting machine simply drops the cells containing seedlings into the holes of the tape as it feeds into the nutrient trough (fig. 5.45). They claim that 154 seedlings can be planted in 20 seconds. Planting is scheduled so that rows of various stages of maturity are mixed to allow maximum light penetration to the lower tier (fig. 5.46). If plants of a similar age were placed in the troughs adjacent to each other, insufficient light would pass to the lower tier as the lettuce matured to full size.

After 6 to 7 weeks mature lettuce is removed by the harvesting machine which pulls the tape of mature heads through the trough at a rate of 40 plants per minute. The operator cuts the heads and places them on a conveyor belt which transports them to stations for inspection, bagging, boxing and subsequent transfer to refrigerated storage (fig. 5.47). In the harvesting process as soon as the lettuce heads and roots are removed from the tape the harvesting

Fig. 5.42 Agri-Systems Lettuce Production in Four Tiers of NFT Troughs. (Courtesy of Whittaker Corporation's Agri-Systems Division, Somis, California).

Fig. 5.43 Bibb Lettuce Production in Two Tiers of NFT Troughs. Note, the Coiled Moveable Tapes for Automatic Planting and Harvesting of the Crop. (Courtesy of Whittaker Corporation's Agri-Systems Division, Somis, California).

Fig. 5.44 Lettuce Seedling Growing in Plastic Cell. (Courtesy of Whittaker Corporation's Agri-Systems Division, Somis, California).

Fig. 5.45. Planting of seedling cells in moveable tape by use of the planting machine. (Courtesy of Whittaker Corporation's Agri-Systems Division, Somis, California).

Fig. 5.47. Harvested lettuce on conveyor belt being transferred to packing area. Note the automatic harvesting machine in the background. (Courtesy of Whittaker Corporation's Agri-Systems Division, Somis, California).

Fig. 5.46. Two tiers of NFT troughs with varying stages of plant maturity from seedlings to mature lettuce. Note the coiled moveable tapes and the recycling closed irrigation system. (Courtesy of Whittaker Corporation's Agri-Systems Division, Somis, California).

machine coils and cleans the tape for re-use in planting at the other end of the troughs. Using their system an annual turnover of 8 to 9 crops can be achieved. Daily planting and harvesting provides continuous production.

A one percent slope of the nutrient troughs with additional aeration of the solution maintains an optimum oxygen level in the solution. The lettuce "factory" is equipped with a complete laboratory for analyzing the nutrient solution and plant tissue by atomic absorption. Data have been recorded and parameters for optimum levels of nutrition have been programmed into a microcomputer. The nutritional levels have been correlated with electrical conductivity which is used as a general indicator of the nutritional status. Also, temperature, relative humidity, carbon dioxide levels and light are monitored by the computer. With programmed tolerance levels for each of these factors, the computer controls the dispensing of nutrients and adjusts the temperature, relative humidity and carbon dioxide levels in the greenhouses.

The company claims that with their system 8 million heads of lettuce can be grown annually on a 2½-acre (1 hectare) operation in comparison with 75,000 produced in the same area by conventional open-field farming. This is equivalent to 9 lettuce per square foot of greenhouse area per crop or 72 head per annum if 8 crops are produced per year. If only 6.5 million are marketable from the total production of 7.5 to 8 million and an estimated 19 people are required to operate a 2.5-acre lettuce module, the estimated labor cost is just over $0.02 per head compared to $0.07 to $0.10 per head for field-grown lettuce.

5.5.8 Rehau NFT Channel System

A rigid PVC extruded growing channel is manufactured by Rehau Plastics, Inc. (Appendix 2). This NFT channel is particularly suited for the growing of European bibb lettuce and herbs. The channels are available in any length but should not exceed 50 feet (15 m) as insufficient oxygenation, blockage of channels by roots, and nutrient gradients may occur. Channels of 50 feet length would be awkward to handle during harvesting and cleaning. The maximum practical length would be about 15 feet (4.6 m). Two sets of channels could be sloped back-to-back to a central catchment channel. In temperature climates the channels could be longer if they were located on the greenhouse floor.

Two cross sectional dimensions are made: a larger channel 2⁹/₁₆ inches in width by 2 inches deep (6.5 cm × 5 cm) and a shallower one 2⁹/₁₆ inches by 1¼ inches deep (6.5 cm × 3 cm). The choice of channel depends upon the propagation block used. For example, the deeper channel is used with 2-inch diameter mesh pots filled with peat medium, rockwool cubes or oasis blocks, while the shallower channel is suitable for "seed cells" made of ultra low density acetate fiber mass, wrapped with cellophane. The channel has a plastic cover 2⁷/₁₆ inches wide (6.2 cm) with a ³/₈-inch (1-cm) leg that sits on a ridge molded into the side of the channel. The smaller channel has the advantage of being 30 percent cheaper in cost than the larger one. Round or square holes may be custom punched in the cover. Seven-inch (18-cm) centers are standard.

Nutrient solution is pumped from a header from the nutrient tank. Emitters of 6 US gallons/hour (22.7 liters/hr) are connected between the header pipe and trickle line (fig. 5.48). Several filters, 100 mesh followed by a 200 mesh, should be installed downstream from the pump to prevent clogging of the emitters.

Fig. 5.48. Rehau NFT channels—trickle irrigation inlet lines from black poly header pipe. European bibb lettuce "Ostinata" about 45 days from seeding, ready for harvesting. Note the use of the "yellow sticky trap" for insect control. (Courtesy of Gourmet Hydroponics, Inc., Lake Wales, Florida).

A commercial grower, Gourmet Hydroponics, Inc., Lake Wales, Florida, uses 12-foot (3.6-m) channels to grow bibb lettuce and herbs (figs. 5.48, 5.49). The channels are supported on a 3-foot (0.9-m) high galvanized steel pipe bench (fig. 5.50). The lettuce is propagated in rockwool cubes (fig. 5.51) and placed directly into the channels after approximately 14 days from germination. The lettuce roots grow along the channel (fig. 5.52). The bottom of the channel is ribbed to give uniform distribution of nutrient flow. The channel has a 2 percent slope from inlet to outlet end. A catchment pipe at the outlet end returns the solution to a cistern.

Plants are spaced at 7.5-inch centers (19-cm) within the rows giving 20 head per 12-foot row, and 8 inches (20 cm) between rows. This system would utilize approximately 80 percent of the greenhouse floor area. In a one-acre greenhouse, allowing for walkways, two sets of 15-foot beds could be oriented perpendicularly to the gutters and posts of the greenhouse. The greenhouse would contain 88,740 plants using 7.5-inch by 8-inch spacing. Plant density would be 2 plants/square foot (21 plants/-sq m) of greenhouse floor area or 2.55 plants/square foot (27 plants/sq m) of growing area. This density is slightly less than the raft system but somewhat greater than the double row NFT system.

During harvesting the channels are removed with the plants intact which are then cut off. The channels are transported to a central cleaning-sterlizing vat where they are rinsed with clean water followed by soaking in a 10 percent chlorox solution for at least one hour. The trays should be rinsed with water upon removing from sterilization and allowed to dry.

Lettuce is packed in polyethylene bags and placed in cardboard boxes for shipping. It must be refrigerated at 35°F (1.7°C). The shelf life for the bibb lettuce is 7–10 days.

5.5.9 Double Row NFT

At least one company in Holland (Reko) (Appendix 2) manufactures an NFT channel and cover to contain two rows of lettuce per channel. The semi-rigid black plastic trough may be used for rockwool culture or NFT culture of other crops such as tomatoes and/or cucumbers.

A white cover is impermeable to light and gives good light reflection (figs. 5.53, 5.54) to reduce heat build-up in the channel.

Fig. 5.49. Basil in 12-feet Rehau channels at 7.5 inches (19 cm) within and 12 inches (30.5 cm) between rows. Note the trickle irrigation inlet lines in the foreground. (Courtesy of Gourmet Hydroponics, Inc., Lake Wales, Florida).

Fig. 5.50. Trickle feeding system to each Rehau channel, supported by a galvanized iron pipe bench. (Courtesy of Gourmet Hydroponics, Inc., Lake Wales, Florida).

Fig. 5.51. Lettuce plant growing in rockwool cube. Plant is about three weeks old from seeding (one week after transplanting). Note the cover of the Rehau channel. (Courtesy of Gourmet Hydroponics, Inc., Lake Wales, Florida).

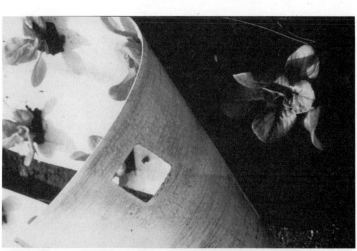

Fig. 5.52. Cover removed from the Rehau channel showing how the lettuce roots grow along the bottom of the channel forming a root mat. (Courtesy of Gourmet Hydroponics, Inc., Lake Wales, Florida).

Fig. 5.53. Double row NFT system with bibb lettuce. The white cover is raised to show the root mat and black NFT channel. The root mat encompasses a paper towel strip set in the channel bottom during transplanting, to obtain uniform solution distribution.

Fig. 5.54. White cover of double row NFT raised to show the size of the hole for inserting the plants. Young transplants are about three weeks old growing in peat blocks.

The white covering can be rolled onto a drum of a planting machine. Two planters sit on the machine while transplanting. The machine travels down the house unrolling four covers as it moves along and places them on the NFT channels as the planters set the plants in the holes. Holes are cut alternatively in the cover at 10 inches (25 cm) between plants within the row and 9 inches (22.5 cm) between rows when used to grow European bibb lettuce. The NFT channels are spaced 8 inches (20 cm) apart to give a row spacing of 9 inches (22.5 cm). No aisles are made so that in effect the entire greenhouse growing area is utilized with lettuce rows 9 inches (22.5 cm) apart (figs. 5.55, 5.56). These channels can easily be sterilized between crops with a 10 percent chlorox solution.

Lettuce can be seeded into compressed peat blocks using an automated block compressor and seeder (fig. 5.57). While most Dutch growers prefer to use a compressed peat block to germinate seedlings, an alternative method is to sow the seeds into rock-wool cubes. A propagation area of approximately 1100 square feet (100 sq m) is sufficient to service 10,760 square feet (1000 sq m) of production area. The propagation area should be provided with supplementary artificial lights and a misting irrigation system. The lettuce seedlings are transplanted to the NFT channels 12 to 40 days after sowing, depending upon the season (summer and winter respectively).

The NFT channels should be a maximum length of 50 feet (15 m) sloping towards a catchment return line. Two sets of channels slope to each catchment trench from each side (fig. 5.55). The catchment trenches return the solution to a cistern where the solution is automatically adjusted with injectors for pH and EC. A pump circulates the nutrient solution continuously 24 hours per day. Uniform distribution of nutrient solution along the NFT channels is achieved by use of a strip of paper towel on the bottom of the channel. Nutrient solution enters the higher end of each channel and is recirculated via the catchment trench, similar to other conventional NFT systems.

A one-acre greenhouse of dimensions 132 feet by 330 feet (40.2 m × 100.6 m) having a 10-foot (3-m) central walkway and 2-foot (0.6-m) end aisles has a useable length of 120 feet (36.6 m) which can contain two 60-foot (18.3-m) NFT channels for every 9 inches (22.5 cm) of greenhouse width.

Access every 27 feet (8.2 m) with 2-foot (0.6-m) wide aisles for pest control is equivalent to 36 rows of plants per 29 feet (8.8m) of

Fig. 5.55. Black plastic NFT channels are spaced 8 inches (20 cm) apart. The channels can easily be sterilized with a 10 percent chlorox solution between crops. The inlet ends of the trickle irrigation system appear in the foreground. NFT channels 50 ft (15 m) long slope towards a central catchment trench.

Fig. 5.56. Maturing lettuce covering most of the greenhouse floor area.

Fig. 5.57. Lettuce is seeded into compressed peat blocks. Lettuce at 2-3 days after germination.

greenhouse width or a total of 410 rows. Rows of 120 feet (36.6 m) in length contain at 10-inch (25-cm) centers 144 plants. Therefore, the total plants per crop in a greenhouse of one acre is: $144 \times 410 = 59,040$ plants. The useable growing area is: 27 feet $\times$ 120 feet $\times$ 11 sections = 35,640 square feet or 82 percent. Productivity is 1.66 plants/square foot (18 head/sq m) of growing area or 1.36 plants/square foot (14.5 head/sq m) of greenhouse floor area.

Of the three systems (cascade, raft, double NFT), this system is the least expensive to set up.

The main advantage of this system is the lower capital cost to achieve a NFT system of relatively high density planting.

5.5.10 PVC Pipe and Gutter NFT Systems

These systems are very similar in principle to the Rehau trough system of NFT. A series of 2-inch (5-cm) diameter PVC pipes have 1½-inch (3.8-cm) diameter holes drilled into the top face at centers equivalent to the appropriate spacing for lettuce within each channel—generally, 6½–7 inches (16.5–18 cm). See figure 5.58. Note that in figure 5.58, while there are 15 channels per bench, only 7 or 8 of them are planted. This was due to the pipes and holes being located too close together. Holes were made at 5½-inch (14-cm) centers within the pipes and pipes spaced 6 inches (15 cm) apart. Each pipe should be spaced 7 inches (18 cm) apart on the supporting bed frame with a total of 15 channels (pipes) so that they may be reached from the aisles on either side. The channels have a 2 percent slope and are 26 feet (7.9 m) long. Feeder tubes run to the inlet end of each pipe from a header and returning nutrient solution is collected in a catchment pipe which conducts the solution to a central cistern of 500 US gallons (1890 liters).

The pH and EC of the cistern are monitored and adjusted by injection of acid and stock solutions.

Lettuce seedlings are grown about 5 weeks (under Florida light conditions) before being transplanted to the growing channels. They are grown initially for 2½–3 weeks in Speedling type trays with a vegetable peat plug mix, then bare-rooted and placed into other larger trays having 1-inch diameter cells (fig. 5.59) for another 1½–2 weeks. These trays are set in shallow beds which can be flooded from the bottom to a level of 1 inch in depth for a period of 15 minutes and then drained for a comparable time. In

Fig. 5.58. A series of 2-inch diameter PVC pipes growing "Ostinata" bibb lettuce. A trickle irrigation inlet system is used. Note that only every other channel was planted due to inadequate spacing between channels. (Courtesy of Garden Patch Produce, Sarasota, Florida).

Fig. 5.59. Lettuce seedlings growing in trays fed by a subirrigation flooding system. The seedlings are about three to four weeks old. (Courtesy of Garden Patch Produce, Sarasota, Florida).

Fig. 5.60. A lettuce transplant with large 1-inch diameter root ball ready for planting into the growing channels. The seedling is about three to four weeks old. (Courtesy of Garden Patch Produce, Sarasota, Florida).

this way, new roots develop, the seedlings grow larger and transplanting into the growing channels can be done bare-rooted without any supporting medium or device. The transplants are about 30–35 days old (fig. 5.60).

The lettuce is grown to maturity within 14 days from transplanting. Two crops per month are possible from any given bed. In a greenhouse floor area of 6800 square feet (632 sq m) Garden Patch Produce of Sarasota, Florida, grows over 11,000 head per month. That is, 5500 head per two-week cropping period within the growing channels which is equivalent to 0.8 head/square foot/ cycle. Since the cycle time in the beds is half that of the other NFT systems and raft system, on a similar monthly basis this production would be 1.6 head/square foot (17 head/sq m). This compares to 2.6 head/square foot (28 head/sq m) and 1.67 plants/ square foot (18 plants/sq m) of the raft and double row NFT systems respectively. The lesser plant density of this NFT system is due to the growing space lost in aisles and the area required to grow the seedlings.

A second growing system used by Garden Patch Produce is a multiple gutter system made from moulded fiberglass (fig. 5.61). This is a series of double channel gutters similar to the double row NFT system described earlier. Channels are 85 feet (26 m) long with a 2 percent slope to the collection channel. Each pair of

Fig. 5.61. Multiple gutter NFT system made of moulded fiberglass. (Courtesy of Garden Patch Produce, Sarasota, Florida).

gutters has a vinyl cover. Plants are spaced at alternating 7-inch × 7-inch (18-cm × 18-cm) centers within each double gutter. Pairs of gutters are 9 inches (23 cm) apart.

Seedlings for the system are started in Speedling trays with a peat mix as for the PVC pipe system. After 21–23 days they are bare-rooted and transplanted to a styrofoam floating system (fig. 5.62). Seedlings are placed in about 1½-inch (4-cm) diameter pots cut from plastic compartmentalized trays. These pots, with a hole in the bottom, are set into the 2-inch (5-cm) thick styrofoam sheets floating on 1 inch of nutrient solution contained in gal-vanized steel beds about 2 ft wide and 2½ inches deep (60 cm × 6 cm). The beds are coated with an epoxy resin to prevent reaction of nutrients with the metal.

After 1½–2 weeks the plants are taken from the transplant beds and placed into the double gutter growing beds. The harvesting time and productivity is very similar to that of the pipe system.

5.5.11 Concrete NFT Channels

While capital costs of constructing concrete NFT channels is higher, maintenance is reduced. The NFT channels are formed in the concrete slab of a greenhouse floor on a 1 in 50 slope. The concrete is coated with epoxy resin to isolate it from the nutrient

Fig. 5.62. Styrofoam floating seedling beds. (Courtesy of Garden Patch Produce, Sarasota, Florida).

solution. Channels 4 inches (10 cm) wide by 1 inch (2.5 cm) deep are formed at 11-inch (28-cm) centers, giving a 7-inch (18-cm) aisle between each channel (fig. 5.63). With a 10-inch (25-cm) spacing between rows, the same plant density is achieved as for the double row NFT system. An operation of 10 acres (4 hectares) built in England produces about 8 million lettuce annually.

Channels are sloped from the inlet end toward a catchment trench at the far end and the solution is monitored, adjusted, and recirculated as for conventional NFT systems (fig. 5.64). A white polyethylene cover through which holes are punched for the placement of lettuce transplants into the NFT channels is spread across the concrete floor (figs. 5.63, 5.64). Lettuce is sown into compressed peat-soil blocks by use of machines as is done for the double row NFT system. Propagation procedures are also the same as for double row NFT. The surface of the blocks are covered with perlite after sowing to maintain moisture and discourage algae growth by keeping the surface dry (fig. 5.65). Irrigation is provided with an overhead misting system (fig. 5.66). As seedlings

Fig. 5.63. A lettuce operation in England using concrete NFT channels. Four-inch-wide concrete channels are covered with white polyethylene through which plants are placed.

Fig. 5.64. Concrete NFT channels at the solution inlet end.

Fig. 5.65. Lettuce seedlings about two to three days after germination, started in compressed peat-soil blocks covered with perlite to maintain moisture and keep the surface dry.

Fig. 5.66. Overhead irrigation-fertilization system for watering the seedlings.

grow, they are spaced further apart in a checkerboard configuration to allow further growth before transplanting to the channels (fig. 5.67).

The white polyethylene cover is used for several crops before replacing it and cleaning the channels. Planting and harvesting can be fully mechanized.

In addition to the higher capital cost, another disadvantage of this system is that it is designed specifically for lettuce or other low profile crops that are planted at similar densities. Thus, its adaptability to growing other crops is limited.

5.5.12 Styrofoam Channel NFT

NFT systems used in tropical countries can result in accumulation of heat in the nutrient solution raising the temperature to supraoptimal levels. In a commercial NFT system designed for the growing of tomatoes, cucumbers, melons, lettuce, and Chinese vegetables in Taiwan, raised styrofoam beds were constructed. A lightweight metal supporting frame (fig. 5.68) was sloped 2 percent to give adequate flow of the solution from the inlet to the catchment trench.

Polyethylene greenhouses 131 feet (40 m) by 16 feet (5 m) were constructed of metal tubing frame. Polyethylene covered the

Fig. 5.67. Lettuce seedlings growing in peat-soil blocks spaced out for further growth.

Fig. 5.68. Lightweight metal frames supporting styrofoam beds.

arched roofs while the 6.5-foot (2-m) sidewalls and gable ends were covered with a nylon insect screen to allow natural ventilation. A saran shade cloth and mist system were set at the peak of the structure to reduce the solar energy entering the house (fig. 5.69).

Two types of styrofoam beds were manufactured, one for low profile plants such as lettuce and Chinese cabbage, the other for vertically-trained plants such as tomatoes, cucumbers, and melons (fig. 5.70). They differed in that the beds for low growing plants did not have a partition in the center and were about one inch (2.5 cm) shallower. The partitioned channels would provide better root aeration to tomatoes, cucumbers, and melons, as roots were prevented from intertwining from one channel to the other. The dimensions of the beds were 64 feet (19.5 m) long by 3 feet (90 cm) wide by 4 inches (10 cm) deep. Partitioned beds had an actual growing NFT channel of 15 inches (38 cm) wide by 2.4 inches (6 cm) deep compared to the low profile beds which were 1.4 inches (3.5 cm) deep. The partitioned beds having separated channels contain two rows of plants, whereas the other beds support 4 to 5 rows of plants, depending on the plant spacing.

Fig. 5.69. Metal frame polyethylene greenhouses covered partially with saran shade cloth and nylon insect screen sidewalls. Note the styrofoam NFT beds inside the house and the nutrient tanks outside.

Fig. 5.70. Two types of styrofoam beds. The one on the right is for low profile plants, and the one on the left is for vine crops. The catchment trench is in the foreground with bed construction not completed at the time of the photo.

The beds were lined with black polyethylene to prevent algae growth and leakage of solution. They were covered with a 1-inch (2.5-cm) thick styrofoam lid through which plants were secured. Seed was sown in plastic mesh pots of 2-inch or 3-inch (5-cm or 8-cm) diameter containing a sand or peat mixture medium. These pots were placed directly into holes in the styrofoam lid during transplanting without disturbing the plant roots (fig. 5.71).

The return solution flows from the catchment tank to a cistern collection tank (fig. 5.72), and then is pumped to an above-ground nutrient tank outside the greenhouse (fig. 5.73). The nutrient solution is gravity fed via the inlet line to the NFT beds (fig. 5.74). No automatic adjustment of pH or EC was installed in this system mainly because such equipment is unavailable in the country.

5.5.13 NFT in Saudi Arabia

During the early 1980's there was a boom in the development of the greenhouse industry in Saudi Arabia, due to the buoyant oil-based economy. Many operations, of a basic size of 5 hectares (about 13 acres), were constructed by Dutch greenhouse builders. Millions of dollars were spent on each of these first-class operations to construct the most up-to-date structures (fig. 5.75). However, limited technology of growing systems existed, as most of the funds were spent on the hardware of the greenhouse. Once the greenhouses were completed, little money remained for growing. Often, qualified horticulturists were not employed, so expected crop production was not achieved.

Inexperienced growers and highly saline waters contributed to substantial reductions in yields. Several well-managed sand culture operations produced high quality crops of peppers, tomatoes, and cucumbers (figs. 5.76–5.78). Some newly constructed greenhouses were completed but not planted as funds tightened with a decline in the economy in 1985. At the same time, competition from the field-grown tomatoes of neighbouring countries, such as Turkey, depressed the market.

Several operations near Riyadh, of 5 hectares each, were growing tomatoes and cucumbers in a NFT system. One company having a technical person from Europe grew relatively good crops while the other suffered badly from excess salt in its well water. Without a reverse-osmosis or other effective treatment unit, the

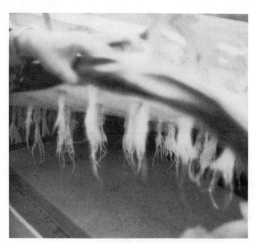

Fig. 5.71. Plants are supported by the styrofoam lids of the beds.

Fig. 5.72.
The catchment trench and cistern collection tank.

Fig. 5.73. An above-ground nutrient tank into which solution is pumped from the collection tank. Solution is gravity fed to the beds in the greenhouse using a solenoid valve.

Fig. 5.74. The inlet ends of the beds on the right and the catchment trenches on the left (construction incomplete).

Fig. 5.75. Dutch-manufactured greenhouses built in Saudi Arabia — reservoir in the foreground is to collect water pumped from wells.

Fig. 5.76. A sand culture operation in Saudi Arabia growing bell peppers.
Fig. 5.77. A sand culture operation in Saudi Arabia growing tomatoes. Note the placement of the ooze hose trickle irrigation system next to the plants on the inside of the rows.

Fig. 5.78. Sand culture of cucumbers in Saudi Arabia.

salt levels were excessive for satisfactory production. Effective cooling with cooling pads was impaired by salt build-up from untreated water. Pad cells would plug within a year, reducing their efficiency to a level where cooling was not achieved and resulting high temperatures, compounded the growing problems.

With competent management and proper desalination equipment, good crops of tomatoes and cucumbers could be grown using the NFT system (figs. 5.79, 5.80). The NFT system was constructed of wooden troughs lined with a black-on-white polyethylene. These NFT channels were sloped from both ends towards a central catchment pipe which returned the solution to the nutrient tank (figs. 5.81, 5.82).

5.5.14 The Ariel NFT

Over the past three to four years, Dr. Allen Cooper working with Nutrient Film Technology, Ltd., in England, has developed a divided channel NFT system. According to Cooper (1985) the Ariel NFT system was developed to overcome a number of limitations inherent in conventional NFT systems:

1. The precise control of solution levels in a conventional NFT system to about one centimeter of depth is difficult to maintain. If the root mat is submerged completely in the nutrient solution, the plant in effect suffers oxygen deficit. The reduction of flow to maintain a one-centimeter depth of solution is difficult especially as the root mat thickens and restricts the flow of solution. The

Fig. 5.79. Cucumbers in a NFT system in Saudia Arabia.

Fig. 5.80. Tomatoes growing in a conventional NFT system in Saudi Arabia. Note that the plants have been harvested at the base and lowered for continued growth. The stems are bent parallel to the NFT troughs with the upper five feet of the plant producing more fruit.

root mat must be only half submerged in the solution to allow diffusion of gases into and out of the top half of the roots not submerged. The reasoning for this is that the diffusion rate of gases in air is 10,000 times more rapid in air than it is in water. If this level adjustment of the solution to keep half of the root mat exposed to the air is not maintained, the submerged roots will rapidly die, the plant wilts, and fungi such as *Pythium* and *Phytophthera* invade the roots, causing further death. This precise regulation of solution level which introduces a high probability of error can be overcome with the Ariel NFT system, Cooper believes.

2. Conventional NFT systems require complex monitoring and injection equipment. Continual maintenance and calibration of pH and EC equipment is necessary to prevent breakdown and loss of accuracy of measurements.

3. The need for continuous recirculation of the nutrient solution in conventional NFT demands an uninterrupted power supply. This is achieved with an automatic start-up standby generator and alarm systems to advise technicians of failures. This is usually part of a computer-operated greenhouse control package.

4. Skilled management is an integral part of successful conventional NFT crop production. Alteration of nutrient formulae

during different crop stages, seasons and weather conditions are decisions made by management.

5. In conventional NFT systems some solid rooting medium is needed for the propagation of the plants. Usually rockwool or compressed peat-soil blocks, peat pellets, or pots filled with a medium of sand, peat, perlite, or a mixture of these components is used. Such use of a propagation medium is often costly. The Ariel NFT system minimizes the use of propagation media and concentrates on bare-rooted seedlings. It should be pointed out, however, that the use of rockwool cubes for propagation of seedlings will reduce transplant "shock" and provide a small reservoir of nutrient solution, preventing desiccation.

The Ariel NFT system grows bare-rooted plants so that any changes in the root environment (adjustment of nutrient solution) will produce a rapid response in the plant. When a solid medium such as rockwool or peat is used, response time is slowed

Fig. 5.81. NFT system constructed of wooden troughs supporting white-on-black polyethylene NFT channels. Rows are paired with an aisle between each set.

Fig. 5.82. NFT channels slope towards a central catchment pipe (6-inch diameter).

due to the interaction with the rooting medium. The significance of this may be questionable. An inexpensive propagation system was developed for the Ariel system by use of "germination pockets" made from an absorbent matting material (Cooper, 1985). The "pockets" with a fold at the top into which the seed is placed are set astride ridges in trays. The trays are placed in germination chambers having controlled optimum temperature for germination. The work of seeding would be tedious if it could not be automated.

Once the seeds germinate, the pockets are removed from the germination chamber and placed at close spacing astride ridges in a propagation bed which has a ridge-and-furrow configuration. Nutrient solution is recirculated down the furrows of the propagation bed. The cost of propagation materials is less than in conventional NFT systems, and labor is less, since large numbers of plants can be transported in trays when they are removed from the propagation beds to the growing channels. But, the labor of sowing seeds may be greater than with conventional NFT. The propagation area with a high density planting can be placed in a small area of the greenhouse having supplementary artificial lighting during the winter months. The space requirements, however, will be a function of the plants grown and to what age they will be grown before transplanting to the final growing beds in the greenhouse. This method of propagation produces a plant with a divided root system necessary for the subsequent growing channels.

The growing channel consists of a divided, metal-channel base of aluminum or galvanized steel (or fired clay), depending upon cost and availability. The base comprises a central ridge with two side channels (fig. 5.83). This cross-sectional configuration adds strength to the base so that it may be placed directly on the ground of a roughly prepared slope without any depressions ocurring. The bases are overlapped down the slope, similar to roofing tiles.

Black-on-white polyethylene is laid in the base channels. Using a wide strip of polyethylene enables it to be rolled above each channel to form two air-filled rolls retained by the walls of the base on either side of the central ridge (fig. 5.83). These rolls provide insulation against solar radiation to prevent overheating of the roots and solution, and at the same time reduces heat loss during the winter months, thus stabilizing the solution temperature.

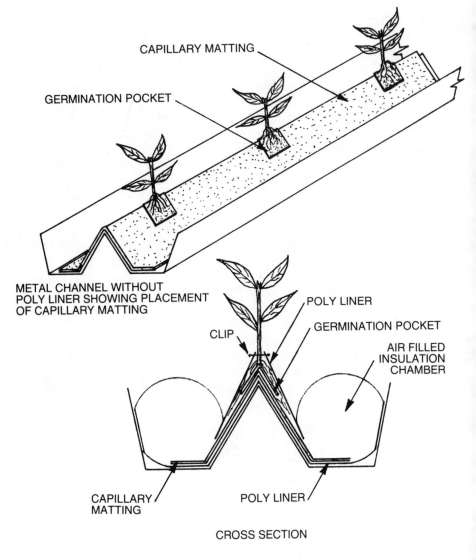

CAPILLARY MATTING

GERMINATION POCKET

METAL CHANNEL WITHOUT
POLY LINER SHOWING PLACEMENT
OF CAPILLARY MATTING

CLIP

POLY LINER

GERMINATION POCKET

AIR FILLED
INSULATION
CHAMBER

CAPILLARY
MATTING

POLY LINER

CROSS SECTION

Fig. 5.83. Profile section of Ariel NFT system.

Capillary matting is placed on the ridge, with its sides reaching to the bottom of each side channel. The plants are then placed astride the ridge with half of the divided root system on either side of the ridge. The polyethylene cover is then clipped together between the plants. These clips serve also as attachment points for support strings of plants normally trained vertically.

In the Ariel NFT system, with plants of a divided root system, the gaseous and aqueous phases are separated. The need to closely regulate the nutrient solution flow-rate in conventional NFT is eliminated. In the Ariel system the nutrient solution flows down only one side of the channel at a time. The time period for alteration of flow down the channels depends upon plant species and weather conditions. This alteration of flow in the channels separates the gaseous and aqueous components of the root environment, and, as a result, at all times one side is fully exposed to the air. The channel receiving the solution can use high-flow rates to completely submerge the roots without causing oxygen deficit to the plant as the other half of the root system has no solution flowing in it. Claims of a 10 percent increase in yields are attributed to this increased root oxygenation. Cooper (1985) has demonstrated that each half of the divided root system is capable of supporting all the plant needs.

Complicated monitoring and injection equipment has been replaced with three plastic bins, one for dilute acid (pH control) and two for nutrient stock solutions. Each bin is connected to the catchment pipe with a narrow bore plastic tube from the side wall near the bottom of the bin. Every morning a solution sample is taken and the pH and EC are determined. The manager then determines the quantities of pH adjuster and stock solutions required for the subsequent 24-hour period. These quantities are placed in the bins each morning and drip slowly via the tubes into the catchment pipe.

Cooper (1985) states that the Ariel system is adaptable to third world countries due to the simplification of the NFT system. He indicates that the need for pumps and electrical power can be eliminated by circulating the solution, using animal-powered water wheels, etc. Edwards (1985) speculates that technology transfer to third world countries is possible whereby several skilled technicians working from a service center can provide the technical inputs to many growers using the Ariel system. Monitoring of nutritional needs and simple adjustment procedures would be provided to the growers.

5.5.15 The Ein Gedi System

The Ein Gedi System (EGS) of water culture was developed in Israel (Soffer and Levinger, 1980) to overcome some of the main disadvantages of hydroponic systems and be applicable to regions

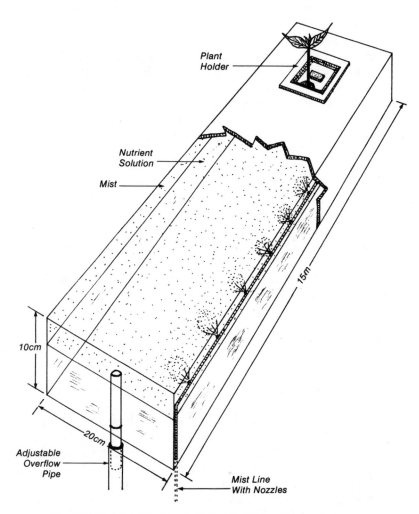

Fig. 5.84 Sketch of the Ein Gedi System Water Culture Bed.

having a limited supply of water. The main disadvantages of hydroponic systems the EGS was to overcome were minimum buffering action of soilless media, small water holding capacity of substrates such as gravel and sand, and insufficient oxygen available to plant roots, especially for full grown plants at increasing water temperatures.

The EGS channel is a self-contained unit so that it can easily be raised from the ground level to any level desired. The system having a cover made of polystyrene allows starting the crop from seeds, bulbs, plants, and rooting of cuttings. Sterilization is fast, simple and inexpensive with a minimum of down time between crops as the channels can be scrubbed clean with a disinfectant. The channel is constructed of durable reinforced double layer polypropylene (fig. 5.84).

The EGS is a system of continually aerated flowing nutrient solution in which plant roots are immersed. A large volume of nutrient solution per plant reduces fluctuations in nutrient levels. Continued flow provides homogeneity of the solution composition and oxygen to the root surface. Aeration of the solution is achieved by spraying the solution throughout the entire growth trough. This produces a nutrient mist on top of a flowing solution. A 7-liter solution per tomato plant (2 plants/sq. m. or 10¾ sq. ft.), at a flow rate of not less than 7 liters (1.8 U.S. gal.)/plant/hour gives good buffering capacity of the root medium. This relatively large volume of solution continuously within the channel gives a safeguard against any mechanical or electrical breakdown.

In 1980 over 30 units of this system of various sizes, were operating in Israel, The Netherlands, Norway, and Italy, for tomatoes, cucumbers, ornamental plants, and propagation. While some were of a semi-commercial scale, all were experimental, to evaluate the economic feasibility of the system.

5.5.16 Advantages of the NFT Systems

The advantages of the nutrient-film technique in glasshouse crop production are:
1. Low capital cost
2. Elimination of soil sterilization and preparation
3. Rapid turnaround between crops
4. Precise control of nutrition
5. Maintenance of optimal root temperatures by heating of the nutrient solution (77° F. for tomatoes, 84° F. for cucumbers)

6. Simplicity of installation and operation

7. Reduction of transplanting shock by use of growing pots or cubes and preheating of nutrient solution to optimal root temperatures

8. Easy adjustment of nutrient solution formulation to control plant growth under changing light conditions.

9. Use of systemic insecticides and fungicides in the nutrient solution to control insects and diseases of ornamental crops

10. Possible energy savings by keeping the greenhouse air temperature at lower than normal levels due to maintenance of optimal root temperatures

11. Elimination of plant water stress between irrigation cycles by continuous watering

12. Conservation of water by use of a cyclic system rather than an open system

The future of successful crop production lies in a universal cropping system in which water and fertilizers can be used efficiently. This is particularly true in arid regions of the world, such as the Middle East, where land is nonarable and water is scarce. In such areas desalinated sea water can be used but is very costly. Sand culture is used in many of these areas, but often it is of calcareous nature which causes rapid changes in pH and tying-up of essential elements such as iron and phosphorus. In these areas of high solar energy, efficient use of costly desalinated water is essential. The nutrient-film technique is the system which makes efficient use of water and fertilizers and at the same time does not rely on a suitable medium such as noncalcareous sand gravel. In my opinion, the future of soilless culture in such harsh environments lies in the NFT systems.

5.6 Tube Culture

Tube culture is a modification of the NFT and water culture. The principles are the same. The nutrient solution is pumped through 4-inch polyvinyl chloride (PVC) drain pipes covered with black polyethylene film. The PVC pipe is cut in half and black polyethylene placed over the top of it to prevent light from entering. Holes are cut in the top of the polyethylene through which seedlings grown in cubes are set into the nutrient solution flowing along the bottom of the PVC pipes. During crop changeover the polyethylene cover and plants are removed, the tube washed with a bleach sterilizing agent and a new polyethylene cover replaced ready for new seedlings.

The "cascade" system of Schippers described earlier is a form of tube culture. Further developments for both commercial and hobby uses have been achieved by Homeland Industries, Inc. of Brooklyn, New York. They term their system "Moduleponic." It consists of two plastic pipes on a supporting stand with an air supply to the lower pipe containing the nutrient solution as shown in figure 5.85. The nutrient reservoir can be constructed of 3-inch (7.6 cm) PVC pipe while the growing bed should be of 4- to 5-inch (10-13 cm) diameter PVC pipe. While the system is not truly a water culture system, since the upper pipe contains a gravel medium, it does closely resemble the tube culture system.

Air is pumped through an air supply pipe into the bottom nutrient reservoir pipe. A filter pipe joins the nutrient reservoir with the growing bed at intervals along the unit. This filter pipe is perforated with small holes. As air is pumped into the sealed nutrient reservoir it is forced up through the filter pipe carrying nutrient solution with it — in principle very similar to the "City Green" indoor units described in Chapter 6. The nutrients are then distributed throughout the gravel bed by escaping through the perforated filter pipe. When the air pressure stops, the excess nutrient solution drains back down to the nutrient reservoir. The pump is activated by a time-clock three to four times a day depending upon the plant stage of growth and weather conditions.

Another recent development is the "Skaife's Pipe Dream." Mesh plugs containing shredded peat moss are fitted into upright sections of 2-inch (5 cm) black, ribbed plastic drainage pipe. These 12-18 inch (30-40 cm) sections fit into a horizontal 6-inch (15 cm) diameter plastic drainage pipe through which the nutrient solution is circulated (fig. 5.86). Plants or seeds are set into each vertical plug. Roots develop downward into the solution, outward into the peat moss and finally through the sides of the mesh into the high relative humidity air between the plug and the pipe. The nutrient solution stored in a reservoir is circulated through the horizontal pipe to keep the pipe half-filled. A pump is not necessary if the solution reservoir is kept slightly above the horizontal pipe.

A modification of tube culture has been used in Kenya in the production of grapes (Barrow, 1980). A gravel substrate was used in a 10-inch (25 cm) PVC pipe. A segment was cut from the top of the pipe, and this segment was placed in the bottom of the pipe to

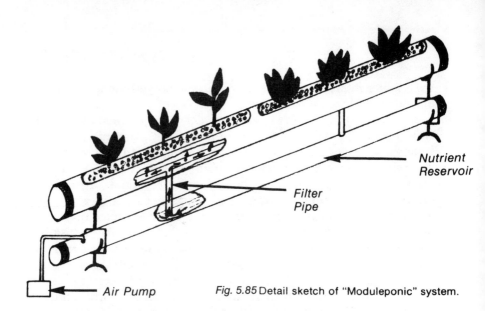

Nutrient
Reservoir

Filter
Pipe

Air Pump

Fig. 5.85 Detail sketch of "Moduleponic" system.

Fig. 5.86 "Skaife's Pipe Dream" system.

facilitate filling and draining of the nutrient solution. Slots were cut at regular intervals along this segment.

Sixty-foot (18.3 m) sections were supported by concrete blocks every ten feet (3 m) to provide a slight slope towards the discharge end. For grapes the spacing between each pair of pipes was 12 feet (3.66 m). A discharge pipe connected all the planting tubes to an underground catchment tank from which the nutrient solution was then pumped back to a storage tank. A main inlet pipe connected to the inlet end of each bed from the storage tank. Rooted cuttings of grapes were planted in the tubes at a spacing of approximately two feet (61 cm). Plants were supported by an overhead trellis.

5.7 Raceway, Raft or Floating System

This system of water culture is a modification of the Japanese system (section 5.3). Dr. Merle Jensen of the Environmental Research Laboratory (ERL) of the University of Arizona, Tucson, Arizona, developed a prototype raceway lettuce production system during 1981–1982. He projected that such a system could produce 4.5 million heads of lettuce per year per hectare.

The system consists of relatively deep (15–20 centimeters or 6–8 inches) beds holding a large volume of nutrient solution. The solution in the beds is fairly static with a circulation of 2–3 liters per minute. The bed dimensions are about 60 centimeters wide by 20 centimeters deep by 30 meters long (24 in × 8 in × 98 ft) (fig. 5.87). Such a bed has a volume of 3.6 cubic meters (127 cubic feet) which is equivalent to 3600 liters (about 950 U.S. gal). Therefore, the flow through each bed at 2–3 liters per minute amounts to an exchange rate of one per 24-hour period.

The nutrient solution from the beds is recirculated through a nutrient tank of 4000 to 5000 liters (1000 to 1250 gallons). There the solution is aerated by an air pump, chilled with a refrigeration unit and is then pumped back to the far ends of each bed. On its return to the beds the nutrient solution is passed through an untraviolet sterilizer (fig. 5.88). These sterilizers are manufactured by several companies (Appendix 2) for use in soft drink, beer, distillery, aquaculture, clothing dye, and cosmetic industries. They are effective against many bacteria, fungi, some viruses, and protozoa such as nematodes. However, their effectiveness against plant pathogenic organisms has not been fully documented.

Fig. 5.87. Raft system of bibb lettuce. Lettuce from far right to left is 4, 3, 2, and 1 day after transplanting. Seedlings are 12-14 days old before transplanting. (Courtesy of Hoppmann Hydroponics, Waverly, Florida).

Some work has been done to evaluate the effectiveness of a UV sterilizer against selected species of pathogenic and non-pathogenic fungi commonly associated with greenhouse crops (Mohyuddin, 1985). The unit significantly reduced or eliminated the following fungi from an aqueous solution: *Botrytis cinerea, Cladosporium* sp., *Fusarium* spp., *Sclerotinia sclerotiorum, Verticillium albo-atrum*, and several others. Similar research is currently being carried out on fungi, bacteria, and algae.

Pythium infection of roots causes stunting of plants (fig. 5.89). Ultraviolet sterilization of nutrient solutions does not combat this disease organism. It can only be controlled by sterilization between crops of all beds, pipes, tanks, etc., with a 10 percent chlorox solution.

The cost of these sterilization units varies with their capacity.

Fig. 5.88. Raft system of water culture. Chiller unit on left in front of acid and stock solution tanks with individual injectors. Circulating pumps in center and U.V. sterilizer on right. (Courtesy of Hoppmann Hydroponics, Waverly, Florida).

Fig. 5.89. Pythium infection of bibb lettuce. Healthy plant on right, infected plant on left. Note the difference in growth of the head and roots between the healthy and infected plants.

The larger volume of water they can effectively treat, the larger the unit and higher the price. For example, a unit capable of handling 50 gpm (gallons per minute) costs about US$3500 while one of 200 gpm costs US$9000.

One side-effect of the use of UV sterilizers is their effect on a few of the micronutrients. Mohyuddin (1985) found that the boron and manganese contents in a nutrient solution were reduced by more than 20 percent over a period of 24 hours of sterilization. The most significant effect was on iron which was precipitated as hydrous ferric oxide. Nearly 100 percent of the iron was affected. The iron precipitate coated lines and the quartz sleeve of the sterilizer thereby reducing the UV transmission. Such precipitate could be removed with a filter. This, however, does not resolve the problem with the loss of iron from the nutrient solution during UV sterilization. Further work is needed to resolve the problem of iron precipitation by the UV sterilizer. Perhaps another form of iron chelate could be used that would not break down.

The pH and electrical conductivity (EC) are monitored with sensors in the return line. Automatic injection of nitric acid (HNO_3), sulfuric acid (H_2SO_4), phosphoric acid (H_3PO_4), or potassium hydroxide (KOH) are used to adjust the pH. Similarly, the EC is raised by injection of calcium nitrate and a mixture of the remaining nutrients from two separate stock concentrate tanks (fig. 5.88) to keep it at 1.2–1.3 mMhos.

Jensen (personal communication) found that the use of a water chiller in the nutrient tank could be used to maintain the temperature of the nutrient solution between 70 and 75°F (21–23°C). This cooling of the solution would prevent bolting of lettuce in desert and tropical regions (fig. 5.88). European bibb lettuce is grown commercially by Hoppmann Hydroponics, Ltd., in Florida, at temperatures exceeding 110°F (43°C) in the greenhouses by use of the floating system using a water chiller in the nutrient tank.

Water chiller units cool, aerate, and circulate the solution. They are available in ⅙, ⅓, and 1 horsepower units. The one horsepower unit is capable of cooling 1000 gallons of water in a temperature range from 35–70°F (2–21°C). For nutrient solutions, units with stainless steel drive shaft, evaporator tube, and circulator blade should be used. These units are used in aquarium tanks for the raising of fish. The one horsepower unit costs US$2000 (see Appendix 2 for manufacturer).

Jensen (1985) successfully grew a leaf lettuce (Waldemann's Green) and three varieties of European bibb (Ostinata, Salina, Summer Bibb). Recent communication with Jensen revealed that an operation in Norway is growing over one acre of head lettuce using the floating system.

Hoppmann Hydroponics in Florida produces bibb lettuce on a 30- to 34-day cycle in the beds after transplanting (figs. 5.90–5.92). Lettuce can be sown using rockwool plugs, jiffy pellets, or directly in a peat mix medium in plastic seeding trays. While rockwool plugs placed in 240 compartment trays are easily sown by automatic sowing equipment, the cost of rockwool is greater than using a peat mix in 273 compartment trays, which can also be sown automatically using pelletized seed.

Fig. 5.90. Lettuce 6 days after transplanting. The solution inlet pipe to the bed is in the foreground. Note the wire hook attached to the first board (raft) to allow pulling of the boards during harvesting.

Fig. 5.91. Lettuce 12 days after transplanting.

Fig. 5.92. Lettuce 32 days after transplanting, ready for harvest. (Courtesy of Hoppmann Hydroponics, Waverly, Florida).

Seedlings should be 12–14 days old before transplanting to the beds. The seedling trays can be bottom irrigated through the use of a capillary mat (fig. 5.93). This prevents overhead watering, which can burn the seedlings under high solar conditions of tropical and desert regions. Seedlings should be irrigated with a dilute nutrient solution when the cotyledons unfold. The capillary mats can either be replaced or sterilized between seedling crops (12–14 days) using a 10 percent chlorox solution to eliminate algae, fungal spores, and insects such as fungus gnats. Seeding and transplanting is carried out daily so that continuous production is achieved. Late evening transplanting after sunset will assure successful "take." Plants will have time to acclimate before full-light conditions of the following day. This is especially significant if transplants are bare-rooted as is the case when the lettuce is sown in a peat medium. Bare-rooted plants are placed in 1-inch (2.5-cm) diameter holes of the styrofoam "rafts" (fig. 5.94).

The "floats" or "rafts" are 1-inch × 6-inches × 24-inches (2.5-cm × 15-cm × 61-cm) boards of styrofoam (fig. 5.95). The styrofoam may be ordered in specific dimensions from the manufacturer if large quantities are purchased. They will cut the boards to the required dimensions with holes for placement of the plants. A high density "roofmate" type material (blue in color) used in house construction is most suitable.

The rafts insulate the underlying solution in the bed and are a moveable system of transplanting and harvesting. Maintenance of cool-solution temperatures (optimum 75°F or 23°C) is a prime factor in preventing bolting of lettuce in hot climates. This is achieved by the water chiller in the nutrient tank, the large

Fig. 5.93. Lettuce seedlings 10-12 days old, in the foreground, are almost ready for transplanting. Lettuce is seeded into a peat plug mix in #273 trays (273 compartments) and set on a capillary mat in beds for watering.

Fig. 5.94. Lettuce seedling being planted into 1-inch holes in "rafts." (Courtesy of Hoppmann Hydroponics, Waverly, Florida).

Fig. 5.95. A "raft" supporting four lettuce plants. Note the vigorous, healthy root growth. (Courtesy of Hoppmann Hydroponics, Waverly, Florida).

volume of solution in the beds, and the insulation from solar radiation by the rafts.

The rafts simplify harvesting. A string placed under the rafts in the bed, attached to three or four wire hooks—in turn attached to the rafts along the entire bed length in several places—can be pulled in by a boat winch at the harvesting end of the greenhouse (figs. 5.90, 5.96). The rafts float the mature lettuce plants *in situ* within the beds. Easier floatation is possible by raising the solution level in the bed prior to harvesting, by plugging the return pipe of the nutrient circulation system.

During transplanting, the boards are pushed along the bed from the harvesting end as the plants are placed in them (fig. 5.94). Long lines of floats with growing lettuce are readily moved.

Between crops, the boards must be cleaned and sterilized by hosing with water prior to dipping them in a 10 percent bleach solution. Similarily, the beds must be drained and cleaned after each harvest (fig. 5.97). A new nutrient solution is prepared in the bed after cleaning and is ready for transplanting the same day.

Sowing, transplanting, and harvesting must be coordinated to get a continuous daily cycle. The growing period in the beds may vary from 28 to 35 days for bibb lettuce, depending on sunlight and temperature conditions. In semi-tropical, tropical, and desert regions where sunlight is abundant and daylength averages between 14 to 16 hours, it is possible to obtain 10 to 12 crops annually, whereas in the temperate climates where sunlight is lower and daylength may be 8 hours or less during the winter months, it may only be possible to reach 7 to 8 crops annually. In temperate regions, winter crops may take 13 weeks (including 40 days from sowing seed to transplanting), whereas summer crops take 5 weeks (including 12 days from sowing to transplanting). By use of supplementary artificial lights, the sowing-transplanting period could be shortened during the winter to perhaps half the time.

Individual heads are packaged in plastic bags. Some growers leave about one inch of roots on the plants when packaging, with the expectation of longer shelf-life than without roots. However, some consumers may not like the presence of roots. In Arizona (Collins and Jensen, 1983) the roots-on package did not increase shelf-life, and it was found to be three times more expensive to prepare and pack. The roots-on packaging was not well accepted by wholesalers or retailers and added to the cost of transportation due to increased volume and weight. Generally, 24 head are packaged to a case.

Fig. 5.96. A boat winch is used to reel in the string which pulls the boards along the bed. (Courtesy of Hoppmann Hydroponics, Waverly, Florida).

Fig. 5.97. Beds are cleaned between crops with a 10 percent chlorox solution. (Courtesy of Hoppmann Hydroponics, Waverly, Florida).

The raceway system maximizes the usage of greenhouse floor space for production of lettuce or other low profile crops. For example, a greenhouse of one acre (43,560 square feet) with dimensions of 108 feet × 403 feet (33 m × 123 m) allowing front and back aisles of 8 feet (2.4 m) and 2 feet (0.6 m) respectively, with 2-foot access aisles every 29 feet (11 sets of beds), has a useable production area of 37,000 square feet (3439 sq m). This is 84 percent utilization of greenhouse floor area. Such a growing area could produce 112,100 head of lettuce per crop. That is, 2.6 head per square foot (28 head/sq m) of greenhouse area or 3 head per square foot (32 head/sq m) of the available growing area.

The main advantage of the raft system is its ability to grow lettuce and cool season crops in tropical climates by use of the chiller unit, cooling the nutrient solution. The high planting density (utilization of greenhouse floor area) is a second factor.

The principal disadvantage is a higher capital cost than conventional NFT systems.

5.8 Aeroponics

Aeroponics is the growing of plants in an opaque trough or supporting container in which their roots are suspended and bathed in a nutrient mist rather than a nutrient solution. This culture is widely used in laboratory studies in plant physiology but not as commonly used as other methods on a commercial scale. Several Italian companies are, however, using aeroponics in the growing of numerous vegetable crops such as lettuce, cucumbers, melons and tomatoes.

Innovative work with aeroponic cultivation continues at the Environmental Research Laboratory (ERL) of the University of Arizona in Tucson. Working with Walt Disney Productions, Dr. Carl Hodges, director of the ERL and Dr. Merle Jensen, research horticulturist, developed concepts for presenting leading-edge agricultural technologies to the public in an entertaining way. The ERL helped create two attractions, the "Listen to The Land" boat cruise and the "Tomorow's Harvest Tour," for The Land—a major facility at Epcot Center at Walt Disney World near Orlando, Florida.

Both Purdue University and the ERL are researching controlled environment life support systems to be used in space stations. These programs sponsored by NASA are called Controlled Ecological Life Support Systems (CELSS). The University of Arizona's Environmental Research Laboratory is developing systems to support visitors to Mars. These experiments must be carried out in completely closed chambers. Closed systems of liquid hydroponics must be used so that surplus solution is recovered, replenished, and recycled. Generally, this is the nutrient film technique (NFT) or modifications of it.

Other work at the ERL includes lettuce growing on styrofoam A-frames in a greenhouse. Roots fall toward an A-frame's center and are periodically misted with nutrients (fig. 5.98). This acroponics system increases the heads of lettuce that can be grown in a greenhouse space, and is similar to the "cascade" and moveable

Fig. 5.98 Styrofoam A-frame with lettuce root systems growing through styrofoam sheet.
Fig. 5.99 Melons on A-frames with lettuce in styrofoam boards floating beneath.

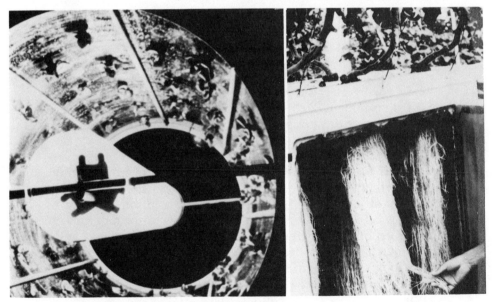

Fig. 5.100 Bibb lettuce growing in rotation drum.
Fig. 5.101 Healthy roots of tomatoes growing in aeroponic A-frame mist cabinet.

NFT systems that decrease unit production costs. Another way ERL scientists increase greenhouse output is to grow melons on A-frames, while lettuce in styrofoam boards is floating on water beneath the melons (fig. 5.99).

They are also growing lettuce on the interior of a large drum rotating around an artificial light source. Lettuce is planted through holes in an inner drum that spins at 50 rpm. As the inner drum spins, the plant tops grow toward the center. The roots, sealed between the two drums, are misted regularly with nutrients (fig. 5.100). As described earlier in the NFT section, the ERL has also experimented with a conveyor-belt plant system of hanging vertical pipes. The plants suspended in the pipes are periodically cycled past spray nozzles that mist nutrients into the pipe tops. At the same time, they pass above an open tank so that excess solution can be recycled (figs. 5.33, 5.34).

Tomatoes are grown in A-frame mist cabinets (fig. 5.101). While such cabinets would not be commercially feasible for growing tomatoes, cucumbers or melons, they demonstrate how aeroponics enables the growth of plants with large, healthy root systems.

With increasing fuel costs for heating greenhouses, new growing systems such as NFT and aeroponics will be rapidly adopted in the future to save energy and increase production volume.

5.9 Hydroponic Grass Units

The growing of grains with a nutrient solution within an en-closed environmentally controlled chamber or unit has become of commercial significance as a source of year-round fresh grass feed for animals.

Grains such as oats, barley, rye, wheat, sorghum or corn are pre-soaked for 24 hours prior to being placed in growing trays (about 0.5 square meters) for 6 days. The trays may be watered manually on shelves with excess nutrient solution draining to waste (fig. 5.102), or the entire system of trays may be mounted on rotating drums which are automatically fed with a nutrient solu-tion which is recycled. Light is provided artificially by use of cool white fluorescent lighting. After 6 days of growth the grain (grass) has grown to 4-5 inches (15-20 centimeters) and is ready for har-vesting and feeding to the animals (fig. 5.103).

Various commercial grass-growing units are available in a number of sizes. A 20-foot long by 8-foot high by 10-foot wide (6.0 meters by 2.4 meters by 3.6 meters) unit is shown in figure 5.104.

Fig. 5.102 Shelves of grass-growing trays. Fig. 5.103 Six-day-old grass ready for feeding to livestock. (Courtesy of La Serenisima, Buenos Aires.)

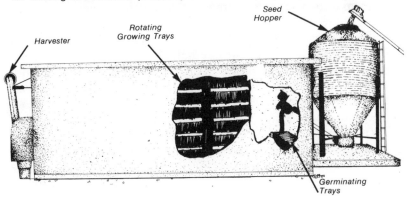

Fig. 5.104 An automated commercial grass-growing unit.

In this unit a four-fold bank of six layered trays separated by about 30 centimeters is rotating under artificial lighting. Each layer has a set of 5 trays 0.9 meters by 0.45 meters (36 inches by 18 inches), giving a total area per layer of 2.0 square meters (22.5 square feet). Into each layer (5 trays) about 11.3 kilograms (25 pounds) of grain is placed daily. The temperature is maintained at 22 to 25° C. and the relative humidity at 65-70 percent.

This unit of four banks of 30 trays is said to produce up to one-half ton (450 kilograms) per day of fresh green grass from100 pounds (45 kilograms) of grain. The grass is fed to animals in its entirety—roots, seed, and green foliage.

The cropping schedule is set up so that one series of trays is harvested each day and at the same time one series is also seeded. In this way continuous production 365 days a year is possible.

It is stated (Arano 1976) that each kilogram (2.2 pounds) of grass is equivalent nutritionally to 3 kilograms (6.6 pounds) of fresh alfalfa. Arano also states that 16 to 18 kilograms (35-40 pounds) of grass is sufficient as the daily food requirement for one cow in milk production.

He speculates that a standard grass-growing unit of 6 separate tiers each having 40 trays could feed 80 cows all year. In a test of milk production with a diet of grass versus one of normal feed (such as grain, hay and silage), the group of 60 cows on the grass diet increased their milk production by 10.07 percent over those on the normal diet. In addition, the group fed on grass produced a butterfat content of 14.26 percent higher than those fed the regular diet.

The grass-growing units have proven to be beneficial to other animals besides dairy cows. Race horses fed on grass performed better, and zoo animals which are accustomed to a grass diet in their normal habitat were more healthy in confinement when fed fresh grass year round.

Evidence is given (Arano 1976) that the hydroponic grass units produce animal feed at about one-half the cost of that produced conventionally. This is based upon the larger amounts of fuel needed in the production and transportation of traditional animal feeds. The grass-growing units enable animal producers to grow feed year round *in situ*. No storage of hay or silage is necessary since fresh grass is produced daily. This grass can be grown in a very small area compared to field-grown grasses and feeds. Costs of insecticides, fertilizers, machinery for cultivation and harvesting, and labor of field-grown feeds are estimated to be at least 10 times greater than that of hydroponically grown grass.

References

Arano, C. A. 1976. Raciones hidropónicas. *La Serenisima* 29:13-19.

———. 1976. Cultivos hidropónico. *La Serenisima* 31:4-19.

———. 1976. Forraje verde hidropónico (FVH). *La Serenisima* 35:19.

Barrow, Joseph M. 1980. Hydroponic culture of grapes in the tropics. *Proc. 5th Int. Congress on Soilless Culture*, Wageningen, May 1980, pp. 443-451.

Cooper, A. J. 1973. Rapid crop turn-round is possible with experimental nutrient film technique. *The Grower*, May 5, 1973, pp. 1048-51.

———. 1974. Soil? Who needs it? Part I. *Am. Veg. Grower*, August 1974, pp. 18-20.

———. 1974. Soil? Who needs it? Part II. *Am. Veg. Grower*, September 1974, pp. 13, 64.

———. 1975. Rapid progress through 1974 with nutrient film trials. *The Grower*, Jan. 25, 1975.

———. 1976. *Nutrient film technique of growing crops*. London: Grower Books.

———. 1985. New ABC's of NFT. *Hydroponics Worldwide: State of the Art in Soilless Crop Production*. Ed., Adam J. Savage. pp. 180-185. Int. Center for Special Studies, Honolulu, Hawaii.

Douglas, J. Sholto. 1976. Hydroponic layflats. *World Crops*, March/April 1976, pp. 82-87.

Edwards, Kenneth. 1985. New NFT breakthroughs and future directions. *Hydroponics Worldwide: State of the Art in Soilless Crop Production*. Ed., Adam J. Savage. pp. 186-192. Int. Center for Special Studies, Honolulu, Hawaii.

Jensen, Merle H. 1980. *Tomorrow's agriculture today. Am. Veg. Grower* 28(3):16-19, 62, 63.

Jensen, Merle H. and W. L. Collins. 1985. Hydroponic vegetable production. *Hort. Reviews.* 7:483-557.

Mohyuddin, Mirza. 1985. Crop cultivars and disease control. *Hydroponics Worldwide: State of the Art in Soilless Crop Production*, Ed., Adam J. Savage. pp. 42-50. Int. Center for Special Studies, Honolulu, Hawaii.

New twist for hydroponics. *Am. Veg. Grower*, November 1976, pp. 21-23.

NFT culture—incalculable potential. *The Grower*, Feb. 14, 1976.

Nutrient film technique: cropping with the hydrocanal commercial system. 1976. *World Crops* 28:212-18.

Resh, H. M. 1976. A comparison of tomato yields, using several hydroponic methods. *Proc. 4th Int. Congress on Soilless Culture*, Las Palmas, Oct. 25-Nov. 1, 1976.

Robinson, Jean. 1976. Soil—a thing of the past. *Gardener's Chronicle*, July 23, 1976, pp. 22-25.

Ruthner, Othmar. 1976. *Phytotechnology–Industrial continuous plant production*. Vienna: F. Pillivein.

Schippers, P. A. 1977. Soilless culture update: Nutrient flow technique. *Am. Veg. Grower*, May 1977, pp. 19, 20, 66.

————. 1980. *Hydroponic lettuce: the latest. Am. Veg. Grower* 28(6):22, 23, 50.

Soffer, H. and D. Levinger. 1980. The Ein Gedi System — Research and development of a hydroponic system. *Proc. 5th Int. Congress on Soilless Culture*, Wageningen, May 1980, pp. 241-252.

Tube Culture—a challenging idea. *Am. Veg. Grower*, November 1974, pp. 46, 47.

Vincenzoni, A. 1976. La colonna di coltura—nuova tecnica aeroponica. *Proc. 4th Int. Congress on Soilless Culture*, Las Palmas, Oct. 25-Nov. 1, 1976.

Zobel, R. W.; Tridici, P. D.; and J. G. Torrey. 1976. Method for growing plants aeroponically. *Plt. Physiol.* 57:344-46.

Chapter 6

Gravel Culture

6.1 Introduction

Gravel culture is one of the most widely used hydroponic techniques. One commercial operation in Arizona has almost 20 acres of greenhouses in gravel culture. Many smaller commercial greenhouses throughout the United States use gravel culture. Gravel culture was one of the first methods used when W. F. Gericke introduced hydroponics commercially. Most outdoor operations established during World War II on nonarable islands, as mentioned in Chapter 1, used gravel culture. Gravel culture is especially useful in areas having an abundance of volcanic rock such as the Canary Islands and Hawaii.

6.2 Media Characteristics

Some of the general characteristics media should possess have been discussed in Chapter 4. The best choice of gravel for a subirrigation system is crushed granite of irregular shape, free of fine particles less than 1/16 inch in diameter and coarse particles more than 3/4 inch in diameter. Over half of the total volume of particles should be about ½ inch in diameter. The particles must be hard enough so they do not break down, able to retain moisture in their void spaces, and drain well to allow root aeration.

The particles should not be of calcareous material—in order to avoid pH shifts. If only calcareous material is available, the amount of calcium and magnesium in the nutrient solution will have to be adjusted according to the levels of these elements released by the aggregate into the nutrient solution. The calcium carbonate in calcareous aggregates such as limestone and coral gravels reacts with the soluble phosphates of the nutrient solutions to produce the insoluble di- and tri-calcium phosphates. This process continues until the surfaces of the calcareous aggregate particles are coated with insoluble phosphates. After they are thoroughly coated, the reaction slows down to a point at which the rate of decrease of phosphates in the nutrient solutions is slow enough to maintain phosphate levels.

A new unused aggregate containing more than 10 percent of acid-soluble materials calculated as calcium carbonate should be pretreated with soluble phosphates to coat the particles with insoluble phosphates (Withrow and Withrow 1948). The aggregate is treated with a solution containing from 500 to 5000 grams of treble superphosphate per 1000 liters or 5 to 50 pounds per 1000 gallons. The new gravel should be soaked for several hours. The pH of the solution will rise as its phosphate content decreases. If the phosphate concentration drops below 300 ppm (100 ppm of P) after one to two hours of soaking, the solution should be drained to the reservoir and and a second phosphate addition made to the solution, which is repumped into the beds. This should be repeated until the phosphate level stays above 100 ppm (30 ppm of P) after several hours of exposure to the gravel. When this occurs, it indicates that all of the carbonate particles have been coated with phosphates. The pH of the solution will then remain about 6.8 or less. The phosphate solution then is drained from the reservoir and the reservoir filled with fresh water. The beds are flushed with this fresh water several times and once again the reservoir drained and refilled with fresh water. The beds then may be planted.

Over time the pH will begin to rise as the phosphates become depleted and free calcium carbonate is exposed on the surface of the aggregate. The process of phosphate treatment will then have to be repeated.

Schwarz and Vaadia (1969) have demonstrated that pretreated calcareous gravel or washed calcareous gravel could not prevent lime-induced chlorosis. The high pH of calcareous gravel also makes iron unavailable to plants. Victor (1973) found that daily addition of phosphorus and iron at the rate of 50 milliliters of phosphoric acid and 12 grams of chelated iron (Fe EDTA) per 1000 gallons of nutrient solution prevented the occurrence of lime-induced chlorosis with tomato plants.

"Haydite" or "Herculite" fired shale, available in a variety of particle sizes, is often used by smaller backyard hydroponic units. It is porous and has given good results in many cases. However, after continued use, the adsorption of fertilizer salts on the surfaces of the particles may cause difficulty. The absorbed salts are not easily removed by washing. Plant roots become lodged in the small pores of the rock surface, making sterilization of the medium between crops difficult. Also, the material fractures and breaks up into small pieces which eventually form a fine sand and silt which plugs feeder lines and pipes.

If a spaghetti feeding system is used rather than a subirrigation system, a smaller medium must be used. For such a system "pea" gravel between ⅛ inch and ⅜ inch in diameter should be used. Over half of the total volume of gravel should have a particle size of ³/₁₆–¼ inch in diameter. No silt or particles larger than ⅜ inch in diameter should be present. The Haydite gravel is particularly suitable to a spaghetti feeding system because its capillary action moves the nutrient solution laterally around the plant root system. However, as plant roots grow laterally they also will intercept the water and cause it to flow laterally.

6.3 Subirrigation Gravel Culture

Almost all gravel culture uses a subirrigation system. That is, water is pumped into the beds and floods them within several inches of the surface, then drains back to the nutrient reservoir. Such a system is termed *closed* or *recycled* since the same nutrient solution is used each pump cycle over a period of from 2 to 6 weeks. Then the solution is disposed of and a new solution made up.

The frequency and length of time of irrigation cycles is important to the success of the system. Each irrigation cycle must provide adequate water, nutrients and aeration to the plant roots.

6.3.1 Frequency of Irrigation

The minimum frequency of irrigation depends upon:

1. The size of the aggregate particles
2. The surfaces of the aggregate particles
3. The nature of the crop
4. The size of the crop
5. Climatic factors
6. Time of day

Smooth, regularly shaped, coarse aggregates must be irrigated more frequently than porous, irregularly shaped, fine aggregates having large surface areas. Tall crops bearing fruit require more frequent irrigation than short-growing leafy crops such as lettuce, due to their greater surface area and therefore higher evapotranspirational losses. Hot, dry weather promotes rapid evaporation and makes more frequent irrigation necessary. During mid-day when light intensities and temperatures are highest the period between irrigation cycles must be reduced.

For most crops the aggregate must be irrigated at least 3 to 4 times per day during dull winter months, and in summer it is often necessary to irrigate at least every hour during the day. Pumping at night is not necessary. In temperate zones, during the summer irrigation should be from 6:00 A.M. to 7:00 P.M., while during the winter an 8:00 A.M. to 4:00 P.M. period may be set up.

Water is absorbed by the plant from the nutrient solution much more rapidly than the inorganic elements. As a result, the films of nutrient solution on the aggregate become concentrated with inorganic salts as absorption takes place. The concentration of the nutrient solution in the aggregate becomes greater as the rate of transpiration of the plants increases and the rate of water absorption thus increases. By increasing the number of irrigation cycles, the high water demand of the plant is met and the water content within the void spaces of the gravel is maintained at a more optimal level. In this way the nutrient solution does not become so concentrated between irrigation cycles. It is also necessary to irrigate frequently so that the films of nutrient solution over the aggregate particles in contact with the root tips are not depleted of any nutrient between irrigations.

Immediately following irrigation, the nutrient solution in the aggregate has nearly the same composition as the reservoir solution. As absorption proceeds, the composition of the nutrient solution in the bed continually changes, including the proportion of the various ions, the concentration of the solution and the pH. If the frequency of irrigation is not sufficient, nutrient deficiencies may develop, even though adequate quantities of the nutrient elements may be present in the reservoir solution. If the aggregate does not contain a large proportion of fine particles, it is unlikely that frequent irrigation will cause aeration problems so long as the beds are completely drained between irrigations and the irrigation period is not too long. The more often the beds are irrigated, the more nearly the composition of the aggregate solution approaches that of the reservoir solution.

6.3.2 Speed of Pumping and Drainage

The speed of pumping and draining of the nutrient solution from the gravel determines the aeration of the plant root system. Roots require oxygen to carry on respiration, which in turn provides energy needed in the uptake of water and nutrient ions. Insufficient oxygen around the plant roots retards their growth or may cause their death, which results in plant injury, reduced yields and eventually plant death.

In a subirrigation system, as the nutrient solution fills the gravel voids from below, it pushes out air which has a relatively low content of oxygen and a high content of carbon dioxide. Then, as the nutrient solution flows from the gravel, it sucks air into the medium. This new supply of air has a relatively high content of oxygen and a low content of carbon dioxide. The greater the speed of solution movement in the gravel medium, the greater the speed of air displacement. Also, since the solubility of oxygen in water is low, the period of low oxygen supply while the free water is in the gravel is shortened if the speed of filling and draining is rapid.

This factor of aeration is also related to the frequency of pumping. When free water is present too often in the gravel, the voids (air spaces between the particles) are filled with water rather than with moist air. Thus the oxygen concentration around the roots is lowered.

A 10- to 15-minute period for filling and draining respectively, or a total time of 20 to 30 minutes, is generally acceptable. In the removal of the free solution from the bed nothing less than complete drainage is recommended. Only a film of moisture on the gravel particles is desired. If puddles of solution remain in the bottom on the plant bed, poor plant growth results. This rapid filling and draining of the growing beds can be achieved by use of large pipes in the bottom of the beds. In summary, proper irrigation cycles should : (a) fill the bed rapidly; (b) drain the bed rapidly and (c) get all the solution out.

6.3.3 Effect of the Irrigation Cycle on Plant Growth

By reducing the number of nutrient solution pumpings, the moisture content in the gravel medium is lowered. This has a concentrating effect on the nutrient ions contained in the water film on the gravel particles. Whenever the osmotic concentration of the nutrient solution is increased, the water-absorbing power of the plant is reduced, also reducing the nutrient ion uptake. Consequently, the rate of plant growth is retarded and a harder and firmer type of growth develops.

In the greenhouse during the dark, cloudy, short days of winter, reduction of the number of irrigation cycles per day will help keep the plants reasonably hard and sturdy.

6.3.4 Height of Irrigation

The nutrient solution should be allowed to come within about only one inch of the surface of the aggregate. This practice keeps the aggregate surface dry, preventing the growth of algae, and reduces the loss of water and high humidity buildup at the base of the plants. It also prevents the growth of roots into the surface inch of the aggregate, which, under conditions of high light intensities, may become too high in temperature for satisfactory root growth. The nutrient level in the beds can be regulated by installation of overflow pipes in the plenum. These construction details are discussed in section 6.3.6.

6.3.5 Nutrient Solution Temperature

In greenhouse culture, the temperature of the nutrient solution should not fall below the night air temperature of the house. The temperature of the solution in the reservoir sump may be raised by use of an immersion heater or electric heating cable. Be careful not to use any heating elements having lead or zinc sheathing as these can be toxic to the plants. Stainless steel or plastic coated cables are best. Electric heating lamps have also been used successfully. In many locations the temperature of outside water used to fill the sump may be as low as 45 to 50° F. If a large reservoir needs to be filled it should be done later in the day after the last irrigation cycle has been completed. Then there will be sufficient time before the next irrigation cycle the following morning for the heating unit to bring the solution temperature to a more optimal level.

In no case should heating cables be placed in the growing beds themselves. This causes localized high temperatures around the heating elements, which injure the roots.

6.3.6 Subirrigation Designs

Construction Materials. Since fertilizer salts used in making up the nutrient solution are corrosive, any metal parts, such as

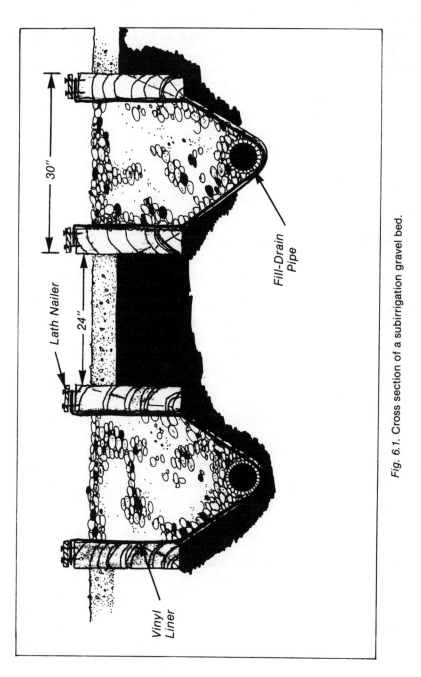

30"

Lath Nailer

24"

Fill-Drain Pipe

Vinyl Liner

Fig. 6.1. Cross section of a subirrigation gravel bed.

pumps, pipes or valves, exposed to the nutrients will wear out in a very short time. Galvanized materials may release sufficient zinc to cause toxicity symptoms in the plants. Copper materials offer the same problem. Plastic pipes and fittings, pumps with plastic impellers, and plastic tanks are noncorrosive and should be utilized. Plant beds can be built of wood and lined with at least 6-mil plastic film, but preferably 20-mil vinyl.

During World War II, concrete was used in numerous commercial operations. It has the advantages of permanence and corrosion resistance, but the cost is the highest of any material. Cedar or redwood is the most often used construction material and direct lining of compacted normal ground substrate is cheapest for bed construction.

Beds. The beds must be designed to provide rapid filling and draining—and complete drainage. The use of a 3-inch diameter PVC pipe and a V-shaped bed configuration will fulfill these watering requirements (fig. 6.1). The beds should have a minimum width of 24 inches, a depth of 12 inches to 14 inches and a maximum length of 120 to 130 feet. The bed slope should be about 1 to 2 inches per 100 feet. Water enters and drains from the beds through small ¼- to ½-inch diameter holes or ⅛-inch-thick sawcuts on the bottom one-third of the PVC pipe. These holes or saw cuts are made every 1 to 2 feet along the entire length of the pipe. The slope can be achieved by sloping the side boards and staking them. In some cases growers may pour concrete walkways between these beds. The beds should be constructed in compacted river sand. A jig containing the desired configuration can be used to dig out the bed (fig. 6.2). Once the proper configuration and slope has been compacted, the beds are lined with a vinyl liner of 20 mil thickness commonly used for swimming pools (fig. 6.3). The 3-inch diameter PVC fill-drain pipe is then set in place with the holes or cuts facing downward to prevent roots readily growing into the pipe. The vinyl is held on the sides of the beds by folding it over the rough 2-inch thick cedar side planks and nailing a wooden strip on top of it the entire length.

The PVC pipe allows water to flow rapidly along the bottom of the beds, and fills and drains the beds equally and vertically along the entire length. With this rapid filling and draining, old air is pushed out of the aggregate and new air is sucked in as discussed earlier.

Fig. 6.2. Digging bed configuration in compacted river sand fill.

Fig. 6.3. Vinyl liner placed into beds and PVC drain pipes located in bottom groove.

The beds should be filled with gravel to within 1 inch of the top at the end near the nutrient tank and within 2 inches at the far end. To prevent uneven near-surface moistening during the irrigation cycles, level the top surface of the gravel. Remember that the beds are not level, but water remains level; so, with the top surface of the gravel leveled, the water level in the flooded beds will be parallel to the gravel surface. (If the gravel were placed to within 1 inch of the top of the bed along the entire length it really would have a 1-inch slope and therefore if during the irrigation cycle the beds were filled to within 1 inch of the gravel surface at the reservoir end of the beds it would be 2 inches from the top at the far end. This would cause uneven watering of the plant roots from one end to the other end of the beds. Recently transplanted seedlings might suffer a water stress at the far end due to insufficient height of water in the bed. If the water level were within 1 inch at the distant end, it would come to the surface at the reservoir end, creating algae problems there.)

The 3-inch PVC pipe should have a 45-degree elbow and project above the gravel surface with a cap at the far end from the tank to allow for cleaning of the pipe. Usually the pipes are cleaned of roots every year or so with a roto-rooter machine. The end of the pipe at the reservoir drains into a plenum.

Plenum. The filling and draining times can be greatly decreased by the use of a plenum rather than solid plumbing from the pump(s). The plenum is simply a trough into which the water is pumped from the tank. The 3-inch PVC pipes running along the bottom of the beds open into this plenum (figs. 6.4, 6.5 and 6.6). The bed pipes must be sealed into the plenum or water will leak behind the tank, resulting in loss of nutrient solution and buildup of water under the greenhouse and tank.

Either sump or submersible pumps may be used to pump the nutrient solution from the reservoir into the plenum. The pump is activated by either a time clock or a feedback mechanism attached to a moisture sensor in the beds. The water level in the beds is regulated by an overflow pipe in the plenum. The plenum and beds will fill to that level which corresponds to 1 inch below the gravel surface in the beds. A dump valve activated by the same time clock or feedback mechanism as the pumps closes the drain holes of the plenum while the pumps are operating (fig. 6.4). The operation is as follows:

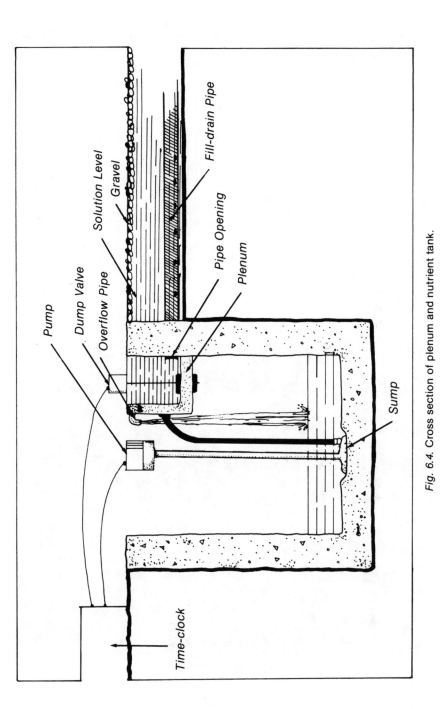

Fig. 6.4. Cross section of plenum and nutrient tank.

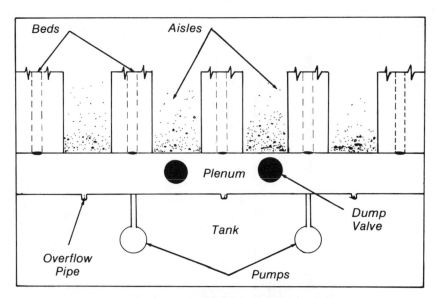

Fig. 6.5. Plan view of plenum and nutrient tank.

Fig. 6.6. Bed fill-drain pipe entering plenum.

1. The moisture sensor in the bed signals the feedback mechanism to turn on the pumps (or the preset time clock strikes an irrigation cycle) and activates the plenum valves.

2. The pumps are activated; the dump valves of the plenum close.

3. The plenum and beds begin to fill.

4. They continue filling until excess solution spills back into the tank via the overflow pipes.

5. The preset irrigation period terminates; the beds are full of solution.

6. The pumps stop, the dump valves fall open, nutrient solution drains from the beds back to the plenum and finally falls into the tank, being well aerated.

7. The whole cycle of pumping and draining should be completed within 20 minutes.

Nutrient Tank. The nutrient tank must be constructed of a watertight material. Steel reinforced concrete 4 inches thick, coated with a bituminous paint to make the concrete watertight, is the most long-lasting material. The plenum should be a part of the tank so that leakage cannot occur between them. The volume of the tank must be sufficient to completely fill the gravel beds, based on the amount of void space in the gravel. This can be determined by taking a sample of the rock (about a cubic foot) and filling it with water, then measuring the volume of water required to fill the void spaces. Then, extrapolate to calculate the total void space in all the beds. The tank should hold a volume 30 to 40 percent greater than the total volume required to fill the beds. For example, a tank of about 2000 Imp. gallons would be required to supply 5 beds 2 feet wide by 12 inches deep by 120 feet long (fig. 6.7).

An automatic float valve could be attached to a water refill line in order to maintain the water level in the tank. In this way water lost during each irrigation cycle through evapotranspiration by the plants would immediately be replaced.

The nutrient tank should have a small sump in which the pumps sit in order to facilitate complete drainage and cleaning of the tank during nutrient changes (fig. 6.4).

The tank-plenum could be changed somewhat in structure to reduce its size. This can be done (as shown in fig. 6.8) by dividing the plenum into two parts, each servicing 3 beds. A three-way automatic valve would discharge the nutrient solution alternately

Fig. 6.7. Nutrient tank construction.

into one plenum upon activation of the pumps and dump valve, filling 3 beds during each cycle (fig. 6.9). In this case a time clock, rather than a moisture sensor feedback system, must be used, with shorter intervals between irrigation cycles than that required for one larger plenum as described earlier.

The pump could also be piped into a discharge line which could be connected to the outside drainage system. Gate valves would be used to control the direction of flow of the nutrient. When the nutrient solution is changed the gate valve in the waste line is opened and the solution is pumped out to waste. Normally during

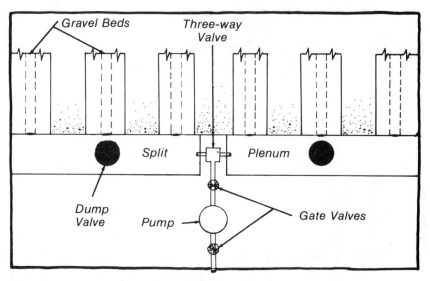

Fig. 6.8. Plan view of nutrient tank with a split plenum.

Fig. 6.9. Three-way automatic valve used with a split-plenum design.

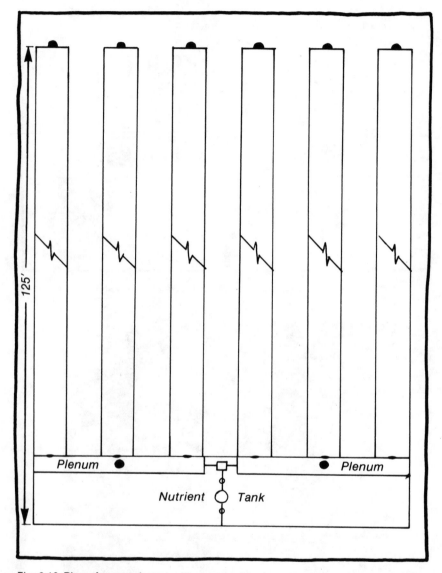

Fig. 6.10. Plan of a greenhouse with six gravel beds and split-plenum nutrient tank.

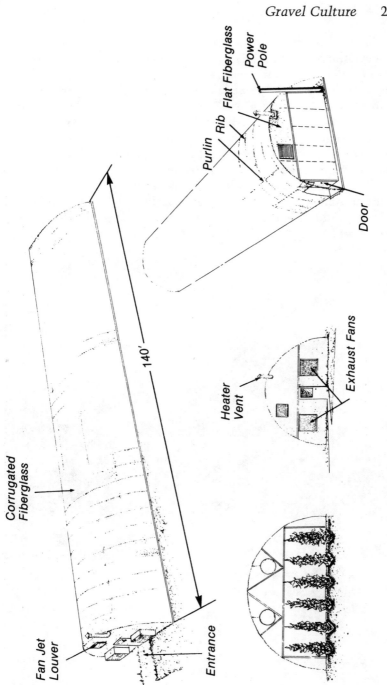

Fig. 6.11. Schematic of an individual quonset style greenhouse using a subirrigation gravel cultural system.

regular feeding cycles this waste valve is closed and the valve between the pump and the three-way valve is open. The three-way valve is available commercially.

By using such a split plenum the tank capacity can be reduced to almost half the volume of one large enough to fill all 6 beds at once. Thus, a tank of 1200 Imp. gallons should easily supply 3 gravel beds 24 inches wide by 12 inches deep by 120 feet long.

An overall plan of a gravel culture system having 6 beds and the attached plenum and nutrient tank is illustrated in figure 6.10. A profile sketch of an individual quonset-style greenhouse which would contain 6 gravel beds is given in figure 6.11. Successful crops of high productivity can be grown with a subirrigation gravel system, as illustrated in figures 6.12 to 6.14.

Fig. 6.12. Crop of tomatoes (about 6 weeks old) growing in a subirrigation gravel culture system.

Fig. 6.13. Crop of cucumbers (about 5 weeks old) growing in a subirrigation gravel culture system.

Fig. 6.14. Crop of mature tomatoes ready for harvesting.

Outdoor Subirrigation Gravel Cultural System

Flume System. The flume system, commonly used outdoors, uses a series of beds built on exactly the same level, parallel with one another. A flume or channel (equivalent to a plenum) at least 10 to 12 inches deep and 18 to 20 inches wide runs perpendicular to the beds. The length of the beds depends upon the size of the reservoir. Usually beds of no longer than 100 to 120 feet are built on both sides of the flume. They must be sloped several inches toward the flume to allow gravitational drainage (fig. 6.15). A reservoir can be constructed above or below ground level into which the flume is connected. If the reservoir is located above ground, a sump must be located at the end of the flume into which nutrient solution will flow from the beds. A pump is then needed to lift the solution from

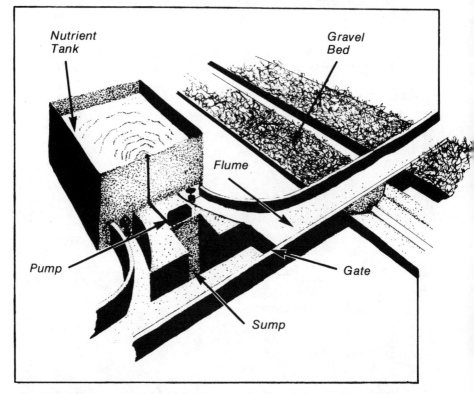

Fig. 6.15. A flume system of subirrigation gravel culture using a sump and above-ground reservoir.

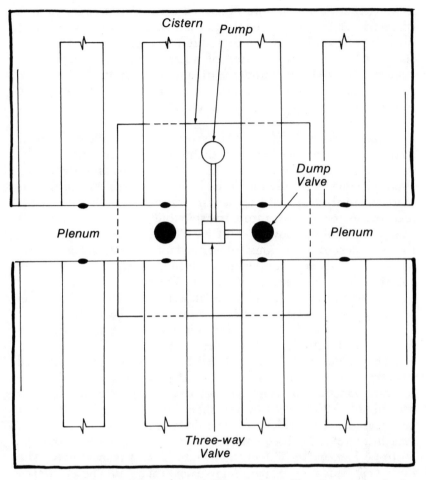

Fig. 6.16. Details of a cistern type of flume system with a three-way valve to control water flow alternately to the flumes.

the sump to the reservoir during the draining cycle. The nutrient solution enters the flume via a valve from the above-ground reservoir and flows along the flume into each bed. A valve or sluice-gate must be used to close the flume off from the sump while the beds are filling. When draining the beds this sluice-gate or valve must be opened.

If a cistern reservoir is built to take the place of the sump, no other reservoir is required. Then a sump or submersible pump is used to pump the water into the flume. This method is very similar in construction to the one described earlier for greenhouses. A three-way valve can be used to alternately direct the flow of water into one of two flumes and therefore twice as many beds can be serviced by the same volume of nutrient tank (fig. 6.16). The cistern could be located underneath and at the ends of the flumes. A dump valve located at the end of each flume over the cistern would open during the drainage cycle.

Terrace System. In the terrace system, a series of beds are made over sloping or terraced ground, each set at a lower level than the previous one, as shown in fig. 6.17. The bottom of a higher bed should be level with the top of the lower bed. Nutrient solution is stored in an above-ground header tank raised several feet above the level of the first bed. An automatic solenoid or manual gate valve is used to control the flow of solution. The beds are constructed on the same design as previously described for a subirrigation system, but a valve is located at each end of the beds to regulate the flow of solution from one bed to the next. The valves may be either manual or automatic. Sometimes an automatic siphon device replaces the valve, but such a system drains the beds very slowly. Finally, the nutrient solution flows into a sump from where it is pumped back into the raised header tank.

Each bed must be filled completely before the solution is allowed to drain into the following bed. Since there is some water loss due to evapotranspiration from one bed to the next, each subsequent bed should be 20 percent shorter than the preceding one. The first bed (nearest to the header tank) should not exceed 100 to 120 feet in length; therefore, subsequent beds in a four-bed system would be 80 to 96 feet, 64 to 77 feet, and 51 to 62 feet respectively. The number of beds running parallel to each other would be a function of the header tank and sump capacity. An automatic float valve could be installed in the sump to maintain the solution level. Automatic solenoid valves would be controlled by one or more time clocks. The valves for each series of beds at the same level should be synchronized to operate simultaneously.

If the sump and header tank were constructed so they did not extend the entire length of the series of beds, return channels (or flumes) could be used to conduct water from the header tank to the beds and from the beds to the sump (fig. 6.18).

The sump is the main storage reservoir for the system. Therefore, the total capacity must be sufficient to fill all the first-level

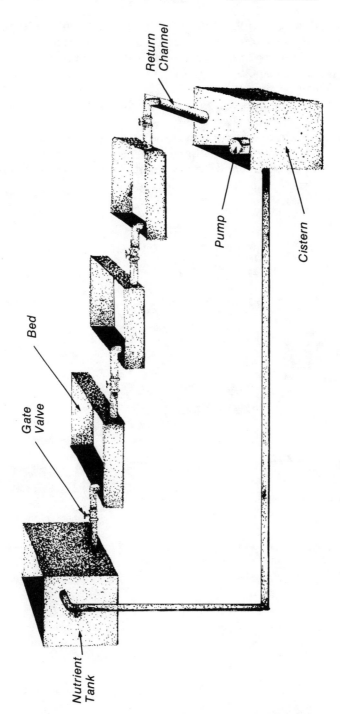

Fig. 6.17. A terrace system of subirrigation gravel culture having a single series of bed levels.

beds with an additional safety factor volume of about 20 percent. Such a gravity system saves reservoir and pump capacity since only the requirements of the first-level beds need to be satisfied. By means of time-clocks, solenoid valves and float valves, the whole system can be automated.

By a further modification, splitting the top flume into two parts and using a three-way valve connected to the header tank and flumes, alternate irrigation of these beds each time could be operated in a similar fashion as that described earlier. This would allow the reduction of tank and sump capacities with resultant savings in water, nutrients and construction costs.

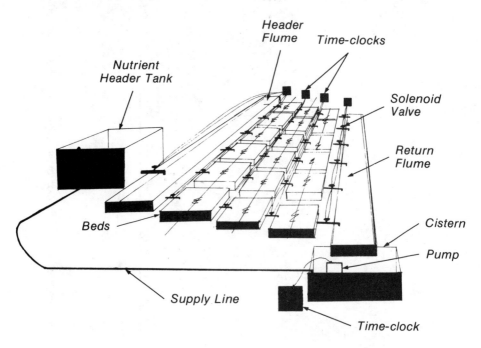

Fig. 6.18. A terraced gravel culture system with six series of bed levels fully automated.

Small-Scale Subirrigation Systems

One of the earliest systems of gravel culture used on a small scale was the bucket system (fig. 6.19). In this system, a plant was grown in a bucket of gravel set on top of a bench. A second bucket, containing the nutrient solution, was connected by a hose to the bucket containing the plant. Normally, the second bucket remained on the floor or on a bench below the bottom of the "growing" bucket. Irrigation was achieved by raising the bucket of nutrient solution above the growing one and attaching it to a hook. After all the nutrient solution drained into the growing bucket, the solution bucket was lowered to the floor and drainage occurred.

This system can be expanded to a series of buckets, each attached to a pulley which can be used to raise and lower the buckets during the feeding-irrigation period. On a larger scale, a bed can be constructed at bench level and a larger reservoir or barrel capable of filling the entire bed can be attached to a pulley system which facilitates the lifting of the reservoir during the irrigation cycle (fig. 6.20). This system could be automated by connecting an electric motor and winch to the pulley ropes. The motor could be activated by a time clock having preset irrigation periods for the whole day.

This system could be simplified by use of a pump in the nutrient reservoir (fig. 6.21). The system would require a tray to hold plants, a tank for the nutrient solution, a pump and control system, and a suitable connecting pipe. The solution is pumped into the plant tray and allowed to drain back to the nutrient reservoir through the pump. A time clock is used to control the pump and thus preset irrigation cycles are programmed for daily watering and feeding. All storage tanks and delivery lines should be opaque to reduce algal growth.

Another simple home unit is one using a trickle feeding system in which the nutrient solution is stored in a reservoir under the tray and is pumped along the gravel surface. Excess water percolates through the perforated bottom of the tray back to the reservoir (fig. 6.22). The irrigation cycles can be operated by a time clock-activated pump.

Several types of small units are available commercially. One is a tray with a water storage tank underneath which uses a common fish aquarium pump to distribute the nutrient solution (fig. 6.23). Self-watering and feeding planters for tropical foliage houseplants are available (figs. 6.24 and 6.25). These work on capillary action of expanded shale for feeding.

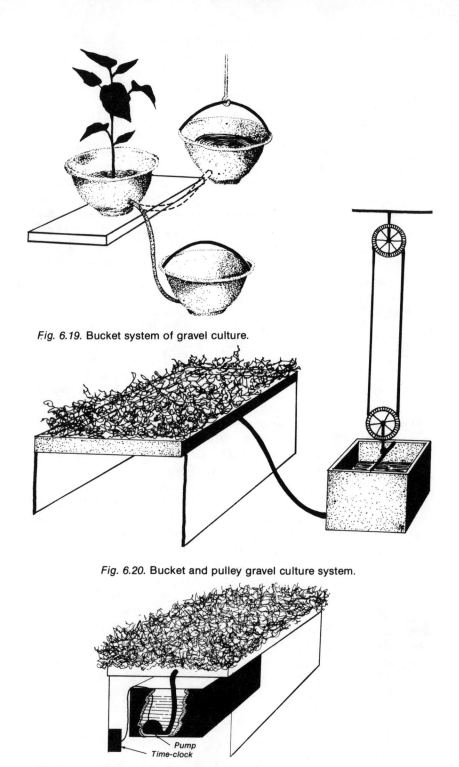

Fig. 6.19. Bucket system of gravel culture.

Fig. 6.20. Bucket and pulley gravel culture system.

Pump
Time-clock

Fig. 6.21. A simple small-scale subirrigation gravel bed with automatic pumping.

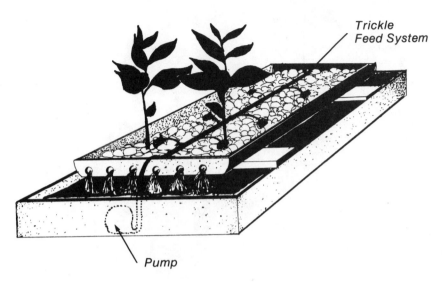

Trickle
Feed System

Pump

Fig. 6.22. A simple small-scale trickle gravel bed with automatic pumping.

Fig. 6.23. "City Green" home hydroponic units.

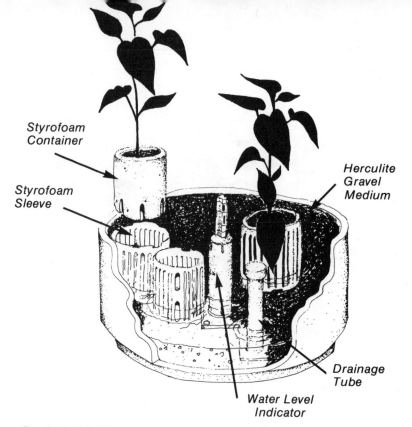

Styrofoam Container

Styrofoam Sleeve

Herculite Gravel Medium

Drainage Tube

Water Level Indicator

Fig. 6.24. "Hydroculture Luwasa" hydroponic planters — cross-sectional sketch.

Fig. 6.25. "Hydroculture Luwasa" planters in an office growing indoor tropical foliage plants. (Courtesy of Hydroculture Luwasa, Downsview, Ontario, Canada.)

6.4 Trickle Irrigation Designs

The bed design and construction of trickle irrigation systems is similar to that of subirrigation systems but can be somewhat simplified, as shown in figure 6.26. The bed may be either round or V-shaped; both configurations will give proper drainage. In this system, the nutrient solution is applied to the base of every plant by either a spaghetti or ooze hose. The solution runs down through the plant roots. The use of smaller gravel (1/8 to 1/4 inch in diameter) with the trickle system is essential to facilitate lateral movement of the nutrient solution through the medium. Lateral distribution of the solution also occurs along the lateral roots of the plants.

The spaghetti system is constructed of 1/2-inch O.D. (outside diameter) thin-wall black polyethylene tubing. Spaghetti tubes of 0.045-inch or 0.060-inch diameter are inserted into the 1/2-inch lateral feed lines by brass inserts (fig. 6.27). These inserts are easily pushed in with a pointed insert tool similar to an awl. The inserts automatically seal themselves in the 1/2-inch pipe (fig. 6.28). A 1-inch piece of the 1/2-inch O.D. pipe is placed on the end of each feeder line to disperse the jet of solution coming out of the line. At the same time this end piece prevents clogging of the feeder line by salt buildup through evaporation between irrigation cycles. Lead end pieces are available commercially. They also serve to keep the spaghetti line in place, but are more costly than the homemade ones.

The spaghetti lines must be long enough to reach the base of the plant they are to feed. Excessively long lines (greater than 3 feet)

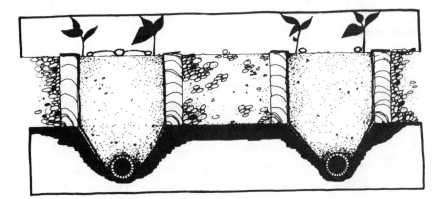

Fig. 6.26. Cross section of a trickle irrigation gravel culture bed.

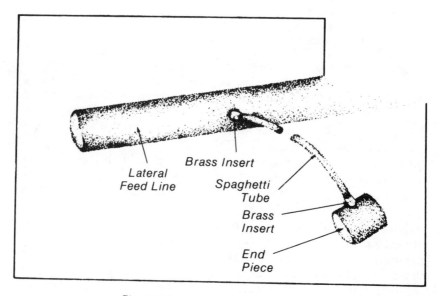

Fig. 6.27 Spaghetti (trickle) feed system.

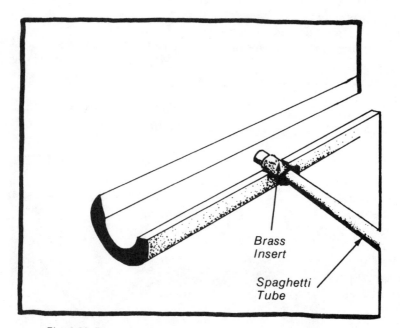

Fig. 6.28. Brass inserts "seal" into the ½-inch lateral feed line.

should be avoided, as the internal friction against the flow of solution will lessen the outflow.

The alternative to a spaghetti system is the ooze hose system. This thin-wall 1/2-inch O.D. tubing is available from several sources. Two commercial types are Chapin Watermatics' "Twin-Wall" and Dupont's "Via-Flow". Both "ooze" or "sweat" water slowly so that it drips from the hose along its entire length at intervals of 6 to 8 inches or whatever spacing you request from the manufacturer. Some complaints against these hoses are that they clog and that algae grows in them. Also, they must be replaced with each crop; however, they are relatively inexpensive (several cents a linear foot).

The disadvantages of the spaghetti system are that the tubes clog, roots grow into them, and they are in the way during the changing of crops. Also, they are often accidentally pulled out by workers passing down the rows. As a result, some plants may suffer from lack of water. Proper filters of 100 to 200 mesh placed in the feed lines after the fertilizer has been injected will overcome a lot of the plugging problems. Since the ooze hoses are thrown away between crops, there is no hindrance to changing of crops and lines are not in workers' way during normal cropping periods.

Another trickle irrigation system common in commercial greenhouses involves the use of 1/2-inch polyethylene pipe for lateral lines and emitters inserted at each plant position along the entire lateral line. About 30 kinds of drip irrigation water emitters, perforated hoses and porous pipes are available for use in drip irrigation systems. A typical system will be discussed in detail in Chapter 7.

The nutrient solution is normally supplied to the plants via the trickle irrigation system from either a storage tank or injectors. This will also be described in detail in chapter 7. However, if a pea gravel culture system is used, a storage tank will have to be used to collect the solution draining through the 3-inch PVC drain pipes in the bottom of the beds. These drain pipes must connect into a main return line which conducts all the solution back to the nutrient tank. The nutrient tank should therefore be placed fairly close to the growing area, preferably at a lower end of the greenhouse so that all drain pipes can slope to that point.

The use of trickle irrigation with a pea gravel system is not commonly practiced on a commercial scale. Trickle irrigation is usually used with sawdust or sand culture. On a small backyard scale, I have found it to work well with pea gravel. In fact, the drainage pipe is not even necessary if the beds are not much longer than 20 feet. A lot of root buildup on the bottom of the beds will occur during cropping and this should be cleaned out at least once a year by turning over the gravel with your hands or a shovel. In a backyard operation this labor is not excessive; however, in a commercial operation it would be prohibitive. Because of this root buildup and resistance of both roots and gravel to the lateral flow of water, in beds greater than 25 feet a drainpipe is absolutely essential.

In the past few years, hydroponics has become available to the general public in the form of backyard hydroponic greenhouses (figs. 6.29 and 6.30), designed in some cases for particular climate areas. For example, Resh Greenhouses Ltd., in Vancouver, B.C., was the first company in Canada to design and manufacture backyard greenhouses specifically for Canadian conditions.

These greenhouses come in an assortment of sizes from 6 feet by 8 feet on up (figs. 6.31–6.33). The units are automated to give optimum growing conditions all year round. Temperature (heating and cooling) is thermostatically regulated. Plants are automatically watered and fed by use of a time clock, pump, and, in the case mentioned above, a spaghetti trickle feeding system (figs. 6.34 and 6.35). Nutrients to feed the plants are usually prepackaged so that the greenhouse operator need merely add these at specified intervals to the water solution.

Results obtained from such greenhouses have been excellent. For example, a 10½-by-12-foot greenhouse can grow 1000 pounds of tomatoes, 2000 cucumbers or 1000 head of lettuce annually, or a combination of crops such as 400 pounds of tomatoes, 700 cucumbers and 400 head of lettuce (figs. 6.36–6.38).

Fig. 6.29. A backyard greenhouse with a trickle feeding system.

Fig. 6.30. A backyard greenhouse growing tomatoes, swiss chard, cabbage, and lettuce with a trickle feeding system.   (*Fig. 6.30-6.38* courtesy of Resh Greenhouses Ltd., Vancouver, Canada.)

Fig. 6.31. A 10½′ by 12′ hydroponic backyard greenhouse.

Fig. 6.32. A 10½′ by 16′ hydroponic backyard greenhouse.

Fig. 6.33. An 8' by 12' hydroponic backyard greenhouse

Fig. 6.34. A completely automated hydroponic backyard greenhouse.

Fig. 6.35. A crop of tomatoes in an automated 8'x 12' hydroponic greenhouse.

Fig. 6.36. Tomatoes grown in a hydroponic backyard greenhouse.

Fig. 6.37. European cucumbers, *Fig. 6.38.* Cauliflower grown in a hydroponic backyard greenhouse.

6.5 Advantages and Disadvantages of Trickle Irrigation

The advantages of the trickle system over the subirrigation system are:

1. Less problems of roots plugging the drain pipes
2. Better aeration to the roots since at no time are they completely submerged in water. Also, water trickles down past the roots, carrying fresh air with it.
3. Lower construction costs since smaller nutrient tanks are needed and no valves or plenums are required
4. A much simpler system with fewer chances of failure. Coordination of valves and pumps, etc., is not involved. It is simple to install, repair and operate.
5. The nutrient solution is fed directly to each plant.

Some disadvantages are also present:

1. Sometimes "coning" of water movement occurs due to the relatively coarse particles of gravel. That is, water does not move laterally in the root zone but flows straight down. This results in water shortage to the plants and roots growing along the bottom of the beds where most water is present, eventually plugging drainage

pipes. A subirrigation system uniformly moistens all plant roots and the medium.

2. The trickle lines sometimes get clogged or pulled out by workers. The use of filters in the main header lines will reduce clogging. The use of sweat hoses or emitters can reduce problems of workers accidentally pulling out lines.

6.6 Sterilization of Gravel Between Crops

The sterilization of gravel between crops can easily be done with household bleach (calcium or sodium hypochlorite) or hydrochloric (muriatic) acid used for swimming pools. A 10,000 ppm of available chlorine solution is made up in the nutrient tank and the beds are flooded several times for 20 minutes each time. The chlorine solution is then pumped to waste and the beds rinsed several times with clean water until all bleach residues are eliminated. The greenhouse then should be allowed to air out for 1 to 2 days before planting the next crop.

In a trickle system, the drain pipe exit must be plugged to allow the beds to fill up and the sterilizing solution can be pumped through the trickle lines. This will take time so it is helpful to use an auxiliary pump and hose and flush the beds from above until they fill up. The same procedure is followed in rinsing the beds with clean water.

With each crop, some roots will be left in the medium. Over the years chlorine sterilization will become less effective unless the roots are removed. Removal would be very costly, therefore eventually a more powerful sterilant will have to be used. Steam sterilization or such chemicals as Vapam, chloropicrin or methyl bromide should be used, observing cautions of the manufacturers as mentioned earlier.

6.7 Advantages and Disadvantages of Gravel Culture

Gravel culture initially is blessed with many advantages, but over time some of these advantages are lost.

Here are the advantages:
1. Uniform watering and feeding of plants.
2. Can be fully automated.
3. Gives good plant root aeration.
4. Adaptable to many types of crops.

5. Has proven to be successful on many commercial crops grown both outdoors and in greenhouses.

6. Can be used in nonarable areas where only gravel is available.

7. Efficient use of water and nutrients by use of a recycle system. Here are the disadvantages:

1. Costly to construct, maintain and repair.

2. With automatic valves, etc., failures occur often.

3. One of the biggest problems is the root buildup in the gravel, which plugs drainage pipes. Each crop leaves some roots behind and the moisture-holding capacity of the medium increases. Consequently, watering frequency may be reduced each year. Watering and aeration stresses occur. Over the years this root buildup results in a graveled soil and the advantages over a soil system will be lost. Eventually the gravel will have to be cleaned of roots, if not completely changed. Sterilization between crops by use of chlorine alone becomes ineffective.

4. Some diseases as *Fusarium and Verticillium* wilts can spread through a cyclic system very rapidly.

References

Schwarz, M., and Vaadia, V. 1969. Limestone gravel as growth medium in hydroponics. *Plant and Soil* 31:122-28.

Victor, Roger S. 1973. Growing tomatoes using calcareous gravel and neutral gravel with high saline water in the Bahamas. *Proc. of Int. Working Group in Soilless Culture Congress,* Las Palmas, 1973.

Withrow, R. B., and A. P. Withrow. 1948. *Nutriculture.* Lafayette, Ind.: Purdue Univ. Agr. Expt. Stn. Publ. S.C. 328.

Chapter 7

Sand Culture

7.1 Introduction

Sand culture is the most widely used method of soilless culture. It is particularly well adapted to desert areas such as the Middle East and North Africa. Some examples of sand culture operations are:

Superior Farming Company, Tucson, Arizona (11 acres) (fig. 7.1)

Quechan Environmental Farms, Fort Yuma Indian Reservation, California (5 acres)

Kharg Environmental Farms, Kharg Island, Iran (2 acres) (fig. 7.2)

Arid Lands Research Institute, Sadiyat, Abu Dhabi, United Arab Emirates (5 acres, presently expanding to 21) (fig. 7.3)

Sun Valley Hydroponics, Fabens, Texas, (10 acres).

The Environmental Research Laboratory, a branch of the University of Arizona, has worked closely with many of these projects and has been instrumental in proving sand culture in these areas. In 1966 the laboratory started a pilot project in Puerto Peñasco, Mexico, to test the feasibility of sand culture and later based the establishment of commercial operations in the U.S. Southwest and in the Middle East on the findings from this project.

7.2 Medium Characteristics

In Mexico and the Middle Eastern countries where greenhouse projects were established on the seacoast, the normal beach sand was used as a medium. Once the growing medium (sand) was leached free of excess salts, vegetables were either seeded directly in the sand or planted as transplants. In the U.S. Southwest a concrete river-wash sand is used, not a mortar sand, as it is too fine and will puddle. Puddling is indicated by water coming to the

239

Fig. 7.1. Aerial view of 11-acre sand culture greenhouse complex of Superior Farming Company, Tucson, Arizona. At the time of the photograph, the air-inflated greenhouses in the foreground were being covered with polyethylene. (Courtesy of Superior Farming Company, The Environmental Research Laboratory and Manley, Inc., Tucson, Arizona.)

Fig. 7.2. Aerial view of 2-acre sand culture greenhouse complex on Kharg Island, Iran. (Courtesy of The Environmental Research Laboratory and Manley, Inc., Tucson, Arizona.)

Fig. 7.3. Aerial view of 5-acre greenhouse complex of Abu Dhabi. Note the barren dunes and proximity to the sea from which water is desalted for use in the growing of crops. At the time of the photograph, a fire had damaged the packing facilities to the rear of the greenhouses. (Courtesy of the government of Abu Dhabi, The Environmental Research Laboratory, Tucson, Arizona, and Gulf Aviation, Bahrain.)

surface upon vibration of the sand. It is a result of a high percentage of silt and fine sand. The aggregate must be washed free of fine silt and clay. It also should be relatively free of particles over 1/16 inch (2 mm) in diameter and under 1/40 inch (0.6 mm). A properly screened sand culture aggregate will drain freely and not puddle after an application of a large amount of water.

Aggregates which are soft and tend to disintegrate should be avoided. However, it may not be possible to avoid using soft particles in areas where only limestone sand is available. In such cases nutrients should be added and the pH adjusted daily, as discussed earlier in Chapter 6.

7.3 Structural Details

Two methods of utilizing sand as a growing medium have proven satisfactory. One is the use of plastic-lined beds; the other involves spreading sand over the entire greenhouse floor.

7.3.1 Beds with Plastic Liner

Growing beds may be built as above-ground troughs with wooden sides similar to those described for gravel culture in chapter 6 (fig. 7.4). Six-mil black polyethylene can be used for the liner, but 20-mil vinyl is better. The bottom of the trough should have a slight slope of 6 inches per 200 feet, so that it can be drained or leached when necessary. The drain pipe should be placed in the

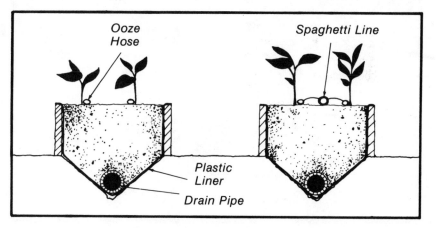

Fig. 7.4. Cross section of sand culture beds.

entire length of the bed. A 3-inch pipe such as that used in gravel culture is not necessary since in sand culture only excess solution (no greater than 8 to 10 percent of that added) is drained. The drain pipes from all beds should be connected to a main at one end which collects the waste water from all beds and conducts it away from the greenhouses.

Similarly to gravel culture, drainage holes are cross-cut with a saw, one-third the distance through the pipe every 18 inches. The cuts must be against the bottom of the bed so that plant roots are discouraged from entering the pipes. Also, as in gravel culture, one end of each pipe should be left above the ground so that a Roto-Rooter can be used to clean the pipes.

The width of the beds may be 24 to 30 inches and the depth 12 to 16 inches. The bottom of the bed may be level, round or V-shaped with the drainage pipe in the middle.

An alternative to above-ground beds would be a trough, with a wire strung 2 inches off the ground on either side of the bed. A 6-mil polyethylene tube is strung over the two wires to form a double-layer barrier between the sand medium and soil (fig. 7.5).

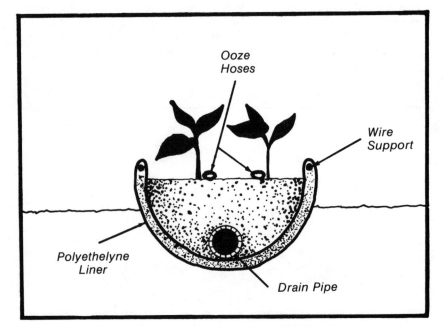

Fig. 7.5. Cross section of bed using wire side supports.

Elevating the edges of the bed above ground level prevents soil from being kicked into the sand beds. In combination, the sides of the trench and the wire support the sides of the polyethylene bed. This replaces wood, which is usually expensive in most desert regions.

7.3.2 Greenhouse Floors Lined with Polyethylene

Construction costs can be reduced in areas where lumber is expensive or difficult to obtain by lining the greenhouse floor with black 6-mil polyethylene and filling it with 12 to 16 inches of sand. The floor should have a slight grade of 6 inches per 100 feet, so that the area may be drained or leached when necessary. Generally, two layers of 6-mil plastic are used to cover the entire floor.

Prior to installing the polyethylene the floor should be graded and packed. Polyethylene sheets should be overlapped several feet when more than one sheet is required in wide houses. The drain pipe, 1¼ to 2 inches in diameter, is then placed on top of the polyethylene at a uniform spacing of 4 to 6 feet between pipes, depending upon the nature of the sand. The finer the particles, the closer the pipes will have to be spaced. These drain lines must run parallel with the slope down into a main drain running across the low end of the greenhouse grade. This drainage water can be stored in a sump, from where it can be used on outside vegetation. The drainage cuts are made in the pipe as described earlier. Once the drain pipes are in place, sand is spread over the entire area to a depth of 12 inches (figs. 7.6 to 7.8).

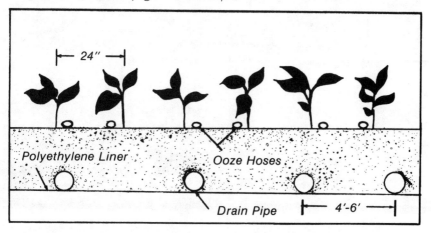

Fig. 7.6. Cross section of greenhouse floor design of sand culture.

Fig. 7.7. The laying of a polyethylene liner and drain pipes. (Courtesy of Superior Farming Company and the Environmental Research Laboratory, Tucson, Arizona.)

Fig. 7.8. Back filling with 12 inches of sand. (Courtesy of Superior Farming Company and the Environmental Research Laboratory, Tucson, Arizona.)

If the medium is spread shallower than 12 inches there will be a problem in obtaining uniform moisture conditions and a greater chance of roots growing into the drain pipes. The surface of the bed should be graded to the same slope as the floor.

7.4 Drip (Trickle) Irrigation System

A drip irrigation system must be used with sand culture. Waste nutrients (no greater than 8 to 10 percent of that applied) are not recycled. Such a system is termed an open system, as opposed to the recycled or closed system of gravel culture. The drip irrigation system feeds each plant individually by use of spaghetti feed lines, sweat (ooze) hoses or emitters (fig. 7.9). If the Chapin Twin-Wall ooze hose is used, a 4-inch spacing between outlets is recommended. If the surface of the bed is level, the tube should not be over 50 feet long. If the surface of the bed is sloped 6 inches, the tube can be 100 feet long, with the supply manifold at the high end.

On a level bed, the supply manifold may run down the center of a

Fig. 7.9. The installation of ooze hoses for an automated drip irrigation-feeding system. (Courtesy of Superior Farming Company and the Environmental Research Laboratory, Tucson, Arizona.)

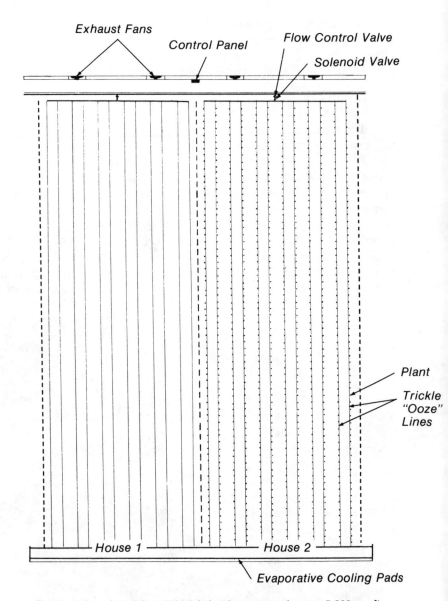

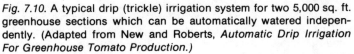

Fig. 7.10. A typical drip (trickle) irrigation system for two 5,000 sq. ft. greenhouse sections which can be automatically watered independently. (Adapted from New and Roberts, *Automatic Drip Irrigation For Greenhouse Tomato Production.)*

100-foot bed, with 50-foot lines off either side. The objective of a greenhouse drip irrigation system is to apply uniform water at optimum levels to all plants.

7.4.1 Planning a Drip Irrigation System

Divide the total greenhouse area into equal or similar crop sections or into individual houses. Plan irrigation systems so that each house or section can be irrigated independently (fig. 7.10). Piping to each section should be capable of distributing 1.6 to 2.4 gallons per minute for each 1000 square feet, or 8 to 12 gallons per minute for each 5000 square feet of growing area.

The rate and length of time for each irrigation cycle will be a function of the type of plant, its maturity, weather conditions and time of day. In all cases a tensiometer system should be set so that no more than 8 to 10 percent of the nutrient solution applied at any irrigation cycle is wasted. This can be determined by measuring the amount of water passing through the main supply line and that flowing out of the main collector drain line.

The volume of water that can enter each greenhouse section should be regulated by a flow control valve which is sized and selected according to plant water requirements of that greenhouse section. Flow valves are usually available in 1- and 2-gallons-per-minute size increments and fit ¾- and 1-inch pipe connections. The flow valve should be located upstream from the solenoid valve where the irrigation cycle is automatically controlled. While a minimum water supply pressure of 15 pounds per square inch is required for proper operation of most flow control valves, for best performance the main water supply line should be maintained at a pressure between 20 and 40 pounds per square inch. The flow control valve assures a constant quantity of water and reduces water pressure in the irrigation system piping to 2 to 4 pounds per square inch which is correct for low-pressure drip irrigation emitters.

Main line piping should be 1¼- to 2-inch diameter PVC, depending upon the area of the largest greenhouse section to be watered at any one time. Since all sections are not irrigated at the same time, the total volume capacity of the main line need satisfy only one section at a time. Header lines should be ¾- to 1-inch PVC pipe for a 5000-square foot section. Larger sections should use larger pipe. The header line is connected to the main line with a tee at its center to equally divide the water supply (fig. 7.10). From this header line ½-inch black polyethylene pipe is run along the inside of each plant row. The emitters are placed in these lateral lines at the base of each plant (fig. 7.11). Flexible polyethylene pipe (usually 80 to 100 pounds per square inch) is normally used for these

Fig. 7.11. Location of ooze hose beside cucumbers. (Courtesy of Superior Farming Company, Tucson, Arizona.)

Fig. 7.12. Automatic proportioner fertilizer injector system used by Superior Farming Company, Tucson, Arizona.

emitter laterals. Where manufactured emitters are used, ½-inch pipe will provide equal water distribution and uniform water application throughout 100- to 150-foot greenhouse irrigation runs.

Most drip emitters can deliver water at a rate of ½ to 3 gallons per hour, depending upon the water pressure in the lateral line. A greenhouse drip irrigation system should be designed so that each drip emitter applies 1 to 1½ gallons per hour.

While spaghetti tubing is more economical than manufactured emitters, more labor is required for its installation and maintenance. Perforated (ooze) hose is installed more easily but is not as durable (it usually must be replaced between crops).

Emitters, pipes and fittings should be black to prevent algae growth inside the piping system.

Water must be filtered before flowing into a drip irrigation system. Y-type, in-line strainers, containing at least 100 mesh screens and equipped with clean-out faucets, should be installed with the screen housing and flush valve down. The filter(s) should be installed downstream from the fertilizer injector in the main supply line. It is wise to also install a filter in the main supply line upstream from the fertilizer injector.

The fertilizer injector or proportioner automatically proportions the right amount of stock solution into the main supply line during every irrigation cycle. Positive displacement pump injectors, venturi proportioners and forced flow batch tanks are some of the types of fertilizer injectors available commercially (fig. 7.12).

Alternatively, a nutrient solution can be pumped into the drip irrigation system directly from a large storage tank. Many growers prefer such a method since they then know the exact formulation of the nutrient solution rather than depend on an automatic proportioner which may sometimes break down or make an error. However, manufacturers of fertilizer injectors claim they are very reliable.

All irrigation may be controlled by time clocks or by a tensiometer feedback system, as described earlier. These control the solenoid valves and the activation of the fertilizer injector or tank pump which allow only one section of the greenhouse to be irrigated at one time.

If calcareous sand is used, the amount of chelated iron going to the plants must be increased, as discussed earlier. If fertilizer proportioners are used, two stock solutions are prepared. One is a calcium nitrate and iron solution and the other contains magnesium sulfate, monopotassium phosphate, potassium nitrate, potassium sulfate, and the micronutrients. The proportioner must be a twin-head type. For example, if each head injects one gallon of stock solution into each 200 gallons of water passing through the water line, then the stock solution will be 200 times the final concentration to reach the plants. In this case, the proportioners would have a ratio of 1:200. Two manufacturers of proportioners in the United States are Anderson and Smith.

7.5 Watering

If a time clock is used, the crop should be watered two to five times per day, depending on the age of the plants, weather and time of the year. As mentioned earlier, enough water is added during each cycle to allow 8–10 percent of the water applied to drain off. Twice a week a sample of this drainage should be tested for total dissolved salts. If the total dissolved salts reaches 2000 ppm, the entire bed should be leached free of salts by using pure water. However, if no extraneous salts such as sodium are found, pure water may be irrigated onto the crop until the plants themselves, over a few days, lower the salt level down to a point at which nutrients can again be added to the irrigation water.

When using a proportioner the total dissolved salts of the nutrient solution going onto the plants should be checked twice each week to be sure that the injector is functioning properly. Also check whether each injector pump is injecting the proper amount of stock solution to the irrigation water.

If a nutrient tank is used to store the nutrient solution, it must be large enough to supply water to all the plants in the greenhouse for at least one week. Its size therefore will depend upon the total greenhouse area. If several crops having very different nutrient requirements are grown, two storage tanks should be used, each having its specific formulation suitable to the crop it is feeding. The entire irrigation system connected to one tank must be independent of the other.

Since a sand culture system is an open system in which excess nutrient solution goes to waste, there will be little change in the formulation of the nutrient solution in the storage tank. The *p*H, however, should be checked daily, especially in areas having highly alkaline waters.

The nutrient solution in the storage tank does not have to be changed regularly as was necessary in gravel culture. It need only be cleaned out periodically of any sludge and sediment due to inert carriers in the fertilizer salts. When the volume of solution in the tank is almost depleted a new batch is mixed up.

Many growers prefer such a storage tank system over the proportioner because they make up their own solution and know exactly what its formulation is. Nonetheless, fertilizer injectors have several advantages over a storage tank: (1) they require less space; (2) the initial capital outlay for an injector is less than for large storage tanks; (3) they are capable of making rapid changes in the nutrient solution formulation to compensate for changes in plant requirements under changing weather conditions. For instance, during a period of dull weather, the rate of nitrogen can be easily reduced, whereas in a storage tank system the entire volume of nutrient (usually at least 1 week's supply) would have to be altered.

7.6 Sterilization of Sand Beds between Crops

While fumigation can rid the sand of any soil-borne disease, plus any nematodes which may have been introduced, it will not rid the sand of tobacco mosaic virus (TMV) or cucumber mosaic virus II (CMV II). One of two fumigants may be used—Vapam, which is added through the irrigation system, or methyl bromide, which is

Fig. 7.13. Injecting methyl bromide under an inflated polyethylene cover.

put through the drain system under pressure. In either case, the entire floor must be covered with polyethylene before the fumigant is applied. Methyl bromide is also available in cannisters which come with a special dispenser hose to inject the fumes into the polyethylene cover. In this case the polyethylene should be inflated with air and sealed with a layer of sand around the edges to hold the air inside before injecting the gas (fig. 7.13). After 48 hours, the cover is removed and the area leached with water. This removes any remaining fumigant and salts. If Vapam is put through the watering system, the system must be flushed with water after application. The beds may be replanted four to five days after fumigation.

To rid sand of TMV or CMV II, steam sterilization must be used. If the greenhouse is heated with a hot water boiler, the boiler should be assembled with a steam converter which can produce sufficient steam for sterilization of the growing beds. The steam may be put through the drain system provided the drain lines will not be damaged by high temperature. Alternatively, pipe can be placed within the top few inches of the sand and the beds covered with heavy canvas or polyethylene before releasing the steam. Pipes are moved along the beds as sterilization is completed for each section of bed.

7.7 Small-Scale Sand Culture System

A simple home unit can be designed similarly to a commercial unit but on a much smaller scale. Basically, it should consist of a bed or growing tray, a nutrient reservoir, and a trickle feeding system operated by a pump energized by a time clock (fig. 7.14).

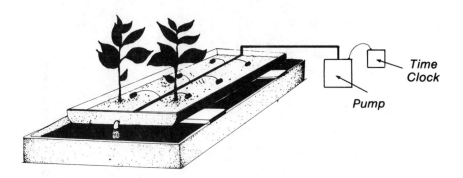

Fig. 7.14. A simple small-scale trickle sand culture system.

The growing tray could have small holes in the bottom of the plastic liner or use a perforated plastic pipe for drainage. One of the oldest and still popular hydroponic methods for individual potted plants is the wick system. Such a system consists of a double pot, one containing the medium and plant and the other the nutrient solution. A fibrous wick is set into the growing pot about one-third of the way with the other end suspended in the nutrient solution below (fig. 7.15). As water evaporates from the plant and moves

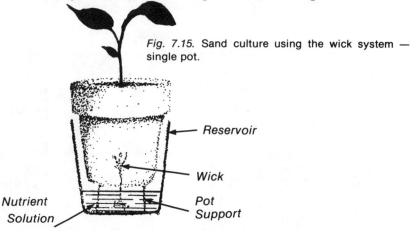

Fig. 7.15. Sand culture using the wick system — single pot.

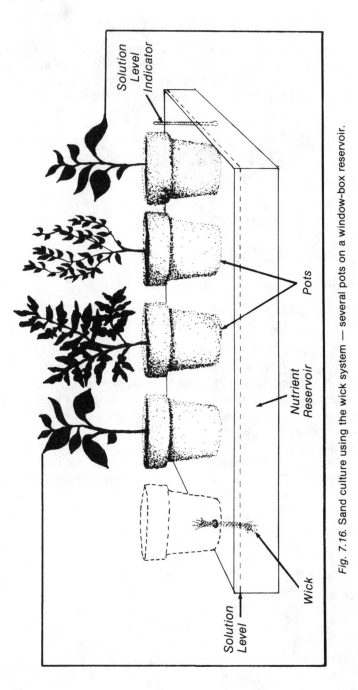

Fig. 7.16. Sand culture using the wick system — several pots on a window-box reservoir.

from the medium to the plant, capillary action moves the solution from the nutrient reservoir through the wick to the plant root zone. The ends of the wick would be teased out so that a tuft of untwined fiber is present at both ends. Be sure that at no time is the solution of the reservoir in contact with the bottom of the growing pot or excess water will be drawn into the root zone, causing puddling. Several pots with wicks may be set up over a window-box reservoir. The reservoir can be covered to prevent evaporation losses, but holes are needed at the location of each pot to allow the wick to pass through (fig. 7.16). Though not essential, it is useful to have a floating marker to indicate the level of liquid in the reservoir.

7.8 Advantages and Disadvantages of Sand Culture

Advantages Over Gravel Culture

1. It is an open system, that is, the nutrient solution is not recycled, so the chances of diseases such as *Fusarium* or *Verticillium* spreading in the medium are greatly reduced.

2. There is less problem with drain pipes getting plugged with roots since the more dense medium of sand favors lateral root growth.

3. The finer sand particles allow lateral movement of water through capillary action so that solution applied at each plant becomes evenly distributed throughout the root zone.

4. With the right choice of sand combined with a drip irrigation system, adequate root aeration is achieved.

5. Each plant is fed individually with a new complete nutrient solution during each irrigation cycle—no nutrient imbalance occurs.

6. Construction costs are lower than for a subirrigation gravel system.

7. The system is simpler, easier to maintain and service and more foolproof than a subirrigation gravel culture system.

8. Due to the smaller particle size of sand, water retention is high and only several irrigations are required each day. If a failure occurs, there is more time available to repair the system before the plants will use up the existing water in the medium and begin to experience water stress.

9. Smaller, centrally located nutrient reservoirs or injectors can be constructed away from the actual growing area of the greenhouse.

10. Sand is readily available in most locations. When using calcareous sand, the formulation can be adjusted to compensate for daily pH changes and shortages of iron and/or other elements.

Disadvantages of Sand Culture Compared with Gravel Culture

1. One of the major disadvantages is that either chemical or steam sterilization methods must be used to fumigate between crops. However, such methods are thorough, even if they are a little more time-consuming than the use of bleach with gravel culture.

2. Drip irrigation lines can become plugged with sediment. This, however, can be overcome by the use of in-line 100- to 200-mesh filters which can be easily cleaned daily.

3. Some claims are made that sand culture uses more fertilizer and water than a cyclic gravel culture system. Again, this can be overcome by good management. The waste should be monitored and feeding adjusted so that no more than 7 to 8 percent of the solution added is actually drained out. Even in gravel culture the waste can be equally as great, if not greater, due to the need to change the nutrient solution periodically.

4. Salt buildup may occur in the sand during the growing period. This can be corrected, however, by flushing the medium periodically with pure water. Again, proper management with monitoring of salt accumulation from the drainage water is important to prevent excess salt problems.

7.9 Operation and Productivity of Sand Culture Greenhouses in Arid Lands

An example of how sand culture can be utilized to produce food on a coastal desert is the commercial-scale power-water-food facility of Abu Dhabi (fig. 7.3). The University of Arizona Environmental Research Laboratory (ERL) with a grant from the ruler of Abu Dhabi in 1972 installed a power-water-food complex which utilizes desalted seawater for the irrigation of vegetable crops in large, controlled-environment greenhouses. With rainfall averaging less than 5 centimeters per year and strong winds occurring frequently, outdoor cultivation is severely limited. Air-inflated polyethylene and structured greenhouses with a desalination plant could meet the needs for producing crops. Half of the 5-acre complex was constructed of air-inflated polyethylene greenhouses connected to two central structured corridors, as shown in figures

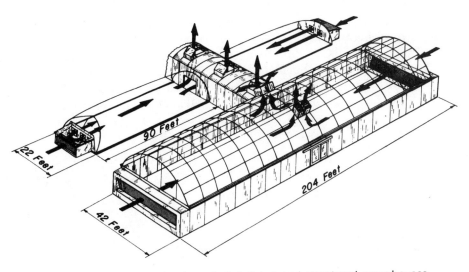

Fig. 7.17. Schematic drawing of air-inflated and structured greenhouses shows air flow pattern. (Courtesy of The Environmental Research Laboratory and Manley, Inc., Tucson, Arizona.)

7.3 and 7.17. Low-growing crops that need no overhead support such as turnips (fig. 7.18), lettuce, peppers, eggplant, radishes, etc. are grown in the air-inflated greenhouses. Crops such as tomatoes, cucumbers and string beans, which are trained vertically on a cordon system, are grown in the structured houses.

The greenhouses are cooled by use of evaporative cooling pads at the ends of each unit. Seawater, rather than fresh water, is distributed over the top of the pad and runs through it as centrally located exhaust fans pull air through the cooling pads and across the houses, exhausting the air in the middle of the structured houses, as shown in figure 7.17. In the inflated greenhouses air is sucked through the cooling pads by fans mounted in the end wall. The air is forced through the house and exhausted through the roof of the central corridor.

The greenhouses protect the plants from blowing sands, drying winds and high and low temperatures, and the high humidity created by seawater cooling systems reduces water consumption.

Crops are grown in the existing sands which is composed of essentially fine calcium carbonate. The pH of the medium consequently is 8.3. Water and fertilizers are applied at regular intervals by dissolving commercial-grade fertilizers in the distilled seawater and distributing them individually to each plant by use of a drip irrigation system and fertilizer injector similar to those shown in figure 7.12.

Plastic-lined beds and a drip irrigation system similar to that described earlier in this chapter are used to grow the crops.

Fontes (1973) points out that production projections for the 2 hectares of greenhouses in Abu Dhabi were an average of 1 ton per day of vegetables, which was accomplished by the middle of 1972. Yields in tons/ha/day for various vegetable crops in 1972 are given in table 7.1.

TABLE 7.1   Comparison of Yields of Various Vegetable Crops Grown in Abu Dhabi Greenhouses

Type of Vegetable	Tons/ha/day
Cabbage	1.4
Cucumber	2.8
Eggplant	1.3
Lettuce	1.5
Okra	0.4
Tomato	1.2
Turnip	2.4

Fig. 7.18. Air-inflated greenhouses are especially suited to low-growing crops such as turnips. (Courtesy of the government of Abu Dhabi, The Environmental Research Laboratory and Manley, Inc., Tucson, Arizona.)

For the first six months of 1973, 230 tons of vegetables were shipped to market. Table 7.2 shows the yields of various crops grown in the Abu Dhabi greenhouses.

TABLE 7.2 Yield of Crops Grown in Abu Dhabi Greenhouses

Type of Vegetable	Yield/ Crop (in tons)	Crops/ Year	Total Yield per Acre Per Year (in tons)
Broccoli	13.0	3	39.0
Bush Beans	4.6	4	18.4
Cabbage	23.0	3	69.0
Chinese Cabbage	20.0	4	80.0
Cucumber	70.0	3	210.0
Radish	9.0	8	72.0
Tomato	45.0	2	90.0

The 1972 production of tomatoes alone exceeded 150,000 kilograms, enough to supply almost 29,000 persons at U.S. levels of consumption.

7.10 Sand Culture in the Tropics

Growing temperate crops in tropical countries presents some unique problems. Certain tropical countries, such as Venezuela, which have a resource-based industrial economy are developing an expanding middle class of people whose demands are similar to those in other industrialized countries throughout the world. They demand similar diets which include fresh fruits, vegetables and similar esthetically pleasing surroundings with the use of flowers.

Such crops which are not native to the tropics require specific growing conditions and culture. Strawberries, sweet peppers, eggplants, tomatoes, cucumbers, lettuce, cabbage, cauliflower, carnations, chrysanthemums and foliage plants are in demand. In many regions of the country the climate is not suitable for growing such crops due to excessive temperatures and high humidity. However, in the mountainous areas with elevations above 1500 meters (4900 feet) the temperatures drop sufficiently to allow the growing of cool-season temperate crops such as lettuce, strawberries, carnations and chrysanthemums. The temperatures in these areas range from 22 to 28 degrees Celsius (72-82°F) during the day and from 16 to 20 degrees Celsius (61-68°F) during the night. The daytime temperatures are at the upper limit of the tolerable range for the growing of cool-season crops such as lettuce, cabbage, cauliflower, carnations and chrysanthemums. Any prolonged variations in daytime temperatures can cause crop failures.

The higher in elevation crops can be located, the less chance of experiencing excessive daytime temperatures which may cause bolting of lettuce or breaking of flower blossoms. By seeking higher elevations, generally steeper terrain is encountered (fig. 7.19). As a result, conventional farming is very difficult. Small plots of land are cultivated by hand repeatedly year after year. Production declines with fertility and soil erosion increases.

Where arable land is very limited and difficult to work as in this case, hydroponic culture for intensive production is the answer. But it is often impossible to obtain local people with the necessary skills for this more technical growing of crops. Fertilizers are often unavailable for months; therefore, large inventories must be maintained. Equipment and materials such as pumps, plastic piping, pesticides and greenhouse supplies are difficult to obtain locally, so they must often be imported from the United States or Europe. All of these factors lead to frustrations and slow progress in a highly technical agriculture such as hydroponics. On the other hand, if technical agriculture is introduced successfully, with time and patience, a vast market awaits to be tapped because presently most fresh vegetables are imported from the United States.

The tropics have an ever present abundance of insects and soil-borne pests such as nematodes. Water is often high in dissolved salts, and soils are shallow and infertile. As a result, growing crops by conventional soil culture produces low yields, with major pest problems.

Hydroponics can overcome these problems of high-salt-content water, soil-borne pests and diseases, shallow infertile soils and limited arable land. Intensive culture under controlled conditions utilizing qualified technologists can open a new era of agricultural production in the tropics.

To demonstrate the problems, possible solutions and the potential of hydroponics in the tropics an example of a sand culture operation in Venezuela is presented. The company involved has been engaged in sand culture production of lettuce for over five years. Most of this time has been devoted to the development of a suitable sand culture system for the local conditions.

Their farm is located on very steep terrain near Caracas. Terraces have been cut to maximize the available level ground (fig. 7.20). Each terrace is about one-third of a hectare. As the soil is very rocky and the use of heavy equipment to level the sites is costly, it was decided to construct raised beds of metal frames. The cost of steel and the labour of welding it is relatively low.

The frames of the beds were welded on-site and set in concrete footings as shown in figure 7.21. The bottoms were constructed of clay bricks and concrete, common building materials of the country (fig. 7.22). The beds were sealed with a bituminous paint (fig. 7.23). The system constructed was basically sand culture with some modifications. Since trickle or drip irrigation systems were not readily available in Venezuela at the time of construction, a sub-irrigation method was used. Large below-ground cisterns of concrete were built for storage of the nutrient solution (fig. 7.24). Water is pumped from several wells to a storage tank above the hydroponic farm. The water from the wells is low in total dissolved salts, a rare and fortunate situation in the tropics. A complex system of piping and plumbing was installed to move the well water to the storage tank and to distribute nutrient solution to each bed from the nutrient solution reservoir (fig. 7.25).

The beds are flooded from one end by spraying the nutrient solution into a plenum (fig. 7.26). Clay tiles cut in half placed along the bottom of the bed (fig. 7.23) join the plenum to the opposite drain end. The drain is plugged manually to allow the water to rise in the bed to within an inch of the sand surface (fig. 7.27). This generally takes about 15-20 minutes. The plug is then removed and the water flows out of the bed within 10 minutes, providing fairly good aeration.

Suitable sand is not available locally and therefore must be hauled by truck a distance of 500 miles. The sand is pure silica of a coarse texture normally used in the glass industry. Its cost is therefore very high, about $50 a cubic meter (slightly greater than a cubic yard). Due to the high cost of sand, the sand requirements were reduced by first putting a 3- to 4-inch (7.6-10.2 cm) layer of crushed clay bricks on the bottom of the beds over the drain tile lines (fig. 7.23). Then about 4 to 5 inches (10.2-12.7 cm) of silica sand was placed on top of the crushed bricks (fig. 7.23). The use of the clay tiles as a lower medium has proved unsatisfactory since over a period of six months to a year it breaks down into a fine powder causing excessive moisture in the roots of the lettuce plants. It contributes to a bacterial soft rot problem from the high

Fig. 7.19 Typical steep terrain of mountainous regions of the tropics with crops grown by hand cultivation in soil. (Courtesy of Hidroponias Venezolanas, S.A., Caracas, Venezuela.)

Fig. 7.20 Hydroponic sand culture beds of head lettuce on terraces in mountainous terrain of Venezuela. (Courtesy of Hidroponias Venezolanas, S.A., Caracas, Venezuela.)

Fig. 7.21 Metal frames for raised sand culture beds. (Courtesy of Hidroponias Venezolanas, S.A., Caracas, Venezuela.)

Fig. 7.22 Bottoms of beds constructed of clay bricks. (Courtesy of Hidroponias Venezolanas, S.A., Caracas, Venezuela.)

Fig. 7.23 Beds sealed with bituminous paint and drainage provided by clay tiles. (Courtesy of Hidroponias Venezolanas, S.A., Caracas, Venezuela.)

Fig. 7.24 Large concrete cisterns for storage of the nutrient solution. (Courtesy of Hidroponias Venezolanas, S.A., Caracas, Venezuela.)

Fig. 7.25 Complex pumping and piping system for distribution of nutrient solution to growing beds. (Courtesy of Hidroponias Venezolanas, S.A., Caracas, Venezuela.)

Fig. 7.26 Distribution of nutrient solution into plenum of each sand bed. (Courtesy of Hidroponias Venezolanas, S.A., Caracas, Venezuela.)

Fig. 7.27 Water regulation and drainage of subirrigated sand culture bed. (Courtesy of Hidroponias Venezolanas, S.A., Caracas, Venezuela.)

moisture content always present in the medium (fig. 7.28). The solution would be to remove the lower clay chard layer and/or convert to a trickle feed system. This would conserve water, reduce puddling, improve root aeration, and minimize the spread of diseases and insects by lowering the relative humidity at the base of the lettuce. With continued use of beds containing clay chard, the clay breakdown caused excessive puddling and it had to be replaced with a layer of coarse granitic rock followed by a layer of smaller pebbles before the top sand layer. Results using this sequence of media have been quite successful with good drainage and aeration (fig. 7.29).

The availability and cost of construction materials, medium, and fertilizers in a specific location will determine the type of hydroponic system that should be used. In many tropical countries lumber is scarce and very costly. Generally, steel products, concrete and clay bricks are readily available and inexpensive. Such is the case in Venezuela where hydroponic beds are constructed of steel frames, clay bricks and concrete as outlined above.

An alternative to this type of construction is to use an asbestos concrete roofing channel ("Canal 90") fabricated by Industrias Eternit, S.A., Caracas, Venezuela. These channels are 1 meter wide by up to 8 meters long. Depth of the channel is 24 centimeters (10 inches) which is sufficient for most crops. The "canal 90" can be lined with heavy (12-mil) black polyethylene or coated with butuminous paint to seal it from chemical reactions with the nutrient solution. It has a shallow "W" shape which is ideal for drainage. Drainage is provided by placing clay tiles end-to-end with several centimeters overlap in each depression of the channel (figs. 7.30, 7.31). A screen is placed immediately over the tiles to prevent sand entering the drainage spaces. The drain tiles are covered with 7-8 centimeters (3 in) of coarse rocks (3-4 cm diameter) followed by 10-12 centimeters (4-5 in) of pea gravel (0.5 cm diameter) and the remainder is filled with coarse sand. All rocks and sand must be of granitic origin, preferrably quartz. Subirrigation or trickle may be used. If a subirrigation system is used, a nutrient solution tank must be located below level unless the beds are raised.

Each bed can grow two rows of tomatoes, cucumbers, egg plants or peppers. If lettuce is grown, two channels should be placed within 5 centimeters (2 in) of each other. Up to four rows of head

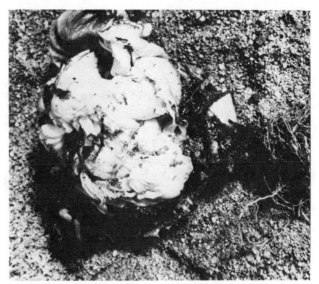

Fig. 7.28 Bacterial soft rot of head lettuce. (Courtesy of
Hidroponias Venezolanas, S.A., Caracas, Venezuela.)

Fig. 7.29. Beds Containing Coarse Gravel, Smaller Pebbles and Coarse Sand.
(Courtesy of Hidroponias Venezolanas, S.A., Caracas, Venezuela).

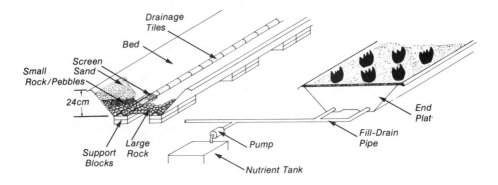

Fig. 7.30. Sketch of "canal 90" Bed.

Fig. 7.31. Watercress Growing in "canal 90" Bed. (Courtesy of Hidroponias Venezolanas, S.A., Caracas, Venezuela).

lettuce can be planted in each bed. The distance between plants within rows should be a minimum of 25 centimeters (10 in) and spacing between rows should be 10 centimeters, 25 centimeters, and 10 centimeters (4 in, 10 in, 10 in, and 4 in). With two channels positioned 5 centimeters (2 in) apart the spacing between all rows of plants will be 25 centimeters (10 in).

Tomatoes, egg plants, and peppers should be spaced 40 centimeters (16 in) apart within the rows and 50 centimeters (20 in) between rows in each bed. Beds should be individually situated with pathways of 65 centimeters (25 in) in width to allow sufficient light penetration in the crop. Cucumbers should also be grown in individual beds placed 65 centimeters (25 in) apart. Spacing within rows should be at least 65 centimeters (25 in) and the distance between rows a minimum of 50 centimeters (20 in).

Watercress is presently being grown successively in "Canal 90" beds of 6-meter length. (figs. 7.31, 7.32) The beds are filled with coarse gravel to just above the level of the drain tiles. A layer (2 cm) of coarse sand is placed on top of the coarse gravel. The watercress seedlings or cuttings are placed on top of the medium and the beds are flooded with nutrient solution to a level of 10 centimeters (4 in) above the medium. This level of solution is maintained constant. Additional solution is pumped up to recycle back to the nutrient tank every hour for 15 minutes during the daylight hours to increase oxygenation to the plants.

Fig. 7.32. Watercress growing in "canal 90" beds. (Courtesy of Hidroponias Venezolanas, S.A., Caracas, Venezuela).

Plants become established within 3-4 weeks and are ready for a continual harvesting program every 7-10 days thereafter. After several months the root mass becomes very dense and thinning is done by rouging out the thicker-stemmed plants. Once the root mass becomes too thick to allow good oxygenation, the plants should be changed. This generally is necessary every 6 months. Beds are cleaned and sterilized before new cuttings or seedlings are transplanted into the beds to begin the production cycle again within 3-4 weeks.

Watercress is packaged in 0.5 kilograms (1.1 lb) bundles for sale to exclusive restaurants in Caracas. The bundles are placed in plastic tote bins having several centimeters of water on the bottom (fig. 7.33). This maintains freshness and, in fact, allows the watercress to take up water and increase its weight. The entire plastic bin is delivered to a restaurant, similar to a case. The client keeps the watercress fresh in the bin until it is used and then returns the bin to the grower at the next delivery.

Fig. 7.33. Packing of watercress in plastic tote bins. (Courtesy of Hidroponias Venezolanas, S.A., Caracas, Venezuela).

In the tropics where daylength and the hours of sunlight vary only slightly from one month to the next an accurate correlation should exist among electrical conductivity (EC), total dissolved solutes (TDS), concentration of various nutrients and plant age as discussed earlier (sec. 3.7.4). There are two seasons in the tropics, a wet season from June through December and a dry season from January through May. While there is more precipitation during the wet season rainfall is very heavy over a short period of time each day. Rapid clearing of the sky follows with full sunlight. Therefore, the number of hours of sunlight for any month during the wet season does not differ greatly from that of the dry season. Consequently, the most significant effect upon nutrient solutions is that of plant growth stage rather than the influence of sunlight. As a result, electrical conductivity can be used to accurately monitor the status of the nutrient solution.

In the tropics year-round warm temperatures generate large insect populations. When crops are grown hydroponically outside without the protection of closed greenhouses, insects quickly invade the crops and rapidly spread with few or no natural predators. The use of pesticides is imperative. Without skilled people knowledgeable in the identification of insects and the use of pesticides, crops infested by one or several pests will soon be destroyed. Such was the case with the lettuce crop in early 1980 when a leaf miner infestation spread throughout the crop causing heavy losses with 70-80 percent of the crop non-marketable (fig. 7.34). Some pesticides were used in an attempt to control the leaf miners but the chemicals were not effective. Often pesticides are not available and those which are may have become ineffective due to the build-up of insect resistance. Without the introduction of new pesticides to overcome such resistance, control diminishes until complete crop losses occur.

Within six weeks after treating the crop weekly with an effective pesticide, complete control was achieved. A backpack "Solo" sprayer was purchased to apply the chemical uniformly over the crop (fig. 7.35). This type of sprayer gives uniform coverage in a fine mist which minimizes the usage of the pesticide. It is simple to use as no hoses or electrical cords need be dragged between the beds and the pesticides can be rapidly applied over large areas.

Leaf miners infest the leaves of plants at an early stage. As larvae they eat the leaf tissue tunnelling between the upper and lower leaf epidermal layers. This produces a characteristic reticulate pattern (fig. 7.34). If the upper and lower leaf surfaces are pulled apart the larvae will be exposed.

The adult female, about 2 mm long, punctures the leaf surface with a tubelike appendage on the abdomen known as an ovipositor and inserts eggs through it. The injection of the eggs into the leaves causes small white blister-like spots on the leaf. The adult males and females feed on the sap which oozes from the punctures. Each female lays about 100 eggs in its two- to three-week life span (see life-cycle in section 10.14 Diseases and Insects). The eggs hatch in 5 to 6 days into soft white maggots (larvae) which reach about 2.5 millimeters in length when mature. The larvae tunnel for up to

Fig. 7.34 Leaf miner damage to lettuce.

Fig. 7.35 Application of insecticide by use of "Solo" backpack sprayer. (Courtesy of Hidroponias Venezolanas, S.A., Caracas, Venezuela.)

two weeks before pupating for two weeks to emerge as adult flies. The female flies then infest new leaves and the cycle is repeated. About five weeks is required for the completion of the life cycle from egg to adult. They infest many crops such as lettuce, tomatoes, carnations and chrysanthemums.

With such a short life cycle the insect can spread rapidly under favorable conditions of warm tropical climates. Populations increase to epidemic proportions in a short time if no insecticide control is practiced; crops can be completely destroyed.

While tropical climates have generally an abundance of sunshine favorable to the growing of crops, they have a wet and dry season. Extremes in rainfall are commonplace. For instance, in the plains of central Venezuela during the dry season precipitation is so low it closely resembles desert conditions with extremely high temperatures over 30°C (86°F), while during the wet season rainfall is so heavy the entire region becomes inundated with several feet of water. In such areas crops can only be grown during the dry season with use of irrgation.

Even in the mountainous regions the wet and dry seasons are distinct. During the wet season temperatures are generally a few degrees warmer and rainfall occurs for several hours almost every day. As a result, crops that cannot tolerate continual moistening soon are damaged and infected with diseases. Such is the case with lettuce, especially head lettuce. Within several weeks of maturity, head lettuce is very sensitive to moisture. Any moisture that penetrates the head causes rotting (fig. 7.28) which spreads rapidly with high temperatures. Losses of up to 40 to 60 percent are not uncommon.

Since many crops cannot be cultivated during the wet season, short supply raises prices dramatically. Head lettuce sells as high as $3.00-$4.00 each during this period of low production. Therefore, an excellent market can be established for hydroponically-grown lettuce and other produce if the market can be reliably supplied year-round.

Using sand culture in raised beds keeps the rainfall from upsetting the growing of crops through excessive root moisture, but moisture onto the plants still causes crop failures. To overcome this a greenhouse type of structure was erected over the beds to prevent the rain from entering the crop as it matures. A closed greenhouse would not be suitable since daily rainfall occurs only for short periods and the sun shines for the majority of the daylight hours. Closed greenhouses would result in high temperature build-up due to the "greenhouse effect" of trapped heat radiation. Unless a cooling system of fans and pads were installed, temperatures would quickly exceed 40 degrees Celsius (104°F) within minutes of the appearance of the sun. While such cooling systems may be the answer to complete environmental control, they are very costly to import and difficult to maintain.

Since the only function of a greenhouse cover was protection from the rain, a better approach was to install a sloped fiberglass roof supported by a steel structure that could be made on-site by local workers. With no sides, free wind movement over the crop allowed natural ventilation for cooling.

The structure was designed in a saw-tooth fashion so that the wind could freely pass through the roof at each "tooth" (fig. 7.36) . They were initially oriented with the "mouths" or high points away from the prevailing wind, assuming that as the wind blew over the top a vacuum effect would suck air outside from underneath through the mouths giving good air exchange. However, with no sides on the structures negative pressure could not be created under the structure. A second reason for orienting the structures away from the prevailing wind was that such orientation would prevent rain from entering during the wet season.

At the low edges the roofs were less than one meter above the top of the growing beds and the distance between the openings was less than one-half of a meter (fig. 7.37). Air exchange was restricted and lack of sufficient ventilation caused temperatures to rise 6 degrees Celsius (11°F) above ambient. With ambient temperatures between 25 and 28 degrees Celsius (77-82°F) the temperatures within the "greenhouse" ranged between 30 to 33 degrees Celsius (86-91°F) exceeding the tolerable range for head lettuce. These high temperatures caused "bolting" of the lettuce (fig. 7.38) so they were not marketable.

Several approaches were taken to rectify the excessive temperatures. First, the structures had to be raised one meter at the lower ends. Second, the "mouths" had to be oriented facing the prevailing winds (opposite to what they were) (figs. 7.39, 7.40) . Third, the openings had to be covered with a screen curtain during rainy periods to prevent water from entering through the "mouths." A screen of polypropylene material would resist breakdown by solar radiation. It would be installed on a cable and pulley system so that it could be opened during sunny periods to allow free air movement through the crop and pulled across only during the rain.

Fig. 7.36 Saw-toothed greenhouse structure for protection against rain during wet season. (Courtesy of Hidroponias Venezolanas, S.A., Caracas, Venezuela.)

Fig. 7.37 Greenhouse structure too low and mouth openings too small for proper ventilation. (Courtesy of Hidroponias Venezolanas, S.A., Caracas, Venezuela.)

Fig. 7.38 "Bolting" of head lettuce caused by excessive heat. (Courtesy of Hidroponias Venezolanas, S.A., Caracas, Venezuela.)

Fig. 7.39 Reconstruction of greenhouses, raising structures and reorienting mouths toward the prevailing wind. (Courtesy of Hidroponias Venezolanas)

Fig. 7.40 Reconstruction of greenhouses to increase height above beds and orient mouths toward prevailing wind. (Courtesy of Hidroponias Venezolanas, S.A., Caracas, Venezuela.)

By raising the structures a meter, ventilation would be greatly improved. At the same time if pockets of stagnant air accumulated just under the covers it would still be kept above the crop. Wind would also enter from the sides more freely resulting in faster air exchange. Overall with rapid air changes of at least one every 10 to 15 seconds temperatures would not rise above the ambient temperatures. By orienting the openings towards the prevailing wind, air is caught and forced down onto the crop moving across the beds. Upon reconstructing the structures in this way (figs. 7.41, 7.42) temperatures were measured under the cover and found to be within one degree of ambient temperatures. Bolting of the lettuce was largely overcome.

The fiberglass coverings have been used successfully, but within several years the material discolors. High humidity and temperatures cause heavy growth of algae on the fiberglass panels. As a result, light transmissibility is greatly reduced. Washing the panels every 3 to 4 weeks to remove the algae became essential. However, such washing with a brush damages the panels by exposing the fibers. Consequently, the panels deteriorate rapidly through wear of the acrylic surface and light passage through the panels is reduced sufficiently to affect crop production.

An alternative to fiberglass is polyethylene. While dust and algae growth are also problems with polyethylene, washing is easier since no corrugations exist. Ultraviolet light from sunlight in the tropics is higher than in temperate regions and breakdown of the polyethylene is more rapid, necessitating changing the polyethylene every year. A more durable grade of polyethylene developed for greenhouses such as "Monsanto 602" has lasted up to two years in some tropical regions, but often if a plastics industry exists in a country, it is difficult or costly to import other polyethylene due to high tariffs protecting the local industry.

With the use of polyethylene instead of fiberglass to cover the protective structures, some modifications in the basic sawtooth design must be made. Its use with roses has been successful in Venezuela (fig. 7.43).

Growing of lettuce in areas of high temperatures, 25 to 28°C, is difficult due to "bolting" which occurs above these temperatures as discussed earlier. With a slight reduction in light from the use of a fiberglass or polyethylene cover, bolting occurs at lower temperatures (25°C to 27°C). For this reason, a temporary cover which could easily be removed would be beneficial to the growing of

Fig. 7.41 Raised structure facing prevailing wind. Compare with Fig. 7.37. (Courtesy of Hidroponias Venezolanas, S.A., Caracas, Venezuela.)

Fig. 7.42 Compare raised and reoriented structures (left) with original structures (right). (Courtesy of Hidroponias Venezolanas, S.A., Caracas, Venezuela.)

Fig. 7.43 Polyethylene Structures Used for the Growing of Roses in the Tropics.

Fig. 7.44 Automated Motorized Polyethylene Cover being Tested in the Tropics. (Courtesy of Hidroponias Venezolanas, S.A., Caracas, Venezuela).

many cool-season crops. A system must be designed that allows the polyethylene cover to be rolled up during sunny weather and quickly cover the beds during rainfall.

A motorized drum system that will automatically roll up the polyethylene within seconds is shown in figure 7.44. However, the cost of such a system is estimated at $250 per bed in Venezuela. This cost could be substantially reduced if a hand crank system were used in place of the motors. The rolls of polyethylene when not extended would be housed in a black case so that ultraviolet light would be excluded. This would greatly extend the longevity of the polyethylene. Head lettuce is very susceptible to bacterial soft rot during the last 15 to 20 days of maturity. It is during that stage that the polyethylene covers would have to be used to prevent rain from entering. Also, the covers would be used during the night and early morning when heavy dew forms.

Since ambient temperatures at the elevation of the hydroponics farm are very close to the upper tolerable limit for heading of lettuce, heat tolerant varieties must be tested to determine a more suitable variety. Some 20 to 25 varieties are presently being tested to determine whether any of them are more resistant to bolting than "Great Lakes 659" presently being grown in Venezuela.

A final approach to solving the problem of bolting is to locate additional growing beds for lettuce production at higher elevation terraces and use the existing terraces for growing carnations, chrysanthemums and warm-season crops such as tomatoes and peppers.

In many tropical countries human sewage is used as fertilizer for field crops. This has resulted in endemic infestations of amoeba causing dysentery. Consequently, many people will not eat fresh salads for fear of becoming ill with dysentery. Hydroponically grown leafy crops such as lettuce and many herbs such as watercress which are very popular in salads, make amoeba-free crops possible. Such sterile products can be easily sold to exclusive restaurants and produce stores for a premium price.

Nematodes infest most soils in tropical countries. These are very small microscopic round worms sometimes called eelworms that infest the roots of plants. Depending upon the species involved they may cause death of roots, injuries to roots which act as ports of entry for fungal diseases or swelling of roots so that they cannot function in normal water and mineral uptake (fig. 7.45). This root damage often causes plants to wilt during the day when

Fig. 7.45 Swelling lettuce roots caused by nematode infection. (Courtesy of Hidroponias Venezolanas, S.A., Caracas, Venezuela.)

Fig. 7.46 Basamid sterilization of sand in bed for elimination of nematodes. Polyethylene cover edges sealed with pipes and sand. (Courtesy of Hidroponias Venezolanas, S.A., Caracas, Venezuela.)

water uptake cannot meet evapo-transpirational losses. If plants do survive the stress, they become stunted and non-marketable.

Soil temperature is critical in the development of nematodes. Females fail to reach maturity at temperatures above 33°C (92°F) or below 15°C (59°F). Soil temperatures in the tropics are near optimum levels for nematode development. It takes about 17 days at 29°C (85°F) for females to develop from infective larvae to egg-laying adults. Spreading within the field occurs through movement of infested soil or plant debris by man, water, and wind.

Even with hydroponic culture nematodes can easily be introduced into a crop by movement through water or wind. Preplanting treatments of steam or chemicals effectively eliminate nematodes from soil and other media such as sand, sawdust or gravel used in hydroponics. Nematodes are killed with steam sterilization by heating the medium under moist conditions for 30 minutes to 49°C (120°F). This and chemical methods of sterilization are described in Chapter 4. A new chemical, Basamid, is a soil fumigant used for the control of unencysted soil-borne nematodes, soil fungi, and germinating weed seeds. It is applied at a rate of 325 to 500 kilograms per hectare or 3 to 5 kilograms per 100 square meters. It must be evenly distributed on the soil surface then worked into the upper 15-23 centimeters (6-9 in) of the medium. The medium is then covered with polyethylene sealing the edges with medium or weights (fig. 7.46). The interval between treatment and planting depends on the temperature, the moisture and nature of the medium. For example, at warm temperatures of above 18°C (64°F) the medium may be opened up 5 to 7 days after the Basamid application. The medium should then be rototilled to release all residual Basamid. A waiting period of 7 to 10 days followed by germination tests must be carried out before planting. The period between treatment and planting depends upon the medium temperature at 10 cm (3.9 in). If it is over 18°C (64°F) a period of 10-12 days is required. Caution must be exercised as Basamid is toxic to all growing plants.

Basamid can be removed from the sand beds within 24 hours by washing the beds with a spreader solution normally used in the application of pesticides. The overall sterilization cycle has been reduced to 3 days: One day of fumigation; one day for cleaning with the spreader and one day to wash with fresh water (at least 4-6 washings are required). No harmful effects of this short fumigation cycle have been found on lettuce production and it has been very effective in the elimination of nematodes from the sand medium.

Steam sterilization is equally effective as chemicals and can be carried out in a shorter period of time especially if the medium is not porous. Steam sterilization can be done with a small portable steam sterilizer (fig. 7.47). Perforated pipes are placed several inches below the surface of the medium in the beds. Then the entire bed is covered with a heavy vinyl or canvas tarpaulin (fig. 7.48).

Generally, it takes several hours to raise the temperature of the medium throughout the bed to 60° to 82°C (140°-180°F). It is best to moisten the medium prior to sterilizing as the moisture carries the heat uniformly throughout the medium. Figure 7.49 outlines the temperatures required to kill various organisms. This process is really pasteurization, not sterilization, as it is best not to use as high a temperature as would be required for sterilization since only the detrimental organisms must be killed. If the lower temperatures between 60° and 80°C (140°-180°F) are used, many beneficial organism will remain alive. It may be a disadvantage to sterilize the medium and kill all organisms as after sterilization any organisms can be easily introduced into the medium. Whereas, with pasteurization at slightly lower temperatures only the pest organisms will be killed. Beneficial organisms can then resist re-inoculation by detrimental organisms.

Once this multitude of problems can be resolved, excellent crops can be grown under tropical conditions using hydroponics (figs. 7.50, 7.51). The disadvantages of unavailability and high costs of materials and equipment can be overcome by use of water cultural and NFT systems of hydroponics. While little commercial application of the nutrient film technique has been carried out in the tropics, it does offer a vast potential by reducing capital costs and dependency upon suitable media such as granitic sand or gravel which is often rare. Hydroponics offers the answer to combating the pests and diseases of the tropics, the lack of good quality water, the presence of steep terrain and relatively small areas for growing at altitudes which have suitable climatic conditions for growing temperate crops.

With high population centers creating strong demands for high quality products normally not obtained from conventional soil culture, superior quality, clean, hydroponically-grown crops find the marketplace willing to pay a premium price. This higher return for products grown hydroponically can justify the high initial capi-

Fig. 7.47 Portable Steam Sterilizer.

Fig. 7.48 Steam sterilization of sand culture beds using a canvas tarpaulin cover.

(Courtesy of Hidroponias Venezolanas, S.A., Caracas, Venezuela).

```
°C          °F
100   ─┼─   212
       ┼
              — Few resistant weed seeds
              — Resistant plant viruses

93.3  ─┼─   200

87.8  ─┼─   190

82.2  ─┼─   180

76.7  ─┼─   170 — Most weed seeds

71.1  ─┼─   160 — All plant pathogenic bacteria
                 — Most plant viruses

65.5  ─┼─   150 — Soil insects

                 — Most plant pathogenic fungi

60.0  ─┼─   140 — Most plant pathogenic bacteria

                 — Worms, slugs, centipedes
                 — Gladiolus yellows Fusarium
54.4  ─┼─   130 — Botrytis gray mold

                 — Rhizoctonia solani
                 — Sclerotium rolfsii and Sclerotinia sclerotiorum
48.9  ─┼─   120 — Nematodes

                 — Water molds

43.3  ─┼─   110

37.8  ─┼─   100
```

Fig. 7.49 Soil temperatures required to kill weed seeds, insects, and various plant pathogens. Temperatures given are for 30 minutes under moist conditions. From: University of California Division of Agricultural Sciences, Manual 23 (4).

Fig. 7.50 Carnations grow well in sand culture in the tropics. (Courtesy of Hidroponias Venezolanas, S.A., Caracas, Venezuela.)

Fig. 7.51 A healthy crop of head lettuce grown in sand culture in the tropics. (Courtesy of Hidroponias Venezolanas, S.A., Caracas, Venezuela.)

Fig. 7.52 High Quality Head Lettuce Produced from Sand Culture in the Tropics. (Courtesy of Hidroponias Venezolanas, S.A., Caracas, Venezuela).

tal costs of establishing a hydroponic farm in tropical countries. It will support imported technology required for successful operation of hydroponics and training of local workers.

The intense solar radiation in tropical countries produces high-yielding crops as long as they can be protected from torrential rainstorms. By choosing the correct altitudes, optimum temperatures can be encountered for growth of the crops. Since any structures need function only for protection of crops from rainstorms and not for heating or cooling, very simple inexpensive covers can be used from locally available materials as much as possible to reduce overall capital costs. With natural ventilation for cooling and no heating system the use of energy from electricity or fossil fuels is minimal. Low cost labour combined with low energy costs of operating a hydroponics farm in the tropics and high prices for produce all contribute to high profits. For this reason, while the initial struggle to overcome many problems and frustrations in establishing a hydroponic operation seem immense, eventual success will lead to handsome returns on the investment.

When all problems were resolved each hydroponic bed 2½ meters by 20 meters by 25 centimeters deep (7.4 ft by 65.6 ft by 9.8 in deep) was capable of producing 310 to 330 head of lettuce each averaging 1 kilogram in weight (fig. 7.52). In a continuous cropping system, new plants were sown every day so that harvesting could be done at least three times a week. In this way the market can be supplied year-round. Consistent supply to the marketplace is essential if long-term contracts are to be met. This reliable servicing of the market is the basis for establishing a strong market with a constant premium price to be received for the hydroponic products.

Lettuce takes between 65 and 70 days from seeding to harvest. Therefore, yearly production of one hydroponic bed would be five crops of on an average of 320 heads or 1670 heads of lettuce annually. With an average wholesale price paid year round for high quality head lettuce in Caracas about $2.00, the annual gross sales per bed would be $3340. The return per square foot of growing area would be $6.89.

The return per square foot for lettuce in North America greenhouses is about $1.50 to $2.00. The gross sales revenue in Venezuela can be three to four times that obtained in North American greenhouses. In addition, since no heating is required and labour is much cheaper in Venezuela, net profits would be six to eight times that of a similar crop grown under greenhouses in North America.

This profit differential between North American and South American growing of vegetable and flower crops hydroponically is the impetus needed to cope with the economic, political and agricultural problems that must be contended with in South America. Once established, hydroponic growing of certain crops offers an attractive return on investment in many tropical countries where arable land is scarce and strong markets exist.

References

Fontes, M.R. 1973. Controlled-environment horticulture in the Arabian Desert at Abu Dhabi. *HortScience* 8:13–16.

Hodges, C. N. and C. O. Hodge. 1971. An integrated system for providing power, water and food for desert coasts. *HortScience* 6:30–33.

Jensen, M. H. 1971. The use of polyethylene barriers between soil and growing medium in greenhouse vegetable production. *Proc. 10th National Agr. Plastics Conf.*, Chicago, Ill., Nov. 2-4, 1971. Ed. J. W. Courter, pp. 144-50.

Jensen, M. H. and N. G. Hicks. 1973. Exciting future for sand culture. *Am. Veg. Grower*, November 1973, pp. 33, 34, 72, 74.

Jensen, M. H., H. M. Eisa and M. Fontes. 1973. The pride of Abu Dhabi. *Am. Veg. Grower*, November 1973, pp. 35, 68, 70.

Jensen, M. H. and Marco Antanio Teran R. 1971. Use of controlled environment for vegetable production in desert regions of the world. *HortScience* 6:33–36.

Massey, P. H., Jr., and Yasin Kamal. 1974. Kuwait's greenhouse oasis. *Am. Veg. Grower,* June 1974, pp. 28, 30.

New, L. and R. E. Roberts. 1973. *Automatic drip irrigation for greenhouse tomato production.* Texas A & M Univ. Ext. bulletin MP-1082.

Chapter 8

Sawdust Culture

8.1 Introduction

Sawdust culture is especially popular in areas having a large forest industry such as the West Coast of Canada and the Pacific Northwest of the United States. In British Columbia, Canada, the Canada Department of Agriculture Research Station at Saanichton carried out extensive research for a number of years to develop a sawdust culture system for greenhouse crops (Maas and Adamson 1971). The need for a soilless culture system became evident with increased soil-borne nematode infestations and diseases coupled with poor soil structure which made the profits from greenhouse crops very marginal. Today, in British Columbia close to 80 percent of all greenhouses use some form of soilless culture for vegetable and flower production. Vegetable growers usually use sawdust culture while flower producers use a peat-sand-pumice mixture.

8.2 The Growing Medium

Sawdust was adopted as a growing medium in the coastal region of British Columbia because of its low cost, light weight and availability. A moderately fine sawdust or one with a good proportion of planer shavings is preferred, because moisture spreads better laterally through these than in coarse sawdust.

Sawdust from Douglas fir (*Pseudotsuga menziesii* [Mirb.] Franco) and western hemlock (*Tsuga heterophylla* [Raf.] Sarg.) were found to give best results (Maas and Adamson 1971). Western red cedar (*Thuja plicata* D.) is toxic and should never be used.

291

While other media such as sphagnum peat, ground fir bark, and mixtures of sawdust with sand and/or peat were tested successfully, they are more expensive and therefore might be used if sawdust is unavailable.

One precaution that should be taken with sawdust is that of determining its sodium chloride content. Logs are floated in barges on the ocean and often remain in the water for many months before going to the sawmill. They will absorb sea water over this time and thus acquire salt (sodium chloride) levels toxic to plants. Therefore as soon as the sawdust is received samples should be taken and the sodium chloride content tested. If any significant amount of sodium chloride is found (greater than 10 ppm) the sawdust should be thoroughly leached with pure fresh water once it is placed in the beds, but before planting. This leaching process may take up to a week in order to reduce the sodium chloride to an acceptable level.

8.3 Bed System

The growing beds are usually constructed of rough cedar and lined with black polyethylene or vinyl similar to those designs discussed under sand culture (fig. 8.1). Rough cedar 1 by 8 inches can be used for the sides. Either a V-bottom or round-bottom bed configuration may be used (fig. 8.1). The depth of the beds should be 10 to 12 inches. A 2-inch drain pipe should be placed on the bottom of the bed. Beds are usually 24 inches wide, however 20-inch wide beds (inside dimension) have been found to be adequate with 32-inch pathways between the beds (fig. 8.2). Studies by Maas and Adamson (1971) have shown that even somewhat narrower and shallower beds, with a volume of ⅓ cubic foot of medium per plant, are satisfactory. If narrower beds are used, the pathways should be widened to provide the same total amount of greenhouse space for each plant, as light requirements for the plants are the same regardless of the ability of the volume of medium required to provide adequate nutrition.

An alternative to these standard bed designs is the use of sloped-bottom beds (fig. 8.1). In this case the beds are constructed of rough cedar 1 by 8 inches on one side and 1 by 12 inches on the other side. The 1-by-12-inch lumber is covered with the liner on the inside face and around the top and bottom edges. The 1-by-8-inch lumber is covered with the liner on one face and then extends on a slope toward the wide side. But a small gap (¼ inch) or the

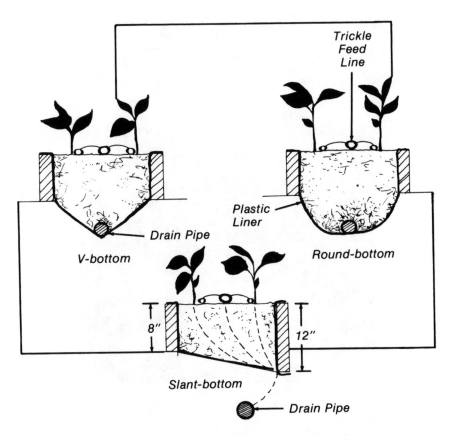

Fig. 8.1. Cross sections of sawdust culture beds.

extension of the liner underneath the wide side allows drainage of excess solution to a drainage pipe located several feet below the beds (fig. 8.1). The drain pipes are installed when the site is leveled prior to the construction of the greenhouse. In this case standard perforated plastic drain pipe is used. It is placed in a ditch dug by an automatic ditch-digging machine (Ditch Witch). When a fine texture (clay loam) soil is present, a filtering material (blinding) placed above and around the pipe will prevent clogging of the holes in the pipe (fig. 8.3). The best material is a composition of varied particle sizes: coarse sand, to fine sand, pea gravel. The material should be installed to a depth of approximately 6 to 8 inches above and around the tile.

Fig. 8.2. Tomato crop in sawdust beds. Note the location of heating pipes and trickle irrigation feed lines. (Courtesy of Seaport Greenhouses Ltd., Vancouver, Canada.)

8.4 Bag System

An alternative to beds is the use of polyethylene bags filled with sawdust (fig. 8.4). Regular "kitchen" garbage bags (1.25 mil thickness, 20 by 26 inches) can be used. Drainage holes must be punched in the bottom to allow good drainage. The bags are often set on top of a poly sheet to prevent any roots growing out of the drainage holes from contacting the underlying soil. Depending upon the bag size, up to three plants may be grown in each bag. The three-plant bags are placed in a single row but the plants are positioned in the bags and trained vertically (e.g., tomatoes) so as to make two rows.

In the growing of European cucumbers bags are set in a single row, then every other bag is planted with one plant (fig. 8.5). These are trained on a sloping trellis. Once this first crop nears completion, new transplants are placed in the alternate empty bags and the process of using alternate bags is repeated after replacing or sterilizing the medium of those plants just removed. In this way up to six short cucumber crops can be grown annually.

A modification of the bag system involves the use of five-gallon plastic pots in place of the polyethylene garbage bags. The use of pots eliminates the cost of replacing the bags annually. Sawdust, sand, pea gravel or a mixture of peat-sand-sawdust may be used as medium in pots. A trickle feeding system must be used with pot culture. If sawdust is used, it is important to spread about ½-inch (1 cm) of sand over the surface to achieve better lateral movement of nutrient solution as it is applied to the surface by the trickle feed system. The use of a shallow layer of sand on top of sawdust applies to bag culture also, to prevent coning of the nutrient solution through the plant roots.

Pots have several advantages over bags. Plastic patio pots, commonly used in the nursery container industry, can be re-used for

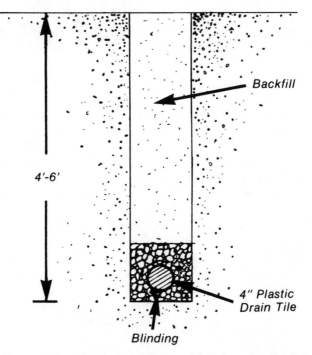

Fig. 8.3. Cross section of a drainage ditch and 4-inch perforated drain pipe.

Fig. 8.4. Bag system of sawdust culture growing tomatoes.
Fig. 8.5. European cucumbers growing in a bag system of sawdust culture.

three to four years. If sawdust is used, it can be emptied from the pots into a pile and easily sterilized by use of steam or chemicals between crops. Even if the medium is discarded annually, pots lend themselves to efficient handling when filling them with new medium. They can be filled by use of mechanized potting machines such as those used in the nursery industry. With such equipment six people can fill and plant over 5000 pots per day. Filling plastic bags is much slower and more difficult. Plastic bags, unlike pots, cannot be easily transported to the greenhouse facilities. Plastic pots of 5-gallon size, having volume of growing medium similar to plastic bags, will produce equally healthy plants (figs. 8.6, 8.7).

Since plastic pots have drainage holes, it is important to closely monitor the amount of nutrient solution applied to be certain that no more than 10 percent waste occurs. Pots, like bags, should be placed on plastic sheets so that roots will not grow into the under-lying medium. If pea gravel is used as the medium, the plastic

Fig. 8.7). Plastic patio pots in vinyl-lined bed for lettuce and tomatoes in a backyard greenhouse.

Fig. 8.6. Five-gallon plastic patio pots filled with pea gravel growing bibblettuce and tomato plants. Trickle feed system.

underlay sheets could be arranged to conduct excess nutrient solution back to the nutrient reservoir. Shallow troughs may be built to house the pots. This arrangement is particularly useful for small systems as used in backyard greenhouses (fig. 8.7). The plastic underlay sheets should be black in color in order to prevent algae growth.

A recent development in sawdust culture is the use of white polyethylene bags similar in dimensions to those used in rockwool culture (fig. 8.8). Bags of approximately 8-10 inches (20-25 cm) wide by 2 feet (60 cm) long by 3-4 inches (8-10 cm) thick are filled with sawdust by a machine and then heat-sealed on the ends. Bags are manufactured by a local company at a cost of about CAN$0.13 (US$0.10). Holes are punched in the bags by the manufacturer for drainage. These bags are particularly suitable for the growing of tomatoes. Each bag contains two tomato plants.

Fig. 8.8. Sawdust culture bags with rockwool cube growing tomato seedling sitting on top. (Courtesy of Gipaanda Greenhouses Ltd., Surrey, B.C., Canada).

Seedlings are started in rockwool plugs, which are transplanted into rockwool blocks, which are then placed into the sawdust bags, similar to rockwool culture. For an early crop (crops seeded by mid-December) the growing blocks are placed on top of the sawdust bags, but not allowed to root out until one flower truss sets fruit. Then holes are cut below the blocks in the plastic bag and the blocks set into the holes.

In British Columbia, where light is limited during the winter months, when tomato seedlings are started it is advisable to use high intensity discharge (HID) sodium vapour 400-watt lights to give 5500 lux (510 foot-candles) intensity at plant surface with a 20-hour photoperiod. Seedlings should be grown under this propagation section of the greenhouse until they are ready for transplanting into the bags. Seedlings are generally sown in mid-December and transplanted in mid-January.

The greenhouse floor is lined with white polyethylene to prevent contact of the roots growing from the bags with the underlying soil. The white polyethylene also serves to reflect light (much needed during the winter months) and seal out any insect and disease organisms present in the underlying soil. Similar to rockwool culture, the floor is sloped to create a swale between each set of two rows of bags for drainage of excess solution out of the greenhouse. Hot water heating pipes conducting heat from a central boiler are laid in the aisles between the double rows of bags (fig. 8.9). The heating pipes also serve as a track for a mobile harvesting-plant maintenance cart to run on (fig. 8.10).

Each plant is fed individually using a sphaghetti trickle feed line placed on the rockwool block in the sawdust bag. The irrigation line runs the length of the rows between each set of two rows

Fig. 8.9. Sawdust culture with hot water heating pipes in aisle next to rows of tomato plants. Note the white poly ground cover on the floor.

Fig. 8.10. Mobile harvesting-working cart running on heating pipes. (Courtesy of Gipaanda Greenhouses Ltd., Surrey, B.C., Canada).

of bags (fig. 8.11). The nutrient solution is pumped from a central injector system using stock solution tanks. Carbon dioxide enrichment is also distributed to the plants by a small polyethylene conduction tube running the length of the beds between each set of two rows of plants (fig. 8.11). The carbon dioxide is generated as a by-product of combustion of natural gas from the central boilers and is piped to each greenhouse (fig. 8.12).

Tomatoes are harvested into 25 pound (11 kg) plastic tote bins (fig. 8.13) using the mobile carts running on the heating pipes. Pollination, suckering, tying string supports, etc. are all made easier by use of a mechanically raised platform running on the heating pipes. Harvested tomatoes in tote bins are moved using a pallet jack (fig. 8.14). Peppers have also been grown successfully using sawdust bags.

In British Columbia, the most common tomato variety used is Dombito. With the sawdust culture system, generally one crop a year of tomatoes is grown. Seeding in mid-December with production beginning by late March and continuing until November.

Plant density of about 8000 plants per acre (20,000 plants/hectare) produces an average of 110-130 tons/acre (255-300 tonnes/hectare). This plant density is 5.45 square feet of greenhouse area per plant, producing 5 to 6 pounds/square foot (25-30

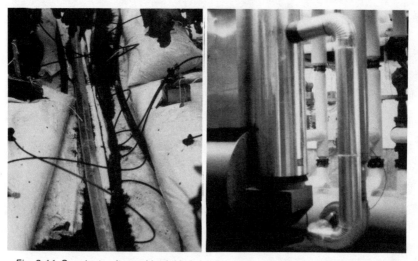

Fig. 8.11. Sawdust culture with trickle irrigation lines to each plant. Carbon dioxide is released through a small polyethylene tube between the rows.

Fig. 8.12. Carbon dioxide recovery unit attached to central boiler. (Courtesy of Gipaanda Greenhouses Ltd., Surrey, B.C., Canada).

Fig. 8.15. A 20-pound case of greenhouse-grown tomatoes packaged by the B.C. Greenhouse Vegetable Growers Cooperative.

Fig. 8.14. A pallet jack is used to transport palletized tote bins to the packing area of the greenhouses. (Courtesy of Gipaanda Greenhouses Ltd., Surrey, B.C., Canada).

Fig. 8.13. Tomatoes are harvested into plastic tote bins. (Courtesy of Gipaanda Greenhouses Ltd., Surrey, B.C., Canada).

kg/sq m). The best growers produce up to 160 tons/acre (370 tonnes/hectare) or 37 kilograms/square meter. This is equivalent to 42 pounds (19 kg) per plant per year. Tomatoes and cucumbers are marketed through a greenhouse vegetable cooperative in British Columbia. The cooperative sells the boxes to the growers, grades, packs, and markets the produce at a cost of about CAN$2.50 (US$1.90) per 20-pound case, in 1986 (fig. 8.15).

8.5 Nutrient Solution Distribution System

In both the bed and bag systems of sawdust culture a trickle irrigation system is used to supply the water and nutrient requirements of the plants (fig. 8.2). As pointed out in Chapter 7, adequately sized main headers and valves are needed to balance the flow to the row headers. Row headers are usually made of ¾-inch plastic hose, which can handle 200 (0.045 inch inside diameter) feeding tubes. Row headers of ½-inch and 1-inch sizes can supply 100 and 300 feeding tubes, respectively.

In the bed system spaghetti feeders, ooze hoses or emitters may be used, but in the bag system spaghetti feeders or emitters are best adapted, due to the distances between bags.

The plants are supplied with nutrient solution directly from a dilute-solution storage tank or through a fertilizer proportioner from containers of concentrated solutions, as described for sand culture. The dilute-solution system needs a storage tank, a pump, and a distribution system, as outlined in figure 8.16.

Determine the capacity of the tank from the number of plants to be fed at one time. The tank should be able to supply at least 1 quart (1 liter) of solution per feeding for each plant for 1 week's total feeding requirements. The total volume needed depends upon the number of irrigation cycles required, which in turn is a function of weather conditions, plant maturity and the nature of the plant. Some growers install more than one tank so that they can prepare the nutrient solution at least a day in advance of the estimated time of depletion of the other tank. In this way the recently made nutrient solution can be heated for at least 12 hours by an immersion heater to bring its temperature to an optimum level (65 to 70°F.) before it is applied to the plants.

Wooden tanks may be constructed of ¾-inch plywood and lined with vinyl or 6-mil polyethylene. Vinyl is a better liner than polyethylene since it does not puncture easily and can be easily repaired with a common swimming pool repair kit should a hole develop.

Fuel oil or gas storage tanks may also be used, but with caution because of the possibility of an explosion if any gases remain in used tanks. These tanks must have a manhole opening cut and holes drilled and tapped for pipe connections. Several coats of epoxy resin or asphaltum should be painted on the inside and one coat on the outside of steel tanks to prevent corrosion and/or rust by the nutrient solution. Also, tanks may be made of concrete and lined with asphalt paint. Large fiberglass tanks, with no corrosion problem, are available commercially. It is a good idea to install an agitator inside the tank to facilitate the mixing of the fertilizers and their dissolution in water. The tank should be supplied with a 50-mesh screen filter at the inlet end to the feeding system and the means for easy cleaning and draining (fig. 8.16). Such tanks should be located in headerhouses near boilers and water supply.

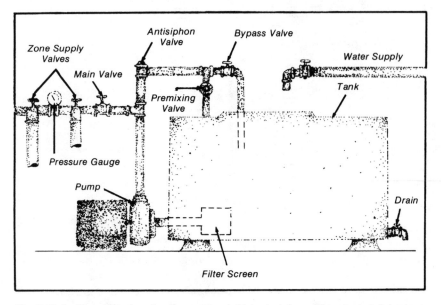

Fig. 8.16 A dilute-solution feeding system. (Adapted from Mason and Adamson, *Trickle Watering and Liquid Feeding System.*)

The distribution system consists of supply lines, main headers, row headers (laterals), leader tubes (spaghetti lines) or emitters, fittings, and controls (fig. 8.17). Gate valves should be installed in the main supply lines so that you have the option of controlling the feed supply to each greenhouse in the range. In this way, you can vary the flow to each house if there are differences between houses in the volume requirements of the plants.

To obtain a more uniform distribution, particularly in green-houses over 100 feet (31 meters) long, locate two main headers

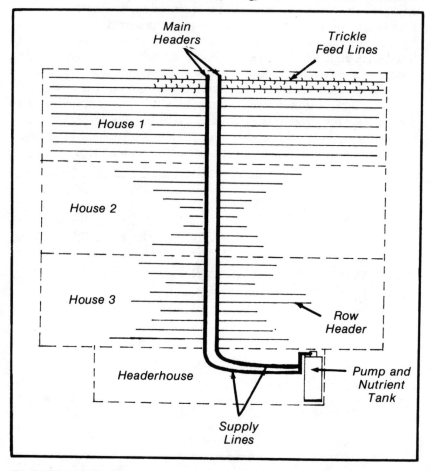

Fig. 8.17 Distribution system layout with main headers on either side of a central aisle with separate supply line from a distributing manifold. (Adapted from Mason and Adamson, *Trickle Watering and Liquid Feeding System.*)

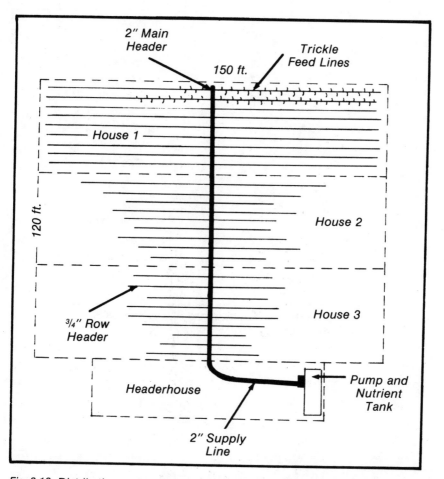

Fig. 8.18 Distribution system layout with a single main header centrally located across the greenhouse. All greenhouses must be level, otherwise separate supply lines at different levels are needed. (Adapted from Mason and Adamson, *Trickle Watering and Liquid Feeding System.*)

in the middle of the greenhouse and extend the row headers from them (fig. 8.17). Or you can install a single main header (fig. 8.18) and connect the row headers (laterals) directly (fig. 8.19a), to a hose Y-fitting with a riser from the main header (fig. 8.19b), or to a sub-main header which is connected to the main header and located underground close to the main header. It is best to bring the main header so that the walkway is unobstructed (fig. 8.20).

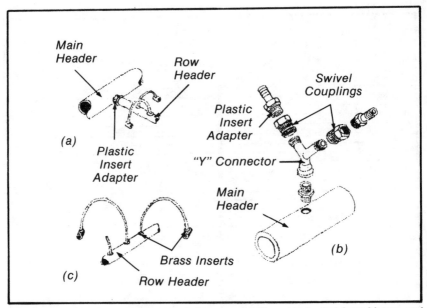

Fig. 8.19 Distribution system pipe, tubing, and fittings. (Adapted from Mason and Adamson, *Trickle Watering and Liquid Feeding System.*)

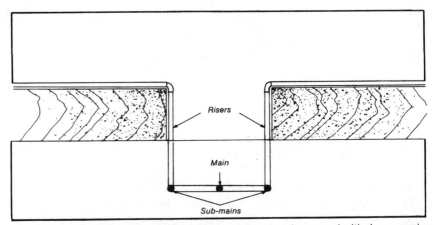

Fig. 8.20 Main header with sub-main headers placed underground with risers coming up from sub-mains to laterals along beds.

Select the main supply pipe and the main header sizes carefully, taking into consideration future expansion. For efficient operation of medium-volume low-pressure pumps, a total friction loss of 25 psi should not be exceeded. For example, the friction loss in 100 feet (31 meters) of 2-inch (5-centimeter) pipe with a flow rate of 60 Imp. gallons (273 liters)/minute is 3.8 psi, whereas in the same length of 1½-inch (3.8-centimeter) pipe at the same flow rate, it is 13 psi, which is impractical, since in 200 feet the total friction loss

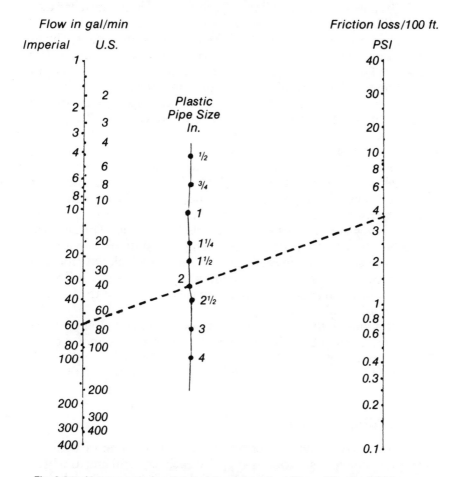

Fig. 8.21 Nomograph for determining pipe size. For a "flow" of 60 Imp. gal/min., and a total friction loss of 3.8 psi/100ft. a suitable pipe diameter is 2 inches. (Adapted from Mason and Adamson, *Trickle Watering and Liquid Feeding System.*)

of 25 psi would be exceeded. A nomograph such as the one in figure 8.21, available from most plastic pipe suppliers, can be used to determine pipe size. By calculating the total friction loss in the supply pipes and the main headers, including couplings and insert fittings, and adding the pressure required at the row headers (usually 1 to 2 psi) and using the total flow requirements in gallons per minute the suitable pipe diameter may be determined from the nomograph.

High spots in the header (lateral) lines should be avoided because trapped air will reduce the flow rate in the system. Install insert adapters with caps at the ends of the main headers for easy flushing. Lateral lines of ½-inch (1.3-centimeter) pipe can supply 150 tubes, at 1 or 2 psi; however, this size is harder to install and keep in position and less troublefree in operation than a ¾-inch (1.9-centimeter) pipe, which is the most suitable size for up to 300 leader tubes. This pipe delivers 20 fluid ounces (0.59 liters) per leader tube at a pressure of 2 psi in 10 minutes or at 1 psi in 13 minutes. To provide for flushing out the row headers (laterals), install an insert adapter and a cap at the ends.

Spaghetti tubes of 0.045-inch (1.1 millimeter) inside diameter are usually cut in lengths of 12 to 15 inches (31 to 38 centimeters). Sloping cuts should be made on the ends to prevent sealing off the tubes if they are inserted too far into the row header. For uniform distribution, cut them all the same length. Install brass inserts in the row header opposite each plant in the 12 o'clock position. An important advantage of this system is the almost instant flow of nutrient solution as soon as the pump is started, since the headers remain full of solution.

At the end of the season, spot check the terminal end of the spaghetti tubes. If there has been a buildup of salts or root growth into them, cut off enough of the tip to clear the inside of the tube (usually ¼ inch). Thoroughly flush the whole system with clean water.

8.6 Feeding Methods

There are two methods of feeding the plants, one in which a complete nutrient solution is supplied each day, and one in which most of the nutrients are mixed with the growing medium before planting.

In the complete nutrient solution method all nutrients are supplied either directly from a storage tank or from concentrated stock solutions passed through an injector. The Saanichton Research Station has prepared formulas to make 600 gallons of diluted nutrient solution (table 8.1). Their formulas are especially suited to Canadian West Coast and U.S. Pacific Northwest conditions.

In the fertilizer premix method the phosphorus, calcium, magnesium, and minor elements are mixed with the medium before each crop is planted. Only nitrogen and potassium are applied throughout the season in a nutrient solution (table 8.2). They state that this method avoids the hazard of precipitation of incompatible fertilizers and reduces the labor required in preparing the nutrient solution. For the spring crop (tomatoes), they recommend incorporating 2.4 ounces of 19 percent superphosphate (0-19-0), 4 ounces

TABLE 8.1 Fertilizers Used in Preparing 600 Imp. Gallons of Complete Nutrient Solution at Three Nitrogen Levels, with Phosphorus at 37 ppm of P (84 ppm P_2O_5), and Potassium at 208 ppm of K (252 ppm of K_2O) for Tomatoes

	Nitrogen Levels		
	126 ppm (up to first truss set)	168 ppm (first to third truss set)	210 ppm (after third truss set)
A			
Potassium chloride (0-0-60)	40 oz	23 oz	nil
Potassium nitrate (13-0-44)	nil	23 oz	55 oz
Magnesium sulfate (Epsom salts)	48 oz	48 oz	48 oz
B			
Diammonium phosphate (21-53-0)	15 oz	15 oz	15 oz
C			
Calcium nitrate (15.5-0-0)	58 oz	64 oz	64 oz
Minor element solution*	20 fl oz	20 fl oz	20 fl oz

*To prepare the minor element solution, dissolve 12 ounces of dry minor element mix in 1 Imperial gallon of boiling water and store in a dark bottle. Twelve ounces of minor element mix contains 57 g boric acid, 72 g manganese sulfate, 9 g zinc sulfate, 3 g copper sulfate, 1 g molybdic acid, and 200 g ferric citrate.
Source: Maas, E. F. and R. M. Adamson. 1971. *Soilless culture of commercial greenhouse tomatoes*. Can. Dept. Agric. Publ. 1460.

TABLE 8.2   Fertilizers Used in Preparing 600 Imp. Gallons of Nitrogen-Potassium Solution at Three Nitrogen Levels and Potassium at 208 ppm of K (252 ppm of K$_2$O) for Tomatoes

	Nitrogen Levels		
	126 ppm (up to first truss set)	168 ppm (first to third truss set)	210 ppm (after third truss set)
Potassium nitrate (13-0-44)	55 oz	55 oz	55 oz
Ammonium nitrate (34-0-0)	14 oz	26 oz	38 oz

Source: Maas, E. F. and R. M. Adamson. 1971. *Soilless culture of commercial greenhouse tomatoes.* Can. Dept. Agric. Publ. 1460.

of dolomite limestone and 1 fluid ounce of minor element solution into each cubic foot of sawdust. To obtain a more uniform admixture of the minor elements, dilute 1 fluid ounce of minor element solution with 3 fluid ounces of water and blend with 1 pint of dry sawdust before incorporating into the medium. The directions for preparing the minor element solution are given in the footnote to table 8.1. If the sawdust is to be reused for a fall crop of tomatoes, apply the premix fertilizers and minor elements at one-half the spring rate.

8.7 Watering and Salt Buildup

When conductivity tests show salt levels above 4 millimhos/cm, plant growth may be suppressed. Salt buildup can be prevented by applying the nutrient solution at a volume 5 percent greater than the requirements of the plants, and allowing the excess solution to drain freely from the bottom of the bed. If salt levels are found to be too high, dilute the nutrient solution by one-quarter and increase the volume by one-third or apply pure water for several days until the conductivity level is reduced sufficiently. The foregoing information has been adapted from several publications by Maas and Adamson (1971) and Mason and Adamson (1973). Further details should be obtained from these publications, which are listed in the bibliography.

8.8 Small-Scale Sawdust Culture Systems

A single home unit can be constructed similar to sand cultural home units. It should consist of a growing tray, a nutrient reservoir, and trickle feeding system operated by a pump on a time clock (fig. 8.22).

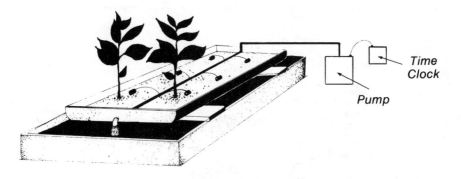

Fig. 8.22 A simple small-scale trickle sawdust culture system.

A small-scale operation can be set up by the use of a trickle feeding system and the bag system of sawdust culture (fig. 8.23). This can be made any size by simply increasing the number of growing bags. It could even be used outdoors for growing vegetables during the summer months in the northerly latitudes. If facilities are not available for sterilizing the sawdust between crops, simply put it in the compost pile and the next season use new sawdust.

8.9 Advantages and Disadvantages of Sawdust Culture

Here are the advantages.

1. Since it, like sand culture, is an open system there is less chance of spread of disease such as *Fusarium* and *Verticillium* wilts, especially in tomatoes.

2. No problem of plugging of drainage pipes with roots.

3. Good lateral movement of nutrient solution throughout the root zone.

4. Good root aeration.

5. A new nutrient solution is added each irrigation cycle.

6. The system is simple, easy to maintain and repair.

7. The high water retention of the sawdust reduces any risk of rapid water stress should a pump fail.

8. It is adaptable to fertilizer injectors and therefore less space for tanks is required.

9. Sawdust has been relatively inexpensive and readily available in areas of extensive forest industries.

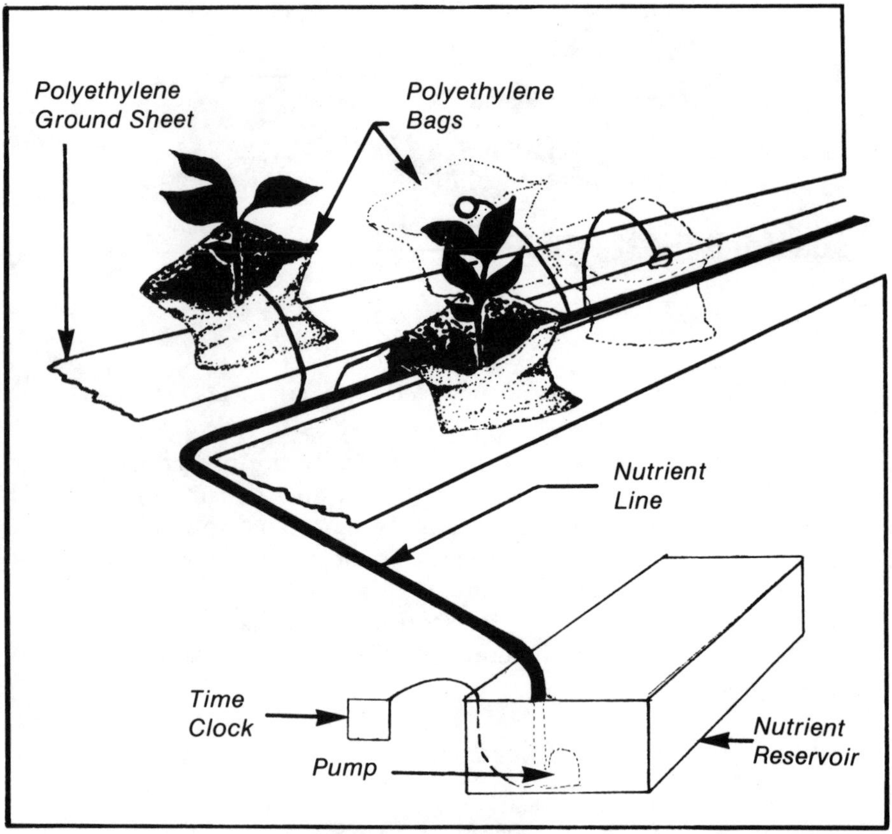

Fig. 8.23 A home unit using sawdust bag culture system.

Here are the disadvantages.

1. It is only applicable to areas having a major forest industry; therefore, it is not feasible to use in arid desert countries.

2. It must be steam or chemically sterilized.

3. The availability of good sawdust, even in areas with an extensive forest industry, is decreasing.

4. Initially, there can be problems of sodium chloride toxicity to plants if the medium is not well leached before planting.

5. Over the cropping season salt accumulation can occur in the medium to levels toxic to the plants. This toxicity can be reduced by leaching with pure water.

6. Plugging of trickle feed lines may occur if proper filters are not used or if cleaning of these filters is neglected.

7. If the sawdust used is very coarse, coning of water may occur, causing roots to grow downward rather than laterally.

8. As sawdust is organic in nature, it decomposes with time. Between crops it must be rototilled and a proportion of new sawdust added to make up for that decomposed and that lost on plant roots during the pulling of the plants at the end of each crop.

REFERENCES
Maas, E. F. and R. M. Adamson. 1971. *Soilless culture of commercial greenhouse tomatoes*. Can. Dept. Agric. Publ. 1460.

Mason, E. B. B. and R. M. Adamson. 1973. *Trickle watering and liquid feeding system for greenhouse crops*. Can. Dept. Agric. Publ. 1510.

Chapter 9

Other Soilless Cultures

9.1 Introduction

Many other methods of soilless culture are being used successfully. Some of the media used are peat, vermiculite, perlite, pumice, and plastic styrofoam. Often mixtures of these media are used in various proportions. Growing trials with various mixtures determine which proportions are most suitable to the plants in question. For example, flowering potted plants such as chrysanthemums, poinsettias and Easter lilies and tropical foliage plants can be grown well in mixtures of peat-sand-pumice in a 2:1:2 ratio.

9.2 Media

9.2.1 Peat

Peat consists of partially decomposed aquatic, marsh, bog, or swamp vegetation. The composition of different peat deposits varies widely, depending upon the vegetation from which it originated, state of decomposition, mineral content and degree of acidity (Lucas et al. 1971; Patek 1965).

Of the three types of peat—moss peat (peat moss), reed sedge, and peat humus—peat moss is the least decomposed and is derived from sphagnum, hypnum, or other mosses. It has a high moisture-holding capacity (10 times its dry weight), is high in acidity (pH of 3.8 to 4.5) and contains a small amount of nitrogen (about 1.0 percent) but little or no phosphorus or potassium. Peat from hypnum and other kinds of mosses breaks down rapidly, as compared with sphagnum, and is not as desirable. Peat from sedges, reeds, and other swamp plants also decomposes rapidly.

314

Sphagnum moss is the dehydrated young residue or living portions of acid-bog plants in the genus *Sphagnum*, such as S. *papillosum*, S. *capillacium*, and S. *palustre*. It is relatively sterile, light in weight, and has a very high water-holding capacity. It is generally shredded before being used as a growing medium.

9.2.2 Vermiculite

This is a micaceous mineral which is expanded when heated in furnaces at temperatures near 2000°F. The water turns to steam, popping the layers apart, forming small, porous, sponge-like kernels. Heating to this temperature gives complete sterilization. Chemically, it is a hydrated magnesium-aluminum-iron silicate. When expanded, it is very light in weight (6 to 10 pounds per cubic foot), neutral in reaction with good buffering properties, and insoluble in water. It is able to absorb large quantities of water— 3 to 4 gallons per cubic foot. It has a relatively high cation exchange capacity and thus can hold nutrients in reserve and later release them. It contains some magnesium and potassium which is available to plants.

Horticultural vermiculite is graded in four sizes: No. 1 has particles from 5 to 8 millimeters in diameter; No. 2, the regular horticultural grade, from 2 to 3 millimeters; No. 3, from 1 to 2 millimeters, and No. 4, which is most useful as a seed-germinating medium, from 0.75 to 1 millimeter. Expanded vermiculite should not be pressed or compacted when wet, as this will destroy its desirable porous structure.

9.2.3 Perlite

Perlite is a silicaceous material of volcanic origin, mined from lava flows. The crude ore is crushed and screened, then heated in furnaces to about 1400°F., at which temperature the small amount of moisture in the particles changes to steam, expanding the particles to small, sponge-like kernels which are very light, weighing only 5 to 8 pounds per cubic foot. The high processing temperature gives a sterile product. A particle size of $1/16$ to $1/8$ inch in diameter is usually used in horticultural applications. Perlite will hold 3 to 4 times its weight of water. It is essentially neutral with a pH of 6.0 to 8.0 but with no buffering capacity; unlike vermiculite, it has no cation exchange capacity and contains no mineral nutrients. It is most useful in increasing aeration in a mixture since it has a very rigid structure. While it does not decay, the particle size can become smaller by fracturing as it is handled. A fine grade is useful primarily for seed germination, while a coarser type or horticultural grade is best suited for mixing with peat, in equal parts, for propagation or with mixtures of peat and sand for growing plants.

9.2.4 Pumice

Pumice, like perlite, is a silicaceous material of volcanic origin. It, however, is the crude ore after crushing and screening without any heating process. It has essentially the same properties as perlite, but is heavier and does not absorb water as readily since it has not been hydrated. It is used in mixtures of peat and sand for the growing of potted plants.

9.2.5 Soilless Mixtures

Most mixtures contain some combination of sand, peat, perlite, pumice and vermiculite. The specific proportions of each used depends upon the plants grown. Some useful mixtures are:

1. peat:perlite:sand   2:2:1 for potted plants
2. peat:perlite   1:1 for propagation of cuttings
3. peat:sand   1:1 for propagation of cuttings and for potted plants
4. peat:sand   1:3 for bedding plants and nursery container-grown stocks
5. peat:vermiculite   1:1 for propagation of cuttings
6. peat:sand   3:1 light weight, excellent aeration, for pots and beds, good for azaleas, gardenias and camellias which like acid conditions
7. vermiculite:perlite   1:1 light weight, good for propagation of cuttings
8. peat:pumice:sand   2:2:1 for potted plants

In general pumice, which costs less, may be substituted for perlite in most mixes.

The most common mixtures are the U.C. mixes of peat and fine sand and the Cornell "Peat-Lite" mixes. The U.C. mixes were derived from the California Agricultural Experiment Station in Berkeley. The U.C. mixes vary from fine sand only to peat moss only, but the mixes that are used more commonly contain from 25 to 75 percent fine sand and 75 to 25 percent peat moss. These mixes are used for growing potted plants and container-grown nursery stock. The Peat-Lite mixes were devised by Cornell University, New York, from equal proportions of peat and vermiculite. They have been used primarily for seed germination, growing of transplants and for container growing of spring bedding plants and annuals. Some growers have used them to grow tomatoes commercially in beds similar to that of sawdust culture.

All the required minerals must be added to these mixes, and some or all of them are added at the time of mixing. The Cornell Peat-Lite mixes are considerably lighter in weight than the U.C. mixes, as either perlite or vermiculite weighs about one-tenth as much as fine sand. The Peat-Lite mixes are made from equal parts of sphagnum peat moss and either horticultural perlite or number 2 vermiculite.

The U.C. Mix. The basic fertilizer additions recommended for a U.C. mix of 50 percent fine sand and 50 percent moss are as follows (Matkin and Chandler 1957).

To each cubic yard of the mix, add
   2½ lb. hoof and horn or blood meal (13 percent nitrogen)
   4 oz. potassium nitrate
   4 oz. potassium sulfate
   2½ lb. single superphosphate
   7½ lb. dolomite lime
   2½ lb. calcium carbonate lime

The fine sand, peat moss, and fertilizer must be mixed together thoroughly. The peat moss should be moistened before mixing. As the crop grows, additional nitrogen and potassium fertilizer must be provided.

The Cornell "Peat-Lite" Mixes. Instructions for three Peat-Lite mixes are as follows (Boodley and Sheldrake 1964; Sheldrake and Boodley 1965).

   1. Peat-Lite Mix A (to make 1 cubic yard):
       11 bu. (88 U.S. gal.) sphagnum peat moss
       11 bu. (88 U.S. gal.) horticultural vermiculite No. 2 grade
       5 lb. ground limestone
       1 lb. superphosphate (20%)
       2 to 12 lb. 5-10-5 fertilizer

2. Peat-Lite Mix B:
    Same as A, except that horticultural perlite is
    substituted for the vermiculite
3. Peat-Lite Mix C (for germinating seeds):
    1 bu. (8 U.S. gal.) sphagnum peat moss
    1 bu. (8 U.S. gal.) horticultural vermiculite No. 4
    1½ oz. ammonium nitrate
    1½ oz. superphosphate (20%)
    7½ oz. ground limestone, dolomitic

The materials should be mixed thoroughly, with special attention given to wetting the peat moss during mixing. Adding a nonionic wetting agent, such as Aqua-Gro (1 ounce per 6 U.S. gallons water) to the initial wetting usually will aid in wetting the peat moss.

Fertilizer, Sphagnum Peat Moss and Vermiculite Mixture. The Vineland Research Station in Ontario, Canada (Sangster 1974), uses a slight modification in fertilizer ingredients for addition to a mixture of equal volumes of sphagnum peat moss and vermiculite (50:50 peat-vermiculite) per cubic yard as shown below.

1¾ 6-cu. ft. compressed bales	Sphagnum peat moss
2 6-cu. ft. bags	Horticultural vermiculite (No. 2)
12 lb.	Ground limestone (dolomitic)
5 lb.	Calcium sulfate (gypsum)
1.5 lb.	Calcium nitrate
2.5 lb.	20% superphosphate
8-10 lb.	Osmocote 18-6-12 (9 month)
6 oz.	Fritted trace elements (FTE 503)
1 oz.	Iron (chelated such as NaFe, 138 or 330)
0.5 lb.	Magnesium sulfate

Osmocote 18-6-12 provides a continuous supply of nitrogen, phosphorus, and potassium throughout the growing season. FTE 503 slowly releases iron, manganese, copper, zinc, boron, and molybdenum.

Mixing the fertilizer ingredients with the peat moss mixture can be done in several ways. Small volumes can be mixed with a shovel on a concrete floor. When mixing on a floor, first disinfect the floor area with a solution of 5 parts water to 1 part Javex (5.25 percent sodium hypochlorite). Spread the fertilizer evenly over the medium and turn the mix back and forth from one pile to another several times with a shovel. A large garbage can is useful for mixing a two-bushel batch. Scoop the mix into the garbage can, pour the mix back onto the floor, and repeat this procedure several times.

A large concrete mixer works well for mixing large amounts. Often commercial growers acquire a "ready-mix" unit from an old concrete truck. This unit can be mounted on a concrete slab and a motor attached to operate it. A series of conveyors can feed in ingredients and also pile the finished product in the potting area of the greenhouse.

If plastic-lined beds are used for the plants, the medium can be mixed directly in the beds. It can be mixed with a padded hoe, taking care not to rupture the plastic liner. For large greenhouses a "ready-mix" unit should be used, with conveyors conducting the finished product directly to the beds.

Dry peat is usually hard to wet. Adding two ounces of a nonionic wetting agent such as Aqua-Gro in ten gallons of water will help wet the peat in one cubic yard of mix. Micronutrients should be dissolved in water, which is then sprinkled over the medium or added directly to the concrete mixer while mixing. For a two-bushel batch the nutrients can be dissolved in one gallon of warm water and then sprinkled over the medium prior to mixing.

9.2.6 Synthetic Foams (Plastoponics)

Attempts are now being made in different parts of the world to develop a completely reproducible synthetic compost in which peat is replaced totally or in part by a synthetic foam which may be urea-formaldehyde, polyurethane or polystyrene.

Foams can be produced with varying proportions of open cells. The thickness of the cell walls and the size of the pores can be varied. This will affect the density of the foam and its water retention capacity. They are excellent aerators of soil and yet they can entrap large volumes of water per unit volume. For example, 1 pound of urea-formaldehyde foam will hold up to 12 gallons of water. The foams are very light and when used for a pot plant compost they must be weighted with dense inert particles such as sand.

Various foam-sand mixtures have been tested successfully in the growing of orchids, carnations, bulbs, numerous houseplants, and tomatoes (Cook 1971). They have also worked well as rooting blocks for the propagation of cuttings.

9.3 Ring Culture

Ring culture was originally developed in England for the growing of tomatoes. The plants are set into a round (8 to 10- inch diameter) ring of plastic film or tar paper filled with a sterile medium such as the Cornell Peat Lite or U.C. mixes. The rings have no top or bottom, and are spaced out on a bed of lightweight aggregate 4 to 6 inches deep. The beds containing the aggregate are lined with a plastic sheeting to prevent roots from penetrating into the infested soil beneath.

The basic difference between "ring" and "bed" culture is that in the bed method, the plants are simply set in a long, narrow trough filled with a growing medium. Both methods work satisfactorily, but in very early plantings during the cold and cloudy periods of February and March, the growing medium in the rings warms up much more readily and the plants begin growth faster due to the higher temperature around the roots. Also, the taller medium column will provide for better root aeration.

Ring Culture Layout. Beds are prepared similarly to that of sand and sawdust culture. The width of the beds should be 24 to 30 inches with 24 to 30-inch walkways. Tomatoes should be set in two rows about 6 inches from the edge of the bed to give 12 to 18 inches between rows. The plants should be 12 to 14 inches apart in each row. The sides of the beds are constructed of 2-by-6-inch or rough 1-by-6 inch cedar lumber on edge, as shown in figure 9.1. The beds are lined with 4-mil polyethylene. While no drainage pipes are needed, holes should be cut in the plastic on the side wall about 1 to 2 inches from the bottom. One-inch holes every 10 feet on each side should be adequate. Plastic rings 9 inches in diameter and 9 inches high are placed on top of the aggregate-filled bed (fig. 9.1).

The beds may be set up on concrete floors or the entire greenhouse floor may be covered with polyethylene prior to constructing the beds. Holes for drainage can be punched in the middle of the aisles.

Rings can be prepared by cutting 9-inch lengths from layflat polyethylene tubing of 2- or 4-mil thickness. If tubing of 14-inch layflat width is used, a 9-inch diameter ring will be produced when opened. The tubing can be either clear or black. Also, rolled roofing paper (about 40-pound grade and usually 36-inch width) can be cut into 9-inch strips and formed around a cylinder such as a stovepipe and the edges of the paper stapled to form the ring.

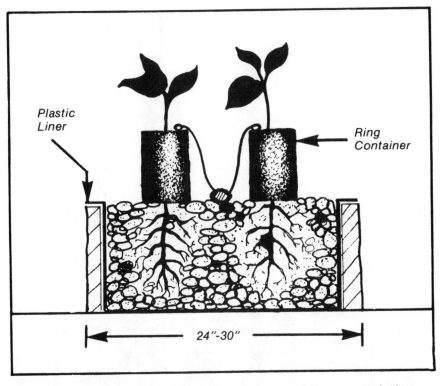

Fig. 9.1. Cross section of ring culture and underneath aggregate bed.

Rings are filled with a sterile medium such as the Cornell Peat-Lite mix. If polyethylene tubing is used for rings, a funnel device is needed, such as a length of stovepipe (8-inch diameter), and a small shovel to handle the medium. If tarpaper rings are used no funnel is needed. The rings are filled about two-thirds full if potted transplants are to be set. They can be filled to within 1 inch of the top after transplanting.

Watering and Feeding. Watering and feeding can be applied by an automatic trickle feeding system using spaghetti tubes, such as outlined for sawdust culture.

9.4 Peat Modules

On Guernsey Island in the United Kingdom, a large number of commercial greenhouse growers use peat modules. The cropping module measures 39 inches long and 7 to 9 inches wide. It was basically designed for the commercial tomato grower, allowing three plants per module. These modules are now being used also by amateur gardeners. They can be used outside over the summer growing season for flowers, bedding plants and vegetables. The modules contain a sterile peat medium.

9.5 Column Culture

The growing of plants in vertical columns has been developed in Europe, particularly in Italy and Spain. This system originated from the use of barrels or metal drums (fig. 9.2) stacked vertically and filled with gravel or a peat mixture. Holes were punched in the sides around the containers in order to place the plants into the medium. Later asbestos cement pipes with spirally positioned holes were used.

Watering and feeding is supplied by a trickle irrigation system mounted at the top of each column. If gravel is used as a medium, the nutrient solution can be recycled by placing the column over a collecting trough which conducts the solution back to a centrally located reservoir (fig. 9.3).

Fig. 9.2. Column culture of strawberries in the Canary Islands using metal drums.

Fig. 9.3. Column culture in Costa Rica using asbestos cement pipes and a cyclic gravel culture system.

In Italy the system has been refined to a column built of smaller modular pipes placed one on top of the other (fig. 9.4). Each module has several cup-shaped protuberances in which the plants are placed rather than merely holes located around the periphery. A peat mixture is used for the medium. It is an open system which allows any excess nutrient solution to drain from the bottom end of the column. This system is particularly useful for the growing of strawberries.

9.6 Sack Culture

Sack culture is a simplification of column culture. The system is basically the same except that polyethylene "sacks" are used instead of rigid drums or pipes. Black layflat 0.15 millimeter thick polyethylene of about 6-inch (150-millimeter) diameter and 6 feet

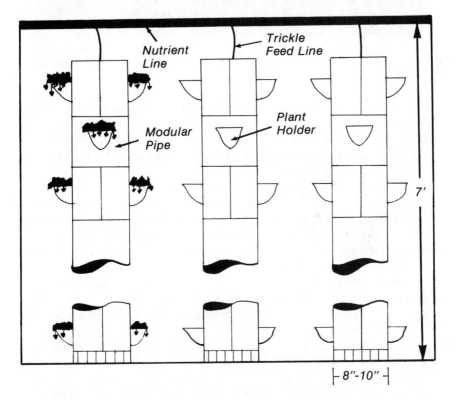

Fig. 9.4. Schematic of Italian column system.

Fig. 9.5. Main irrigation pipe and lateral lines running along the greenhouse superstructure above the "sacks." (Courtesy of M. Tropea, University of Catania, Italy.)

(2.0 meters) in length is filled with a peat-vermiculite mixture. The bottom end is tied to prevent the medium from falling through and the top end is tied to constrain the medium into a sausage-like form. The top end is tied by a wire or rope to the greenhouse and the sack hangs down, giving a column effect.

Watering and feeding is automated by use of a trickle spaghetti tube system to each sack from a central nutrient reservoir or fertilizer injector (fig. 9.5). Small holes 1 to 2 inches in diameter are cut around the sack's periphery, into which plants are placed (fig. 9.6). The nutrient solution is applied at the top end of the sack and percolated down through the entire sack.

The plant-holding containers or sacks supported by the greenhouse superstructure are spaced 80 centimeters (32 inches) apart within the rows and the rows are spaced at 1.2 meters (about 4 feet), as shown in figure 9.7.

Watering and feeding cycles are generally from 2 to 5 minutes, giving a volume of 1 to 2 liters of nutrient solution per sack per irrigation cycle. Nutrients are not recycled but allowed to percolate from the top to the bottom of the sack and out the drainage holes. Once a month the system is flushed with pure water to

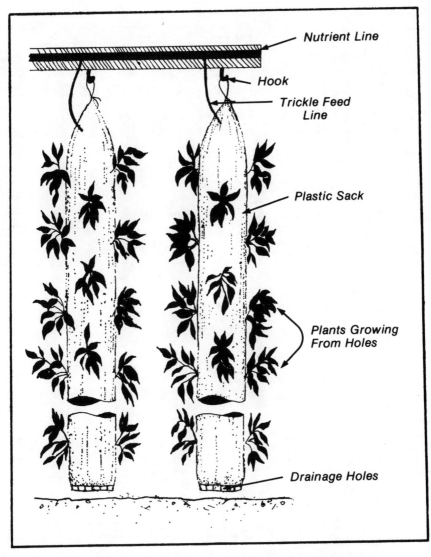

Fig. 9.6. Schematic of hanging sack culture system.

Fig. 9.7. Rows of "sacks" supported by the greenhouse superstructure. (Courtesy of M. Tropea, University of Catania, Italy.)

Fig. 9.8. Mixing medium and filling "sacks" for next crop. (Courtesy of M. Tropea, University of Catania, Italy.)

Fig. 9.9. Strawberries growing in vertical sacks. *Fig. 9.10.* Tomatoes. *Fig. 9.11.* Peppers. *Fig. 9.12.* Eggplants. (Courtesy of M. Tropea, University of Catania, Italy.)

remove any salt buildup. At the end of each growing period the entire sack and substrate is disposed of and new ones are made up with sterile medium (fig. 9.8).

This system is particularly useful for lettuce and strawberries which normally require a lot of greenhouse floor area with little utilization of the vertical space (fig. 9.9). However, tests with tomatoes (fig. 9.10), peppers (fig. 9.11), eggplant (fig. 9.12), cucumbers and other vegetables have also been very successful (Tropea 1976).

At present one industrial installation is operating in Campania, Italy, growing about 8 hectares (about 20 acres) of sack culture in polyethylene greenhouses. They are growing mainly strawberries, but have experimented successfully with many other crops. They have developed an "electronic brain" which is programmed to automatically feed the entire 20-acre complex, which is divided into 32 sections, each of them covering an area of 2500 square meters (about 0.6 acre) (fig. 9.13). The electronic brain controls the timing of irrigation cycles according to the environmental conditions and plant stage of development.

The cost of the entire system, including the metal framed greenhouses, heating, irrigation system and electronic brain, have been moderate and operating costs are substantially reduced by the efficient use of the vertical space within the greenhouse and by reduction of labor.

Fig. 9.13. An "electronic brain" controls the irrigation cycles. (Courtesy of M. Tropea, University of Catania, Italy.)

9.7 Small-Scale Units

Single home units may be constructed very similar to those outlined in chapter 8 on sawdust culture. Either growing trays or plastic bags may be used (fig. 9.14). On a small scale sterilization should not be attempted. Merely replace the medium with each new crop.

Fig. 9.14. Small "home units" about 2 feet long by 10 inches wide (60 cm. by 25 cm.) using a perlite-vermiculite medium. Ideal for use on windowsills or balconies of homes and apartments.

The simplest and most inexpensive method of growing herbs, lettuce and bedding plants hydroponically is the use of a plastic flat, "com-pack" filler tray and one-gallon nutrient bottle reservoir. A 10½-inch by 21-inch plastic flat with no drainage holes is used with a 48-compartment "com-pack" tray (Chapter 10). One of the eight sections (6 compartments) is removed at one corner and the nutrient tank is placed in that location. The nutrient tank can be a rigid polyethylene bottle with a large plastic cap through which a small hole is drilled and a split cork ring glued. The bottle is filled with nutrient solution and inverted into the flat. The hole in the cap allows solution to flow out of the bottle until the level in the flat reaches that of the hole; then, with the air supply cut off, the solution stops draining from the reservoir bottle.

The compartments of the "com-pack" are filled with coarse vermiculite. Seeds are planted, covered with a shallow layer of additional vermiculite, then moistened with water alone. A black plastic cover may be placed on top of the tray for several days until germination takes place. This prevents desiccation of the seedlings during germination. Once the seeds have germinated the cover is removed and the growing tray exposed to full light.

Such a nursery tray is meant to grow small plants such as herbs or bedding plants which will later be transplanted. However, the tray can be used to grow rapid crops of leaf lettuce. The lettuce must be harvested within several weeks of seeding when it reaches three to four inches in height (fig. 9.15).

Fig.9.15. Hydroponic nursery tray for bedding plants, herbs (sweet basil) and lettuce. One-gallon nutrient reservoir.

A sack culture system has been developed for the growing of foliage house plants, annuals, flowering plants, vegetables, small fruits and herbs. These "Gro-Tubes" have specifically been designed for the hobbyist and interior landscaping trades. The plastic tubes are approximately 2½ inches (6 cm) in diameter by 4 feet (1.2 m) in length filled with a medium of peat, sand, and vermiculite. Osmocote, fritted trace elements and lime fertilizers added to the medium provide the basic plant nutrients in some makes of plastic tubes while others may have less fertilizers incorporated into the mix and therefore require a liquid fertilizer on a regular basis several weeks after planting. A water reservoir secured on the top of the sack and a collecting cup at the bottom provide ease of watering and prevention of loss of drainage water. The water percolates from the reservoir bottle through a wick which is incorporated in the medium the entire length of the sack.

Such sacks are ideal for the growing of herbs, lettuce, strawberries, and houseplants such as coleus, pepperomia, begonias, ferns, wandering Jew, pathos, petunias, marigolds and impatiens. Most houseplants are set in the bags as unrooted cuttings through slits made in the sides of the bags. The bags will contain 30 to 50 coleus cuttings, 40 to 60 wandering Jew cuttings, or 12 to 20 fibrous begonias. They root and grow laterally and vertically from the suspended bag. Many vegetables and flowering plants can be placed in the bags as seedling transplants. As the plants grow to maturity they fill the sacks making a very showy display of massive vertical plants as illustrated in figures 9.16, 9.17.

Fig. 9.16. Coleus Growing in Sacks Showing Recently Planted Cuttings on the Right in the Foreground. (Courtesy of Poly-Tech Growing Systems Ltd.)

Fig. 9.17. Fully Grown Coleus Plants in a Sack Showing the Water Reservoir at the Top. (Courtesy of Poly-Tech Growing Systems Ltd.)

9.8 Sterilization of the Medium

All the media mentioned in this chapter must be sterilized either chemically or by steam, as outlined in Chapter 7.

9.9 Advantages and Disadvantages of Peat Mixtures

Advantages:

1. Like sand and sawdust cultures, they are open systems, therefore there is less spread of diseases such as *Fusarium* and *Verticillium* wilts, especially in tomatoes.

2. No problem of plugging drainage pipes with roots.

3. Good lateral movement of nutrient solution throughout the root zone.

4. Good root aeration.

5. A new nutrient solution is added each irrigation cycle.

6. The system is simple, easy to maintain and repair.

7. The high water-holding capacity of the medium reduces risk of water stress should a pump fail.

8. It is adaptable to fertilizer injectors and therefore less space is required for storage tanks.

9. Peat, perlite and vermiculite are generally readily available in most regions of the world.

10. Sack culture enables a greenhouse operator to utilize efficiently vertical space for crops such as lettuce and strawberries which normally use a large amount of floor area. Therefore, a much greater number of plants can be grown in a given area of greenhouse.

11. Sack and column cultures keep plant parts and fruit off the underlying medium, thus reducing disease problems of fruit and vegetation.

Disadvantages:

1. The medium must be sterilized between crops by steam or chemically, which requires more time than in gravel culture. However, sterilization is very thorough.

2. Peat, pumice and vermiculite are more costly than sawdust in areas having a large forest industry.

3. Over the cropping season salt accumulation can build up in the medium to toxic levels. Proper and regular leaching with pure water can overcome this problem.

4. Plugging of trickle feed lines may occur if proper filters are not used or if cleaning of these filters is neglected.

5. Since peat is organic in nature, it decomposes over time with continual cropping. Between crops it should be rototilled and additional peat must be added.

6. Perlite, pumice and vermiculite break down with continued use, resulting in compaction of the medium. For this reason, the peat mixtures are generally replaced between crops, resulting in replacement costs (of both medium and labor) each year.

7. If compaction occurs during the cropping period root aeration will be greatly restricted, resulting in poor crop yields. Both the original mixture ratios and handling are important to prevent compaction.

In summary, peat mixtures are used extensively in container-grown plants. In beds, other than ring culture, another medium such as sand or sawdust would be more suitable. In sack culture peat or sawdust mixtures are most suitable because of their light weight.

9.10 Rockwool Culture

Over the past ten years rockwool culture has become one of the principal techniques for the growing of vine crops, especially tomatoes and cucumbers. According to a recent survey (May 1986) by C. J. Graves of the Glasshouse Crops Research Institute in Littlehampton, England, the total area (hectares) of tomato production in Great Britain using rockwool in 1978 was less than 1 hectare (2 acres). This increased to 77.5 (197 acres), 126 (320 acres), and 148 hectares (376 acres) from 1984 through 1986, respectively. Similarly, the area of cucumbers under rockwool increased from less than one hectare (2 acres) to 68 hectares (173 acres) over the same period from 1978 to 1986.

Presently, rockwool culture is the most extensively used form of hydroponics in the world, with more than 2000 hectares (5000 acres) of greenhouse crops being grown by this system in the Netherlands. The technology originated in Denmark in 1969 with the growing of tomatoes and cucumbers.

Rockwool is an inert fibrous material produced from a mixture of volcanic rock, limestone, and coke, melted at 1500° to 2000°C. It is extruded as fine threads and pressed into loosely woven sheets. Surface tension is reduced by the addition of a phenol resin during cooling. While the composition of rockwool varies slightly from one manufacturer to another, it basically consists of silica dioxide (45 percent), aluminum oxide (15 percent), calcium oxide (15 percent), magnesium oxide (10 percent), iron oxide (10 percent), and other oxides (5 percent). Rockwool is slightly alkaline, but inert and biologically nondegradable. It has good water-holding capacity, with about 95 percent pore spaces. All fertilizers must be added to the irrigation water for plant growth. Rockwool has about an 80 percent water holding capacity. The pH of rockwool is between 7 and 8.5. Since it has no buffering capacity, the pH can easily be reduced to optimal levels of 6.0 to 6.5 for tomatoes and cucumbers by the use of a slightly acid nutrient solution.

Rockwool culture is an open, nonrecycling hydroponic system, generally, with nutrients fed to the base of each plant with a drip irrigation spaghetti line and emitter. Approximately a 10–15 percent excess of solution is supplied during each watering to allow leaching of minerals from the rockwool slabs.

Plants may be seeded into small rockwool plugs, granular rockwool, or a peat-lite plug mix placed in styrofoam trays of 240 cells (fig. 9.18) or plastic cell-pacs and flats. This system allows the grower to use automatic sowing equipment. The trays are watered with raw water until germination takes place, then with a dilute nutrient solution thereafter until first true leaves begin to unfold. Then these plugs are transplanted into larger rockwool cubes available in a number of sizes, $7.5 \times 7.5 \times 6.5$ centimeters $(3 \times 3 \times 2.5$ in$)$, $7.5 \times 7.5 \times 10$ centimeters $(3 \times 3 \times 4$ in$)$, $10 \times 10 \times 6.5$ centimeters $(4 \times 4 \times 2.5$ in$)$, and $10 \times 10 \times 8$ centimeters $(4 \times 4 \times 3$ in$)$ (length $\times$ width $\times$ height). The choice of growing block is determined by the plant being grown and at which stage the grower wishes to transplant to the final rockwool slabs. The longer he wishes to hold the plants in a seedling area, the larger blocks he should use (figs. 9.19, 9.20). The growing blocks are manufactured in strips, each block individually surrounded by a plastic wrapping. They are placed in holes cut into the plastic on top of the rockwool slabs (fig. 9.21). Slabs are available as unsleeved or sleeved with a white polethylene sheet. They come in a number of sizes, $90 \times 30 \times 5$ centimeters $(35.5 \times 12 \times 2$ in$)$, $90 \times 15 \times 7.5$ centimeters $(35.5 \times 6 \times 3$ in$)$, $90 \times 20 \times 7.5$ centimeters $(35.5 \times 8 \times 3$ in$)$, $90 \times 30 \times 7.5$ centimeters $(35.5 \times 12 \times 3$ in$)$ and $90 \times 45 \times 7.5$ centimeters $(35.5 \times 18 \times 3$ in$)$ (length $\times$ width $\times$ thickness).

The slabs of 15-20 centimeters (6-8 in) width are generally recommended for tomatoes, those of 20-30 centimeters (8-12 in)

Fig. 9.18. Tomato plants seeded in styrofoam trays, using a granular rockwool medium.

Fig. 9.19. Tomato plants transplanted into rockwool blocks after first true leaves have developed.

for cucumbers and the 30 centimeters (12 in) width for melons. Wider slabs for tomatoes can lead to excessive vegetative growth. Wrapped slabs are ready to use for annual crops such as tomatoes, cucumbers, and melons. They are designed for growers wishing to use a fresh growing medium each year to assure an ideal air/water ratio and sterile medium. Turn-around time between cropping can be saved, as it is not necessary to dry out, sterilize, and re-wrap the slabs.

A typical layout for an open-system rockwool culture is shown in figure 9.22. Prior to placing out the growing slabs the greenhouse floor area should be disinfected with a 2 percent formaldehyde solution. The soil surface (floor) should be leveled. Beds consist of two rockwool slabs set 60–75 cm (2–2.5 ft) apart. Soil or sand makes the best floor as it can be easily formed to obtain good drainage. A slight slope towards the center between the two slabs will provide adequate drainage away from the slabs (fig. 9.23). The entire greenhouse floor area is covered with a white polyethylene of 6-mil thickness to provide light reflection and good hygiene (fig. 9.24). If the drainage conditions in the greenhouse are poor, it is necessary to lay a drainage pipe in the middle of the bed. The drainage pipe should be covered with pea gravel and/or

Fig. 9.20. Tomato seedlings growing in rockwool blocks under supplementary artificial lighting in a nursery area of the greenhouse. (Courtesy of Gipaanda Greenhouses, Surrey, B.C., Canada).

Fig. 9.21. Tomato plants growing in rockwool slabs. Note that the rockwool cubes have been placed on top of the slab after cutting several slits in the slab.

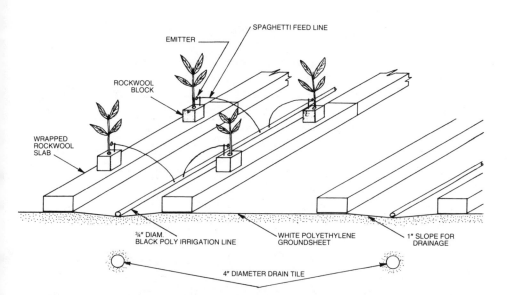

Fig. 9.22. Sketch of an open system of rockwool culture.

Labels in figure:

EMITTER

SPAGHETTI FEED LINE

ROCKWOOL BLOCK

WRAPPED ROCKWOOL SLAB

¾" DIAM. BLACK POLY IRRIGATION LINE

WHITE POLYETHYLENE GROUNDSHEET

1" SLOPE FOR DRAINAGE

4" DIAMETER DRAIN TILE

Fig. 9.23. Sloping of floor to provide drainage for each two rows of slabs.

coarse sand and the white ground sheet placed on top of it. If this method is used, the ground sheet should have small holes punched in it to allow percolation of the excess nutrient solution to the drain pipe. Alternatively, the unpunched polyethylene sheet will act as a drainage channel to conduct excess solution to a drain pipe at the far end of the greenhouse. But problems with algae may develop if stagnant water remains in the channel.

If the underlying greenhouse floor is backfilled with a sand or gravel base of high percolation, the rockwool slabs could be placed directly on the floor without a polyethylene ground sheet. Excess nutrients would drain away rapidly; however, weed growth

Fig. 9.24. Laying of white polyethylene groundsheet.

would be promoted in these areas immediately adjacent to the growing slabs.

If bottom heat is required, the rockwool slabs could be placed on top of styrofoam sheets grooved in the upper surface to accommodate hot water pipes.

The rockwool slabs must be soaked with nutrient solution prior to transplanting (fig. 9.25). The slabs must be soaked with nutrient solution for 24–48 hours. This will adjust the pH and uniformly moisten the slabs. To do this, place the slabs in their final position with three drip lines entering the top of each slab at equal spacing. Do not cut the drainage holes in the slabs until they have been soaked. In transplanting simply set the rockwool cubes growing the seedlings on top of the slabs through holes cut in the plastic sleeve (fig. 9.26). Little transplant shock is encountered by the plants. The roots will grow from the cubes into the slabs within several days.

Each plant is fed nutrient solution via a drip line and emitter (fig. 9.27). Either dripper or spitter type emitters may be used. A spitter gives a small spray of nutrient solution near the base of the plant. It has the advantage of giving wider application of solution and thus eliminating dry spots, but excessive amounts could easily be applied and moisture at the stem base will promote diseases. Following the first irrigation after transplanting, the slabs should be checked for dry spots between the emitters, as the slabs must be fully saturated to ensure sufficient solution reserves for the plant during the initital post-transplant period. Drainage holes must be cut on the slab sides at the bottom edge. They should be in the shape of an inverted "T" or an angled straight cut approximately 4–5 centimeters (2 in.) in height. Three holes should be made in each slab on the inside face.

More frequent irrigation is necessary immediately after transplanting until the plants become established. Later a frequency of 5 to 10 times per day should be adequate, with rates varying according to plant stage of growth and environmental conditions. Irrigation should be continued until a 15-20 percent excess of water drains from the slabs. Smith (1987) states that watering should be done before the slabs have lost more than 5-10 percent of their water-holding capacity. Daily waterings up to 20 times may be needed for summer crops.

Monitoring of salt levels in the rockwool slabs should be carried out several times a week. A sample solution taken from the slab with a small syringe should be tested for its pH and electrical conductivity (EC). Values should be close to those of the nutrient solution provided to the plants. If significantly high levels of conductivity or nonoptimal pH levels are detected, the slabs must be irrigated more often until their solution concentration approaches that of the input solution. "Clear" water should not be

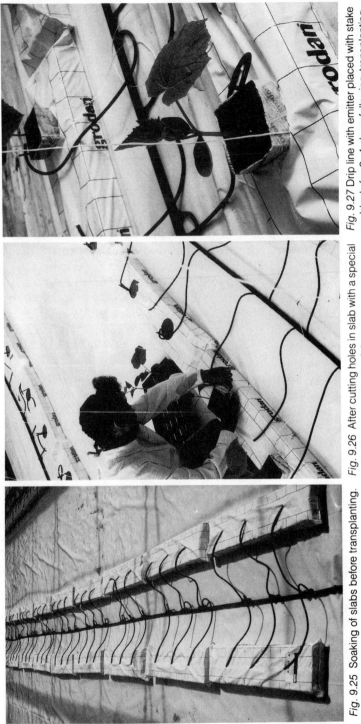

Fig. 9.25 Soaking of slabs before transplanting.

Fig. 9.26 After cutting holes in slab with a special tool, plants are set onto slabs.

Fig. 9.27 Drip line with emitter placed with stake on block for 3–4 days following transplanting, then moved to slab next to block for continued feeding.

used as it often contains sodium, calcium, and magnesium. These ions will accumulate in the slabs, and other nutrients such as potassium, nitrates, and phosphates will be depleted causing an imbalance in the slab nutrition.

9.11 Advantages and Disadvantages of Rockwool Culture

Advantages:

1. As an open system there is less chance for disease spread throughout the crop.

2. Uniform application of nutrients to the plants; each plant is fed individually.

3. Since rockwool is light in weight, it can easily be handled.

4. It is simple to provide bottom heat.

5. It is easily steam-sterilized if the grower wishes to use it several times. Structurally, it will not break down for up to three to four years.

6. Rapid crop turn-around is possible at a minimal labor cost.

7. It provides good root aeration.

8. There is less risk of crop failure due to mechanical break-down in the system, than with NFT.

9. Little growth setback occurs during transplanting.

10. With the use of the plug trays the sowing of seeds can be automated.

11. It requires less capital cost for equipment and installation than many NFT systems.

Disadvantages:

1. Rockwool is relatively expensive in countries not manufac-turing it locally.

2. Accumulation of carbonates and sodium may occur in the rockwool slabs in regions having high salts in the raw water. In such areas a reverse osmosis water purifier would be required.

Overall, rockwool culture offers many positive factors in its rapidly accepted use in the growing of not only vine crops, but also cut flowers such as roses and potted flowering plants. It is also widely used as a propagation medium for vegetables such as lettuce, spinach and other low profile crops.

References

Boodley, J. W. and R. Sheldrake, Jr. 1964. *Cornell "Peat-Lite" mixes for container growing*. Dept. Flor. and Orn. Hort., Cornell Univ. Mimeo Rpt.

Cook, C.D. 1971. Plastoponics in ornamental horticulture. *Gardeners Chronicle/HTJ*, Oct. 7, 1971, Oct. 15, 1971.

Graves, C. J. 1986. Growing Plants without soil. *The Plantsman*, May 1986, pp. 43-57.

Hartmann, H. T. and D. E. Kester. 1975. *Plant propagation principles and practices*. 3rd ed. Englewood Cliffs, N.J.: Prentice-Hall.

Irish peat modules for amateurs. *Gardeners Chronicle/HTJ*, Aug. 10, 1973, p. 17.

Lucas, R.E.; P. E. Riecke and R. S. Farnham. 1971. *Peats for soil improvement and soil mixes*. Mich. Coop. Ext. Ser. Bull. No. E-516.

Matkin, O. A. and P. A. Chandler. 1957. *The U.C. type soil mixes*. Section 5 in Calif. Agr. Exp. Sta. Man. 23.

Patek, J. M. 1965. Peat moss. *Amer. Hort. Mag.* 44: 132–41.

Sangster, D. M. 1974. *Soilless culture of tomatoes with slow-release fertilizers*. Ontario Min. of Agric. and Food Factsheet 73–057.

Sheldrake, R., Jr. and J. W. Boodley. 1965. *Commercial production of vegetable and flower plants*. Cornell Ext. Bull. 1056.

Sheldrake, R., Jr. and S. Dallyn. 1969. *Production of greenhouse tomatoes in ring culture or in trough culture*. Cornell Veg. Crops Mimeo No. 149.

Smith, Dennis L. 1987. *Rockwool in Horticulture*. 153 pp. London: Grower Books.

Tropea, M. 1976. The controlled nutrition of plants. II - A new system of "vertical" hydroponics. *Proc. 4th Int. Congress on Soilless Culture*, Las Palmas, pp. 75–83.

Chapter 10

Plant Culture

10.1 Introduction

While this book is an outline and review of soilless culture methods, it is appropriate to discuss briefly some of the methods and products available for the growing of seedlings to be transplanted into a soilless culture system. In order to successfully grow plants you must start out with vigorous and healthy disease-free seedlings. Tomatoes are used as an example. We shall then proceed to other aspects of successful plant cultures.

10.2 Seeding of Tomatoes

Three basic systems maybe used for growing tomato transplants. One approach is to broadcast seed or sow it in rows in flats of a soilless mix. Either the U.C. or Cornell Peat-Lite mixes may be used (see Chapter 9). When the seedlings reach the cotyledon stage (fig. 10.1), they are transplanted at wider spacing in other flats or in individual plant-growing containers.

Another system is to seed directly into the growing flats or containers. Many types of containers are on the market. Plastic "com-packs" and "multi-pots" are shaped like ice cube trays with from 1 large compartment to 12 compartments per pack (5¼ inches by 5¼ inches by 2⁵/₁₆ inches deep) (fig. 10.2). These come in 8 packs per 10½-inch-by-21-inch sheet which fits into a corresponding plastic flat. A similar product (Jiffy strips) is made of peat rather than plastic. Also individual plastic and peat pots of various sizes are available. In all of these containers a soilless mix must be used. Most vegetable plants can be grown satisfactorily in

343

2¼- or 3-inch square or round pots. In the peat pots and strips transplanting is done by placing the pot and medium into the beds. The plant roots will grow through the peat container walls.

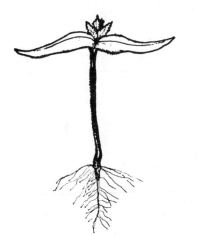

Fig. 10.3. Jiffy-7 pellets.

Fig. 10.1. Tomato seedling in cotyledon and early first true-leaf stage.

Fig. 10.2. Com-pack and multi-pack containers.

The third system is to seed directly into Jiffy peat pellets, Kys cubes or BR-8 blocks. The latter two are about 1½-inch paper fiber cubes. Seeds are placed in small precut seeding holes and filled with a peat mix. Peat pellets are compressed peat discs contained by a nylon mesh. These discs are about 1½ inches in diameter and ¼ inch thick when shipped dry. After soaking in water for 5 to 10 minutes they swell to about 1½ inches in height (fig. 10.3). Seeds are placed in the top and covered with their peat medium. They contain sufficient nutrients to carry most plants for 3-4 weeks. Plant roots grow out through the nylon mesh. During transplanting the peat pellet (Jiffy-7) or paper cube (Kys cube, BR-8) with the plant is placed in the growing bed. In Europe rockwool pellets with black polyethylene cover are used as growing blocks in a similar fashion.

Several very popular growing blocks used with NFT are rockwool and oasis blocks. Use of rockwool blocks originated in Denmark and Sweden. They have been used on a commercial scale for tomatoes and cucumbers in The Netherlands and England.

Rockwool is composed of coke and limestone molten at 1600°C (2912° F) and spun into fibers. The fibers are woven into slabs, stabilized with phenolic resin and provided with a wetting agent. The most widely used rockwool block is manufactured under the trade mark "Grodan."

Chemically, rockwool blocks are relatively inert as the elements they contain are practically unavailable to plants. While they are slightly alkaline in pH, they are quickly neutralized after a short time of passing nutrient solutions of lower pH through them.

Rockwool blocks have good physical properties of a low volume weight, a large pore volume and a great water retention capacity. Both rockwool cubes and oasis blocks are often used with NFT systems. Both of these growing blocks are sterile, so that disinfecting measures are unnecessary.

Rockwool blocks are available as propagation blocks and growing blocks. The propagation blocks are provided with a hole to facilitate placing cuttings into the blocks. The growing blocks are large enough to allow growing on by use of a "pot-in-pot" system. Seeds can be sown in propagation blocks which in turn can be placed into growing blocks after several weeks of growth. In this way plants can continue growing in the same medium with a minimum of transplanting shock by means of the "pot-in-pot" system. Growing blocks are 10 centimeters by 10 centimeters (4 in by 4 in) surrounded by black polyethylene wrapping on the four sides. Rockwool blocks can be placed directly into NFT troughs. Rockwool blocks are completely dry and therefore, like peat pellets, must be properly moistened before seeding.

Oasis "Horticubes" are widely used in North America specifically for hydroponic and NFT applications. These cubes have good drainage making them ideal for seed germination. The "Horticube" medium is available in 1 inch by 1 inch by 1½ inches (2.5 cm by 2.5 cm by 3.8 cm) blocks for maximum planting density. Each medium tray is composed of 162 cubes joined at their bases to allow easy separation for transplanting. Their main advantages are that they are sterile, easy to handle, and have a balanced pH.

They, like peat pellets, must be saturated with water prior to seeding. This can be accomplished in several ways: misting for one hour, soaking through hand submersion, or by overhead watering until the cubes are completely saturated. Seeds can then be placed in the pre-punched hole in each block. When roots appear on the outside of the cubes and true leaves develop, the plants are ready for transplanting. Since the plants are transplanted intact with their blocks a minimum of transplant setback will occur.

Usually it is wise to sow at least two seeds per pot or pellet and as soon as the plants reach their cotyledon stage simply cut the less vigorous ones out at "soil" level with a scissors, leaving the desired number (1 per pot or pellet for tomatoes). If this is not done at an early stage, the seedlings will compete for light and nutrients, resulting in spindly, thin-stemmed transplants.

A seedling house temperature range of 65°F. night minimum to 80°F. day maximum will provide good germination and growth of tomatoes. Optimum germination temperature will vary with different plant species.

Plant tomato seed ¼ to ⅜ inch deep. Most larger-seeded vegetables should be covered about ¼ inch deep. A good rule-of-thumb is to cover the seed about twice its greatest diameter. Very fine seed, such as petunias, begonias, and snapdragons, should be pressed into the soil with a board, but should not be covered. After watering the flats or containers, cover them with a sheet of clear plastic in order to prevent their medium from drying out during germination and emergence. This will save the labor of daily watering to maintain moisture. Clear plastic should not be used during hot weather unless shading from direct sunlight is provided. Otherwise, soil temperature under the plastic film may become too hot for proper germination. The plastic sheet must be removed at the first signs of seedling emergence.

Some growers use a low-pressure, intermittent mist system to provide uniform moisture levels for seed germination. The mist cycle should be 4 seconds every 6 minutes from approximately 8:30 A.M. until 4:00 P.M. or it can be operated from an automatic moisture sensor. If mist is used, bottom heat should be supplied by steam pipes under the bench, or by imbedding electric heating cables under the flats and covering with 1-inch of gravel. As soon as seedlings emerge, flats should be removed from under the mist and grown under full light at the proper temperature.

In northerly latitudes, during winter months when cloudy weather prevails, supplementary artificial lighting should be installed in the seedling house. Cool-white, high-output fluorescent tubes, metal-halide or mercury vapor lamps should be used in sufficient numbers to obtain at least 1000 foot-candles of light intensity at plant surface. The lights should operate at least 14 hours per day for tomatoes. Lighting requirements, particularly day length (photoperiod), are very important for many plant species such as chrysanthemums and poinsettias; therefore, check out such factors before deciding on the type and amount of lighting needs.

Recent evidence by Dr. Gerald Wilcox of Purdue University (personal communication) has shown that wind action causes the development of a hormone within the plant that thickens its stem. Wind action can be duplicated in the greenhouse by use of blowers in the seedling area or by drawing a foam rubber mat across the seedlings for one minute per day over a period of three weeks. The result is a shortening of the internodes which produces a shorter, stalkier plant that will be more productive at later stages.

10.3 Plant-Growing Temperature

Usually better quality plants are grown when night temperature is 10°F. lower than day temperature. The best temperature range for warm season crops is 60°F. night and 75°F. day. Cool-season crops will do better at 50°F. night and 60°F. day temperature. A 10-degree lower day temperature is best during periods of cloudy weather. If the day-night temperature differential is too great, long upright clusters form that will later kink and possibly break under fruit development.

If temperature is too low, plant growth will be slower and some purpling of leaves may occur, especially on tomatoes. If the temperature is too high, plant growth will be soft and "leggy," resulting in poor-quality plants.

Cold Treatment. Cold treatment subjects young tomato seedlings just after the seed leaves unfold (fig. 10.1) to temperatures of 52 to 56°F. for ten days to three weeks. Cold temperatures during both day and night are effective. Ten days are sufficient in bright, sunny weather; three weeks are necessary in cloudy, dark or winter weather. The duration of the cold treatment is determined by the time required for the plant to develop to the two-leaf stage. The optimum temperature for the tomato plant varies with the stage of plant development (table 10.1). Tomato plants properly exposed to a cold treatment develop large cotyledons and thick stems, with fewer leaves formed before the first flower cluster, up to double the number of flowers in the first, and often the second clusters, and higher early and total yields.

TABLE 10.1 Night and Day Temperatures from Seed Germination to Fruiting of Greenhouse Tomatoes

Growth Stage	Sunlight Conditions	Temperature (°F.)	
		Night	Day
Seed germination	Not critical	65-70	65-70
After seed leaves unfold, begin "cold treatment" and continue for: 10 days to 2 weeks during	Sunny or partly cloudy days	52-56	55-60
2 to 3 weeks during	Cloudy or dull days	52-56	55-58
After "cold treatment" until plants are transplanted into beds	Sunny or partly cloudy days Cloudy or dull days	58-62 58-60	65-75 60-62
During flowering and fruiting	Sunny or partly cloudy days Cloudy or dull days	60-65 60-62	65-75 60-62

Source: Adapted from Wittwer, S. H. and S. Honma, 1969. *Greenhouse tomatoes: guidelines for successful production*. East Lansing: Michigan State Univ. Press.

10.4 Watering

It is important that each watering soaks the medium thoroughly. Water should be applied uniformly over all plants or uneven growth is likely to occur. Plants should be watered early enough so foliage will dry before dark. Remember that plants require less water during periods of dark, cloudy weather than during periods of bright, warm weather. As plants grow larger, they require more water. Normally, increasing day length and average temperature will increase water needs of plants.

Excess moisture may result in fast growth and poor fruit set in tomatoes, especially when combined with higher nitrogen levels and poor light conditions. The fertilizer program is most effective when moisture and temperature are controlled to fit available light conditions. Water requirements vary, depending on size of plant, day length, light intensity, and temperature.

Overhead irrigation systems for watering plants have been used by some growers. This type of watering saves considerable time, but it is difficult to obtain completely uniform distribution. Uniform watering is especially critical where plants are grown in small, individual containers or multi-packs.

Large greenhouse operations such as Superior Farming Company in Tucson, Arizona, use an overhead traveling boom sprinkler irrigation system. In this way seedlings can be placed over the entire greenhouse area rather than leaving pathways for people to walk for manual watering.

10.5 Light

During cloudy weather, tomato leaves become low in sugars. Leaves and stems become pale and thin and the fruit clusters may be smaller or fail to set. Excess nitrogen during such a period can be harmful. Supplementary artificial lighting has generally been found to be economically impractical except in the raising of the seedlings, as mentioned earlier.

During bright, sunny weather sugar production in the leaves is high. The leaves are dark and thick, stems dark green and sturdy, fruit sets well with large clusters, and root systems vigorous. Nitrogen can be supplied at a heavier rate during this period.

When the weather is cloudy for more than 1 or 2 days, it may be necessary to:

1. Reduce day and night temperatures in the greenhouse 3 to 4 degrees F.

2. Use as little water as possible but do not let the plants wilt.

3. Cut the recommended fertilizer application by half, and if the cloudy weather lasts more than 5 days, skip the odd fertilizer application completely.

These steps will help to keep plant growth balanced between leaf growth and fruit production. If they are not observed, the plants are likely to be very dark green and healthy, but are not likely to set many fruit.

During seedling stage plants should be transplanted to wider spacing in flats (at least 2 inches apart) or individual containers at full cotyledon development or very early first-true-leaf stage (fig. 10.1) to reduce mutual shading. In flats, plants should be set out in about 3 weeks to avoid spindly development. In individual small containers or growing pellets plants can develop longer than 3 weeks, provided they are spaced out as they grow to avoid crowding. Excellent plants can be grown in 3- or 4-inch pots, but they require more nursery space than do smaller containers. Containers should be spaced to prevent leaf overlapping during growth. Good pot-grown plants have pencil-size stems and are about as wide, from leaf tip to leaf tip, as they are tall (fig. 10.4).

Fig. 10.4. Vigorous, healthy tomato plants (5-6 weeks old) ready for transplanting. Plant on the left was grown in a 3-inch square peat pot, while the one on the right was grown in a Jiffy-7 peat pellet. Note roots emerging from the containers.

10.6 Carbon Dioxide Enrichment

In northern regions, carbon dioxide enrichment in greenhouses has improved productivity substantially. Commercial greenhouse operators claim a 20 to 30 percent increase in tomato yields; better fruit set in early clusters, especially when low light levels would normally reduce fruit setting; and larger fruits. In Ohio, cucumber yields have increased as much as 40 percent. Lettuce yields have increased 20 to 30 percent per crop, and faster growth rates have allowed production of an extra crop each year.

Carbon dioxide enrichment and supplementary artificial lighting may be economic in greenhouses used to produce vegetable seedlings and bedding plants. These practices produce sturdier plants in much less time than conventional systems.

For maximum profits there is an optimum CO_2 concentration inside the greenhouse that depends upon the stage of growth and species of crop, as well as the location, time of year, and type of greenhouse. Generally levels at 2 to 5 times the normal atmospheric levels (1000 to 1500 ppm CO_2) may be taken as the optimum levels.

On cool days, when greenhouses are being heated and air vents are closed, plants will deplete the CO_2 in the greenhouse atmosphere. In 1 hour, plants in a closed greenhouse may lower the CO_2 concentration enough to significantly reduce growth rates. Air venting to maintain CO_2 concentration at outside levels would increase heating costs substantially. In these circumstances, special heaters using propane, natural gas, or fuel oil can supply CO_2 while simultaneously raising temperatures.

Carbon dioxide enrichment may be expected to increase fertilizer and water requirements, since plants will be growing more vigorously. Young tomato plants are especially responsive to CO_2 enrichment. Wittwer and Honma (1969) claim that growth rates can be increased by 50 percent and early flowering and fruiting accelerated by a week or 10 days. Effects are carried into the fruiting period. Not only is top growth and flower formation accelerated, but root growth is promoted even more. Carbon dioxide enrichment is of special significance in hydroponic culture since one of the sources of the gas, decaying organic matter in the soil, is not present.

10.7 Transplanting

Good quality transplants are essential to a good greenhouse crop. They must be set into the beds properly and cared for afterward to avoid any check in growth. For the least amount of transplanting shock, plants should be the right age and moderately hardened. Tomato or pepper plants should not have any fruit set. Cabbage, cauliflower, and broccoli plants should have a stem diameter about one-half as large as a pencil and have 6 to 8 true leaves.

Less transplant shock will be undergone by containerized plants than by bare-root plants because there is little or no disturbance to the root system. The transplanting shock of bare-root plants can be minimized, however, with proper planting and care.

With tomatoes, regardless of growing medium, the transplant should be set into the bed with some of its stem below the bed surface. The upper surface of solid containers, or the upper surface of the root ball from a potted plant, should be 2 to 3 inches below the bed surface. Bare-root plants should be planted to an equivalent depth. Ordinarily, this means burying the cotyledons (seed leaves). This provides better initial support for the plant, and allows new roots to develop on the buried stem section. Shallow troughs limit depth of planting, but 4 or 5 inches of stem can be buried in deep beds. If very tall spindly plants must be used, it is best to set a portion of the stem at an angle. The above-ground portion will grow vertically from where it enters the medium.

Irrigate the plants as soon as possible after they are set to avoid or minimize wilting. In gravel culture the beds can be flooded while transplanting to maintain a high level of water in the coarse medium. Before planting, keep the containers or flats of plants moist. Properly set container plants will not wilt following transplanting, if their root balls are moist when planted and irrigation follows soon afterward. Bare-root plants may wilt after planting, even though irrigated immediately, but they will recover overnight.

10.8 Spacing

Most publications on greenhouse tomato production suggest space allowances of 3 to 4 square feet per plant under soil culture. This is a population of 14,520 or 10,890 plants per acre, respectively. Plantings as dense as 18,500 per acre (about 2 square feet per plant) have been used in hydroponic culture in California and Arizona with good yields and quality. Plants are placed in double rows per bed. Plant rows should be 16 to 18 inches apart and plants 12 to 14 inches apart within each row. Plants may be placed in staggered positions in adjacent rows, in order to maximize the exposure of the leaves to sunlight, and to minimize physical interference of the leaves between adjacent plants.

European cucumbers require a minimum row width of 5 feet. For the spring/summer crop, the plants require 7 to 9 square feet for each plant, for the fall crop 9 to 10 square feet. Plants can be placed in single rows 14 to 16 inches apart within the row. The plants are then tied alternately to overhead wires spaced 2½ to 3 feet apart so that the plants are inclined away from the row on each side. They will then be growing in a V-arrangement down the row, allowing light to fall more uniformly on the plants.

10.9 Feeding and Watering

Once the plants have been transplanted, the feeding-irrigation system cycles must be set. The time between irrigation cycles depends on a number of factors, as discussed earlier, including the type of growing medium used. In sand and sawdust culture several irrigations per day will be sufficient while gravel culture requires watering every few hours during the daylight period. A typical watering program for a trickle gravel culture system is given in table 10.2.

TABLE 10.2   Annual Watering Scheme: Tomatoes, Cucumbers, Lettuce

Date	Plant Stage	Cycle Frequency Per Day	Cycle Duration
Feb. 1-15	Transplants	2 hr. 8:00 A.M. - 5:00 P.M.	15 min.
March 1	Seedlings	3 hr. 7:00 A.M. - 6:00 P.M.	15 min.
March 31	Mature Plants	2 hr. 7:00 A.M. - 7:00 P.M.	15 min.
April 15	Mature Plants	2 hr. 7:00 A.M. - 7:00 P.M.	15 min.
May 15 - July 15	Mature Plants	1½ hr. 7:00 A.M. - 7:00 P.M.	15 min.
July 15	Transplants	1 hr. 7:00 A.M. - 8:00 P.M.	15 min.
July 31 - Sept. 1	Mature Plants	2 hr. 7:00 A.M. - 7:00 P.M.	15 min.
Sept. 1 - Oct.1	Mature Plants	2 hr. 8:00 A.M. - 6:00 P.M.	15 min.
Oct. 1 - Jan. 1	Mature Plants	3 hr. 8:00 A.M. - 5:00 P.M.	15 min.

Note: These timings are only approximate. Plants should be watched closely, especially during the long, hot, summer days and after transplanting. If any wilting of the tops of the plants occurs, it is likely that they need to be irrigated more frequently.

During winter months, particularly just after transplanting, care should be taken not to overwater. Water only several times a day.

After transplanting, irrigate once every 2 hours during the day-light hours for 15 minutes each time for the first two weeks until the plants take hold, that is, until the roots start growing out of the peat pellets and into the gravel. This condition will be expressed as vigorous leafy growth. After this initial hold period, regular irrigation cycles similar to those outlined in table 10.2 should be followed. If the plants wilt at any time during the day, increase the frequency of irrigation cycles.

10.10 Plant Support

Plants such as tomatoes and cucumbers which are trained vertically must be strung and clamped. Use plastic twine and plastic clips (Stem Gems). The string should be tied to support cables directly above the plants. Leave 1 to 2 feet extra length of the string at the cable end in case you wish to carry the plants for a longer than normal growing period. In this way they can be lowered once they have grown as high as the cable.

The plants must be clamped to the string before they fall over. Secure the first clamp under a pair of large leaves pulling the twine taut, but not so tight that when released it will pull the leaves of the plant up. Clamping should be done as shown in figure 10.5.

The clamps should be placed directly under the leaf petioles, not above them, as such a position gives no support. Clamps should not be placed under flower clusters as the weight of maturing tomatoes later may break off the fruit cluster or fruit may be punctured by the clamps. Clamps should be secured along the plant every foot or so to give adequate support as fruit matures. The back (hinge) of the clamp must pinch the string, as shown in figure 10.5.

Clip
Hinge

Support
String

Fig. 10.5. The use of plastic plant clips to support plants vertically.

A more recent method of stringing is especially useful with one-year single crops of tomatoes. Extra string is wound on a thick wire hook having a flat spool shape (fig. 10.6). Using this method, plants can easily be lowered with the additional string available. The string may be attached to the bottom of the plant by use of a plant clip or simply by tying a loose loop around the stem below a healthy leaf. The string is then wound around the stem of the plant always in the same direction (generally clockwise), and occasionally a plant clip may be placed under a leaf petiole to give additional support (fig. 10.7).

Fig. 10.6. Wire spools with a hook on one end are used for extra support-string required during lowering of plants.

Fig. 10.7. Support-string wound around tomato plant in a clockwise direction. Several plastic plant clips are attached to the plant for additional support. Flower trusses are pruned to four or five fruit per truss.

10.11 Suckering and Trimming (Tomatoes and Cucumbers)

Suckers are the small shoots which grow between the main stem and the leaf petioles. They must be removed before they grow too large as they drain the nutrients of the plant which could otherwise go into fruit development. With tomatoes they should be removed when they are about 1 inch long. At this stage they can be easily snapped off by hand without creating a large scar of the axillary region (area between stem and petiole), as shown in figure 10.8.

Removing suckers by hand rather than using a knife presents less hazard of spreading disease. Rubber or plastic gloves can be worn to protect your hands from the acidic sap of the plants. Larger suckers which may develop due to late suckering will have to be removed with pruning shears or a knife.

Often terminated plants, those no longer having a growing point, will be encountered. Select a vigorous sucker near the growing

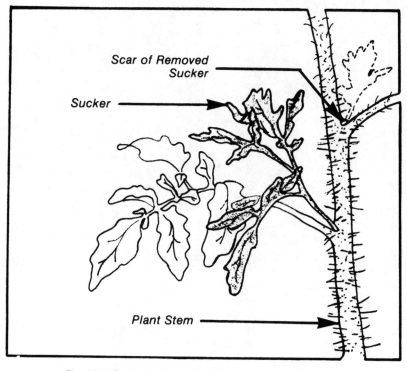

Fig. 10.8. Removal of tomato suckers at an early stage.

point and allow it to continue growing, but remove other less vigorous suckers. Some plants may fork or split. Again select the most vigorous branch and prune off the other growing point (plant apex).

As the plant matures and the fruit has been harvested from the lower trusses, the older leaves on the bottom of the plant will begin to senesce (yellow) and die. These leaves should be removed to allow better air ventilation and thus lower the relative humidity around the base of the plants. These leaves should be removed from the time the second truss (fruit cluster) has been completely harvested. After that continue removing leaves which turn yellow up to the truss presently bearing mature fruit. Simply snap off the leaves with your fingers to get a clean break to minimize scars. Remove all the dead leaves from the greenhouse and dispose of them. This leaf pruning can be repeated several times as the plants mature, but never prune out green leaves, as they nourish the maturing fruit. Generally, no more than 3–4 leaves should be removed at any time and not more frequently than once per week.

As the plants reach the support cables above, loosen the support strings and lower the plants about a foot each time. Since the lower leaves and fruit have been removed, the stems can be twisted or coiled around on top of the bed. If care is not taken stems may break. If a stem cracks, lower the plant enough to bury the broken part into the medium. Place a feeder line nearby and within several weeks roots will develop from this broken stem. At all times about 4 feet of foliage and fruit clusters should remain on the upper part of the plant (fig. 5.80).

Flower trusses on tomatoes should be pruned to select the most uniform four or five set fruit on a truss (fig. 10.7). Any misshapen flowers, double set fruit, and often the furthest flower out on the truss are removed. This gives uniform fruit development, shape, size, and color of tomatoes. Blossoms and small fruit should be removed as soon as two or three fruit set to pea size.

Long English (European) cucumbers are grown in greenhouses since they can be trained vertically and cannot withstand the temperature fluctuations they would encounter under outside conditions.

Fig. 10.9 Renewal umbrella system of training European cucumbers.

European cucumbers should be trained under two systems, the renewal umbrella system (fig. 10.9), and the V-cordon system (fig. 10.10). A V-cordon system trains the plants to make best use of available light within the greenhouse. Two support wires are placed 6½ to 7 feet above the ground over each row of plants. The wires are spaced 2½ to 3 feet apart. The support strings are then tied alternately to the two overhead wires so that the plants are inclined away from the row on each side (fig. 10.10). Suckering and trimming of cucumbers is necessary to obtain a balance between the vegetative vigor and fruit load of each plant. Suckers and also all blossoms and fruit should be removed up to the fifth true leaf.

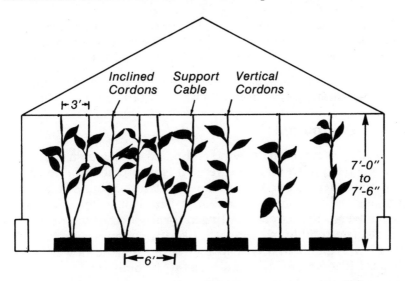

Fig. 10.10 V-cordon system of training European cucumbers.

If too many fruits are allowed to form at any one time, a large proportion will abort because the plant may not have sufficient food reserves to develop them. If a heavy load of fruit sets, often malformed or poorly colored fruits develop which are unmarketable. Remove them at an early stage. Multiple fruits in one axil should be thinned to one.

The renewal umbrella system of training plants is achieved by the following steps (Loughton 1975):

1. The main stem should be stopped at one leaf above the support wire. Pinch out the growing point at that level. Tie a small

loop of string around the wire and below the top leaf so that the plant will not slide down the main string.

2. Do not allow fruits to develop on the main stem up to about 4 feet.

3. Remove all laterals in the leaf axils on the main stem, except 2 at the top.

4. Train the top 2 laterals over the wire to hang down on either side of the main stem. Allow these to grow to two-thirds of the way down the main stem.

5. Remove all secondary laterals, except 2 at the top.

6. While the fruit on the first laterals are maturing, allow the second laterals to grow out and downward.

7. When the fruits on the first laterals have been harvested, remove them completely, allowing the second laterals to develop.

8. Repeating steps 5, 6 and 7 will maintain fruit production.

Some growers carry a cucumber crop for 10 months using this renewal umbrella system and obtain over 100 cucumbers per plant.

10.12 Pollination

Tomatoes are normally wind pollinated when grown outside. In greenhouses, however air movement is insufficient for flowers to pollinate themselves. Vibration of the flower clusters is essential for good pollination in a greenhouse. This can be done by tapping the flowers with a stick, your fingers, or an electric vibrator such as an electric toothbrush which has had its bristles removed. The vibrator is momentarily held lightly against the flower cluster branch. If environmental conditions are favorable and the flower is receptive, the fine yellow pollen can be seen flowing from the flower upon vibration.

Pollinating must be done while the flowers are in a receptive state. This is indicated by their petals curling back. Plants should be pollinated at least every other day, since blossoms remain receptive for about two days. Pollinating should be done between 11:00 A.M. and 3:00 P.M. under sunny conditions for best results. Research has shown that relative humidity of 70 percent is optimum for pollination, fruit set, and fruit development. High humidity keeps pollen damp and sticky, except around midday, and lessens the chances of sufficient pollen transfer from anthers to stigma. Too dry conditions (relative humidity less than 60 to 65 percent) cause desiccation of pollen.

Greenhouse temperatures should not fall below 60°F. at night nor exceed 85°F. during the day. At higher or lower temperatures, pollen germination and pollen tube growth are greatly reduced. Chemical growth regulators can be used to induce fruit development under lower than optimum temperatures, but these fruit are usually seedless. Open locules and thin outer walls may make the fruit soft and greatly reduce their quality.

Prolonged dark cloudy weather retards pollen development and germination, resulting in poor fruit set. Even if weather conditions are not ideal, pollination must be done at least every other day during the early afternoon to assist fruit set.

If pollination has been done correctly, small bead-like fruit will develop within a week or so. This is called fruit set. When young plants produce their first trusses, pollinate each day until fruit set is visible. It is important to get the fruit set on these first trusses as it throws the plant into a reproductive state which favors greater flower and fruit production as the plant ages. After the first few trusses have set, pollinating can be done every other day.

European cucumbers, unlike the regular North American seeded cucumbers, do not require pollinating to set fruit and the fruits are therefore seedless. Pollination may occur by the presence of bees and from male flowers on the same or neighboring plants in the greenhouse. Pollination causes seeds to form, and the fruits become clubbed at the end and develop a bitter taste. To prevent pollination, bees must not be allowed to enter the greenhouse, and male blossoms should be removed from the plants as soon as they develop. Now all-female and gynoecious (less than 10 percent male blooms) varieties have been developed so that male blossoms seldom, if at all, develop. In this way self-pollination is reduced, if not eliminated.

10.13 Physiological Disorders

Hydroponics has many advantages but it does not free the grower from the need for alertness in dealing with many physiological disorders common to all forms of food production. Physiological disorders are those fruit quality defects caused by undesirable temperatures, faulty nutrition, or improper irrigation. Some varieties are more susceptible than others to some of these disorders. Because we are using tomatoes and cucumbers as examples, we will present as a reference source several disorders common to those fruits.

1. *Blossom-end rot (tomatoes)*. This disorder appears as a brown, sunburned, leathery tissue at the blossom end of the fruit. (fig. 10.11). In the early stages the affected area will have a green, water-soaked appearance. While the cause of blossom-end rot is a low supply of calcium in the fruit, the indirect cause is plant stress. This stress may be due to: (a) low soil moisture, (b) excess soluble salts in the growing medium, (c) high rates of transpiration, and (d) high soil moisture, which leads to poor root aeration. Prevention involves avoiding these conditions.

2. *Fruit cracking (tomatoes)*. Symptoms are cracks radiating from the stem, almost always on maturing fruit, at any time during ripening. This is usually caused by a water deficit and excessively high fruit temperatures followed by a sudden change in moisture supply to the plants. Prevention is by avoidance of high fruit temperatures and maintenance of uniform soil (medium) moisture conditions.

3. *Blotchy ripening (tomatoes)*. This is uneven coloring of the fruit wall in the form of irregular, light green to colorless areas with brown areas in the vascular tissue inside the fruit. It is associated with low light intensity, cool temperatures, high soil moisture, high nitrogen, and low potassium. It can be avoided under low light intensity conditions by less frequent applications of irrigation and fertilizer (especially nitrogen).

4. *Green shoulder, sunscald (tomatoes)*. These disorders are associated with high temperature or high light intensity. Avoid removing leaves which offer protection to fruit clusters during the spring and summer months when sunlight is intense and keep greenhouse temperatures down.

5. *Roughness and catfacing (tomatoes)*. This is radial wrinkling of the fruit shoulders and walls and fruit shape distortion due to protuberances and indentations (fig. 10.12). This is caused by poor pollination and environmental factors such as low temperatures and high relative humidity which cause the flower parts to develop abnormally.

6. *Crooking (cucumbers)*. This is excessive fruit curvature. It can be caused by a leaf or stem interfering with the growth of the young fruit or the sticking of a flower petal on the spines of a leaf stem or another young fruit. Adverse temperature, excessive soil moisture, and poor nutrition have also been suggested as causes. Remove severely curved fruit from the plant immediately.

Fig. 10.11 Blossom-end-rot of tomatoes showing leathery, brown tissue at the blossom end of the fruit.

Fig. 10.12 Catfacing of tomato.

10.14 Diseases and Insects

Since the control of diseases and insects is very specific, only a brief description of the most common problems are given here.

Some common tomato diseases.

1. Leaf mold (Cladosporium). This starts as a small gray spot on the lower side of the leaf and spreads until a definite pale area also develops on the upper surface (fig. 10.13). Additional infection sites develop and the initially small spots expand. The basic control measure is sanitation within the greenhouse and careful ventilation and temperature control to prevent high humidity. Some fungicide sprays can be helpful.

2. Wilt (Fusarium and Verticillium). Initially plants wilt on hot days, then eventually they wilt all the time and the leaves become yellow. If the plant is cut just above the soil surface, a darkened ring is visible inside the outer green layer of cells. No spray or cultural treatment will control these diseases. They can only be controlled through sterilization of the growing medium.

Greenhouse growers of tomatoes in British Columbia lose about 10-15 percent of their plants annually to *Fusarium* wilt when growing in soilless culture. Experimental work supports the possibility of reducing infection through intercropping several lettuce plants in each row with the tomatoes. Apparently, lettuce gives off an exudate that slows the activity of *Fusarium* in the medium and thereby reduces infection of tomatoes.

3. *Early blight and leaf spot (Alternaria* and *Septoria)*. These cause discolored or dead spots on the leaves. Early blight has dark rings on a brown background. Leaf spot has small black dots on the affected area. Both organisms attack the oldest leaves first and cause severe defoliation of the lower part of the plant. Proper ventilation and removal of lower senescing leaves to improve air circulation and reduce relative humidity helps reduce the disease.

4. *Gray mold (Botrytis)*. Under high humidity conditions fungal spores infect wounds such as leaf scars and a watery rot and fluffy gray growth forms over the affected area. The disease may develop along the stem for several inches and eventually girdle it, killing the plant. Proper ventilation to reduce the relative humidity will prevent the spread of the disease. Remove infected plants immediately. Affected areas at early stages of infection can be scraped and covered with a fungicide (Ferbam) paste or the plants can be sprayed with Ferbam.

5. *Virus (Tobacco mosaic virus, TMV)*. Several viruses will attack tomatoes. TMV is the most common, causing distortion of the leaves and stunting of growth with resultant yield reductions (fig. 10.14). Plant juice containing the virus is spread by sucking insects or on the hands or tools of the people working in the crop. Sanitation, control of sucking insects and no smoking (TMV is present in tobacco) in greenhouses will help to avoid infection. Presently, an antibody type of spray has been used successfully. The plants are inoculated with an attenuated (mild) strain of TMV which offers cross-protection against infection by the severe strain. This use of TMV protection is no longer required as most commercial tomato varieties have TMV resistance bred into them.

Some common cucumber diseases.

1. *Powdery mildew*. Small snowy white spots initially appear on the upper surface of the leaves. They quickly spread in size and to other leaves (fig. 10.15). Proper sanitation and adequate ventilation are the primary control measures. Chemical control is also possible.

2. *Cucumber mosaic virus (CMV)*. Some of the same strains of virus found on tomatoes also infect cucumbers. The affected leaves are dwarfed or become long and narrow. No control measure other than prevention through sanitation is known.

Fig. 10.13. Leaf mold of tomato plant. Lower side of leaf showing pale colored areas and brown lesions.

Fig. 10.14. TMV infected tomato leaf. Distorted leaf pattern and mosaic appearance.

Fig. 10.15. Powdery mildew of cucumber with white spots (lesions) on upper leaf surface.

3. *Wilt (Fusarium)*. This is the same wilt disease as found commonly in tomatoes. Proper sterilization of the growing medium between crops and sanitation are the only control measures.

4. *Gray Mold (Botrytis)*. Again the symptoms and control measure are the same as for tomatoes.

Tomato and Cucumber Insects.

Biological control of insect pests is now widely accepted in the greenhouse industry. A number of companies (Appendix 2) sell these biological agents. Biological control refers to the use of living organisms to control other living pest organisms.

There are a number of advantages to using biological control agents. Pests cannot build up resistance against biological agents as easily as they can with pesticides. The cost of biological control is less than with the use of pesticides. There is no fear of phytotoxicity or persistence of chemicals potentially hazardous to human health. Generally, biological control does not completely eliminate the pest, as a certain level of pest population is necessary to sustain the predator population. For this reason, emphasis is on integrated control, using biological control agents with cultural and chemical control measures. The objective is not complete pest elimination, but pest management, whereby pest populations are maintained at a level below any significant plant damage.

With an integrated pest management program, only certain pesticides must be used which do not harm the predatory agents. However, spot treatment of highly infested areas may be controlled by other more poisonous pesticides if pest populations cannot be controlled by the biological agents. Once such infestations are reduced, the use of these chemicals should be restricted. Such pesticides as insecticidal soaps, insect growth regulators or hormones, sticky yellow strip traps and bacterial or fungi insecticides may be used with the biological agents without harming them. The grower must check with government agencies and the companies selling biological agents to determine which pesticides may be used without harming the specific predators in their integrated pest management program. For example, if a program of mite control using the predatory mite *Phytoseiulus persimilis* has been introduced into the greenhouse, outbreaks of the two-spotted mite may be controlled using fenbutatin-oxide (Vendex), which is harmless to the predatory mite. Yellow sticky traps (fig. 5.48) may be used to trap adult whiteflies. These traps are available commercially or may be made from pieces of stiff cardboard painted a bright yellow and coated with vaseline, vaseline/mineral oil mix, or other sticky material.

1. *Whitefly (Trialeurodes vaporariorum).* The whitefly life cycle is four to five weeks during which time it undergoes a number of molts in its nymph stage as shown in figure 10.16. This is the most common pest in the greenhouse tomato crop. It is usually located on the undersides of the leaves. When at rest on a leaf its triangular white body makes it easy to identify. The insect secretes a sticky substance on the leaves and fruit in which a black fungus later grows, making it necessary to clean the fruit before marketing. Several pesticides such as parathion, pyrethrin and vapona can be used for control. However, the insects quickly build up resistance, making it necessary to use different pesticides to obtain reasonable control. Whitefly is also a common pest on cucumbers.

Biological control may be achieved by use of the chalcidoid wasp *Encarsia formosa.* This parasite is available from biological control agent suppliers. Adult female wasps lay eggs in the whitefly larvae and also eat early larval stages of the whitefly. The parasitic grub feeds within the larva, which turns black within two weeks providing an easy method of determining the success of the *Encarsia.* Successful control is temperature and humidity dependent, as the wasp reproduces best at a mean temperature of 23°C (73°F) and a relative humidity not exceeding 70 percent. *Encarsia* are purchased as pupae stuck to paper strips (fig. 10.17) which are hung on plants in the greenhouse. Each card contains the black pupae from which the parasite emerges. As soon as the first whiteflies are found, a program of repeated introductions of the wasp must be initiated.

To use *Encarsia formosa* successfully a number of steps must be followed:

a. No residual pesticides should be used a month prior to introduction.

b. Existing whitefly populations should be reduced, using insecticidal soap or insect hormones, to an average of less than one adult per upper leaf.

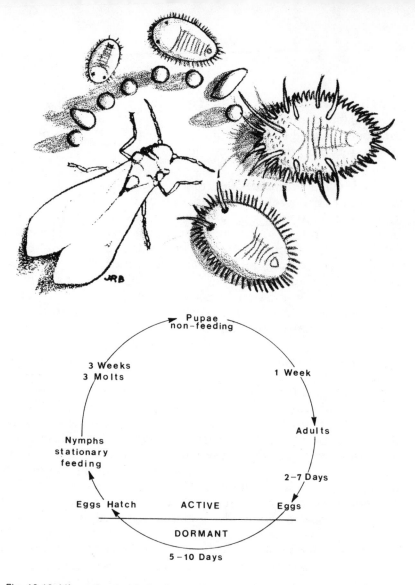

Fig. 10.16. Life cycle of whitefly. (Insect drawings courtesy of J. R. Baker, North Carolina Agricultural Extension Service, Raleigh, NC 27695-7613.)

   c. Adjust temperature and humidity to 23-27°C (73°-81°F) and 50-70 percent respectively.

   d. Introduce *Encarsia* at the rate of 10/square meter (1/sq ft) of planted area or 1-5/infested plant.

   e. Reintroduce *Encarsia* every 10-14 days for a total of four introductions.

   f. Monitor plants weekly for the number of whitefly and black scales.

Fig. 10.17. Paper containing *Encarsia* pupae attached to a leaf petiole of a tomato plant.

Several parasitic fungi, *Verticillium lecanii* and *Achersonia aleyrodis,* are being tested commercially for their effectiveness in controlling whitefly. They are safe to use with *Encarsia formosa.*

2. *Two-spotted spider mite (Tetranychus urticae).* Mites are closely related to spiders and ticks having four pair of legs, unlike insects which have three pair of legs. Their life cycle goes through a number of nymph stages, as indicated in figure 10.18. Their life cycle is from 10 to 14 days, depending upon temperature. At 26°C (80°F) the cycle is shortened to 10 days; whereas, at lower temperatures the cycle may be up to 2 months. Low relative humidity also favors their development. Misting plants frequently during dry periods will discourage spider mites as they dislike high humidity.

This pest is particularly common on cucumbers. A webbing appearance on the undersides of leaves indicates an already heavy infestation. A magnifying glass is needed to observe the mite closely in order to see the dark-colored spot on each side of its body. The mite causes a yellowing of leaves starting as very small yellow pin-sized dots which coalesce to eventually form a very characteristic bronzed appearance (fig. 10.19). Severe infestations will cause leaves to become entirely bleached as the mites suck the contents of the leaf cells, leaving a dead shell.

Mites live on plant refuse and on the greenhouse framework between crops. A thorough eradication and sterilization between crops is necessary. Clear the greenhouse of all plant material and

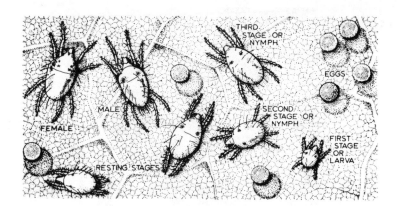

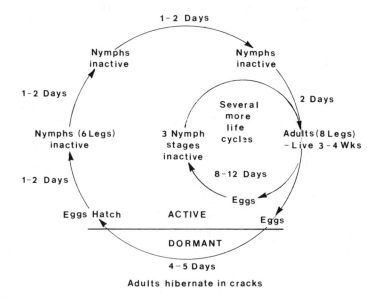

Fig. 10.18. Life cycle of two-spotted spider mite. (Insect drawings courtesy of J. R. Baker, North Carolina Agricultural Extension Service, Raleigh, NC 27695-7613.)

fumigate or spray with appropriate chemicals. If populations are very large they will spread to tomatoes, lettuce, chard and almost all vegetables and flowers. Control by chemical miticides such as "Pentac," "Vendex," and "Mavrik" are effective only against adults.

A predatory mite, *Phytoseiulus persimilis,* is available commercially. *Phytoseiulus* differs from the two-spotted mite by its lack of spots, pear-shaped body, longer front legs, and especially its rapid movement when disturbed. It prefers temperatures in the range of 21–27°C (70–81°F). Adults develop from eggs in less than a week. This is twice as fast as their prey. However, since bright light and high temperatures are unfavorable to their development, such hot conditions should be avoided, since these conditions also favor spider mites.

Other predatory mites are available: *Metaseiulus occidentalis*, which performs well under cooler temperatures, and *Amblyseius californicus*, which prefers warmer temperatures.

These predators are applied mainly to cucumbers and peppers but may also be used on tomatoes, beans, gherkins, melons, grapes, strawberries, and various flower crops.

To use *Phytoseiulus persimilis* or others:

a. For one month prior to introduction do not use residual pesticides.

b. Introduce the predator at the first sign of spider mite damage. If there is greater than 1 mite/leaf, reduce the population with insecticidal soap or fenbutatin-oxide (Vendex), until only 10 percent of the leaves are infested.

c. Maintain optimum temperatures for the predator and high relative humidity.

d. Generally, 8–10 predators/square meter (80–100/sq ft) should be introduced. Release in early morning onto the mid and upper foliage. Predator mites are available in shaker bottles.

e. Monitor spider mite populations once per week.

f. Reintroduce the predator at monthly intervals. Populations of predators should be roughly maintained at one predator for every five spider mites. Good control should be achieved within four to six weeks.

Fig. 10.19 Spider mite infestation of cucumber leaf. Severe infestation causing yellowing of leaves as pin-sized dots coalesce.

3. *Aphids-green peach aphid (Myzus persicae),* foxglove aphid *(Alacorthum solani),* and potato aphid *(Macrosiphum euphorbiae).*

The life cycle varies in length from 7–10 days to three weeks depending upon temperature and season, as shown in figure 10.20.

Aphids are usually clustered in large colonies on new succulent growth, at the base of buds, and on the underside of leaves. The most common greenhouse species is the green peach aphid. The wingless forms are yellowish green in summer and pink to red in the fall and spring. The winged forms are brown. They have a pear-shaped body 1–6 millimeters in length with four wings, if winged. They excrete "honeydew" from their abdomen, which is a food for ants. The presence of large ant populations on plants often indicates aphid infestation. Aphids feed by sucking out plant sap with their tubelike, piercing mouthpart. This causes distorted leaves when they feed on young leaf buds. Under short food supply winged females appear and migrate.

A number of types of aphids including pink, black and dark green feed on most greenhouse vegetables. They suck the juices out of the plant and cause the leaves to become distorted and sticky from a honeydew deposit. They can be controlled with a weekly spray program using chemicals such as pyrethrin, malathion and rotenone.

Some biological control can be achieved using various lady beetles and the green lacewing, *Chrysopa carnea.* A predaceous midge larva, *Aphidoletes aphidimyza,* is being marketed in Finland and Canada. The adult midge, a small black, delicate fly lives only a few days. The female lays 100–200 eggs on the underside of leaves close to aphid colonies, which hatch in three to four days. A large orange or red larve up to three millimeters long matures in three to five days and drops to the ground where it forms a cocoon. Pupation takes about 10–14 days completing a total life cycle of three weeks.

The threshold temperature for larval development is approximately 6°C (43°F), with optimum temperatures between 23° and 25°C (73°–77°F) at 80–90 percent relative humidity. Adult midges feed on aphid honeydew excretions. The larva feeds on aphids, killing from 4–65 aphids each.

To use *Aphidoletes aphidimyza:*

a. Control ants which may protect the aphids.

b. Avoid using residual pesticides one month prior to introduction.

c. Reduce heavy aphid populations with Enstar (insect growth regulator) or insecticidal soap. Areas of at least 10 aphids/plant or one aphid/square centimeter should be left to encourage egg laying by the midge.

d. Maintain temperatures between 20°–27°C (68°–81°F).

e. Introduce the predator at a rate of 1 pupa/3 aphids or 2–5 pupae/square meter (2–5 pupae/10 sq ft) of planted area.

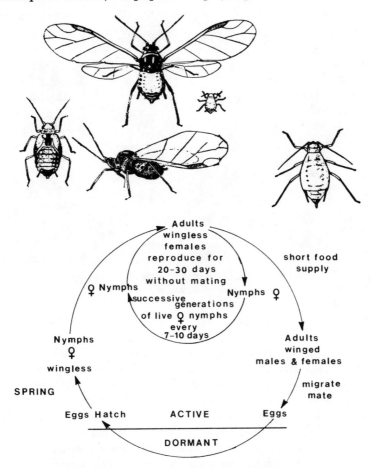

Fig. 10.20. Life cycle of aphid. (Insect drawings courtesy of J. R. Baker, North Carolina Agricultural Extension Service, Raleigh, NC 27695-7613.)

f. Spread the pupae in shady areas near aphid-infested plants and repeat introductions in 7–14 days and thereafter as necessary.
g. Monitor plants for infestation weekly.

In Europe and possibly Canada a parasitic fungus, *Verticillium lecanii*, trade name Vertalec, is available commercially as a biological control agent of aphids.

Spot spraying in localized infestations may be done with chemical pesticides such as insecticidal soap, Enstar and Pirimor, but avoid spraying the *Aphidoletes* larvae. Reintroduction of the predatory larvae will be necessary in areas sprayed with chemical pesticides.

Fig. 10.21. Leafminer damage to tomato plant with distinct "mines" or "tunnels" appearing between the leaf epidermal tissues.

4. *Tomato leafminer (Liriomyza bryoniae)* and the American serpentine leafminer *(Liriomyza trifolii)*. *Liriomyza bryoniae* is common on tomatoes, especially in the tropics. Adult flies are yellow-black in color and about two millimeters in length. The female deposits its eggs in the leaf, causing a small white puncture-protuberance. When the larvae hatch they eat "tunnels" through the leaf between the upper and lower leaf epidermis creating "mines" (fig. 10.21). These tunnels may coalesce resulting in large areas of damage until the entire leaf dries up. The maturing larva drops from the leaves to the ground where it

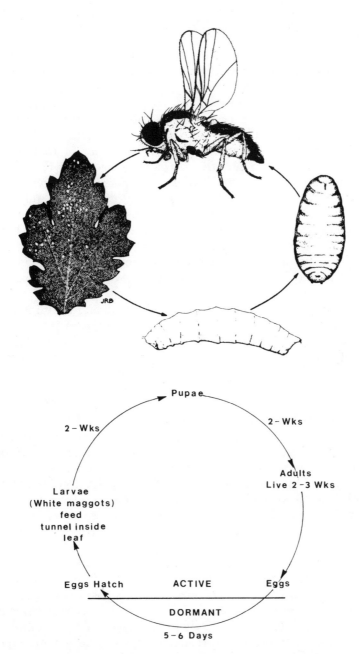

Fig. 10.22. Life cycle of leafminer. (Insect drawings courtesy of J. R. Baker, North Carolina Agricultural Extension Service, Raleigh, NC 27695-7613.)

pupates. Within 10 days the adult emerges, the whole cycle from egg to adult fly takes three to five weeks, as shown in figure 10.22.

The leafminer has become resistant to many chemical pesticides. The leafminer of lettuce in Venezuela *(Liriomyza huidobrensis)* is very resistant to most pesticides. While a number of biological control agents have been identified and are presently available commercially for leafminer of tomato and flower crops, there is no effective control agent for the lettuce leafminer. The two insects, *Dacnusa sibirica* and *Diglyphus isaea* parasitize both leafminer species *Liriomyza bryoniae* and *L. trifolii*. A third, *Opius pallipes*, only parasitizes the tomato leafminer. *Opius* and *Dacnusa* lay eggs in the leafminer larva. As the leafminer larva pupates, the parasite emerges instead of the leafminer. *Diglyphus isaea* kills the leafminer in its tunnel and lays an egg beside it. The wasp (parasite) develops in the tunnel, feeding on the dead larva.

Leaf samples must be taken from the crop and examined in a laboratory to identify the species of leafminer, parasites present, and level of parasitism. If there are insufficient natural parasites present, *Dacnusa* or *Diglyphus* are introduced. The introduction depends on the season, the species of leafminer, and the level of infestation.

5. *Thrips (Heliothrips haemorrhoidalis)* and flower thrips *(Frankliniella tritici* and *F. occidentalis).* Thrips *(Heliothrips haemorrhoidalis)* is becoming a problem on cucumbers. Adults are attracted to the yellow cucumber flower. Adult thrips are 0.75 millimeters long with feathery wings. They develop outside the greenhouse on weeds and invade the greenhouse. Feeding on leaf undersides, growing tips, and flowers, they cause small, bleached dead spots on leaves and damage growing tips and flowers. Nymphs with rasping mouth parts scrape the leaf surface and suck the plant sap, causing a white, silvery, discoloration resulting in streaks. Thrips feed like spider mites by puncturing and sucking the leaf contents. Damage appears as narrow crevices and a silvery appearance on leaves. They feed in narrow crevices between the calyx and the newly forming fruit of the cucumbers, causing curled and distorted fruits. Thrips similarly damage peppers.

Their two- to three-week life cycle begins with the adult female depositing eggs under the leaf surface (fig. 10.23). After four days

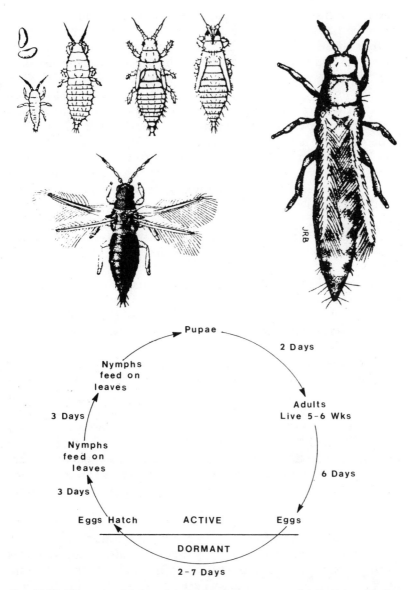

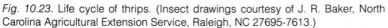

Fig. 10.23. Life cycle of thrips. (Insect drawings courtesy of J. R. Baker, North Carolina Agricultural Extension Service, Raleigh, NC 27695-7613.)

they hatch into nymphs which feed on the leaves for three days before molting into larger more active nymphs that feed for another three days before dropping to the ground to pupate and emerge as adults within two days. They feed for about six days before beginning to lay from 50 to 100 eggs over 40 days.

Yellow sticky traps should be used for early detection and monitoring of the pest population. *Amblyseius cucumeris*, a predatory mite, is available commercially to control thrips. The predatory mite is similar in appearance to *Phytoseiulus*, differing only in its lighter pale pink color and shorter legs. Its life cycle is similar to *Phytoseiulus*. The predator mite must be introduced in the crop at an early stage for preventive action so that a large population can be built up in order to control the thrips as soon as they appear. Their introduction and management is similar to that of *Phytoseiulus*. They should be introduced on a weekly basis until population levels reach 100 per plant.

6. *Caterpillars and cutworms.* Caterpillars are larvae of butterflies, and cutworms are larvae of moths. These are common in most greenhouse crops. The larvae feed on aerial plant parts. Their presence is indicated by notches in leaves and cut stems and petioles.

Cutworms climb up the plant and feed on the foliage during the night and are found in the soil or medium in the day. Caterpillars are not nocturnal like cutworms but feed on above-ground plant parts day and night.

Adult moths and butterflies fly into the greenhouse from outdoors and quickly lay eggs on the plants, where they hatch into feeding larvae within several days during high temperatures. Entry of adults should be prevented by using screens over shutters, vents, etc. The time of their life cycle varies with season, temperature, and the species (fig. 10.24).

Control may be achieved by use of a number of effective chemical pesticides such as Lannate, Diazinon, Malathion, etc., as well as biological control with a parasitic bacterium, *Bacillus thuringiensis*, marketed as Dipel or Thuricide. This bacterium must be sprayed on a regular weekly basis, as new growth occurs to protect all surfaces. It is active only upon ingestion by the caterpillar or cutworm. The larvae are paralyzed so they stop eating a few hours after spraying. They die within one to five days. The bacterium is harmless to mammals, fishes, birds and leaves no toxic residue in the environment.

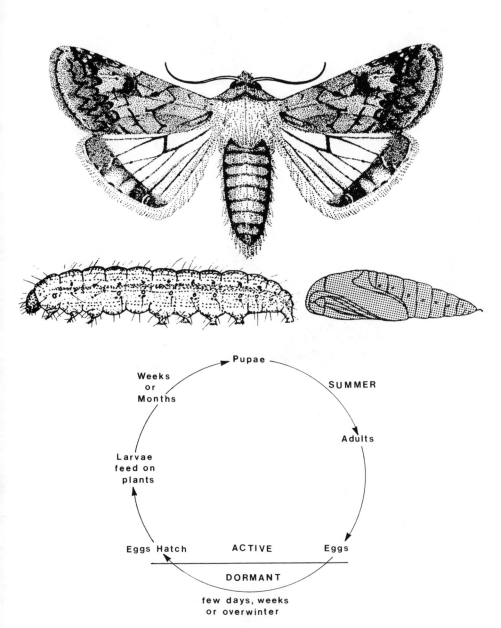

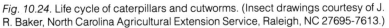

Fig. 10.24. Life cycle of caterpillars and cutworms. (Insect drawings courtesy of J. R. Baker, North Carolina Agricultural Extension Service, Raleigh, NC 27695-7613.)

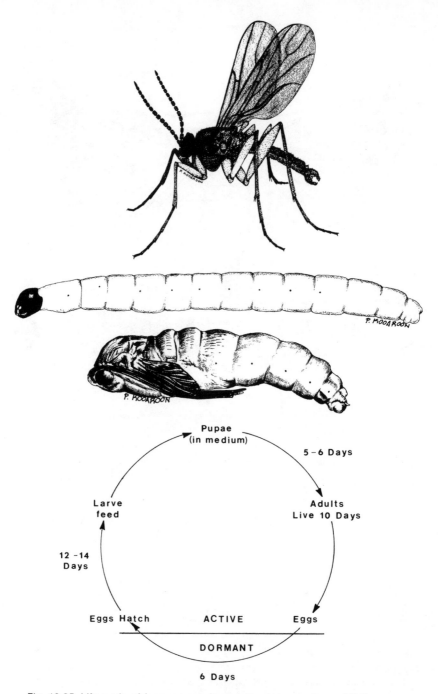

Pupae
(in medium)

5 – 6 Days

Larve
feed

Adults
Live 10 Days

12 –14
Days

Eggs Hatch   ACTIVE   Eggs

DORMANT

6 Days

Fig. 10.25. Life cycle of fungus gnat. (Insect drawings courtesy of P. Kooaroon, North Carolina Agricultural Extension Service, Raleigh, NC 27695-7613.)

7. *Fungus gnats* (*Bradysia* species and *Sciara* species). The larvae of these small, dark grey or black flies feed normally on soil fungi and decaying organic matter, but as populations increase, they attack plant roots. They are legless white worms about six millimeters (¼ in) in length with a black head. Adults have long legs and antennae, about three millimeters long, with one pair of clear wings. They attack all seedlings and are favored by the presence of moisture such as exists with capillary mats and the growth of algae. They also feed on the tap roots, stem cortex, and root hairs of mature cucumbers. They have a four-week life cycle as shown in figure 10.25.

Control by use of yellow sticky traps and chemical pesticides such as Diazinon are effective. Also, avoid moist areas in the greenhouse; keep medium surfaces dry. Some success has been achieved using a predatory mite which feeds on the eggs and pupae in the soil. *Bacillus* bacterium may provide some control of the larvae. Vectobac, produced by Abbott Laboratories, is an effective *Bacillus* subspecies against fungus gnats.

In general, life cycles of insects can be shortened under optimal temperature and relative humidity conditions. Control of insect pests must be carried out at the most susceptible stage of their life cycle. This is usually the adult or active nymph or larval stages that are feeding. For successful integrated pest control using biological agents, the predator and prey populations must be in balance. Use of selective chemical pesticides for control of localized population outbreaks of the pest is necessary. Before using any chemical pesticides, the grower must check with manufacturers, the supplier of biological agents and/or agricultural extension personnel to determine which may be used safely. Environmental conditions within the greenhouse must be maintained at levels favorable to the predator. Weekly monitoring of predator-prey populations is needed to maintain equilibrium and new introductions of predators made to achieve successful integrated pest management.

Hydroponic culture minimizes pests and diseases in the growing medium by efficient sterilization between crops. The pests and diseases of the aerial part of the plant, however, are not influenced by hydroponic culture. Therefore, if proper preventive programs are not followed, severe infestations may occur similar to those in regular soil culture field conditions.

10.15 Vegetable Varieties

Many varieties of vegetables are available from seed houses. While both field and greenhouse varieties can be grown in a greenhouse, it is advantageous to use greenhouse varieties whenever possible since they are often bred to yield very heavily under controlled environment conditions. That is, in a greenhouse higher yields generally could be expected from greenhouse varieties than from field varieties. In most cases greenhouse varieties cannot be easily grown under field conditions since they are unable to withstand the temperature fluctuations encountered there.

A number of greenhouse varieties of vegetables perform particularly well in hydroponic culture. These along with other acceptable greenhouse varieties are given in table 10.3.

Older tomato varieties such as Vendor, Vantage, Tropic, Manapel are being replaced by the Dutch varieties Dombito, Caruso, Larma, and Perfecto which are superior in vigor, yields, and disease resistance. These varieties are resistant to Tobacco Mosaic Virus (TMV), *Cladosporium* leaf mold, *Fusarium*, and *Verticillium* crown rots. Seed companies give symbols to each variety indicating which diseases it is resistant to. For example, the

TABLE 10.3 Recommended Vegetable Varieties for Greenhouse and Hydroponic Culture

Vegetable	Varieties
Cucumbers—European	*Toska 70, Rocket, Brilliant, *Pandex, Farbio, La Reine, Sandra, * Uniflora D, *Corona, *Farona, *Marillo, *Fidelio
Lettuce—European —Novelty —Looseleaf	*Deci-Minor, *Ostinata Buttercrunch *Domineer, *Black Seeded Simpson, Grand Rapids, Waldmann's Dark Green
Tomatoes	*Vendor, Vantage, *Tropic, Manapel, Michigan-Ohio Hybrid, Ohio WR-25, *Dombito, *Caruso, *Larma, *Perfecto, *Laura
Peppers, Belltypes —Green to red, use: —Green to yellow, use:	 *Delphin, *Plutona, *Tango *Luteus, *Goldstar

*Varieties particularly suitable to hydroponic culture

tomato variety Caruso is given the symbol "TmC$_5$VF$_2$" indicating it is resistant to: TMV, *Cladosporium* races A,B,C,D, and E, *Verticillium*, and *Fusarium* races 1 and 2. The most popular cucumber varieties now used are Farona, Corona, and Farbio. They are all female, seedless varieties that set fruit without pollination. Peppers are becoming an important greenhouse crop. These are the sweet bell peppers which are green, maturing either to red or yellow. The more popular green-to-red use varieties are Delphin, Plutona, and Tango, while the green-to-yellow use ones are Luteus and Goldstar.

10.15.1 Lettuce

Lettuce grows very well in hydroponic culture. There are four basic types of lettuce: European or bibb lettuce; looseleaf lettuce; head lettuce or iceberg; and cos or romaine lettuce. While many varieties of each type are available from seed houses there are a few of each type which are particularly well suited to hydroponic culture and greenhouse environments. The most suitable varieties of European or bibb lettuce are Deci-minor, Capitan and Ostinata. They should be planted at 20 cm by 20 cm (8 in. by 8 in.) spacing. Bibb lettuce requires a night temperature of 18°C (65°F), a day temperature of 17° to 19°C (63°–66°F) on dull days and 21° to 24°C (70°–75°F) on sunny days. They take about 60 days from seeding to maturity.

Looseleaf varieties are generally the easiest to grow. Varieties such as Slo Bolt, Black Seeded Simpson, Grand Rapids, and Waldmann's Dark Green are very vigorous in hydroponic culture. They require between 45 and 50 days to mature. Their spacing and temperature requirements are similar to European lettuce. Looseleaf varieties require night temperatures of 10° to 13°C (50°–55°F) and 13° to 21°C (55°–70°F) during the day depending upon sunlight. However, they will tolerate higher temperatures to 27°C (75°–80°F) without wilting, bolting or slowing growth. But if higher temperatures occur, "burning" of the leaf tip or margin may result. Some varieties are more tolerant to higher temperatures and resist "tip-burn."

Of the many head lettuce varieties available, Great Lakes 659 grows best in hydroponics and greenhouse environments. It takes between 80 to 85 days to mature and will tolerate higher day temperatures up to 27° to 28° C (77°–78°F) without bolting provided that it receives full sunlight. Head lettuce should be spaced slightly wider apart at 25 centimeters by 25 centimeters (10 in by 10 in).

Valmaine Cos and Parris Island Cos have similar temperature requirements to looseleaf lettuce. They take about 75 days to mature and require similar spacing as looseleaf lettuce.

Lettuce should be seeded in peat pellets, rockwool blocks, oasis blocks or flats of artificial medium as discussed earlier. Transplanting into growing beds should take place once the seedlings are 5–6 centimeters (2–2½ in) in height (about 20 to 23 days after seeding).

All lettuce is susceptible to rot on the lower leaves when inadequate ventilation causes the lower leaves to remain moist. Since the fibrous root system of lettuce does not penetrate the medium very deeply, good drainage with frequent, uniform, moderate applications of the nutrient solution is better than longer periods of less frequent cycles.

10.16 Planting Schedules

A number of planting schedules are possible depending upon what crop or combination of crops is to be grown over the entire year. If only tomatoes are to be grown, a spring and fall crop system is used, as shown in table 10.4. Particularly when growing on a backyard scale, intercropping of lettuce is recommended for the spring crop of tomatoes. Lettuce should be seeded and transplanted into the beds at the same time. One to two lettuce plants can be placed between each pair of tomato plants. The tomatoes will soon grow above the lettuce so they will not be shaded by it. While the tomatoes are still small (12-18 inches in height) the lettuce will receive sufficient light to produce well. In this way a crop of lettuce can be harvested at least one month before the tomatoes will be ready. After this initial intercropping of lettuce further intercrops can be placed under the tomatoes once the tomatoes are fully mature and several trusses of fruit and all the leaves up to the maturing truss have been removed. This will be about May, as shown in table 10.4. One intercrop of lettuce could be grown with the fall crop through July and August (table 10.4).

A combination crop of late spring tomatoes and two fall lettuce crops is practical on a commercial scale, as shown in table 10.5. As in the two-crop tomato schedule, lettuce could be intercropped from January to March while the tomatoes are growing.

TABLE 10.4   Planting Schedule for a Spring and Fall Crop of Tomatoes (Two Crops Annually)

Date	Activity
Dec. 20-31	Sow lettuce and tomato seeds in peat pellets
Feb. 1-15	Transplant seedlings into hydroponic beds
March 15	Harvest lettuce
April 15	Begin harvesting tomatoes
May 15	Terminate tomato plants, seed lettuce
June 1	Sow tomato seeds in peat pellets for fall crop; transplant lettuce intercrop under existing tomatoes
July 1	Harvest lettuce, pull tomato plants of spring crop, clean greenhouse, sterilize, etc.
July 15	Transplant fall tomato crop and lettuce intercrop into greenhouse beds
Aug. 15-30	Harvest lettuce
Sept. 15	Begin harvesting ripe tomatoes
Nov. 1	Terminate tomato plants
Dec. 20-31	Pull plants of fall crop, clean up, sterilize, etc., sow lettuce and tomato seeds of spring crop

TABLE 10.5 Combination Crop of Late Spring Tomatoes and Two Fall Lettuce Crops

Date	Activity
Late Spring Tomatoes:	
Dec. 20-31	Sow tomato seeds
Feb. 1-15	Transplant tomatoes into beds
May-July	Harvest tomatoes
July 20-31	Remove plants, clean up, etc.
Fall Lettuce:	
First Crop:	
Aug. 10-15	Sow lettuce seeds
Sept. 5-10	Transplant lettuce into greenhouse beds
Oct. 10-20	Harvest crop
Second Crop:	
Sept. 15-20	Sow second crop lettuce seeds
Oct. 15-25	Transplant lettuce into beds
Dec. 12-15	Harvest crop

TABLE 10.6   Combination Crop of Spring Cucumbers and Fall Tomatoes

Date	Activity
Spring Cucumbers:	
Dec. 25-31	Sow cucumber seeds (and lettuce seeds)
Feb. 1-15	Transplant cucumbers (and lettuce) into greenhouse beds
March 1-15	Harvest lettuce and begin harvesting cucumbers
June 25-15	Remove cucumbers, clean up, sterilize, etc.
Fall Tomatoes:	
June 15-30	Sow tomato (and lettuce) seeds
July 20-31	Transplant tomatoes (and lettuce)
Sept. 15	Harvest lettuce
Oct. 1	Begin harvesting tomatoes
Dec. 15-25	Remove tomato plants, clean up, sterilize, etc.

A third schedule is one using a spring cucumber crop with a fall tomato crop, as shown in table 10.6. Lettuce once again could be intercropped with the initial planting of both the cucumbers and the tomatoes.

Cucumbers, if grown as the only crop year round, may be scheduled in numerous ways. Some growers prefer to grow 3 to 5 crops a year while others may grow only one long crop from February through October using the renewal umbrella system. Those using the single long crop often close their greenhouses down from November through January, saving on heating bills and carrying out only a maintenance and repair program to their greenhouse during these winter months. Table 10.7 gives a schedule for a 3-crop system of cucumbers. Lettuce could be intercropped during the first and second crops, but not during the third crop when lighting conditions are poor.

Over the past few years it has become common practice to grow a single crop of tomatoes or cucumbers per year. Tomatoes are sown in mid-December and grow through November of the following year, while cucumbers are sown a little later, in early January, as shown in table 10.8.

10.17 Crop Termination

In the growing of tomatoes the growing point of each plant should be cut off 60 days prior to the expected date for pulling of the

TABLE 10.7   A Three-Crop Schedule for Annual Cucumber Production

Date	Activity
Jan. 1	Sow cucumber (and lettuce) seeds (first crop)
Feb. 1-15	Transplant into beds (first crop)
March 1	Harvest lettuce
March 31	Begin harvesting cucumbers
May 1	Sow cucumber (and lettuce) seeds (second crop)
May 31	Pull cucumbers of first crop, clean up, etc.
June 1-10	Transplant cucumbers (and lettuce) into beds (second crop)
July 1	Harvest lettuce
July 15	Begin harvesting cucumbers (second crop)
Aug. 1	Sow cucumber seeds (third crop)
Aug. 31	Pull cucumber plants of second crop, clean up, etc.
Sept. 1-10	Transplant cucumbers into beds (third crop)
Oct. 15	Begin harvesting cucumbers
Dec. 20-31	Pull plants (third crop), clean up, sterilize, etc.

TABLE 10.8 Single Crop of Tomatoes or Cucumbers

Date	Activity
Tomatoes:	
Dec. 15–20	Sow tomato seeds
Jan. 1–5	Transplant to larger rockwool blocks keep under HID supplementary lighting with minimum 5500 lux (510 ft. candles) intensity in seedling area of greenhouse
Jan. 20–Feb. 1	Transplant tomatoes into beds when flower buds appear
April–Nov.	Harvest tomatoes
Nov. 15–Dec. 15	Remove plants, clean up, etc.
Cucumbers:	
Jan. 1–10	Sow cucumber seeds
Feb. 1–15	Transplant into beds
March 15–31	Begin harvesting cucumbers
April–Nov. 15	Harvest cucumbers
Nov. 15–Dec. 31	Remove plants, clean up, etc.

plants (table 10.4). During this 60-day period remove the many suckers which will develop at the tops of the plants.

Several days before physically removing the plants from the greenhouse, pull out the roots and stop the flow of water and nutrients to the beds. Leave the rest of the plant still supported by the string and clamps. This will result in the plants losing a lot of water and thus reduce the overall plant weight to be removed from the greenhouse. Shake the gravel from the roots and wedge the plastic clamps apart with a spoon or knife edge when the plants are ready to be transported out of the greenhouse. The plastic support clamps can be reused after soaking and washing them in a bleach solution. Dispose of the plants in the garbage, on a compost pile or bury them some distance from the greenhouse to avoid any disease or insect reinfestation of the new crop. After all the plants have been removed from the greenhouse, sweep all the floors, etc., clean so that no plant debris remains. The beds, nutrient tank and growing medium must then be thoroughly sterilized according to measures given in earlier chapters. Once everything has been completely sterilized, the system is ready for its next crop.

A hydroponic system, if properly sterilized and cleaned between each crop, will continuously yield heavy crops over the years, giving its operator higher returns than could be achieved over the long run with soil.

10.18 Concluding Remarks

Whether plants are grown hydroponically or in soil, their cultural requirements are the same. Specific information on the growing of various plants is available from gardening books and various extension bulletins issued by universities and agricultural departments. A list of some university extension offices is given in the Appendix.

Hydroponic gardening differs from soil growing in its effective control of watering, nutrition, diseases and pests. It is this control which provides it with the potential of becoming the solution to intensive crop production under adverse conditions throughout the world and in man's future travels to other planets.

References

Johnston, H., Jr. 1973. *Cultural practices for tomatoes*. Univ. of Calif. Agric. Extension Bulletin, Nov. 1973.

────── 1975. *Greenhouse tomato production*. Univ. of Calif. Leaflet 2806.

────── 1975. *Greenhouse cucumber production*. Univ. of Calif. Coop. Ext. Leaflet 2775.

Larson, J. E. 1970. *Growing tomatoes in plastic greenhouses*. Texas A&M Univ. Agric. Ext. Bulletin, June 1970.

Loughton, A. 1975. The "How-To" of European cucumbers. *Am. Veg. Grower*, November 1975, pp. 16, 18, 58 and 60.

Schales, F. D. and P. H. Massey, Jr. 1968. *Tomato production in plastic greenhouses*. Virginia Polytechnic Inst. Ext. Div. Publ. 154, July 1968.

────── 1969. *Starting early plants*. Virginia Polytechnic Inst. Ext. Div. Publ. 226, Jan. 1969.

Stoner, A. K. 1971. *Commercial production of greenhouse tomatoes*. U.S.D.A. Handbook No. 382, Washington, D.C.: Gov. Printing Office.

Tiessen, H., J. Wiebe and C. Fisher. 1976. *Greenhouse vegetable production in Ontario*. Ontario Min. of Agric. and Food Publ. 526.

Wittwer, S. H. and S. Honma. 1969. *Greenhouse tomatoes: guidelines for successful production*. East Lansing: Michigan State Univ. Press.

Wittwer, S. H., S. Honma and W. M. Robb. 1964. *Practices for increasing yields of greenhouse lettuce*. East Lansing: Michigan State Univ. Research Rept. 22.

APPENDIX 1

Hydroponic and Soilless Culture Societies

The International Society for Soilless Culture (ISOSC) is an organization of people (growers, hobbyists, scientists) active in some way in various forms of soilless culture. The purpose of ISOSC is worldwide promotion of research and application of soilless culture. It operates as an information center on such culture. Every three to four years ISOSC organizes an international congress on soilless culture and publishes the proceedings of theses congresses.

Any person who is actively engaged in research, advisory work or commercial application of soilless culture is elegible to become a member of ISOSC. Information may be obtained from: Secretariat of ISOSC, P.O. Box 52, Wageningen, The Netherlands.

A similar society exists in North America. It is the Hydroponic Society of America. Information and membership may be obtained from: Hydroponics Society of America, P.O. Box 6067, Concord, Calif. 94524.

APPENDIX 2

Research Extension Services for Publications on Greenhouse Production

Extension Division
Virginia Polytechnical Institute and
   State University
Blacksburg, VA 24061

Agricultural Engineering Cooperative
   Extension Service
The Pennsylvania State University
University Park, PA 16802

Cooperative Extension Service
Department of Agricultural Engineering
University of Kentucky
Lexington, KY 40506

Department of Vegetable Crops
New York State College of Agriculture
Cornell University
Ithaca, NY 14850

Cooperative Extension Service
Rutgers University
New Brunswick, NJ 08903

Cooperative Extension Service
College of Agriculture and
   Natural Resources
University of Connecticut
Storrs, CT 06268

Superintendent of Documents
U.S. Government Printing Office
Washington, DC 20402

Agricultural Extension Service
University of California
Riverside, CA 92502

Agricultural Experiment Station
Mississippi State University
State College, MS 39762

Cooperative Extension Service
College of Agriculture
University of Illinois
Urbana, IL 61801

Agricultural Extension Service
University of California
Davis, CA 95616

Agricultural Extension Service
Purdue University
Lafayette, IN 47907

Agricultural Extension Service
Texas A&M University
College Station, TX 77843

Ontario Department of Agriculture
and Food
Parliament Buildings
Toronto, Ontario

Light and Plant Growth Lab.
VSDA-ARS, Building 046 A Arcw
Beltsville, MD 20705

Agricultural Extension Service
The University of Arizona
4201 East Broadway
Phoenix, AZ 85040

Cooperative Extension Service
The Ohio State University
Columbus, OH 43210

Ontario Department of Agriculture
and Food
Horticultural Research Institute
Vineland Station, Ontario

Agricultural Experiment Station
Michigan State University
East Lansing, MI 48823

Cooperative Extension Service
Washington State University
Pullman, WA 99163

Cooperative Extension Service
Ohio State University
Wooster, OH 44691

Department of Floriculture
Colorado State University
Fort Collins, CO 80521

Department of Horticulture
Oregon State University
Corvallis, OR 97331

Department of Horticulture
Oklahoma State University
Stillwater, OK 74074

Department of Ornamental
Horticulture
University of Florida
Gainsville, FL 32611

Department of Horticultural Science
North Carolina State University
Raleigh, NC 27607

Some Soil and Plant Tissue Testing Laboratories

Soil and Plant Laboratory, Inc.
P.O. Box 11744, Santa Ana, CA
92711
P.O. Box 153, Santa Clara, CA
95052
P.O. Box 1648, Bellevue, WA 98009

Peninsu-LAB (Disease and Pest Lab)
23976 N.E. Newellhurst Court
Kingston, WA. 98346

Norwest-Priva Plant LaboratoriesInc.
203-20771 Langley Bypass
Langley, B.C., Canada

Soil Testing Laboratory
Purdue University
Agronomy Dept.
Lafayette, IN 47907

Griffin Laboratories
1875 Spall Rd.
Kelowna, B.C. Canada
V1Y 4R2

Department of Land Resource Science
University of Guelph
Guelph, Ontario, Canada

Soil Testing Laboratory
Texas A&M University
College Station, TX 77843

Ohio State University
Ohio Agricultural Research and
Development Center
Research-Extension Analytical
Laboratory
Wooster, OH 44691

Biological Control Agents

Note: This is not a complete list of companies selling biological control agents.

Applied Bio-Nomics Ltd.
P.O. Box 2637
Sidney, B.C.
Canada V8L 4C1

Beneficial Insectory
245 Oak Rum Rd.
Oak Rum, CA 96069

Bio Insect Control
710 South Columbia
Plainview, TX 79072

Biosis
1057 East Meadow Circle
Palo Alto, CA 95303

Gerhart Inc.
6346 Avon Belden Rd.
North Ridgeville, OH 44039

Koppert (UK) Ltd.
Biological Control
P.O. Box 43
Tunbridge Wells
Kent TN2 5BX
United Kingdom

Organic Pest Management
P.O. Box 55267
Seattle, WA 98155

Richters
P.O. Box 26
Goodwood, Ontario
Canada L0C 1A0

Safer Ltd.
6761 Kirkpatrick Cres.
Victoria, B.C. Canada V8X 3X1

Beneficial Bugs
P.O. Box 1627
Apopka, FL 32703

Better Yield Insects
13310 Riverside Dr. East
Tecumseh, Ontario
Canada N8N 1B2

Bio-Resources
P.O. Box 92
Santa Paula, CA 93060

Biotactics Inc.
7765 Lakeside Dr.
Riverside, CA 92509

Hydro-Gardens Inc.
P.O. Box 9707
Colorado Springs, CO 80932

Nature's Control
P.O. Box 35
Medford, OR 97501

Necessary Trading Co.
P.O. Box 603
New Castle, VA 24127

Praxis
P.O. Box 4164
Auburn Heights, MI 48051

Rincon-Vitova Insectories Inc.
P.O. Box 95
Oak View, CA 93022

Unique Insect Control
P.O. Box 15376
Sacramento, CA 95851

Special Hydroponic Equipment

1. NFT Troughs:

Rehau Plastics Inc.
P.O. Box 1706
Leesburg, VA 22075

Hydro-Gardens, Inc.
P.O. Box 9707
Colorado Springs, CO 80932

CropKing, Inc.
P.O. Box 310
Medina, OH 44258

Clover Greenhouses
200 Weakley Lane
Smyrna, TN 37167

Troy Hygro-Systems, Inc.
4096 Hwy. ES
East Troy, WI 53120

Westbrook Greenhouse Systems
Ltd.
270 Hunter Rd.
Grimsby, Ontario
Canada L3M 5G1

2. Reko Double Row NFT Troughs:

ADJ Horti-Projects Inc.
P.O. Box 3004
Langley, B.C.
Canada V3A 4R3

Reko bv
P.O. Box 191
6190 AD Beek (L)
Holland

Other Related Equipment

1. UV Sterilizers:

Trojan Technologies
845 Consortium Court
London, Ontario
Canada N6B 2S8

Aquafine Corporation
25230 West Ave. Stanford
Valencia, CA 91355

2. Water Chiller Units:

Frigid Units, Inc.
3214 Sylvania Ave.
Toledo, OH 43613

3. Hobby Units:

Aqua Culture, Inc.
P.O. Box 26467
Tempe, AZ 85282

APPENDIX 3

Units of Measurement – Conversion Factors

Units of		To Convert ⟶	Into ⟶	Multiply by
Length	25.401	Millimeters	Inches	0.0394
	2.5401	Centimeters	Inches	0.3937
	0.3048	Meters	Feet	3.2808
	0.9144	Meters	Yards	1.0936
	1.6093	Kilometers	Miles (statute)	0.6214
Area	645.160	Sq. Millimeters	Sq. Inches	0.001550
	6.4516	Sq. Centimeters	Sq. Inches	0.1550
	0.0929	Sq. Meters	Sq. Feet	10.7639
	0.8361	Sq. Meters	Sq. Yards	1.1960
	0.004046	Sq. Kilometers	Acres	247.105
	2.5900	Sq. Kilometers	Sq. Miles	0.3861
	0.4046	Hectares	Acres	2.4710
Volume	16.3872	Cub. Centimeters	Cubic Inches	0.0610
	0.0283	Cubic Meters	Cubic Feet	35.3145
	0.7646	Cubic Meters	Cubic Yards	1.3079
	0.003785	Cubic Meters	Gallons (U.S.)	264.178
	0.004545	Cubic Meters	Gallons (U.K.)	219.976
	0.01639	Liters	Cubic Inches	61.0238
	28.3205	Liters	Cubic Feet	0.03531
	3.7850	Liters	Gallons (U.S.)	0.2642
	4.5454	Liters	Gallons (U.K.)	0.2200
Weight	28.3495	Grams	Ounces (Av.)	0.0353
	31.1035	Grams	Ounces (Troy)	0.0321
	0.4536	Kilograms	Pounds (Av.)	2.2046
	0.0004535	Metric Tons	Pounds (Av.)	2204.62
	0.907185	Metric Tons	Tons (U.S.)	1.1023
	1.016047	Metric Tons	Tons (U.K.)	0.9842
	Multiply by	⟵ Into	⟵ To Convert	

APPENDIX 4

Physical Constants of Inorganic Compounds

Name	Formula	Density or Sp. Gravity	Solubility (gm/100 ml) Cold Water	Solubility (gm/100 ml) Hot Water
Ammonium Nitrate	NH_4NO_3	1.725	118.3	871
Ammonium dihydrogen phosphate	$NH_4H_2PO_4$	1.803	22.7	173.2
Ammonium molybdate	$(NH_4)_6Mo_7O_{24}\cdot4H_2O$		43	
Ammonium monohydrogen phosphate	$(NH_4)_2HPO_4$	1.619	57.5	106.0
Ammonium sulfate	$(NH_4)_2SO_4$	1.769	70.6	103.8
Boric acid	H_3BO_3	1.435	6.35	27.6
Calcium carbonate	$CaCO_3$	2.710	0.0014	0.0018
Calcium chloride	$CaCl_2$	2.15	74.5	159
Calcium chloride, hexahydrate	$CaCl_2\cdot6H_2O$	1.71	279	536
Calcium hydroxide	$Ca(OH)_2$	2.24	0.185	0.077
Calcium nitrate	$Ca(NO_3)_2$	2.504	121.2	376
Calcium nitrate tetrahydrate	$Ca(NO_3)_2\cdot4H_2O$	1.82	266	660
Calcium oxide	CaO	3.25-3.38	0.131	0.07
Calcium monophosphate	$Ca(H_2PO_4)_2\cdot H_2O$	2.220	1.8	decomposes
Calcium sulfate	$CaSO_4$	2.960	0.209	0.1619
Calcium sulfate dihydrate	$CaSO_4\cdot2H_2O$	2.32	0.241	0.222
Copper sulfate pentahydrate	$CuSO_4\cdot5H_2O$	2.284	31.6	203.3
Iron (II) hydroxide	$Fe(OH)_2$	3.4	0.00015	—
Iron (II) nitrate	$Fe(NO_3)_2\cdot6H_2O$	1.6	83.5	166.7
Iron (II) sulfate heptahydrate	$FeSO_4\cdot7H_2O$	1.898	15.65	48.6
Magnesium oxide	MgO_2	3.58	0.00062	0.0086
Magnesium orthophosphate	$Mg_3(PO_4)_2$	—	insoluble	insoluble
Magnesium mono hydrogen phosphate heptahydrate	$MgHPO_4\cdot7H_2O$	1.728	0.3	0.2
Magnesium orthophosphate tetrahydrate	$Mg_3(PO_4)_2\cdot4H_2O$	1.64	0.0205	—
Magnesium sulfate heptahydrate	$MgSO_4\cdot7H_2O$	1.68	71	91
Manganese dichloride tetrahydrate	$MnCl_2\cdot4H_2O$	2.01	151	656

APPENDIX 4

Physical Constants of Inorganic Compounds

Name	Formula	Density or Sp. Gravity	Solubility (gm/100 ml) Cold Water	Hot Water
Manganous (II) hydroxide	$Mn(OH)_2$	3.258	0.0002	—
Manganous nitrate	$Mn(NO_3)_2 \cdot 4H_2O$	1.82	426.4	∞
Manganous dihydrogen phosphate	$Mn(H_2PO_4)_2 \cdot 2H_2O$	—	soluble	—
Manganous monohydrogen phosphate	$MnHPO_4 \cdot 3H_2O$	—	slightly soluble	decomposes
Manganous sulfate	$MnSO_4$	3.25	52	70
Manganous sulfate tetrahydrate	$MnSO_4 \cdot 4H_2O$	2.107	105.3	111.2
Nitric acid	HNO_3	1.5027	∞	∞
Phosphoric acid (ortho)	H_3PO_4	1.834	548	very sol.
Phosphoric anhydride	P_2O_5	2.39	decomposes to H_3PO_4	decomposes
Potassium carbonate	K_2CO_3	2.428	112	.156
Potassium carbonate dihydrate	$K_2CO_3 \cdot 2H_2O$	2.043	146.9	331
Potassium hydrogen carbonate	$KHCO_3$	2.17	22.4	60
Potassium carbonate trihydrate	$2K_2CO_3 \cdot 3H_2O$	2.043	129.4	268.3
Potassium chloride	KCl	1.984	34.7	56.7
Potassium hydroxide	KOH	2.044	107	178
Potassium nitrate	KNO_3	2.109	13.3	247
Potassium orthophosphate	K_3PO_4	2.564	90	soluble
Potassium dihydrogen phosphate	KH_2PO_4	2.338	33	83.5
Potassium monohydrogen phosphate	K_2HPO_4	—	167	very soluble
Potassium sulfate	K_2SO_4	2.662	12	24.1
Zinc carbonate	$ZnCO_3$	4.398	0.001	—
Zinc chloride	$ZnCl_2$	2.91	432	615
Zinc orthophosphate	$Zn_3(PO_4)_2$	3.998	insoluble	insoluble
Zinc dihydrogen phosphate	$Zn(H_2PO_4)_2 \cdot 2H_2O$	—	decomposes	—
Zinc orthophosphate tetrahydrate	$Zn_3(PO_4)_2 \cdot 4H_2O$	3.04	insoluble	insoluble
Zinc sulfate heptahydrate	$ZnSO_4 \cdot 7H_2O$	1.957	96.5	663.6

APPENDIX 5

Greenhouse suppliers (Adapted from American Vegetable Grower and Greenhouse Grower). *Subject to change.*

Fertilizers

AMMONIUM NITRATE

Agrico Chemical Co.
American Cyanamid Co.
BFG Supply Co.
H. G. German Seeds, Inc.
W. R. Grace & Co.
Hydro-Gardens, Inc.
Kaiser
Occidental Chemical
Penn State Seed Co.
Phillips Chemical Co., Fertilizer Div.
USS Agri-Chemicals

AMMONIUM NITRATE LIMESTONE

Agrico Chemical
Kaiser

AMMONIUM PHOSPHATE

W. R. Grace & Co.
Hydro-Gardens, Inc.
Kerr-McGee
Occidental Chemical

AMMONIUM POLY-PHOSPHATE

Allied Chemical Corp.

AMMONIUM POLYSULFIDE

Agrico Chemical Co.

AMMONIUM SULFATE

Agrico Chemical Co.
Allied Chemical Corp.
Occidental Chemical
Penn State Seed Co.
Phillips Chemical Co., Fertilizer Div.
USS Chemicals, Div. of United States Steel Corp.
Wilson & Geo. Meyer & Co.

AMMONIUM THIOSULFATE (Amthio®)

Allied Chemical Corp.

ANHYDROUS AMMONIA

Agrico Chemical Co.
Agway Inc.
Allied Chemical Corp.
American Cyanamid Co., Agricultural Div.
W. R. Grace & Co.
Occidental Chemical
Phillips Chemical Co., Fertilizer Div.

Reichhold Chemicals, Inc.
Smith-Douglass
USS Agri-Chemicals

BORAX

Bioferm International
Hydro-Gardens, Inc.
Kerr-McGee
Miller Chemical & Fertilizer Corp.
U. S. Borax

CALCIUM CYANAMID

Miller Chemical & Fertilizer Corp.

CALCIUM NITRATE

Geo. Ball Pacific, Inc.
Ball Seed Co.
BFG Supply Co.
H. G. German Seeds, Inc.
Hydroculture, Inc.
Hydro-Gardens, Inc.
Miller Chemical & Fertilizer Corp.
Penn State Seed Co.
Seaborn Inc.
Wilson & Geo. Meyer & Co.

CHELATED COMPOUNDS

BFG Supply Co.
Bioferm International
CIBA-GEIGY Corp.
Dow
Hydroculture, Inc.
Hydro-Gardens, Inc.
Kaiser
Miller Chemical & Fertilizer Corp.
Occidental Chemical
Plant Marvel Laboratories
SESCO Enterprises Inc.
Stoller Chemical Co., Inc.

CONTROLLED RELEASE FERTILIZERS

Geo. Ball Pacific, Inc.
Ball Seed Co.
BFG Supply Co.
Bioferm International
Hydroculture, Inc.
Geo. W. Park Seed Co., Inc.
Penn State Seed Co.
Harry Sharp & Son
Sierra Chemical Co.

COPPER SULFATE

Chemical & Pigment Co.
Cities Service Co.
Hydroculture, Inc.
Hydro-Gardens, Inc.

Penn State Seed Co.
Phelps Dodge Refining Corp.
Stoller Chemical Co., Inc.
Wilson & Geo. Meyer & Co.

DIAMMONIUM PHOSPHATE

Agrico Chemical Co.
W. R. Grace & Co.
Hydroculture, Inc.
Hydro-Gardens, Inc.
International Minerals & Chemical Corp.
Kerr-McGee
Occidental Chemical

FERRIC SULFATE

Cities Service Co.
Hydro-Gardens, Inc.

FERROUS SULFATE

Hydro-Gardens, Inc.
Stoller Chemical Co., Inc.
Wilson & Geo. Meyer & Co.

FOLIAR NUTRITIONAL TRACE ELEMENTS

Allied Chemical Corp.
Bioferm International
Hydro-Gardens, Inc.
Leffingwell Div.
Plant Marvel Laboratories
Rohm & Haas Co.
SESCO Enterprises Inc.
Harry Sharp & Son
Thompson-Hayward Chemical Co.

GYPSUM, AGRICULTURAL

Hydroculture, Inc.
Hydro-Gardens, Inc.
Occidental Chemical
Penn State Seed Co.
United States Gypsum Co.

HYDROPONIC FERTILIZERS

Geo. Ball Pacific, Inc.
Ball Seed Co.
BFG Supply Co.
Bioferm International
Clover Garden Products
Hydroculture, Inc.
Hydro-Gardens, Inc.
Penn State Seed Co.
Plant Marvel Laboratories
Pronto Plant Food Co.
SESCO Enterprises Inc.
Rambridge Structure & Design Ltd

LIME, AGRICULTURAL

Agway Inc.
Hydroculture, Inc.
Penn State Seed Co.
United States Gypsum Co.

LIQUID FERTILIZERS

Agrico Chemical Co.
Agway Inc.
Allied Chemical Corp.
Geo. Ball Pacific, Inc.
Ball Seed Co.
BFG Supply Co.
Bioferm International
Chemical & Pigment Co.
Hettich Mfg. Co.
Hydroculture, Inc.
Kaiser
Occidental Chemical
Organic Laboratories, Inc.
Penn State Seed Co.
Phillips Chemical Co., Fertilizer Div.
Plant Marvel Laboratories
Ra-Pid-Gro Corp.
SESCO Enterprises Inc.
Stoller Chemical Co., Inc.
USS Agri-Chemicals

MAGNESIUM SULFATE

BFG Supply Co.
Hydroculture, Inc.
Hydro-Gardens, Inc.
Penn State Seed Co.
Stoller Chemical Co., Inc.
Wilson & Geo. Meyer & Co.

MANGANESE SULFATE

Hydroculture, Inc.
Hydro-Gardens, Inc.
Stoller Chemical Co., Inc.
Wilson & Geo. Meyer & Co.

MANGANOUS OXIDE

Hydroculture, Inc.
International Minerals & Chemical Corp.

MIXED FERTILIZERS

Agrico Chemical Co.
Agway Inc.
American Cyanamid Co. (Vegetables)
Bioferm International
W. R. Grace & Co.
Hydroculture, Inc.
Hydro-Gardens, Inc.
International Minerals & Chemical Corp.
J. M. McConkey & Co., Inc.
Miller Chemical & Fertilizer Corp.
Occidental Chemical
Penn State Seed Co.
Plant Marvel Laboratories

MONOAMMONIUM PHOSPHATE

Chevron Chemical Co.
International Minerals & Chemical Corp.
Stauffer Chemical Co.

MURIATE OF POTASH

BFG Supply Co.
Hydro-Gardens, Inc.
International Minerals & Chemical Corp.
Kerr-McGee
Penn State Seed Co.
U.S. Borax
USS Agri-Chemicals

NITRATE OF POTASH

H. J. Baker & Bro.
Hydro-Gardens, Inc.
Penn State Seed Co.
Reichhold Chemicals, Inc.

NITRATE OF SODA

Chilean Nitrate Sales Corp.

NITRATE OF SODA/POTASH 15-0-14

Chilean Nitrate Sales Corp.

NITRIFICATION INHIBITOR

Dow (*N-Serve)
Kalo Laboratories (Extend)

NITROGEN SOLUTIONS

Agway Inc.
Allied Chemical Corp.
American Cyanamid Co., Agricultural Div.
W. R. Grace & Co.
International Minerals & Chemical Corp.
Occidental Chemical
Reichhold Chemicals, Inc.
USS Agri-Chemicals

NUTRITIONAL FOLIAR PLANT FOODS AND STARTER SOLUTIONS

Agrotec Inc.
Agway Inc.
Allied Chemical Corp.
Bioferm International
W. R. Grace & Co., Horticultural Products
Hettich Mfg. Co.
Hydro-Gardens, Inc.
Kaiser
Leffingwell Div.
McCormick and Co.
Miller Chemical & Fertilizer Corp.
Occidental Chemical
Plant Marvel Laboratories
Pronto Plant Food Co.
Ra-Pid-Gro Corp.
Rohm and Haas Co.
Seaborn Inc.
SESCO Enterprises Inc.
Harry Sharp & Son
Stoller Chemical Co., Inc.
USS Agri-Chemicals

NUTRITIONAL TRACE ELEMENTS

BORON

Bioferm International
W. R. Grace & Co., Horticultural Products
Hydroculture, Inc.
Hydro-Gardens, Inc.
Kerr-McGee
Leffingwell Div.
Penn State Seed Co.
Stoller Chemical Co., Inc.
U. S. Borax & Chemical Corp.
Wilson & Geo. Meyer & Co.

COPPER

Bioferm International
CIBA-GEIGY Corp.
W. R. Grace & Co., Horticultural Products
Hydroculture, Inc.
Hydro-Gardens, Inc.
Leffingwell Div.
Penn State Seed Co.
Phelps Dodge
Stoller Chemical Co., Inc.
Wilson & Geo. Meyer & Co.

IRON

Allied Chemical Corp.
BFG Supply Co.
Bioferm International
CIBA-GEIGY Corp.
Cities Service Co.
Eagle-Picher Industries, Inc.
W. R. Grace & Co., Horticultural Products
Hydroculture, Inc.
Hydro-Gardens, Inc.
Leffingwell Div.
Penn State Seed Co.
Stoller Chemical Co., Inc.
Wilson & Geo. Meyer & Co.

MAGNESIUM

Allied Chemical Corp.
Bioferm International
W. R. Grace & Co., Horticultural Products
Hydroculture, Inc.
Hydro-Gardens, Inc.
Leffingwell Div.
Penn State Seed Co.
SESCO Enterprises Inc.
Stoller Chemical Co., Inc.
Wilson & Geo. Meyer & Co.

MANGANESE

BFG Supply Co.
Bioferm International
CIBA-GEIGY Corp.
Eagle-Picher Industries, Inc.
W. R. Grace & Co., Horticultural Products
Hydroculture, Inc.
Hydro-Gardens, Inc.
Leffingwell Div.
Penn State Seed Co.

SESCO Enterprises Inc.
Stoller Chemical Co., Inc.
Wilson & Geo. Meyer & Co.

MIXTURES

BFG Supply Co.
Bioferm International
W. R. Grace & Co., Horticultural Products
Hydroculture, Inc.
Hydro-Gardens, Inc.
Leffingwell Div.
Occidental Chemical
Plant Marvel Laboratories
SESCO Enterprises Inc.
Sierra Chemical Co.
Stoller Chemical Co., Inc.
Occidental Chemical
SESCO Enterprises Inc.
Woolfolk Chemical Works Inc.

SUPERPHOSPHATE

American Cyanamid Co.
BFG Supply Co.
W. R. Grace & Co.
International Minerals & Chemical Corp.
Miller Chemical & Fertilizer Corp.
Occidental Chemical
Penn State Seed Co.
USS Agri-Chemicals

TABLETS, ROOT ZONE

Harry Sharp & Son
Sierra Chemical Co.

UNIPELS

Chevron Chemical Co.

UREA

Agway Inc.
Allied Chemical Corp.
American Cyanamid Co.
BFG Supply Co.
W. R. Grace & Co.
Hydro-Gardens, Inc.
Miller Chemical & Fertilizer Corp.
Occidental Chemical
Penn State Seed Co.
Reichhold Chemicals, Inc.
USS Agri-Chemicals
Wilson & Geo. Meyer & Co.

UREA-FORM

Boots Hercules Agrochemicals
J. M. McConkey & Co., Inc.

ZINC COMPOUNDS

Allied Chemical Corp.
Bioferm International
Chemical & Pigment Co.
Plant Marvel Laboratories
SESCO Enterprises Inc.
Sierra Chemical Co.
Stoller Chemical Co.
Wilson & Geo. Meyer & Co.
Woolfolk Chemical Works, Inc.

Fungicides

ANILAZINE

*Dyrene .... Mobay

ANTIBIOTICS

Actidione
*Acti-dione .... TUCO

Copper-Streptomycin-Terramycin
Agri-mycin 500 .... Pfizer

Streptomycin
Agri-Strep .... Harry Sharp
FMC Streptomycin .... FMC

Streptomycin-Terramycin
Agri-mycin 100 .... Pfizer

BENOMYL

*Benlate .... Du Pont
Benlate .... Harry Sharp
Benlate .... Siegers Seed
Benomyl .... Agway
Benomyl .... Geo. Ball Pacific
Benomyl .... Ball Seed
Benomyl .... BFG Supply
Benomyl .... DAC
Benomyl .... FMC, Citrus Machinery Div.
Benomyl .... Hydro-Gardens
Benomyl .... Geo. W. Park
Benomyl .... Penn State
Benomyl .... Pennwalt, Decco

CAPTAFOL

Captafol .... Agway
*Difolatan 4 Flowable .... Chevron Chemical

CAPTAN

Captan .... Agway
Captan .... BFG Supply
Captan .... Geiger
Captan .... H. G. German Seeds
Captan .... Hopkins
Captan .... Hydro-Gardens
Captan .... Geo. W. Park
Captan .... Penn State
Captan .... Rohm and Haas

*Company's brand name

Captan .... Harry Sharp
Captan .... Siegers Seed
FMC Captan .... FMC
Occidental Captan .... Occidental
Orthocide 50 Wettable .... Chevron Chemical
Orthocide 80 Wettable .... Chevron Chemical
Orthocide Seed Protectants .... Chevron Chemical
Security Captan ....Woolfolk
Stauffer Captan .... Stauffer

CHLOROPICRIN

Chlor-O-Pic.................. Great Lakes Chemical
Chloropicrin .... Agway
Chloropicrin ....Hendrix & Dail
Picfume .... Dow

CHLOROTHALONIL

Bravo ....Diamond Shamrock
Daconil 2787 ....Diamond Shamrock
Daconil 2787 ....Harry Sharp
Exotherm Termil.....................Harry Sharp

CITCOP 4E

Citcop 4E ....Cities Service
Citcop 4E .... Siegers Seed

COPPER COMPOUNDS

Agway   Kocide Chemical
Amvac Chemical   Leffingwell
Bioferm International   Miller Chemical
FMC   Phelps Dodge
Hercules   Stoller Chemical
Hydro-Gardens, Inc.

COPPER-COUNT-N

Copper-Count-N .... Mineral Research & Devel.
Copper-Count-N .... Siegers Seed

COPPER HYDROXIDE

Cumin.......................Bioferm International
Kocide 101 .... Kocide Chemical

COPPER SULFATE

Copper Sulfate .... Agway
Copper Sulfate .... Chemical & Pigment
Copper Sulfate ....Hydro-Gardens
Copper Sulfate .... Penn State
Copper Sulfate .... Siegers Seed
Triangle .... Phelps Dodge
Tri-Basic ....Cities Service

CNA

Botec .... TUCO
Botran .... TUCO
FMC Botran .... FMC
Occidental Botran .... Occidental
Security Botran ....Woolfolk

DICHLONE

Dichlone .... Agway
Dichlone .... Siegers Seed
FMC Dichlone (Vegetables) .... FMC
FMC Kolodust 100 .... FMC
Quintar .... Hopkins

DICHLOROPROPENE

*Telone II .... Dow

DICHLOROPROPENE & CHLOROPICRIN MIXTURE

Telone* C-17 .... Dow

*DIKAR

Dikar .... Agway
Dikar .... Penn State
*Dikar ....Rohm and Haas
Dikar .... Siegers Seed

DODINE

*Cyprex ....American Cyanamid
Dodine .... Agway
Dodine .... Penn State

FENAMINOSULF

*Lesan .... Mobay
Lesan ... .Harry Sharp

FENTIN HYDROXIDE

*Du-Ter .. ..Thompson-Hayward

FERBAM

*Carbamate .... FMC
Ferbam .... Agway
Ferbam .... BFG Supply
Ferbam .... Geiger
Ferbam .... H. G. German Seeds
Ferbam .... Penn State
Ferbam ....Harry Sharp
Ferbam .... Siegers Seed
Security Ferbam ....Woolfolk
Velsicol Ferbam .... Velsicol

FOLPET

Folpet .... Agway
Folpet .... H. G. German Seeds
Folpet .... Penn State
Folpet .... Siegers Seed
*Phaltan 50 Wettable .... Chevron Chemical
Stauffer Folpet .... Stauffer

*GLYODEX

Glyodex............................. Agway

GLYODIN

Glyodin .... Agway
Glyodin .... Penn State

IPRODIONE

*Chipco 26019 .... Rhone-Poulenc
*Rovral .... Rhone-Poulenc

LIME SULFUR SOLUTION

FMC Lime Sulfur .... FMC
Lime Sulfur Solution .... Agway
Lime Sulfur Solution .... Miller Chemical
Lime Sulfur Solution .... Penn State
Lime Sulfur Solution .... Siegers Seed
Security Lime Sulfur ....Woolfolk

MANCOZEB

*Dithane M-45 ....Rohm and Haas

Mancozeb .... Agway
Mancozeb .... Geiger
Mancozeb .... Hopkins
*Manzate 200 .... Du Pont

MANEB

BASF Maneb .... BASF
Dithane .... Harry Sharp
*Dithane M-22 .... Rohm and Haas
Maneb .... Agway
Maneb .... BFG Supply
Manab .... Geiger
Maneb .... Penn State
Maneb .... Siegers Seed
*Manzate .... Du Pont
Manzate .... Harry Sharp
*Manzate D .... Du Pont
Pennwalt Maneb 80 .... Pennwalt
Security Maneb Dust .... Woolfolk

OXYTHIOQUINOX

*Morestan .... Mobay

PCNB

FMC PCNB .... FMC
PCNB .... Agway
*Terraclor .... Olin
Terraclor .... Harry Sharp
Terraclor .... Siegers Seed

POLYRAM

Occidental Polyram .... Occidental
Polyram .... Agway
*Polyram .... FMC
Polyram .... Hopkins
Polyram .... Penn State
Polyram .... Siegers Seed

SULFUR

Agway	Miller Chemical
Chevron Chemical	Sandoz
Dow	Stoller Chemical
Drexel Chemical	Woolfolk
FMC	

THIABENDAZOLE

*Ap-Lustr .... Pennwalt, Decco
Thiabendazole .... Agway
Thiabendazole ...... FMC, Citrus Machinery Div.

THIOPHANATE

*Pennwalt Topsin-M .... Pennwalt
Thiophanate .... Agway

TRIFORINE

*Funginex .... Chevron Chemical
*Ortho Triforine E.C. .... Chevron Chemical

THIRAM

*Arasan .... Du Pont
*Chipco Thiram .... Rhone-Poulenc
FMC Thiram .... FMC
Pennwalt Thiram .... Pennwalt
*Tersan 75 .... Du Pont
Thiram .... Agway

Thiram .... Penn State
Thiram .... Siegers Seed
Thiram 42-S .... Hopkins
*Thylate .... Du Pont

TRIZIMAN

Triziman .... Pennwalt

ZINEB

BASF Zineb .... BASF
FMC Zineb .... FMC
Miller Zineb .... Miller Chemical
Pennwalt Zineb .... Pennwalt
Zineb .... BFG Supply
Zineb .... Geiger
Zineb .... Penn State
Zineb .... Harry Sharp
Zineb .... Siegers Seed

ZIRAM

Velsicol Ziram .... Velsicol
Ziram Spray .... FMC
*Ziram Technical .... Pennwalt

Fumigants and Nematicides

ALDICARB

Aldicarb .... Agway
Aldicarb .... BFG Supply
Aldicarb .... Siegers Seed
*Temik .... Union Carbide

CARBOFURAN

*Furadan .... FMC
Furadan .... Mobay

CHLOROPICRIN

*Chlor-O-Pic .... Great Lakes Chemical
Chloropicrin .... Agway
Chloropicrin .... Hendrix & Dail
*Picfume .... Dow

DAZOMET

*Micofume .... Miller Chemical
*Mylone .... Hopkins

DIBROMOCHLOROPROPANE

Dibromochloropropane .... Harry Sharp
*Fumazone 86E .... Dow
*Nematocide .... Amvac Chemical
Oxy DBCP .... Occidental

DICHLOROPROPENE

*Telone II .... Dow

**DICHLOROPROPENE & CHLORO-
PICRIN MIXTURE**

*Telone C-17 .... Dow

EDB

*Dowfume W-85 .... Dow
EDB .... Agway
*Soilbrom .... Great Lakes Chemical

FENAMIPHOS

*Nemacur .... Mobay

FENSULFOTHION

*Dasanit .... Mobay

GELLED METHYL BROMIDE

Gelled Methyl Bromide .... Hendrix & Dail
*Terr-O-Gel .... Great Lakes Chemical

METAM-SODIUM

*Vapam .... Stauffer

METHYL BROMIDE

*Dow Methyl Bromide .... Dow
*Meth-O-Gas .... Great Lakes Chemical
Methyl Bromide .... Agway
Methyl Bromide .... BFG Supply
Methyl Bromide .... Geiger
Methyl Bromide .... Hendrix & Dail
Methyl Bromide .... Penn State
Methyl Bromide .... Harry Sharp
*Pestmaster .... Velsicol

METHYL BROMIDE & CHLOROPICRIN

*Brom-O-Gas .... Great Lakes Chemical
*Brom-O-Sol .... Great Lakes Chemical
*Brozone .... Dow
*Dowfume MC-2 .... Dow
*Dowfume MC-33 .... Dow
MBC Soil Fumigant .... Hendrix & Dail
MBC Concentrate Soil Fumigant ...... Hendrix & Dail
MBC-33 Soil Fumigant .... Hendrix & Dail
Methyl Bromide & Chloropicrin .... Agway
Methyl Bromide & Chloropicrin .... Harry Sharp
Methyl Bromide & Chloropicrin .... Siegers Seed
*Terr-O-Gas .... Great Lakes Chemical

**METHYL ISOTHIOCYANATE and
CHLORINATED C3 HYDROCARBONS**

*Vorlex .... Nor-Am

OXAMYL

*Vydate .... Du Pont

*TERR-O-CIDE

*Terr-O-Cide .... Great Lakes Chemical
Terr-O-Cide .... Hendrix & Dail

Growth Regulators

ABSCISSION AGENTS

CYCLOHEXIMIDE

*Acti-Aid Citrus Abscission Agent .... TUCO

*RELEASE

*Release .... Abbott Labs

2, 4-D ISOPROPYL ESTER (Technical)

Isopropyl Ester of 2,4-D (Technical) .. Amvac Chemical
Citrus Fix .... Amvac Chemical

ANTI-TRANSPIRANTS

Agrotec Inc. (Agrotec Anti-Transpirants)
Bioferm International (Phyto-Seal)
Miller Chemical Co. (Vapor Gard*)
Nursery Specialty Products (Wilt-Pruf*)
Penn State Seed Co.

BENEFICIAL BACTERIA

Materials Science Co.

DPA

DPA .... Agway
*No Scald DPA .... Chemley

ETHEPHON

*CEPHA .... GAF
Ethephon .... Agway
Ethephon .... BFG Supply
*Ethrel .... Union Carbide
Florel .... Harry Sharp
*Florel .... Union Carbide

FRUIT SHAPING & SIZING

*Promalin .... Abbott Labs

FRUIT THINNING SPRAYS

DINITROS
FMC

NAPHTHALENEACETIC ACID
Amvac Chemical Corp.
Chevron Chemical Co.
FMC Corp.
Miller Chemical & Fertilizer Corp.
Union Carbide Agricultural Products Co., Inc.

GIBBERELLIC ACID

Abbott Laboratories
Agway Inc.
BFG Supply Co.
Bioferm International
Elanco Products Co.
Penn State Seed Co.
Pfizer, Inc.
Harry Sharp & Son
Siegers Seed

GROWTH RETARDERS

MALEIC HYDRAZIDE
Agway Inc.
BFG Supply Co.
Drexel Chemical Co.
Penn State Seed Co.
Harry Sharp & Son
Woolfolk Chemical Works, Inc.

INDOLE BUTYRIC ACID

Agrotec Inc.
Bioferm International
Harry Sharp & Son

POTATO SPROUT INHIBITOR

Agway Inc.
PPG Industries

SADH

*ALAR-85

BFG Supply Co.
Penn State Seed Co.
Uniroyal, Inc.

*B-NINE

Agrotec
Geo. Ball Pacific, Inc.
Ball Seed Co.
BFG Supply Co.
Geiger Corp.
Penn State Seed Co.
Harry Sharp & Son

STOP DROP SPRAYS AND DUSTS

NAPHTHALENEACETIC ACID
See FRUIT THINNING SPRAYS

Agway Inc.
Amvac Chemical Corp.
Miller Chemical & Fertilizer Corp.
Union Carbide Agricultural Products Co., Inc.

TRANSPLANT HORMONES

Agrotec Inc.
Bioferm International
Union Carbide Agricultural Products Co., Inc.

Insecticides and Miticides

ACEPHATE
*Orthene . . . . Chevron Chemical

ALDICARB
Aldicarb . . . . BFG Supply
Aldicarb . . . . Geiger
Temik . . . . Harry Sharp
Temik . . . . Siegers Seed

ALFA-TOX
*Alfa-Tox . . . . CIBA-GEIGY
Alfa-Tox . . . . Siegers Seed

AMITRAZ
*BAAM E.C. . . . . TUCO

ARSENICALS
Security Calcium Arsenate . . . . Woolfolk
Security Lead Arsenate . . . . Woolfolk

AZINPHOS-METHYL
Azinphos-Methyl . . . . Rohm and Haas
*Guthion . . . . Mobay

BACILLUS THURINGIENSIS (Biological Insecticide)
Bacillus Thuringiensis . . . . Geo. Ball Pacific
Bacillus Thuringiensis . . . . Ball Seed
Bacillus Thuringiensis . . . . BFG Supply
Bacillus Thuringiensis . . . . . . Johnny's Selected Seeds
Bacillus Thuringiensis . . . . Penn State
Bacillus Thuringiensis . . . . Harry Sharp
*Dipel . . . . Abbott Laboratories
Dipel . . . . Geo. W. Park
Occidental Bacillus Thuringiensis . . . . Occidental
Security Dipel Dust . . . . Woolfolk
Security Dipel Spray . . . . Woolfolk
*Thuricide . . . . Sandoz Inc.

BOMYL
*Bomyl . . . . Hopkins

CARBARYL
Carbaryl . . . . Penn State
FMC Sevin . . . . FMC
Occidental Sevin . . . . Occidental
*Ortho Sevin 50 Wettable . . . . Chevron Chemical
Security Sevin . . . . Woolfolk
Sevin . . . . Amvac Chemical
Sevin . . . . PureGro
Sevin . . . . Harry Sharp
Sevin . . . . Siegers Seed
*Sevin . . . . Union Carbide
Sevin 5% Bait . . . . Hopkins

CARBOFURAN
*Furadan . . . . FMC
Furadan . . . . Mobay

CARBOPHENOTHION
FMC Trithion . . . . FMC
Occidental Trithion . . . . Occidental
*Trithion . . . . Stauffer

CHLORDANE
Chlordane . . . . BFG Supply
Chlordane . . . . Penn State
Chlordane . . . . Siegers Seed
Chlordane . . . . Velsicol
Occidental Chlordane . . . . Occidental
Security Chlordane . . . . Woolfolk

CHLORPYIFOS
Dursban Granules 1 . . . . Amvac Chemical
*Lorsban 4E . . . . Dow
*Lorsban 15G . . . . Dow

CRYOLITE
*Kryocide . . . . Pennwalt
Occidental Cryolite . . . . Occidental

CYHEXATIN
*Ortho Plictran 50W . . . . Chevron Chemical
*Plictran 50W . . . . Dow

DDVP
DDVP . . . . Amvac Chemical
DDVP . . . . BFG Supply
DDVP . . . . H. G. German Seeds

DDVP .... Hydroculture
DDVP .... Harry Sharp
Occidental DDVP .... Occidental
Vapona Insecticide .... Miller Chemical
*Vapona .... Shell Chemical

DEMETON

*Systox .... Mobay
Systox .... Harry Sharp

DIAZINON

Diazinon .... Geo. Ball Pacific
Diazinon .... Ball Seed
Diazinon .... BFG Supply
Diazinon .... FMC
Diazinon .... Hopkins
Diazinon .... Hydroculture
Diazinon .... Hydro-Gardens
Diazinon .... Penn State
Diazinon .... Harry Sharp
Diazinon .... Siegers Seed
Occidental Diazinon .... Occidental
*Sarolex .... CIBA-GEIGY
Security Diazinon .... Woolfolk
*Spectracide .... CIBA-GEIGY

DICOFOL

FMC Kelthane .... FMC
Kelthane .... Harry Sharp
Kelthane EC .... Rohm and Haas
Kelthane 35 .... Rohm and Haas
Occidental Kelthane .... Occidental

DIMETHOATE

*Cygon .... American Cyanamid
Cygon .... Harry Sharp
*De-Fend E-267 .... Thompson-Hayward
*De-Fend W-25 .... Thompson-Hayward
*Dimate 267 .... Custom Chemicides
Dimethoate .... Hopkins
FMC Dimethoate 247 .... FMC
*Rebelate .... BASF
Security Cygon .... Woolfolk

DISULFOTON

*Di-Syston .... Mobay
Occidental Di-Syston .... Occidental

ENDOSULFAN

Endosulfan .... Hopkins
Miller Thiodan .... Miller Chemical
Security Endosulfan .... Woolfolk
Security Thiodan .... Woolfolk
Thiodan .... FMC
Thiodan .... Harry Sharp
Thiodan .... Siegers Seed

ENDRIN

Endrin .... H. G. German Seeds
Endrin .... Velsicol
FMC Endrin .... FMC
Miller Endrin .... Miller Chemical
Occidental Endrin .... Occidental

EPN

Du Pont EPN .... Du Pont
EPN-5 .... Drexel
FMC EPN .... FMC
Occidental EPN .... Occidental
Security EPN .... Woolfolk

ETHION

*Ethion .... FMC

FENSULFOTHION

*Dasanit .... Mobay

FORMETANATE HYDROCHLORIDE

*Carzol .... Nor-Am

HEPTACHLOR

Heptachlor .... Velsicol
Occidental Heptachlor .... Occidental

LINDANE

FMC Lindane .... FMC
*Isotox Lindane 25 Wettable .... Chevron Chemical
*Isotox Lindane Spray No. 200 ...... Chevron Chemical
Lindane .... BFG Supply
Lindane .... Geiger
Lindane .... Hydroculture
Lindane .... Geo. W. Park
Lindane .... Penn State
Lindane .... Harry Sharp
Security Lindane .... Woolfolk

MALATHION

*Cythion .... American Cyanamid
FMC Malathion .... FMC
Malathion .... BFG Supply
Malathion .... DAO
Malathion .... Geiger
Malathion .... Hopkins
Malathion .... Hydroculture
Malathion .... Geo. W. Park
Malathion .... Penn State
Malathion .... Harry Sharp
Malathion .... Siegers Seed
Malathion ULV* Concentrate ...... American Cyanamid
Miller Malathion .... Miller Chemical
Occidental Malathion .... Occidental
*Ortho Malathion 5 Emulsive .... Chevron Chemical
*Ortho Malathion 8 Emulsive .... Chevron Chemical
*Ortho Malathion 25 Wettable .... Chevron Chemical
Security Malathion .... Woolfolk

MERCAPTODIMETHUR

*Mesurol .... Mobay

METALDEHYDE

Metaldehyde .... Amvac Chemical
Metaldehyde .... Penn State
Occidental Metaldehyde .... Occidental
*Ortho Metaldehyde 4% Bait .... Chevron Chemical

METHAMIDOPHOS

*Monitor .... Mobay
*Ortho Monitor .... Chevron Chemical

METHIDATHION
*Supracide .... CIBA-GEIGY

METHOMYL
Lanna Bait .... Hopkins
*Lannate .... Du Pont
Lannate .... Harry Sharp
*Nudrin .... Shell Chemical
Security Methomyl Dust .... Woolfolk

METHOXYCHLOR
FMC Methoxychlor .... FMC
*Marlate .... Du Pont
Methoxychlor .... Chemical Formulators
Methoxychlor .... Hopkins
Methoxychlor .... Penn State
Methoxychlor .... Siegers Seed
Miller Methoxychlor .... Miller Chemical
Occidental Methoxychlor .... Occidental

METHYL PARATHION
FMC Methyl Parathion .... FMC
Methyl Parathion .... American Cyanamid
Methyl Parathion .... Hopkins
Methyl Parathion .... Siegers Seed
Methyl Parathion .... Velsicol
Methyl Parathion 4-E .... Drexel
*Metron Methyl Parathion .... Kerr-McGee
Monsanto Niran .... Monsanto
Occidental Methyl Parathion .... Occidental
Penncap-M .... Pennwalt
Security Methyl Parathion .... Woolfolk

MEVINPHOS
Duraphos .... Amvac Chemical
FMC Phosdrin .... FMC
Mevinphos Technical .... Amvac Chemical
Miller Phosdrin .... Miller Chemical
Occidental Phosdrin .... Occidental
*Phosdrin Insecticide .... Shell Chemical

MILKY DISEASE SPORES (Biological Insecticide)
Milky Spore .... Mellinger's

MONOCROTOPHOS
*Azodrin .... Shell Chemical

NALED
Dibrom .... Harry Sharp
FMC Dibrom .... FMC
Naled .... Amvac Chemical
Naled .... BFG Supply
Occidental Dibrom .... Occidental
*Ortho Dibrom .... Chevron Chemical

OILS: EMULSIONS, MISCIBLE, SUMMER, DORMANT, TAR EMULSIONS
BFG Supply	Miller Chemical
Chevron Chemical	Penn State
Dow	Pennwalt
FMC	Woolfolk
Hopkins	

OXAMYL
*Vydate .... Du Pont
Vydate L .... Harry Sharp

OXYDEMETON-METHYL
*Metasystox R .... Mobay

OXYTHIOQUINOX
*Morestan .... Mobay

PARATHION
Miller Parathion .... Miller Chemical
*Niran .... Monsanto
Occidental Parathion .... Occidental
*Ortho Parathion 8 Flow Conc. .... Chevron Chemical
*Ortho Parathion 15 Wettable .... Chevron Chemical
*Ortho Parathion 25 Wettable .... Chevron Chemical
Parathion .... BFG Supply
Parathion .... Geiger
Parathion .... Hopkins
Parathion .... Penn State
Parathion .... Harry Sharp
Parathion .... Siegers Seed
Parathion 8E .... Drexel
*Phoskil .... FMC
Security Parathion .... Woolfolk
*Thiophos .... American Cyanamid

PERMETHRIN
*Ambush ICI
Permethrin .... Agway
Permethrin .... Geo. Ball Pacific
Permethrin .... Ball Seed
*Pounce .... FMC

*PERTHANE
Occidental Perthane .... Occidental
Pennwalt Perthane .... Pennwalt
Perthane .... Agway

PHORATE
FMC Thimet .... FMC
Occidental Thimet .... Occidental
*Thimet .... American Cyanamid

PHOSALONE
*Zolone .... Rhone-Poulenc

PHOSPHAMIDON
FMC Phosphamidon 8 Spray .... FMC
Miller Phosphamidon .... Miller Chemical
Occidental Phosphamidon .... Occidental
Phosphamidon .... Agway
Phosphamidon .... Penn State

PIRIMICARB
*Pirimor ICI

PROPARGITE
FMC Omite .... FMC
*Omite .... Uniroyal

PYRETHRUM & ROTENONE

Agrico .... Penn State
Miller Chemical .... Plant Marvel Lab
Penick .... Harry Shar

ROTENONE

Rotenone .... Agway
Rotenone .... Penn State
Rotenone .... Siegers Seed
Security Rotenone .... Woolfolk

TEPP

*Kilmite-40 .... Miller Chemical

TETRADIFON

Tedion .... Harry Sharp

Miller Tetradifon .... Miller Chemical
Tetradifon .... Agway

TOXAPHENE

Occidental Toxaphene .... Occidental
*Ortho Toxaphene 6 Emulsive .... Chevron Chemical
*Ortho Toxaphene 8 Emulsive .... Chevron Chemical
Security Toxaphene .... Woolfolk
*Toxakil .... FMC
Toxaphene .... Agway
Toxaphene .... Hopkins
Toxaphene 6E .... Drexel

TRICHLORFON

*Dylox .... Mobay
*Proxol 80 SP .... TUCO

Addresses of Chemical Suppliers

A & L Agricultural Laboratories, 2176 Dunn Ave., Memphis TN 38114

Abbott Laboratories, CAPD, Dept. 44A, R1B, 3rd Fl., 14th & Sheridan Rd., N. Chicago IL 60064

Agrico Chemical Co., P.O. Box 3166, Tulsa OK 74101

Agri-Sul Canada, P.O. Box 1180, Didsbury, Alberta, Canada T0M 0W0

Agrotec Inc., Box 215, Salisbury MD 21801

Agway Inc., Box 4933, Syracuse NY 13221

Allied Chemical Corp., Box 2120, Houston TX 77001

AMAX Chemical Corp., 35 Mason St., Greenwich CT 06830

American Cyanamid Co., P.O. Box 400, Princeton NJ 08540

Amvac Chemical Corp., 4100 E. Washington Blvd., Los Angeles CA 90023

H. J. Baker & Bro., 100 E. 42nd St., New York NY 10017

Geo. Ball Pacific, Inc., P.O. Box 9055, Sunnyvale CA 94088

Ball Seed Co., P.O. Box 335, West Chicago IL 60185

BASF Wyandotte Corp., Box 181, Parsippany NJ 07054

Bell Laboratories, Inc., 3699 Kinsman Blvd., Madison WI 53704

BFG Supply Co., Box 479, Burton OH 44021

Bioferm International, Heritage Building, Suite #6, Stokes Rd., Medford NJ 08055

Boots Hercules Agrochemicals, Box 7489, Wilmington DE 19803

Chemical Formulators, Inc., Box 26, Nitro WV 25143

Chemical & Pigment Co., A Div. of ESI Chemicals, Inc., 600 Nichols Rd., Pittsburg CA 94565

Chemley Products Co., Box 14, North Town Station, Chicago IL 60625

Chempar Chemical Co., Inc., 60 E. 42nd St., Suite 652, New York NY 10017

Chevron Chemical Co., 575 Market St., San Francisco CA 94105

Chilean Nitrate Sales Corp., One World Trade Center, Suite 5167, New York NY 10048

CIBA-GEIGY Corp., Box 11422, Greensboro NC 27409

Cities Service Co., P.O. Box 50360, Atlanta GA 30302

Clements Associates, Inc., P.O. Box 398, Grinnell IA 50112

Climax Molybdenum Co., One Greenwich Plaza, Greenwich CT 06830

Clover Garden Products, Inc., Box 874, Smyrna TN 37167

Corning Medical & Scientific, Corning Glass Works, MP 21-5, Corning NY 14830

Custom Chemicides Inc., 1495 Railroad Ave., Clovis CA 93612

Diamond Shamrock Corp., 1100 Superior Ave., Cleveland OH 44114

Dow Chemical U.S.A., Ag-Products Dept., Box 1706, Midland MI 48640

Drexel Chemical Co., P.O. Box 9306, Memphis TN 38109

E. I. Du Pont de Nemours & Co., Inc., 1007 Market St., Wilmington DE 19898

Duval Sales Corp., P.O. Box 2967, Houston, TX 77001

Eagle-Picher Industries Inc., P.O. Box 83, Joplin MO 64801

Edwards Laboratory, 219 Fremont Ave., Sandusky OH 44870

Elanco Products Co., Div. of Eli Lilly, Box 1750, Indianapolis IN 46206

FMC Corp., Agricultural Chemical Group, 2000 Market St., Philadelphia PA 19103

FMC Corp., Citrus Machinery Div., 3075 12th St., Riverside CA 92502

GAF Corp., 140 W. 51st St., New York NY 10020

Geiger Corp., P.O. Box 2853, Harleysville PA 19438

H. G. German Seeds, Inc., 103 Bank St., Smethport PA 16749

B. F. Goodrich Chemical Co., 6100 Oak Tree Blvd., Cleveland OH 44131

W. R. Grace & Co., Box 277, Memphis TN 38101

W. R. Grace & Co., Horticultural Products, 62 Whittemore Ave., Cambridge MA 02140

Great Lakes Chemical Corp., Box 2200, West Lafayette IN 47906

Hach Agricultural Div., P.O. Box 907, Ames IA 50010

Harshaw Chemical Co., 1945 E. 97th St., Cleveland OH 44106

Hendrix & Dail, Inc., P.O. Box 631, Greenville NC 27834

Hettich Mfg. Co., Box 237, Dousman WI 53118

Hopkins Agricultural Chemical Co., Box 7532, Madison WI 53707

A. H. Hummert Seed Co., 2746 Chouteau Ave., St. Louis MO 63103

Hydroculture, Inc., P.O. Box 1655, Glendale AZ 85311

Hydro-Gardens, Inc., P.O. Box 9707, Colorado Springs CO 80932

ICI Americas Inc., Agricultural Chemicals Div., Wilmington DE 19897

International Minerals & Chemical Corp., 421 E. Hawley St., Mundelein IL 60060

Johnny's Selected Seeds, Box 32, Albion ME 04910

Kaiser Agricultural Chemicals, Box 246, Savannah GA 31402

Kalo Laboratories Inc., 10236 Bunker Ridge Rd., Kansas City MO 64137

Kay-Fries Inc., Member Dynamit Nobel Group, 200 Summit Ave., Montvale NJ 07645

Kerr-McGee Chemical Corp., Kerr-McGee Center, Oklahoma City OK 73125

Kocide Chemical Corp., P.O. Box 45539, Houston TX 77045

Koppers Co., Inc., 1900 Koppers Bldg., Pittsburgh PA 15219

LaMotte Chemical Products Co., Box 329, Chestertown MD 21620

Leffingwell Div., Thompson-Hayward Chemical Co., 111 S. Berry St., Brea CA 92621

Mallinckrodt Inc., P.O. Box 5439, St. Louis MO 63147

Materials Science Co., P.O. Box 3391, Santa Barbara CA 93105

J. M. McConkey & Co., Inc., P.O. Box 309, Sumner WA 98390

McCormick and Co., McCormick Bldg., Baltimore MD 21202

Medina Agriculture Prods. Co., Inc., P.O. Box 309, Hondo TX 78861

Mellinger's Inc., 2324M Range, N. Lima OH 44452

Merck and Co., Inc., P.O. Box 2000, Rahway NJ 07065

Miller Chemical & Fertilizer Corp., Box 333, Hanover PA 17331

Mineral Research & Development Corp., P.O. Box 31711, Charlotte NC 28231

Mobay Chemical Corp., Agricultural Chemicals Div., Box 4913, Kansas City MO 64120

Monsanto Agricultural Products Co., 800 N. Lindbergh Blvd., St. Louis MO 63166

National Spectographic Labs., Inc., 19500 S. Miles, Cleveland OH 44128

Nor-Am Agricultural Products Inc., 350 W. Shuman Blvd., Naperville IL 60540

Nursery Specialty Products, P.O. Box 4280, Greenwich CT 06830

Oakfield Apparatus Co., P.O. Box 65, Oakfield WI 53065

Occidental Chemical Co., Box 1185, Houston TX 77001

Olin Corp., Box 991, Little Rock AR 72203

Organic Laboratories, Inc., 1656 E. Townhurst, Houston TX 77043

Geo. W. Park Seed Co., Inc., Wholesale Div., P.O. Box 31, Greenwood SC 29647

Penick Corp., 1050 Wall St. W., Lyndhurst NJ 07071

Penn State Seed Co., 906 Wyoming Ave., Forty Fort PA 18704

Pennwalt Corp., Agrochemical Div., Pennwalt Bldg., 3 Parkway, Philadelphia PA 19102; Decco Div., 1713 S. California Ave., Monrovia CA 91016

Pfizer, Inc., 235 E. 42nd St., New York NY 10017

Phelps Dodge Refining Corp., 300 Park Ave., New York NY 10022

Phillips Chemical Co., Fertilizer Div., Bartlesville OK 74004

Plant Marvel Laboratories, 624 W. 119th St., Chicago IL 60628

Potash Co. of America, 630 Fifth Ave., New York NY 10020

PPG Industries, Inc., 1 Gateway Center, Pittsburgh PA 15222

Premier Brands, Inc., 145 Hugenot St., New Rochelle NY 10801

Pronto Plant Food Co., Inc., P.O. Drawer V, Wisner LA 71378

Rambridge Structure & Design Ltd. 1316 Centre St., NE Calgary, Alberta T2E 2A7

Ra-Pid-Gro Corp., P.O. Box 370, Dansville NY 14437

Red's Package, Inc., Rt. 9W, Milton NY 12547

Reichhold Chemicals, Inc., 525 N. Broadway, White Plains NY 10602

Rhone-Poulenc Chemical Co., Agrochemical Div., P.O. Box 125, Monmouth Junction NJ 08852

Rohm and Haas Co., Independence Mall West, Philadelphia PA 19105

Sandoz, Inc., 480 Camino Del Rio South, Suite 204, San Diego CA 92108

Seaborn Inc., 2000 Rockford Rd., Charles City IA 50616

SESCO Enterprises Inc., 12100 S. Peoria, Chicago IL 60643

Harry Sharp & Son, 420 8th Ave. N., Seattle WA 98109

Shell Chemical Co., Agricultural Chemicals, P.O. Box 3871, Houston TX 77001

Siegers Seed Co., 7245 Imlay City Rd., Imlay City MI 48444

Sierra Chemical Co., 1001 Yosemite Dr., Milpitas CA 95035

Slater Supply Co., 143 Allen Blvd., Farmingdale NY 11735

Stauffer Chemical Co., Agricultural Chemical Div., Westport CT 06880

Stoller Chemical Co., Inc., 8582 Katy Freeway, Suite 200, Houston TX 77024

Stoller Research Co., P.O. Box 1071, Santa Cruz CA 95060

Sudbury Laboratory, Box 2127, Sudbury MA 01776

Thompson-Hayward Chemical Co., Box 2383, Kansas City KS 66110

TUCO Agricultural Chemicals, Div. of The Upjohn Co., 9823-190-1, Kalamazoo MI 49001

Union Carbide Agricultural Products Co., Inc., Brookside Ave., Ambler PA 19002

Uniroyal Chemical, Div. of Uniroyal, Inc., 32 Spencer St., Naugatuck CT 06770

U.S. Borax & Chemical Corp., P.O. Box 75128, Sanford Sta., Los Angeles CA 90010

U.S. Gypsum Co., 101 S. Wacker Dr., Chicago IL 60606

USS Agri-Chemicals, Div. of U.S. Steel Corp., P.O. Box 1685, Atlanta GA 30301

USS Chemicals, Div. of United States Steel Corp., P.O. Box 86, Pittsburgh PA 15230

United States Testing Co., Inc., 3765 Premier Cove, Memphis TN 38118

Velsicol Chemical Co., 341 E. Ohio St., Chicago IL 60611

Wilson & Geo. Meyer & Co., 270 Lawrence Ave., So. San Francisco CA 94080

Woolfolk Chemical Works, Inc., P.O. Box 938, Ft. Valley GA 31030

Greenhouses

AIR CIRCULATORS

AAA Associates Inc.
1445 South 3rd St., Niles, MI 49120
Acme Engineering and Mfg. Corp.
P.O. Box 978, Muskogee, OK 74402
American Horticultural Supply, Inc.
25603 West Ave. Stanford, Valencia, CA 91355
Conley's Greenhouse Mfg. and Sales
4344 Mission Blvd., Pomona, CA 91766
DACE
1937 High St., Longwood, FL 32750
E.C. Geiger, Inc.
P.O. Box 285, Harleysville, PA 19438
Harnois Industries Inc.
1044 Principale, Saint-Thomas-of-Joliette, PQ
J0K 3L0
Ludy Greenhouse Mfg. Corp.
143 West Washington St., New Madison, OH
45346
J.M. McConkey and Co., Inc.
P.O. Box 309, Sumner, WA 98390
Reznor
McKinley Ave., Mercer, PA 16137
Sharp and Son
19219 62nd Ave. S., Kent, WA 98032
Simburg Co.
2646 Pacific Park Dr., Whittier, CA 90601
X.S. Smith Inc.
P.O. Drawer X, Red Bank, NJ 07701
Specialty Products and Services Corp.
P.O. Box 20909, San Jose, CA 95160
Structures Unlimited
2740 Leonard Reid Ave., Sarasota, FL 33580
Jack Van Klaveren Ltd. (JVK)
P.O. Box 910, St. Catharines, ON L2R 6Z4
Van Wingerden Greenhouse Co.
4078 Haywood Rd., Horse Shoe, NC 28742
Vary Industries
P.O. Box 248, Lewiston, NY 14092
Vent-Tech U.S.A.
Drawer Q, Richmond, IL 60071
Westbrook Greenhouse Systems Ltd.
270 Hunter Rd., Grimsby, ON L3M 4G1

BOILERS

Bio-Energy Systems Co.
221 Canal St., Ellenville, NY 12428
CanaBurn Bioenergy Inc.
P.O. Box 2037, Windsor, ON N8Y 4R5
CASSCO
P.O. Box 3508, Montgomery, AL 36193
Dalsem Greenhouses USA Inc.
P.O. Box 54039, Jacksonville, FL 32245
Delta T Sales
3576 Empleo, Suite 2, San Luis Obispo, CA
93401
Eshland Enterprises Inc.
P.O. Box 8A, Greencastle, PA 17225

Firetender-Stokermatic Mfg.
1610 South Industrial Rd., Salt Lake City, UT
84104
E.C. Geiger, Inc.
P.O. Box 285, Harleysville, PA 19438
McCalif
2215 Ringwood Ave., San Jose, CA 95131
J.M. McConkey and Co., Inc.
P.O. Box 309, Sumner, WA 98390
Nepco International
P.O. Box 33918, Seattle, WA 98188
Sharp and Son
19219 62nd Ave. S., Kent, WA 98032
Simburg Co.
2646 Pacific Park Dr., Whittier, CA 90601

United Greenhouse Systems, Inc.
708 Washington St., Edgerton, WI 53534
Van Wingerden Greenhouse Co.
4078 Haywood Rd., Horse Shoe, NC 28742
Vary Industries
P.O. Box 248, Lewiston, NY 14092
Waldo & Associates, Inc.
28214 Glenwood Rd., Perrysburg, OH 43551
Winandy Greenhouse Co., Inc.
2211 Peacock Rd., Richmond, IN 47374

BOTTOM HEATING

Aluminum Sun-Fin Radiation
4302 Woodland Ave., Kansas City, MO 64110
Ball Seed Co.
250 Town Rd., West Chicago, IL 60185
Bio-Energy Systems Co.
221 Canal St., Ellenville, NY 12428
CASSCO
P.O. Box 3508, Montgomery, AL 36193
Conley's Greenhouse Mfg. and Sales
4344 Mission Blvd., Pomona, CA 91766
CropKing Inc.
P.O. Box 310, Medina, OH 44258
DACE
1937 High St., Longwood, FL 32750
Dalsem Greenhouses USA Inc.
P.O. Box 54039, Jacksonville, FL 32245
Delta T Sales
3576 Empleo, Suite 2, San Luis Obispo, CA
93401
Hydro-Gardens, Inc.
P.O. Box 9707, Colorado Springs, CO 80932
McCalif
2215 Ringwood Ave., San Jose, CA 95131
Mee Industries Inc.
4443 North Rowland Ave., El Monte, CA
91731
Nepco International
P.O. Box 33918, Seattle, WA 98188
Park Seed Co., Wholesale Div.
Cokesbury Rd., Greenwood, SC 29647-0001
Penn State Seed Co.
Route 309, Box 390, Dallas, PA 18612

Reznor
  McKinley Ave., Mercer, PA 16137
Sharp and Son
  19219 62nd Ave. S., Kent, WA 98032
Simburg Co.
  2646 Pacific Park Dr., Whittier, CA 90601
United Greenhouse Systems, Inc.
  708 Washington St., Edgerton, WI 53534
Vary Industries
  P.O. Box 248, Lewiston, NY 14092
Vaughan's Seed Co.
  5300 Katrine Ave., Downers Grove, IL 60515
Winandy Greenhouse Co., Inc.
  2211 Peacock Rd., Richmond, IN 47374

CLIMATE CONTROLLERS

AAA Associates Inc.
  1445 South 3rd St., Niles, MI 49120
Acme Engineering and Mfg. Corp.
  P.O. Box 978, Muskogee, OK 74402
American Coolair Corp.
  P.O. Box 2300, Jacksonville, FL 32203
American Horticultural Supply, Inc.
  25603 West Ave. Stanford, Valencia, CA 91355
Atomizing Systems Inc.
  1 Hollywood Ave., Hohokus, NJ 07423
Automata, Inc.
  19393 Redberry Rd., Grass Valley, CA 95945
BFG Supply Co.
  P.O. Box 479, Burton, OH 44021
Chicago Climate Systems, Inc.
  1675 Glen Ellyn Rd., Glendale Heights, IL 60139
CropKing Inc.
  P.O. Box 310, Medina, OH 44258
DACE
  1937 High St., Longwood, FL 32750
Dalsem Greenhouses USA Inc.
  P.O. Box 54039, Jacksonville, FL 32245
E.C. Geiger, Inc.
  P.O. Box 285, Harleysville, PA 19438
Growers Technical Services Ltd.
  2245 Dunwin Dr., Mississauga, ON L5L 1A3
Harnois Industries Inc.
  1044 Principale, Saint-Thomas-of-Joliette, PQ JOK 3L0
Hydro-Gardens, Inc.
  P.O. Box 9707, Colorado Springs, CO 80932
McCalif
  2215 Ringwood Ave., San Jose, CA 95131
J.M. McConkey and Co., Inc.
  P.O. Box 309, Sumner, WA 98390
Mee Industries Inc.
  4443 North Rowland Ave., El Monte, CA 91731
Midwest Growers Supply, Inc.
  2613 Kaneville Court, Geneva, IL 60134
Priva Computers Inc.
  4556 Steinhauer Rd., Marietta, GA 30066
Q-Com Corp.
  2050 South Grand Ave., Santa Ana, CA 92705

Sharp and Son
  19219 62nd Ave. S., Kent, WA 98032
Simburg Co.
  2646 Pacific Park Dr., Whittier, CA 90601
X S. Smith Inc.
  P.O. Drawer X, Red Bank, NJ 07701
Specialty Products and Services Corp.
  P.O. Box 20909, San Jose, CA 95160
Structures Unlimited
  2740 Leonard Reid Ave., Sarasota, FL 33580
United Greenhouse Systems, Inc.
  708 Washington St., Edgerton, WI 53534
Jack Van Klaveren Ltd. (JVK)
  P.O. Box 910, St. Catharines, ON L2R 6Z4
Van Wingerden Greenhouse Co.
  4078 Haywood Rd., Horse Shoe, NC 28742
Vary Industries
  P.O. Box 248, Lewiston, NY 14092
Waldo & Associates, Inc.
  28214 Glenwood Rd., Perrysburg, OH 43551
Westbrook Greenhouse Systems Ltd.
  270 Hunter Rd., Grimsby, ON L3M 4G1
Winandy Greenhouse Co., Inc.
  2211 Peacock Rd., Richmond, IN 47374

COMPUTER CONTROLS

Acme Engineering and Mfg. Corp.
  P.O. Box 978, Muskogee, OK 74402
Agro-Dynamics Inc., Eastern Div.
  Building #3, Navy Yard, Brooklyn, NY 11205
Agro-Dynamics Inc., Western Div.
  6492 South Heritage Place E., Englewood, CO 80111
American Horticultural Supply, Inc.
  25603 West Ave. Stanford, Valencia, CA 91355
Automata, Inc.
  19393 Redberry Rd., Grass Valley, CA 95945
Conley's Greenhouse Mfg. and Sales
  4344 Mission Blvd., Pomona, CA 91766
CropKing Inc.
  P.O. Box 310, Medina, OH 44258
DACE
  1937 High St., Longwood, FL 32750
Dalsem Greenhouses USA Inc.
  P.O. Box 54039, Jacksonville, FL 32245
Growers Technical Services Ltd.
  2245 Dunwin Dr., Mississauga, ON L5L 1A3
Hydro-Gardens, Inc.
  P.O. Box 9707, Colorado Springs, CO 80932
J.M. McConkey and Co., Inc.
  P.O. Box 309, Sumner, WA 98390
Mee Industries Inc.
  4443 North Rowland Ave., El Monte, CA 91731
Oglevee Computer Systems
  151 Oglevee Lane, Connellsville, PA 15425
Priva Computers Inc.
  4556 Steinhauer Rd., Marietta, GA 30066
Q-Com Corp.
  2050 South Grand Ave., Santa Ana, CA 92705
Simburg Co.
  2646 Pacific Park Dr., Whittier, CA 90601

Specialty Products and Services Corp.
P.O. Box 20909, San Jose, CA 95160
United Greenhouse Systems, Inc.
708 Washington St., Edgerton, WI 53534

Jack Van Klaveren Ltd. (JVK)
P.O. Box 910, St. Catharines, ON L2R 6Z4
Van Wingerden Greenhouse Co.
4078 Haywood Rd., Horse Shoe, NC 28742

COOLING EQUIPMENT .

AAA Associates Inc.
1445 South 3rd St., Niles, MI 49120
Acme Engineering and Mfg. Corp.
P.O. Box 978, Muskogee, OK 74402
AGRITECH
P.O. Box 577, Broadway, NC 27505
American Coolair Corp.
P.O. Box 2300, Jacksonville, FL 32203

American Horticultural Supply, Inc.
25603 West Ave. Stanford, Valencia, CA 91355
Atomizing Systems Inc.
1 Hollywood Ave., Hohokus, NJ 07423
Ball Seed Co.
250 Town Rd., West Chicago, IL 60185
Baumac International
1500 Crafton Ave., Mentone, CA 92359
BFG Supply Co.
P.O. Box 479, Burton, OH 44021
CASSCO
P.O. Box 3508, Montgomery, AL 36193
Conley's Greenhouse Mfg. and Sales
4344 Mission Blvd., Pomona, CA 91766
CropKing Inc.
P.O. Box 310, Medina, OH 44258

DACE
1937 High St., Longwood, FL 32750
Dalsem Greenhouses USA Inc.
P.O. Box 54039, Jacksonville, FL 32245
E.C. Geiger, Inc.
P.O. Box 285, Harleysville, PA 19438
Growers Technical Services Ltd.
2245 Dunwin Dr., Mississauga, ON L5L 1A3
Harnois Industries Inc.
1044 Principale, Saint-Thomas-of-Joliette, PQ
J0K 3L0
Hobbs Bonded Fibers
P.O. Box 34888, Houston, TX 77234
Hydro-Gardens, Inc.
P.O. Box 9707, Colorado Springs, CO 80932
Ludy Greenhouse Mfg. Corp.
143 West Washington St., New Madison, OH
45346
McCalif
2215 Ringwood Ave., San Jose, CA 95131
J.M. McConkey and Co., Inc.
P.O. Box 309, Sumner, WA 98390
Mee Industries Inc.
4443 North Rowland Ave., El Monte, CA
91731

Microcool-Environmental Cooling Concepts Inc.
653 Commercial Rd., Palm Springs, CA 92262
Park Seed Co., Wholesale Div.
Cokesbury Rd., Greenwood, SC 29647-0001
Reznor
McKinley Ave., Mercer, PA 16137
Rounhouse
P.O. Box 1744, Cleveland, TX 77327
Sharp and Son
19219 62nd Ave. S., Kent, WA 98032
Simburg Co.
2646 Pacific Park Dr., Whittier, CA 90601
X.S. Smith Inc.
P.O. Drawer X, Red Bank, NJ 07701
Structures Unlimited
2740 Leonard Reid Ave., Sarasota, FL 33580
United Greenhouse Systems, Inc.
708 Washington St., Edgerton, WI 53534
Jack Van Klaveren Ltd. (JVK)
P.O. Box 910, St. Catharines, ON L2R 6Z4
Van Wingerden Greenhouse Co.
4078 Haywood Rd., Horse Shoe, NC 28742
Vary Industries
P.O. Box 248, Lewiston, NY 14092
Vaughan's Seed Co.
5300 Katrine Ave., Downers Grove, IL 60515-
4095
Waldo & Associates, Inc.
28214 Glenwood Rd., Perrysburg, OH 43551
Westbrook Greenhouse Systems Ltd.
270 Hunter Rd., Grimsby, ON L3M 4G1
Western Farm Service, Inc.
1015 Linda Vista Dr., Bldg. B, San Marcos, CA
92069
Winandy Greenhouse Co., Inc.
2211 Peacock Rd., Richmond, IN 47374

CO_2 CONCENTRATION METERS

Dalsem Greenhouses USA Inc.
P.O. Box 54039, Jacksonville, FL 32245
Growers Technical Services Ltd.
2245 Dunwin Dr., Mississauga, ON L5L 1A3
Harnois Industries Inc.
1044 Principale, Saint-Thomas-of-Joliette, PQ
J0K 3L0
Hydro-Gardens, Inc.
P.O. Box 9707, Colorado Springs, CO 80932
Oglevee Computer Systems
151 Oglevee Lane, Connellsville, PA 15425
Priva Computers Inc.
4556 Steinhauer Rd., Marietta, GA 30066
Sharp and Son
19219 62nd Ave. S., Kent, WA 98032
Jack Van Klaveren Ltd. (JVK)
P.O. Box 910, St. Catharines, ON L2R 6Z4

CO_2 GENERATORS

American Horticultural Supply, Inc.
25603 West Ave. Stanford, Valencia, CA 91355
Dalsem Greenhouses USA Inc.
P.O. Box 54039, Jacksonville, FL 32245

Harnois Industries Inc.
1044 Principale, Saint-Thomas-of-Joliette, PQ J0K 3L0
McCalif
2215 Ringwood Ave., San Jose, CA 95131
Priva Computers Inc.
4556 Steinhauer Rd., Marietta, GA 30066
Jack Van Klaveren Ltd. (JVK)
P.O. Box 910, St. Catharines, ON L2R 6Z4

CO_2, LIQUID

Dalsem Greenhouses USA Inc.
P.O. Box 54039, Jacksonville, FL 32245

ENVIRONMENTAL MONITORING SYSTEMS

AAA Associates Inc.
1445 South 3rd St., Niles, MI 49120
Acme Engineering and Mfg. Corp.
P.O. Box 978, Muskogee, OK 74402
Automata, Inc.
19393 Redberry Rd., Grass Valley, CA 95945
Conley's Greenhouse Mfg. and Sales
4344 Mission Blvd., Pomona, CA 91766
Growers Technical Services Ltd.
2245 Dunwin Dr., Mississauga, ON L5L 1A3
McCalif
2215 Ringwood Ave., San Jose, CA 95131
Priva Computers Inc.
4556 Steinhauer Rd., Marietta, GA 30066
Q-Com Corp.
2050 South Grand Ave., Santa Ana, CA 92705
Simburg Co.
2646 Pacific Park Dr., Whittier, CA 90601
Specialty Products and Services Corp.
P.O. Box 20909, San Jose, CA 95160
Jack Van Klaveren Ltd. (JVK)
P.O. Box 910, St. Catharines, ON L2R 6Z4

EVAPORATIVE COOLING PADS

AAA Associates Inc.
1445 South 3rd St., Niles, MI 49120
AAA Brokers, Inc.
P.O. Box 3250, Jackson, TN 38303-0250
Acme Engineering and Mfg. Corp.
P.O. Box 978, Muskogee, OK 74402
American Coolair Corp.
P.O. Box 2300, Jacksonville, FL 32203
American Horticultural Supply, Inc.
25603 West Ave. Stanford, Valencia, CA 91355
Ball Seed Co.
250 Town Rd., West Chicago, IL 60185
BFG Supply Co.
P.O. Box 479, Burton, OH 44021

E.C. Carson and Associates
P.O. Box 3095, Greenwood, SC 29648
CASSCO
P.O. Box 3508, Montgomery, AL 36193
Caves Enterprises Inc.
2464 Pumpkin Center Rd., Hammond, LA 70401

Conley's Greenhouse Mfg. and Sales
4344 Mission Blvd., Pomona, CA 91766
CropKing Inc.
P.O. Box 310, Medina, OH 44258
Eng-Cor Inc.
1149 Central Ave., University Park, IL 60466
E.C. Geiger, Inc.
P.O. Box 285, Harleysville, PA 19438
Harnois Industries Inc.
1044 Principale, Saint-Thomas-of-Joliette, PQ J0K 3L0
Hobbs Bonded Fibers
P.O. Box 34888, Houston, TX 77234
Hydro-Gardens, Inc.
P.O. Box 9707, Colorado Springs, CO 80932
McCalif
2215 Ringwood Ave., San Jose, CA 95131
J.M. McConkey and Co., Inc.
P.O. Box 309, Sumner, WA 98390
The Munters Corp.
P.O. Box 6428, Ft. Myers, FL 33911
Packer Greenhouses
9308 CTH H, Cuba City, WI 53807
Reznor
McKinley Ave., Mercer, PA 16137
Sharp and Son
19219 62nd Ave. S., Kent, WA 98032
X.S. Smith Inc.
P.O. Drawer X, Red Bank, NJ 07701
Structures Unlimited
2740 Leonard Reid Ave., Sarasota, FL 33580
United Greenhouse Systems, Inc.
708 Washington St., Edgerton, WI 53534
Van Wingerden Greenhouse Co.
4078 Haywood Rd., Horse Shoe, NC 28742
Simburg Co.
2646 Pacific Park Dr., Whittier, CA 90601
Vary Industries
P.O. Box 248, Lewiston, NY 14092
Westbrook Greenhouse Systems Ltd.
270 Hunter Rd., Grimsby, ON L3M 4G1
Western Farm Service, Inc.
1015 Linda Vista Dr., Bldg. B, San Marcos, CA 92069
Winandy Greenhouse Co., Inc.
2211 Peacock Rd., Richmond, IN 47374

FANS

Air circulation

AAA Associates Inc.
1445 South 3rd St., Niles, MI 49120
Acme Engineering and Mfg. Corp.
P.O. Box 978, Muskogee, OK 74402
American Horticultural Supply, Inc.
25603 West Ave. Stanford, Valencia, CA 91355
E.C. Carson and Associates
P.O. Box 3095, Greenwood, SC 29648
Chicago Climate Systems, Inc.
1675 Glen Ellyn Rd., Glendale Heights, IL 60139
Conley's Greenhouse Mfg. and Sales
4344 Mission Blvd., Pomona, CA 91766

DACE
1937 High St., Longwood, FL 32750
E.C. Geiger, Inc.
P.O. Box 285, Harleysville, PA 19438
Ludy Greenhouse Mfg. Corp.
143 West Washington St., New Madison, OH 45346
Packer Greenhouses
9308 CTH H, Cuba City, WI 53807
Priva Computers Inc.
4556 Steinhauer Rd., Marietta, GA 30066
Simburg Co.
2646 Pacific Park Dr., Whittier, CA 90601
Vary Industries
P.O. Box 248, Lewiston, NY 14092
Vaughan's Seed Co.
5300 Katrine Ave., Downers Grove, IL 60515-4095
Vent-Tech U.S.A.
Drawer Q, Richmond, IL 60071
Westbrook Greenhouse Systems Ltd.
270 Hunter Rd., Grimsby, ON L3M 4G1
Winandy Greenhouse Co., Inc.
2211 Peacock Rd., Richmond, IN 47374

Ducted, fresh air ventilating

AAA Associates Inc.
1445 South 3rd St., Niles, MI 49120
Acme Engineering and Mfg. Corp.
P.O. Box 978, Muskogee, OK 74402
American Horticultural Supply, Inc.
25603 West Ave. Stanford, Valencia, CA 91355
BFG Supply Co.
P.O. Box 479, Burton, OH 44021
CASSCO
P.O. Box 3508, Montgomery, AL 36193
Conley's Greenhouse Mfg. and Sales
4344 Mission Blvd., Pomona, CA 91766
Harnois Industries Inc.
1044 Principale, Saint-Thomas-of-Joliette, PQ J0K 3L0
Hydro-Gardens, Inc.
P.O. Box 9707, Colorado Springs, CO 80932
Keeler-Glasgow
P.O. Box 234, Hartford, MI 49057
Ken-Bar Inc.
24 Gould St., Reading, MA 01867
Ludy Greenhouse Mfg. Corp.
143 West Washington St., New Madison, OH 45346
Penn State Seed Co.
Route 309, Box 390, Dallas, PA 18612
Sharp and Son
19219 62nd Ave. S., Kent, WA 98032
X.S. Smith Inc.
P.O. Drawer X, Red Bank, NJ 07701
Structures Unlimited
2740 Leonard Reid Ave., Sarasota, FL 33580
Van Wingerden Greenhouse Co.
4078 Haywood Rd., Horse Shoe, NC 28742
Vent-Tech U.S.A.
Drawer Q, Richmond, IL 60071

Waldo & Associates, Inc.
28214 Glenwood Rd., Perrysburg, OH 43551
Western Farm Service, Inc.
1015 Linda Vista Dr., Bldg. B, San Marcos, CA 92069
Winandy Greenhouse Co., Inc.
2211 Peacock Rd., Richmond, IN 47374

Exhaust

AAA Associates Inc.
1445 South 3rd St., Niles, MI 49120
Acme Engineering and Mfg. Corp.
P.O. Box 978, Muskogee, OK 74402
American Coolair Corp.
P.O. Box 2300, Jacksonville, FL 32203
American Horticultural Supply, Inc.
25603 West Ave. Stanford, Valencia, CA 91355
Baumac International
1500 Crafton Ave., Mentone, CA 92359
BFG Supply Co.
P.O. Box 479, Burton, OH 44021
Brady Mfg. Co.
210 R.D. #1, Jackson, NJ 08527
CASSCO
P.O. Box 3508, Montgomery, AL 36193
Caves Enterprises Inc.
2464 Pumpkin Center Rd., Hammond, LA 70401
Chicago Climate Systems, Inc.
1675 Glen Ellyn Rd., Glendale Heights, IL 60139
Conley's Greenhouse Mfg. and Sales
4344 Mission Blvd., Pomona, CA 91766
CropKing Inc.
P.O. Box 310, Medina, OH 44258
DACE
1937 High St., Longwood, FL 32750
Florist Products, Inc.
2242 North Palmer Dr., Schaumburg, IL 60173
E.C. Geiger, Inc.
P.O. Box 285, Harleysville, PA 19438
Harnois Industries Inc.
1044 Principale, Saint-Thomas-of-Joliette, PQ J0K 3L0
Hydro-Gardens, Inc.
P.O. Box 9707, Colorado Springs, CO 80932
Keeler-Glasgow
P.O. Box 234, Hartford, MI 49057
Ludy Greenhouse Mfg. Corp.
143 West Washington St., New Madison, OH 45346
McCalif
2215 Ringwood Ave., San Jose, CA 95131
J.M. McConkey and Co., Inc.
P.O. Box 309, Sumner, WA 98390
Packer Greenhouses
9308 CTH H, Cuba City, WI 53807
Park Seed Co., Wholesale Div.
Cokesbury Rd., Greenwood, SC 29647-0001
Penn State Seed Co.
Route 309, Box 390, Dallas, PA 18612
Rounhouse
P.O. Box 1744, Cleveland, TX 77327

Sharp and Son
19219 62nd Ave. S., Kent, WA 98032
Simburg Co.
2646 Pacific Park Dr., Whittier, CA 90601
X.S. Smith Inc.
P.O. Drawer X, Red Bank, NJ 07701
Structures Unlimited
2740 Leonard Reid Ave., Sarasota, FL 33580
Stuppy Inc.
1212 Clay St., North Kansas City, MO 64116
United Greenhouse Systems, Inc.
708 Washington St., Edgerton, WI 53534
Van Wingerden Greenhouse Co.
4078 Haywood Rd., Horse Shoe, NC 28742
Vary Industries
P.O. Box 248, Lewiston, NY 14092
Vaughan's Seed Co.
5300 Katrine Ave., Downers Grove, IL 60515-4095
Waldo & Associates, Inc.
28214 Glenwood Rd., Perrysburg, OH 43551
Westbrook Greenhouse Systems Ltd.
270 Hunter Rd., Grimsby, ON L3M 4G1
Winandy Greenhouse Co., Inc.
2211 Peacock Rd., Richmond, IN 47374

Horizontal air flow

Acme Engineering and Mfg. Corp.
P.O. Box 978, Muskogee, OK 74402
American Horticultural Supply, Inc.
25603 West Ave. Stanford, Valencia, CA 91355
Conley's Greenhouse Mfg. and Sales
4344 Mission Blvd., Pomona, CA 91766
Ludy Greenhouse Mfg. Corp.
143 West Washington St., New Madison, OH 45346
Midwest Growers Supply, Inc.
2613 Kaneville Court, Geneva, IL 60134
Simburg Co.
2646 Pacific Park Dr., Whittier, CA 90601
Jack Van Klaveren Ltd. (JVK)
P.O. Box 910, St. Catharines, ON L2R 6Z4
Vaughan's Seed Co.
5300 Katrine Ave., Downers Grove, IL 60515-4095
Westbrook Greenhouse Systems Ltd.
270 Hunter Rd., Grimsby, ON L3M 4G1
Winandy Greenhouse Co., Inc.
2211 Peacock Rd., Richmond, IN 47374

Jet system

AAA Associates Inc.
1445 South 3rd St., Niles, MI 49120
Acme Engineering and Mfg. Corp.
P.O. Box 978, Muskogee, OK 74402
AGRITECH
P.O. Box 577, Broadway, NC 27505
Ball Seed Co.
250 Town Rd., West Chicago, IL 60185
BFG Supply Co.
P.O. Box 479, Burton, OH 44021
E.C. Carson and Associates
P.O. Box 3095, Greenwood, SC 29648

Conley's Greenhouse Mfg. and Sales
4344 Mission Blvd., Pomona, CA 91766
CropKing Inc.
P.O. Box 310, Medina, OH 44258
Florist Products, Inc.
2242 North Palmer Dr., Schaumburg, IL 60173
E.C. Geiger, Inc.
P.O. Box 285, Harleysville, PA 19438
Hydro-Gardens, Inc.
P.O. Box 9707, Colorado Springs, CO 80932
Keeler-Glasgow
P.O. Box 234, Hartford, MI 49057
Sharp and Son
19219 62nd Ave. S., Kent, WA 98032
X.S. Smith Inc.
P.O. Drawer X, Red Bank, NJ 07701
Structures Unlimited
2740 Leonard Reid Ave., Sarasota, FL 33580
Stuppy Inc.
1212 Clay St., North Kansas City, MO 64116
United Greenhouse Systems, Inc.
708 Washington St., Edgerton, WI 53534
Van Wingerden Greenhouse Co.
4078 Haywood Rd., Horse Shoe, NC 28742
Vaughan's Seed Co.
5300 Katrine Ave., Downers Grove, IL 60515-4095
Westbrook Greenhouse Systems Ltd.
270 Hunter Rd., Grimsby, ON L3M 4G1
Western Farm Service, Inc.
1015 Linda Vista Dr., Bldg. B, San Marcos, CA 92069
Winandy Greenhouse Co., Inc.
2211 Peacock Rd., Richmond, IN 47374

Power tube

AAA Associates Inc.
1445 South 3rd St., Niles, MI 49120
Acme Engineering and Mfg. Corp.
P.O. Box 978, Muskogee, OK 74402
American Coolair Corp.
P.O. Box 2300, Jacksonville, FL 32203
BFG Supply Co.
P.O. Box 479, Burton, OH 44021
E.C. Carson and Associates
P.O. Box 3095, Greenwood, SC 29648
Conley's Greenhouse Mfg. and Sales
4344 Mission Blvd., Pomona, CA 91766
CropKing Inc.
P.O. Box 310, Medina, OH 44258
Harnois Industries Inc.
1044 Principale, Saint-Thomas-of-Joliette, PQ J0K 3L0
Hydro-Gardens, Inc.
P.O. Box 9707, Colorado Springs, CO 80932
Keeler-Glasgow
P.O. Box 234, Hartford, MI 49057
Ken-Bar Inc.
24 Gould St., Reading, MA 01867
Rounhouse
P.O. Box 1744, Cleveland, TX 77327
Simburg Co.
2646 Pacific Park Dr., Whittier, CA 90601

X.S. Smith Inc.
P.O. Drawer X, Red Bank, NJ 07701
Structures Unlimited
2740 Leonard Reid Ave., Sarasota, FL 33580
United Greenhouse Systems, Inc.
708 Washington St., Edgerton, WI 53534
Van Wingerden Greenhouse Co.
4078 Haywood Rd., Horse Shoe, NC 28742
Vary Industries
P.O. Box 248, Lewiston, NY 14092
Western Farm Service, Inc.
1015 Linda Vista Dr., Bldg. B, San Marcos, CA 92069
Winandy Greenhouse Co., Inc.
2211 Peacock Rd., Richmond, IN 47374

FERTILIZER EQUIPMENT

Applicators

Agrotec Inc.
P.O. Box 49, Pendleton, NC 27862-0049
BFG Supply Co.
P.O. Box 479, Burton, OH 44021
International Irrigation Systems
LPO 160, 1555 3rd Ave., Niagara Falls, NY 14304

J.M. McConkey and Co., Inc.
P.O. Box 309, Sumner, WA 98390
Plant Nurturing Service
P.O. Box 12683, Salem, OR 97309
Sharp and Son
19219 62nd Ave. S., Kent, WA 98032
Jack Van Klaveren Ltd. (JVK)
P.O. Box 910, St. Catharines, ON L2R 6Z4

Dispensers

BFG Supply Co.
P.O. Box 479, Burton, OH 44021
Bouldin and Lawson, Inc.
Route 10, Box 208, McMinnville, TN 37110
Gleason Industries, Inc.
13670 Southeast 132nd Ave., Clackamas, OR 97015
Javo USA, Inc.
1900 Albritton Dr., Suite G & H, Kennesaw, GA 30144
J.M. McConkey and Co., Inc.
P.O. Box 309, Sumner, WA 98390
Plant Nurturing Service
P.O. Box 12683, Salem, OR 97309
Sharp and Son
19219 62nd Ave. S., Kent, WA 98032
Jack Van Klaveren Ltd. (JVK)
P.O. Box 910, St. Catharines, ON L2R 6Z4

Injectors

American Horticultural Supply, Inc.
25603 West Ave. Stanford, Valencia, CA 91355
Ball Seed Co.
250 Town Rd., West Chicago, IL 60185
BFG Supply Co.
P.O. Box 479, Burton, OH 44021

BrushKing Div. of Loos & Co., Inc.
924 Industrial Blvd., Naples, FL 33942
CASSCO
P.O. Box 3508, Montgomery, AL 36193
CropKing Inc.
P.O. Box 310, Medina, OH 44258
Dalsem Greenhouses USA Inc.
P.O. Box 54039, Jacksonville, FL 32245
Dosatron International, Inc.
1610 North Fort Harrison Ave., Clearwater, FL 34615
Florist Products, Inc.
2242 North Palmer Dr., Schaumburg, IL 60173
E.C. Geiger, Inc.
P.O. Box 285, Harleysville, PA 19438
Growers Technical Services Ltd.
2245 Dunwin Dr., Mississauga, ON L5L 1A3
Growing Systems, Inc.
2950 North Weil St., Milwaukee, WI 53212
Harnois Industries Inc.
1044 Principale, Saint-Thomas-of-Joliette, PQ J0K 3L0
Hydro-Gardens, Inc.
P.O. Box 9707, Colorado Springs, CO 80932
J-F Equipment Co.
896 North Mill St., Suite 201, Lewisville, TX 75067

J-M Trading Corp.
241 Frontage Rd., Suite 31, Burr Ridge, IL 60521
Keeler-Glasgow
P.O. Box 234, Hartford, MI 49057
McCalif
2215 Ringwood Ave., San Jose, CA 95131
J.M. McConkey and Co., Inc.
P.O. Box 309, Sumner, WA 98390
Midwest Growers Supply, Inc.
2613 Kaneville Court, Geneva, IL 60134
Netafim Irrigation, Inc.
104 South Central Ave., Valley Stream, NY 11580
Park Seed Co., Wholesale Div.
Cokesbury Rd., Greenwood, SC 29647-0001
Penn State Seed Co.
Route 309, Box 390, Dallas, PA 18612
Sharp and Son
19219 62nd Ave. S., Kent, WA 98032
Jack Van Klaveren Ltd. (JVK)
P.O. Box 910, St. Catharines, ON L2R 6Z4
Van Wingerden Greenhouse Co.
4078 Haywood Rd., Horse Shoe, NC 28742
Van Wingerden Greenhouse Co.
4078 Haywood Rd., Horse Shoe, NC 28742
Vaughan's Seed Co.
5300 Katrine Ave., Downers Grove, IL 60515-4095
Waldo & Associates, Inc.
28214 Glenwood Rd., Perrysburg, OH 43551
Western Farm Service, Inc.
1015 Linda Vista Dr., Bldg. B, San Marcos, CA 92069

Young Industries
1033 Wright Ave., Mountain View, CA 94043

Mixers

BFG Supply Co.
P.O. Box 479, Burton. OH 44021
Dalsem Greenhouses USA Inc.
P.O. Box 54039, Jacksonville, FL 32245
Growers Technical Services Ltd.
2245 Dunwin Dr., Mississauga, ON L5L 1A3
J-M Trading Corp.
241 Frontage Rd., Suite 31, Burr Ridge, IL 60521
J.M. McConkey and Co., Inc.
P.O. Box 309, Sumner. WA 98390
Sharp and Son
19219 62nd Ave. S., Kent, WA 98032
Jack Van Klaveren Ltd. (JVK)
P.O. Box 910, St. Catharines, ON L2R 6Z4

Monitors

BFG Supply Co.
P.O. Box 479, Burton, OH 44021
CropKing Inc.
P.O. Box 310. Medina, OH 44258
E.C. Geiger, Inc.
P.O. Box 285, Harleysville, PA 19438
Growers Technical Services Ltd.
2245 Dunwin Dr., Mississauga, ON L5L 1A3
Hydro-Gardens, Inc.
P.O. Box 9707, Colorado Springs, CO 80932
J-M Trading Corp.
241 Frontage Rd.. Suite 31, Burr Ridge, IL 60521
Myron L Co.
6231 C Yarrow Dr., Carlsbad, CA 92009
Sharp and Son
19219 62nd Ave. S., Kent, WA 98032
Jack Van Klaveren Ltd. (JVK)
P.O. Box 910, St. Catharines, ON L2R 6Z4

Pumps

Agrotec Inc.
P.O. Box 49, Pendleton, NC 27862-0049
BFG Supply Co.
P.O. Box 479, Burton, OH 44021
Dalsem Greenhouses USA Inc.
P.O. Box 54039, Jacksonville, FL 32245
Dosatron International, Inc.
1610 North Fort Harrison Ave., Clearwater, FL 34615
Growers Technical Services Ltd.
2245 Dunwin Dr., Mississauga, ON L5L 1A3
J-M Trading Corp.
241 Frontage Rd., Suite 31, Burr Ridge, IL 60521
J.M. McConkey and Co., Inc.
P.O. Box 309, Sumner. WA 98390
Sharp and Son
19219 62nd Ave. S., Kent, WA 98032
Jack Van Klaveren Ltd. (JVK)
P.O. Box 910, St. Catharines, ON L2R 6Z4

Spreaders

E.C. Geiger, Inc.
P.O. Box 285, Harleysville, PA 19438
McCalif
2215 Ringwood Ave., San Jose, CA 95131
Penn State Seed Co.
Route 309, Box 390, Dallas. PA 18612
Sharp and Son
19219 62nd Ave. S., Kent, WA 98032
Jack Van Klaveren Ltd. (JVK)
P.O. Box 910, St. Catharines, ON L2R 6Z4
Western Farm Service, Inc.
1015 Linda Vista Dr., Bldg. B, San Marcos, CA 92069

GREENHOUSE GLASS

DACE
1937 High St., Longwood, FL 32750
Dalsem Greenhouses USA Inc.
P.O. Box 54039, Jacksonville, FL 32245
Harnois Industries Inc.
1044 Principale, Saint-Thomas-of-Joliette, PQ J0K 3L0
Ludy Greenhouse Mfg. Corp.
143 West Washington St., New Madison, OH 45346
J.M. McConkey and Co., Inc.
P.O. Box 309, Sumner, WA 98390
Jack Van Klaveren Ltd. (JVK)
P.O. Box 910, St. Catharines, ON L2R 6Z4
Van Wingerden Greenhouse Co.
4078 Haywood Rd., Horse Shoe, NC 28742
Winandy Greenhouse Co., Inc.
2211 Peacock Rd., Richmond, IN 47374

GREENHOUSE PLASTICS

Acrylic and polycarbonate

Agra Tech Inc.
2131 Piedmont Way, Pittsburg, CA 94565
American Horticultural Supply, Inc.
25603 West Ave. Stanford, Valencia. CA 91355
BFG Supply Co.
P.O. Box 479, Burton, OH 44021
CASSCO
P.O. Box 3508, Montgomery, AL 36193
Conley's Greenhouse Mfg. and Sales
4344 Mission Blvd., Pomona, CA 91766
CropKing Inc.
P.O. Box 310, Medina, OH 44258
CYRO Industries
25 Executive Blvd., Orange, CT 06477
Florist Products, Inc.
2242 North Palmer Dr., Schaumburg, IL 60173
E.C. Geiger, Inc.
P.O. Box 285, Harleysville, PA 19438
General Electric Co.
1 Plastic Ave., Pittsfield, MA 01201
Harnois Industries Inc.
1044 Principale, Saint-Thomas-of-Joliette, PQ J0K 3L0

Hydro-Gardens, Inc.
P.O. Box 9707, Colorado Springs, CO 80932
McCalif
2215 Ringwood Ave., San Jose, CA 95131
J.M. McConkey and Co., Inc.
P.O. Box 309, Sumner, WA 98390
Midwest Growers Supply, Inc.
2613 Kaneville Court, Geneva, IL 60134
Penn State Seed Co.
Route 309, Box 390, Dallas, PA 18612
Poly Grower Greenhouse Co.
P.O. Box 359, Muncy, PA 17756
Rounhouse
P.O. Box 1744, Cleveland, TX 77327
Sharp and Son
19219 62nd Ave. S., Kent, WA 98032
Simburg Co.
2646 Pacific Park Dr., Whittier, CA 90601
X.S. Smith Inc.
P.O. Drawer X, Red Bank, NJ 07701
Structures Unlimited
2740 Leonard Reid Ave., Sarasota, FL 33580
Stuppy Inc.
1212 Clay St., North Kansas City, MO 64116
United Greenhouse Systems, Inc.
708 Washington St., Edgerton, WI 53534
Van Wingerden Greenhouse Co.
4078 Haywood Rd., Horse Shoe, NC 28742
Vary Industries
P.O. Box 248, Lewiston, NY 14092
Vaughan's Seed Co.
5300 Katrine Ave., Downers Grove, IL 60515-4095
Waldo & Associates, Inc.
28214 Glenwood Rd., Perrysburg, OH 43551
Westbrook Greenhouse Systems Ltd.
270 Hunter Rd., Grimsby, ON L3M 4G1
Wetsel Seed Co. Inc.
P.O. Box 791, Harrisonburg, VA 22801
Winandy Greenhouse Co., Inc.
2211 Peacock Rd., Richmond, IN 47374

Copolymer

American Horticultural Supply, Inc.
25603 West Ave. Stanford, Valencia, CA 91355
BFG Supply Co.
P.O. Box 479, Burton, OH 44021
CropKing Inc.
P.O. Box 310, Medina, OH 44258
Midwest Growers Supply, Inc.
2613 Kaneville Court, Geneva, IL 60134
Monsanto Co.
800 North Lindbergh Blvd., St. Louis, MO 63167
Morton's Horticultural Products
P.O. Box 24, McMinnville, TN 37110
Penn State Seed Co.
Route 309, Box 390, Dallas, PA 18612
Sharp and Son
19219 62nd Ave. S., Kent. WA 98032
Simburg Co.
2646 Pacific Park Dr., Whittier, CA 90601

X.S. Smith Inc.
P.O. Drawer X, Red Bank, NJ 07701
Structures Unlimited
2740 Leonard Reid Ave., Sarasota, FL 33580
Van Wingerden Greenhouse Co.
4078 Haywood Rd., Horse Shoe, NC 28742
Waldo & Associates, Inc.
28214 Glenwood Rd., Perrysburg, OH 43551
Western Farm Service, Inc.
1015 Linda Vista Dr., Bldg. B, San Marcos, CA 92069
Wetsel Seed Co. Inc.
P.O. Box 791, Harrisonburg, VA 22801
Winandy Greenhouse Co., Inc.
2211 Peacock Rd., Richmond, IN 47374

Fiberglass

Agra Tech Inc.
2131 Piedmont Way, Pittsburg, CA 94565
American Horticultural Supply, Inc.
25603 West Ave. Stanford, Valencia, CA 91355
BFG Supply Co.
P.O. Box 479, Burton, OH 44021
CASSCO
P.O. Box 3508, Montgomery, AL 36193
Conley's Greenhouse Mfg. and Sales
4344 Mission Blvd., Pomona, CA 91766
CropKing Inc.
P.O. Box 310, Medina, OH 44258
Florist Products, Inc.
2242 North Palmer Dr., Schaumburg, IL 60173
E.C. Geiger, Inc.
P.O. Box 285, Harleysville, PA 19438
Harnois Industries Inc.
1044 Principale, Saint-Thomas-of-Joliette, PQ J0K 3L0
Hydro-Gardens, Inc.
P.O. Box 9707, Colorado Springs, CO 80932
McCalif
2215 Ringwood Ave., San Jose, CA 95131
J.M. McConkey and Co., Inc.
P.O. Box 309, Sumner, WA 98390
Packer Greenhouses
9308 CTH H, Cuba City, WI 53807
Penn State Seed Co.
Route 309, Box 390, Dallas, PA 18612
Poly Grower Greenhouse Co.
P.O. Box 359, Muncy, PA 17756
Sharp and Son
19219 62nd Ave. S., Kent, WA 98032
Simburg Co.
2646 Pacific Park Dr., Whittier, CA 90601
X.S. Smith Inc.
P.O. Drawer X, Red Bank, NJ 07701
Structures Unlimited
2740 Leonard Reid Ave., Sarasota, FL 33580
Stuppy Inc.
1212 Clay St., North Kansas City, MO 64116
United Greenhouse Systems, Inc.
708 Washington St., Edgerton, WI 53534
Van Wingerden Greenhouse Co.
4078 Haywood Rd., Horse Shoe, NC 28742

Vary Industries
P.O. Box 248, Lewiston, NY 14092
Vaughan's Seed Co.
5300 Katrine Ave., Downers Grove, IL 60515-4095
Waldo & Associates, Inc.
28214 Glenwood Rd., Perrysburg, OH 43551
Westbrook Greenhouse Systems Ltd.
270 Hunter Rd., Grimsby, ON L3M 4G1
Winandy Greenhouse Co., Inc.
2211 Peacock Rd., Richmond, IN 47374

Polyethylene

AAA Associates Inc.
1445 South 3rd St., Niles, MI 49120
Agra Tech Inc.
2131 Piedmont Way, Pittsburg, CA 94565
Agro-Dynamics Inc., Eastern Div.
Building #3, Navy Yard, Brooklyn, NY 11205
Agro-Dynamics Inc., Western Div.
6492 South Heritage Place E., Englewood, CO 80111
American Horticultural Supply, Inc.
25603 West Ave. Stanford, Valencia, CA 91355
Armin Plastics Corp.
414 Alaska Ave., Torrance, CA 90503
Ball Seed Co.
250 Town Rd., West Chicago, IL 60185
BFG Supply Co.
P.O. Box 479, Burton, OH 44021
Brady Mfg. Co.
210 R.D. #1, Jackson, NJ 08527
E.C. Carson and Associates
P.O. Box 3095, Greenwood, SC 29648
Caves Enterprises Inc.
2464 Pumpkin Center Rd., Hammond, LA 70401
C-I-L Plastics Inc.
142 Kennedy Rd. S., Brampton, ON L6W 3G5
Conley's Greenhouse Mfg. and Sales
4344 Mission Blvd., Pomona, CA 91766
CropKing Inc.
P.O. Box 310, Medina, OH 44258
FVG America
P.O. Box 21276, Minneapolis, MN 55421
E.C. Geiger, Inc.
P.O. Box 285, Harleysville, PA 19438
Harnois Industries Inc.
1044 Principale, Saint-Thomas-of-Joliette, PQ J0K 3L0
Hendrix and Dail, Inc.
P.O. Box 648, Greenville, NC 27835-0648
Hydro-Gardens, Inc.
P.O. Box 9707, Colorado Springs, CO 80932
J-M Trading Corp.
241 Frontage Rd., Suite 31, Burr Ridge, IL 60521
Keeler-Glasgow
P.O. Box 234, Hartford, MI 49057
McCalif
2215 Ringwood Ave., San Jose, CA 95131

J.M. McConkey and Co., Inc.
P.O. Box 309, Sumner, WA 98390
Monsanto Co.
800 North Lindbergh Blvd., St. Louis, MO 63167
Morton's Horticultural Products
P.O. Box 24, McMinnville, TN 37110
Packer Greenhouses
9308 CTH H, Cuba City, WI 53807
Park Seed Co., Wholesale Div.
Cokesbury Rd., Greenwood, SC 29647-0001
Reddick Fumigants
P.O. Box 391, Williamston, NC 27892
Rounhouse
P.O. Box 1744, Cleveland, TX 77327
Sharp and Son
19219 62nd Ave. S., Kent, WA 98032
Simburg Co.
2646 Pacific Park Dr., Whittier, CA 90601
X.S. Smith Inc.
P.O. Drawer X, Red Bank, NJ 07701
Structures Unlimited
2740 Leonard Reid Ave., Sarasota, FL 33580
Stuppy Inc.
1212 Clay St., North Kansas City, MO 64116
Jack Van Klaveren Ltd. (JVK)
P.O. Box 910, St. Catharines, ON L2R 6Z4
Van Wingerden Greenhouse Co.
4078 Haywood Rd., Horse Shoe, NC 28742
Vary Industries
P.O. Box 248, Lewiston, NY 14092
Vaughan's Seed Co.
5300 Katrine Ave., Downers Grove, IL 60515-4095
Vent-Tech U.S.A.
Drawer Q, Richmond, IL 60071
VisQueen
P.O. Box 2448, Richmond, VA 23218
Waldo & Associates, Inc.
28214 Glenwood Rd., Perrysburg, OH 43551
Westbrook Greenhouse Systems Ltd.
270 Hunter Rd., Grimsby, ON L3M 4G1
Winandy Greenhouse Co., Inc.
2211 Peacock Rd., Richmond, IN 47374

Polyethylene with UV stabilizers

AAA Associates Inc.
1445 South 3rd St., Niles, MI 49120
Agra Tech Inc.
2131 Piedmont Way, Pittsburg, CA 94565
Agro-Dynamics Inc., Eastern Div.
Building #3, Navy Yard, Brooklyn, NY 11205
Agro-Dynamics Inc., Western Div.
6492 South Heritage Place E., Englewood, CO 80111
American Horticultural Supply, Inc.
25603 West Ave. Stanford, Valencia, CA 91355
CASSCO
P.O. Box 3508, Montgomery, AL 36193

C-I-L Plastics Inc.
142 Kennedy Rd. S., Brampton, ON L6W 3G5
Conley's Greenhouse Mfg. and Sales
4344 Mission Blvd., Pomona, CA 91766
Dalsem Greenhouses USA Inc.
P.O. Box 54039, Jacksonville, FL 32245
Florist Products, Inc.
2242 North Palmer Dr., Schaumburg, IL 60173
FVG America
P.O. Box 21276, Minneapolis, MN 55421
E.C. Geiger, Inc.
P.O. Box 285, Harleysville, PA 19438
Harnois Industries Inc.
1044 Principale, Saint-Thomas-of-Joliette, PQ
J0K 3L0
J-M Trading Corp.
241 Frontage Rd., Suite 31, Burr Ridge, IL
60521
Monsanto Co.
800 North Lindbergh Blvd., St. Louis, MO
63167
Morton's Horticultural Products
P.O. Box 24, McMinnville, TN 37110
Packer Greenhouses
9308 CTH H, Cuba City, WI 53807
PAK Unlimited Inc.
3300 Holcomb Bridge Rd., Suite 230, Norcross,
GA 30092
Penn State Seed Co.
Route 309, Box 390, Dallas, PA 18612
Poly Grower Greenhouse Co.
P.O. Box 359, Muncy, PA 17756
Rounhouse
P.O. Box 1744, Cleveland, TX 77327
Simburg Co.
2646 Pacific Park Dr., Whittier, CA 90601
X.S. Smith Inc.
P.O. Drawer X, Red Bank, NJ 07701
Structures Unlimited
2740 Leonard Reid Ave., Sarasota, FL 33580
Vary Industries
P.O. Box 248, Lewiston, NY 14092
Vaughan's Seed Co.
5300 Katrine Ave., Downers Grove, IL 60515-
4095
Vent-Tech U.S.A.
Drawer Q, Richmond, IL 60071
VisQueen
P.O. Box 2448, Richmond, VA 23218
Westbrook Greenhouse Systems Ltd.
270 Hunter Rd., Grimsby, ON L3M 4G1
Western Farm Service, Inc.
1015 Linda Vista Dr., Bldg. B, San Marcos, CA
92069

Polyvinyl chloride

J.M. McConkey and Co., Inc.
P.O. Box 309, Sumner, WA 98390
Packer Greenhouses
9308 CTH H, Cuba City, WI 53807
Sharp and Son
19219 62nd Ave. S., Kent, WA 98032

Simburg Co.
2646 Pacific Park Dr., Whittier, CA 90601
X.S. Smith Inc.
P.O. Drawer X, Red Bank, NJ 07701
Structures Unlimited
2740 Leonard Reid Ave., Sarasota, FL 33580
Van Wingerden Greenhouse Co.
4078 Haywood Rd., Horse Shoe, NC 28742

Polyvinyl fluoride

E.C. Geiger, Inc.
P.O. Box 285, Harleysville, PA 19438
Serac Corp.
10 Farrell St., South Burlington, VT 05403

Vinyl

CropKing Inc.
P.O. Box 310, Medina, OH 44258
Ken-Bar Inc.
24 Gould St., Reading, MA 01867
X.S. Smith Inc.
P.O. Drawer X, Red Bank, NJ 07701
Structures Unlimited
2740 Leonard Reid Ave., Sarasota, FL 33580
Van Wingerden Greenhouse Co.
4078 Haywood Rd., Horse Shoe, NC 28742
Van Wingerden Greenhouse Co.
4078 Haywood Rd., Horse Shoe, NC 28742

GREENHOUSE STRUC-
TURES
Aluminum/steel

AAA Associates Inc.
1445 South 3rd St., Niles, MI 49120
Agra Tech Inc.
2131 Piedmont Way, Pittsburg, CA 94565
Agro-Dynamics Inc., Eastern Div.
Building #3, Navy Yard, Brooklyn, NY 11205
Agro-Dynamics Inc., Western Div.
6492 South Heritage Place E., Englewood, CO
80111
American Horticultural Supply, Inc.
25603 West Ave. Stanford, Valencia, CA 91355
Ball Seed Co.
250 Town Rd., West Chicago, IL 60185
Beck Greenhouse Co.
P.O. Box 650, Auburn, AL 36831-0650
BFG Supply Co.
P.O. Box 479, Burton, OH 44021
Brady Mfg. Co.
210 R.D. #1, Jackson, NJ 08527
CASSCO
P.O. Box 3508, Montgomery, AL 36193
Caves Enterprises Inc.
2464 Pumpkin Center Rd., Hammond, LA
70401
Conley's Greenhouse Mfg. and Sales
4344 Mission Blvd., Pomona, CA 91766
CropKing Inc.
P.O. Box 310, Medina, OH 44258
DACE
1937 High St., Longwood, FL 32750

Dalsem Greenhouses USA Inc.
P.O. Box 54039, Jacksonville, FL 32245
Florist Products, Inc.
2242 North Palmer Dr., Schaumburg, IL 60173
E.C. Geiger, Inc.
P.O. Box 285, Harleysville, PA 19438
Harnois Industries Inc.
1044 Principale, Saint-Thomas-of-Joliette, PQ
J0K 3L0
Hydro-Gardens, Inc.
P.O. Box 9707, Colorado Springs, CO 80932
Keeler-Glasgow
P.O. Box 234, Hartford, MI 49057
Ludy Greenhouse Mfg. Corp.
143 West Washington St., New Madison, OH
45346
McCalif
2215 Ringwood Ave., San Jose, CA 95131
J.M. McConkey and Co., Inc.
P.O. Box 309, Sumner, WA 98390

Midwest Growers Supply, Inc.
2613 Kaneville Court, Geneva, IL 60134
Nexus Greenhouse Systems
10983 Leroy Dr., Northglenn, CO 80233

Oehmsen Plastic Greenhouse Mfg. Inc.
50 Carlough Rd., Bohemia, NY 11716
Poly Grower Greenhouse Co.
P.O. Box 359, Muncy, PA 17756
Rough Brothers Inc.
P.O. Box 16010, Cincinnati, OH 45216

Rounhouse
P.O. Box 1744, Cleveland, TX 77327
Sharp and Son
19219 62nd Ave. S., Kent, WA 98032
Simburg Co.
2646 Pacific Park Dr., Whittier, CA 90601

X.S. Smith Inc.
P.O. Drawer X, Red Bank, NJ 07701
Structures Unlimited
2740 Leonard Reid Ave., Sarasota, FL 33580
Stuppy Inc.
1212 Clay St., North Kansas City, MO 64116
United Greenhouse Systems, Inc.
708 Washington St., Edgerton, WI 53534
Jack Van Klaveren Ltd. (JVK)
P.O. Box 910, St. Catharines, ON L2R 6Z4
Van Wingerden Greenhouse Co.
4078 Haywood Rd., Horse Shoe, NC 28742

Vary Industries
P.O. Box 248, Lewiston, NY 14092
Vaughan's Seed Co.
5300 Katrine Ave., Downers Grove, IL 60515-
4095
Waldo & Associates, Inc.
28214 Glenwood Rd., Perrysburg, OH 43551
Westbrook Greenhouse Systems Ltd.
270 Hunter Rd., Grimsby, ON L3M 4G1
Winandy Greenhouse Co., Inc.
2211 Peacock Rd., Richmond, IN 47374

Free-standing

AAA Associates Inc.
1445 South 3rd St., Niles, MI 49120
Agra Tech Inc.
2131 Piedmont Way, Pittsburg, CA 94565
American Horticultural Supply, Inc.
25603 West Ave. Stanford, Valencia, CA 91355

Ball Seed Co.
250 Town Rd., West Chicago, IL 60185
Beck Greenhouse Co.
P.O. Box 650, Auburn, AL 36831-0650
BFG Supply Co.
P.O. Box 479, Burton, OH 44021
Brady Mfg. Co.
210 R.D. #1, Jackson, NJ 08527

Caves Enterprises Inc.
2464 Pumpkin Center Rd., Hammond, LA
70401
Conley's Greenhouse Mfg. and Sales
4344 Mission Blvd., Pomona, CA 91766
CropKing Inc.
P.O. Box 310, Medina, OH 44258
Dalsem Greenhouses USA Inc.
P.O. Box 54039, Jacksonville, FL 32245
Florist Products, Inc.
2242 North Palmer Dr., Schaumburg, IL 60173
E.C. Geiger, Inc.
P.O. Box 285, Harleysville, PA 19438

Harnois Industries Inc.
1044 Principale, Saint-Thomas-of-Joliette, PQ
J0K 3L0
Hydro-Gardens, Inc.
P.O. Box 9707, Colorado Springs, CO 80932
Keeler-Glasgow
P.O. Box 234, Hartford, MI 49057
Ludy Greenhouse Mfg. Corp.
143 West Washington St., New Madison, OH
45346
McCalif
2215 Ringwood Ave., San Jose, CA 95131
J.M. McConkey and Co., Inc.
P.O. Box 309, Sumner, WA 98390
Oehmsen Plastic Greenhouse Mfg. Inc.
50 Carlough Rd., Bohemia, NY 11716
Park Seed Co., Wholesale Div.
Cokesbury Rd., Greenwood, SC 29647-0001
Penn State Seed Co.
Route 309, Box 390, Dallas, PA 18612
Poly Grower Greenhouse Co.
P.O. Box 359, Muncy, PA 17756
Poly-Tex, Inc.
P.O. Box 458, Castle Rock, MN 55010
Rough Brothers Inc.
P.O. Box 16010, Cincinnati, OH 45216
Sharp and Son
19219 62nd Ave. S., Kent, WA 98032
Simburg Co.
2646 Pacific Park Dr., Whittier, CA 90601

X.S. Smith Inc.
P.O. Drawer X, Red Bank, NJ 07701
Structures Unlimited
2740 Leonard Reid Ave., Sarasota, FL 33580
Stuppy Inc.
1212 Clay St., North Kansas City, MO 64116
United Greenhouse Systems, Inc.
708 Washington St., Edgerton, WI 53534
Jack Van Klaveren Ltd. (JVK)
P.O. Box 910, St. Catharines, ON L2R 6Z4
Van Wingerden Greenhouse Co.
4078 Haywood Rd., Horse Shoe, NC 28742
Vary Industries
P.O. Box 248, Lewiston, NY 14092
Vaughan's Seed Co.
5300 Katrine Ave., Downers Grove, IL 60515-4095
Waldo & Associates, Inc.
28214 Glenwood Rd., Perrysburg, OH 43551
Westbrook Greenhouse Systems Ltd.
270 Hunter Rd., Grimsby, ON L3M 4G1
Wetsel Seed Co. Inc.
P.O. Box 791, Harrisonburg, VA 22801
Winandy Greenhouse Co., Inc.
2211 Peacock Rd., Richmond, IN 47374

Gutter connected

AAA Associates Inc.
1445 South 3rd St., Niles, MI 49120
Agra Tech Inc.
2131 Piedmont Way, Pittsburg, CA 94565
American Horticultural Supply, Inc.
25603 West Ave. Stanford, Valencia, CA 91355
Ball Seed Co.
250 Town Rd., West Chicago, IL 60185
Beck Greenhouse Co.
P.O. Box 650, Auburn, AL 36831-0650
BFG Supply Co.
P.O. Box 479, Burton, OH 44021
Brady Mfg. Co.
210 R.D. #1, Jackson, NJ 08527
Caves Enterprises Inc.
2464 Pumpkin Center Rd., Hammond, LA 70401
Conley's Greenhouse Mfg. and Sales
4344 Mission Blvd., Pomona, CA 91766
CropKing Inc.
P.O. Box 310, Medina, OH 44258
DACE
1937 High St., Longwood, FL 32750
Dalsem Greenhouses USA Inc.
P.O. Box 54039, Jacksonville, FL 32245
Dillen Products, Inc.
P.O. Box 738, Middlefield, OH 44062
Florist Products, Inc.
2242 North Palmer Dr., Schaumburg, IL 60173
E.C. Geiger, Inc.
P.O. Box 285, Harleysville, PA 19438
Harnois Industries Inc.
1044 Principale, Saint-Thomas-of-Joliette, PQ J0K 3L0

Hydro-Gardens, Inc.
P.O. Box 9707, Colorado Springs, CO 80932
Keeler-Glasgow
P.O. Box 234, Hartford, MI 49057
Ludy Greenhouse Mfg. Corp.
143 West Washington St., New Madison, OH 45346
McCalif
2215 Ringwood Ave., San Jose, CA 95131
J.M. McConkey and Co., Inc.
P.O. Box 309, Sumner, WA 98390
Midwest Growers Supply, Inc.
2613 Kaneville Court. Geneva, IL 60134
Nexus Greenhouse Systems
10983 Leroy Dr., Northglenn, CO 80233
Oehmsen Plastic Greenhouse Mfg. Inc.
50 Carlough Rd., Bohemia, NY 11716
Packer Greenhouses
9308 CTH H, Cuba City, WI 53807
Park Seed Co., Wholesale Div.
Cokesbury Rd., Greenwood, SC 29647-0001
Penn State Seed Co.
Route 309, Box 390, Dallas, PA 18612
Poly Grower Greenhouse Co.
P.O. Box 359, Muncy, PA 17756
Poly-Tex, Inc.
P.O. Box 458, Castle Rock, MN 55010
Rough Brothers Inc.
P.O. Box 16010, Cincinnati, OH 45216
Rounhouse
P.O. Box 1744, Cleveland, TX 77327
Sharp and Son
19219 62nd Ave. S., Kent, WA 98032
Simburg Co.
2646 Pacific Park Dr., Whittier, CA 90601
X.S. Smith Inc.
P.O. Drawer X, Red Bank, NJ 07701
Structures Unlimited
2740 Leonard Reid Ave., Sarasota, FL 33580
Stuppy Inc.
1212 Clay St., North Kansas City, MO 64116
United Greenhouse Systems, Inc.
708 Washington St., Edgerton, WI 53534
Jack Van Klaveren Ltd. (JVK)
P.O. Box 910, St. Catharines, ON L2R 6Z4
Van Wingerden Greenhouse Co.
4078 Haywood Rd., Horse Shoe, NC 28742
Vary Industries
P.O. Box 248, Lewiston, NY 14092
Vaughan's Seed Co.
5300 Katrine Ave., Downers Grove, IL 60515-4095
Waldo & Associates, Inc.
28214 Glenwood Rd., Perrysburg, OH 43551
Westbrook Greenhouse Systems Ltd.
270 Hunter Rd., Grimsby, ON L3M 4G1
Wetsel Seed Co. Inc.
P.O. Box 791, Harrisonburg, VA 22801
Winandy Greenhouse Co., Inc.
2211 Peacock Rd., Richmond, IN 47374

Portable

AAA Associates Inc.
1445 South 3rd St., Niles, MI 49120

BFG Supply Co.
P.O. Box 479, Burton, OH 44021

Brady Mfg. Co.
210 R.D. #1, Jackson, NJ 08527

Brummel Design & Mfg. Co., Inc.
1170 74th Ave., Zeeland, MI 49464

Conley's Greenhouse Mfg. and Sales
4344 Mission Blvd., Pomona, CA 91766

CropKing Inc.
P.O. Box 310, Medina, OH 44258

Dalsem Greenhouses USA Inc.
P.O. Box 54039, Jacksonville, FL 32245

Florist Products, Inc.
2242 North Palmer Dr., Schaumburg, IL 60173

Keeler-Glasgow
P.O. Box 234, Hartford, MI 49057

J.M. McConkey and Co., Inc.
P.O. Box 309, Sumner, WA 98390

Poly-Tex, Inc.
P.O. Box 458, Castle Rock, MN 55010

Sharp and Son
19219 62nd Ave. S., Kent, WA 98032

X.S. Smith Inc.
P.O. Drawer X, Red Bank, NJ 07701

Structures Unlimited
2740 Leonard Reid Ave., Sarasota, FL 33580

Stuppy Inc.
1212 Clay St., North Kansas City, MO 64116

United Greenhouse Systems, Inc.
708 Washington St., Edgerton, WI 53534

Jack Van Klaveren Ltd. (JVK)
P.O. Box 910, St. Catharines, ON L2R 6Z4

Van Wingerden Greenhouse Co.
4078 Haywood Rd., Horse Shoe, NC 28742

Vaughan's Seed Co.
5300 Katrine Ave., Downers Grove, IL 60515-4095

Quonset

AAA Associates Inc.
1445 South 3rd St., Niles, MI 49120

Agra Tech Inc.
2131 Piedmont Way, Pittsburg, CA 94565

American Horticultural Supply, Inc.
25603 West Ave. Stanford, Valencia, CA 91355

Ball Seed Co.
250 Town Rd., West Chicago, IL 60185

BFG Supply Co.
P.O. Box 479, Burton, OH 44021

Brady Mfg. Co.
210 R.D. #1, Jackson, NJ 08527

Brummel Design & Mfg. Co., Inc.
1170 74th Ave., Zeeland, MI 49464

Caves Enterprises Inc.
2464 Pumpkin Center Rd., Hammond, LA 70401

Canadian Hydrogardens Limited
411 Book Road West
Ancaster, Ontario L9G 3L1

Conley's Greenhouse Mfg. and Sales
4344 Mission Blvd., Pomona, CA 91766

CropKing Inc.
P.O. Box 310, Medina, OH 44258

Dalsem Greenhouses USA Inc.
P.O. Box 54039, Jacksonville, FL 32245

Dillen Products, Inc.
P.O. Box 738, Middlefield, OH 44062

Florist Products, Inc.
2242 North Palmer Dr., Schaumburg, IL 60173

E.C. Geiger, Inc.
P.O. Box 285, Harleysville, PA 19438

Harnois Industries Inc.
1044 Principale, Saint-Thomas-of-Joliette, PQ J0K 3L0

Hydro-Gardens, Inc.
P.O. Box 9707, Colorado Springs, CO 80932

Keeler-Glasgow
P.O. Box 234, Hartford, MI 49057

McCalif
2215 Ringwood Ave., San Jose, CA 95131

J.M. McConkey and Co., Inc.
P.O. Box 309, Sumner, WA 98390

Midwest Growers Supply, Inc.
2613 Kaneville Court, Geneva, IL 60134

Morton's Horticultural Products
P.O. Box 24, McMinnville, TN 37110

Oehmsen Plastic Greenhouse Mfg. Inc.
50 Carlough Rd., Bohemia, NY 11716

Packer Greenhouses
9308 CTH H, Cuba City, WI 53807

Penn State Seed Co.
Route 309, Box 390, Dallas, PA 18612

Poly Grower Greenhouse Co.
P.O. Box 359, Muncy, PA 17756

Rounhouse
P.O. Box 1744, Cleveland, TX 77327

Sharp and Son
19219 62nd Ave. S., Kent, WA 98032

Simburg Co.
2646 Pacific Park Dr., Whittier, CA 90601

X.S. Smith Inc.
P.O. Drawer X, Red Bank, NJ 07701

Structures Unlimited
2740 Leonard Reid Ave., Sarasota, FL 33580

Stuppy Inc.
1212 Clay St., North Kansas City, MO 64116

United Greenhouse Systems, Inc.
708 Washington St., Edgerton, WI 53534

Jack Van Klaveren Ltd. (JVK)
P.O. Box 910, St. Catharines, ON L2R 6Z4

Van Wingerden Greenhouse Co.
4078 Haywood Rd., Horse Shoe, NC 28742

Vaughan's Seed Co.
5300 Katrine Ave., Downers Grove, IL 60515-4095

Westbrook Greenhouse Systems Ltd.
270 Hunter Rd., Grimsby, ON L3M 4G1

GROWING BLOCKS

Agro-Dynamics Inc., Eastern Div.
Building #3, Navy Yard, Brooklyn, NY 11205
Agro-Dynamics Inc., Western Div.
6492 South Heritage Place E., Englewood, CO 80111
CropKing Inc.
P.O. Box 310, Medina, OH 44258
Fibrex, Inc.
P.O. Box 1148, Aurora, IL 60507
Grow-Tech, Inc. of California
56 Peckham Rd., Watsonville, CA 95076
Hydro-Gardens, Inc.
P.O. Box 9707, Colorado Springs, CO 80932
Rambridge Structure & Design Ltd.
1316 Centre St., NE
Calgary, Alberta T2E 2A7
Sharp and Son
19219 62nd Ave. S., Kent, WA 98032
Smithers-Oasis
P.O. Box 118, Kent, OH 44240
Waldo & Associates, Inc.
28214 Glenwood Rd., Perrysburg, OH 43551

GROWTH MEDIA

Agro-Dynamics Inc., Eastern Div.
Building #3, Navy Yard, Brooklyn, NY 11205
Agro-Dynamics Inc., Western Div.
6492 South Heritage Place E., Englewood, CO 80111
ASB Greenworld Inc.
82 Cherrywood Dr., Somerset, NJ 08873
Ball Seed Co.
250 Town Rd., West Chicago, IL 60185
BFG Supply Co.
P.O. Box 479, Burton, OH 44021
Conrad Fafard Inc.
P.O. Box 3190, Springfield, MA 01101
CropKing Inc.
P.O. Box 310, Medina, OH 44258
ENP
200 North Main St., Mendota, IL 61342
Fibrex, Inc.
P.O. Box 1148, Aurora, IL 60507
Fisons Western Corp.
120-1100 31st St., Downers Grove, IL 60515
E.C. Geiger, Inc.
P.O. Box 285, Harleysville, PA 19438
W.R. Grace & Co.
62 Whittemore Ave., Cambridge, MA 02140
Grow-Tech, Inc. of California
56 Peckham Rd., Watsonville, CA 95076
The Heflin Co.
P.O. Box 1485, Rockville, MD 20850
Hydro-Gardens, Inc.
P.O. Box 9707, Colorado Springs, CO 80932
J-M Trading Corp.
241 Frontage Rd., Suite 31, Burr Ridge, IL 60521
Keeler-Glasgow
P.O. Box 234, Hartford, MI 49057

Mantis Mfg. Co.
1458 County Line Rd., Huntingdon Valley, PA 19006
Michigan Peat Co.
P.O. Box 980129, Houston, TX 77098-0129
Mr. Mulch Soils, Inc.
Rt. 2, Box 381, Effingham, SC 29541
Park Seed Co., Wholesale Div.
Cokesbury Rd., Greenwood, SC 29647-0001
Penn State Seed Co.
Route 309, Box 390, Dallas, PA 18612
Premier Brands, Inc.
145 Huguenot St., New Rochelle, NY 10801
Rambridge Structure & Design Ltd.
1316 Centre St., NE
Calgary, Alberta T2E 2A7
Sharp and Son
19219 62nd Ave. S., Kent, WA 98032
Smithers-Oasis
P.O. Box 118, Kent, OH 44240
Sogevex
326 Main St., Red Hill, PA 18076
Touchstone Corp.
Route 2, Box 158, Columbia, MO 65201
Jack Van Klaveren Ltd. (JVK)
P.O. Box 910, St. Catharines, ON L2R 6Z4

HEATING EQUIPMENT

Biomass

CanaBurn Bioenergy Inc.
P.O. Box 2037, Windsor, ON N8Y 4R5
Eshland Enterprises Inc.
P.O. Box 8A, Greencastle, PA 17225

Coal

CanaBurn Bioenergy Inc.
P.O. Box 2037, Windsor, ON N8Y 4R5
Dalsem Greenhouses USA Inc.
P.O. Box 54039, Jacksonville, FL 32245
Eshland Enterprises Inc.
P.O. Box 8A, Greencastle, PA 17225
Firetender-Stokermatic Mfg.
1610 South Industrial Rd., Salt Lake City, UT 84104

Gas-fired

AAA Associates Inc.
1445 South 3rd St., Niles, MI 49120
American Horticultural Supply, Inc.
25603 West Ave. Stanford, Valencia, CA 91355
Ball Seed Co.
250 Town Rd., West Chicago, IL 60185
BFG Supply Co.
P.O. Box 479, Burton, OH 44021
Brady Mfg. Co.
210 R.D. #1, Jackson, NJ 08527
CASSCO
P.O. Box 3508, Montgomery, AL 36193
Caves Enterprises Inc.
2464 Pumpkin Center Rd., Hammond, LA 70401
Combustion Research
2516 Leach Rd., Pontiac, MI 48057

Conley's Greenhouse Mfg. and Sales
4344 Mission Blvd., Pomona, CA 91766
CropKing Inc.
P.O. Box 310, Medina, OH 44258
Dalsem Greenhouses USA Inc.
P.O. Box 54039, Jacksonville, FL 32245
Delta T Sales
3576 Empleo, Suite 2, San Luis Obispo, CA 93401
Florist Products, Inc.
2242 North Palmer Dr., Schaumburg, IL 60173
E.C. Geiger, Inc.
P.O. Box 285, Harleysville, PA 19438
Hydro-Gardens, Inc.
P.O. Box 9707, Colorado Springs, CO 80932
Keeler-Glasgow
P.O. Box 234, Hartford, MI 49057
Ludy Greenhouse Mfg. Corp.
143 West Washington St., New Madison, OH 45346
McCalif
2215 Ringwood Ave., San Jose, CA 95131

J.M. McConkey and Co., Inc.
P.O. Box 309, Sumner, WA 98390
Midwest Growers Supply, Inc.
2613 Kaneville Court, Geneva, IL 60134
Modine Mfg. Co. - Heating Div.
1500 De Koven Ave., Racine, WI 53401
Nepco International
P.O. Box 33918, Seattle, WA 98188
Packer Greenhouses
9308 CTH H, Cuba City, WI 53807
Penn State Seed Co.
Route 309, Box 390, Dallas, PA 18612
Reznor
McKinley Ave., Mercer, PA 16137
Rounhouse
P.O. Box 1744, Cleveland, TX 77327
Sharp and Son
19219 62nd Ave. S., Kent, WA 98032
Siebring Mfg. Co.
303 South Main St., Box 658, George, IA 51237
Simburg Co.
2646 Pacific Park Dr., Whittier, CA 90601
X.S. Smith Inc.
P.O. Drawer X, Red Bank, NJ 07701
Structures Unlimited
2740 Leonard Reid Ave., Sarasota, FL 33580
Stuppy Inc.
1212 Clay St., North Kansas City, MO 64116
Sunderman Mfg. Co.
Rt. 1, Box 14, Baltic, SD 57003
United Greenhouse Systems, Inc.
708 Washington St., Edgerton, WI 53534
Van Wingerden Greenhouse Co.
4078 Haywood Rd., Horse Shoe, NC 28742
Vary Industries
P.O. Box 248, Lewiston, NY 14092
Vaughan's Seed Co.
5300 Katrine Ave., Downers Grove, IL 60515-4095
Waldo & Associates, Inc.
28214 Glenwood Rd., Perrysburg, OH 43551

Western Farm Service, Inc.
1015 Linda Vista Dr., Bldg. B, San Marcos, CA 92069
Wetsel Seed Co. Inc.
P.O. Box 791, Harrisonburg, VA 22801
Winandy Greenhouse Co., Inc.
2211 Peacock Rd., Richmond, IN 47374

Hot water

Aluminum Sun-Fin Radiation
4302 Woodland Ave., Kansas City, MO 64110
American Horticultural Supply, Inc.
25603 West Ave. Stanford, Valencia, CA 91355
BFG Supply Co.
P.O. Box 479, Burton, OH 44021
Bio-Energy Systems Co.
221 Canal St., Ellenville, NY 12428
CanaBurn Bioenergy Inc.
P.O. Box 2037, Windsor, ON N8Y 4R5
Conley's Greenhouse Mfg. and Sales
4344 Mission Blvd., Pomona, CA 91766
CropKing Inc.
P.O. Box 310, Medina, OH 44258
DACE
1937 High St., Longwood, FL 32750
Dalsem Greenhouses USA Inc.
P.O. Box 54039, Jacksonville, FL 32245
Delta T Sales
3576 Empleo, Suite 2, San Luis Obispo, CA 93401
Firetender-Stokermatic Mfg.
1610 South Industrial Rd., Salt Lake City, UT 84104
E.C. Geiger, Inc.
P.O. Box 285, Harleysville, PA 19438
Hydro-Gardens, Inc.
P.O. Box 9707, Colorado Springs, CO 80932
Ludy Greenhouse Mfg. Corp.
143 West Washington St., New Madison, OH 45346
McCalif
2215 Ringwood Ave., San Jose, CA 95131
J.M. McConkey and Co., Inc.
P.O. Box 309, Sumner, WA 98390
Modine Mfg. Co. - Heating Div.
1500 De Koven Ave., Racine, WI 53401
Nepco International
P.O. Box 33918, Seattle, WA 98188
Reznor
McKinley Ave., Mercer, PA 16137
Rough Brothers Inc.
P.O. Box 16010, Cincinnati, OH 45216
Sharp and Son
19219 62nd Ave. S., Kent, WA 98032
Simburg Co.
2646 Pacific Park Dr., Whittier, CA 90601
X.S. Smith Inc.
P.O. Drawer X, Red Bank, NJ 07701
Structures Unlimited
2740 Leonard Reid Ave., Sarasota, FL 33580
Stuppy Inc.
1212 Clay St., North Kansas City, MO 64116
United Greenhouse Systems, Inc.
708 Washington St., Edgerton, WI 53534

Van Wingerden Greenhouse Co.
4078 Haywood Rd., Horse Shoe, NC 28742
Vary Industries
P.O. Box 248, Lewiston, NY 14092
Waldo & Associates, Inc.
28214 Glenwood Rd., Perrysburg, OH 43551
Winandy Greenhouse Co., Inc.
2211 Peacock Rd., Richmond, IN 47374

Infrared

AAA Associates Inc.
1445 South 3rd St., Niles, MI 49120
BFG Supply Co.
P.O. Box 479, Burton, OH 44021
Combustion Research
2516 Leach Rd., Pontiac, MI 48057
Conley's Greenhouse Mfg. and Sales
4344 Mission Blvd., Pomona, CA 91766
CropKing Inc.
P.O. Box 310, Medina, OH 44258
Galaxie Radiant Systems
1144 Millburn Court, St. Charles, IL 60174
J.M. McConkey and Co., Inc.
P.O. Box 309, Sumner, WA 98390
Modine Mfg. Co. - Heating Div.
1500 De Koven Ave., Racine, WI 53401
Nepco International
P.O. Box 33918, Seattle, WA 98188
Reznor
McKinley Ave., Mercer, PA 16137
Sharp and Son
19219 62nd Ave. S., Kent, WA 98032
Simburg Co.
2646 Pacific Park Dr., Whittier, CA 90601
X.S. Smith Inc.
P.O. Drawer X, Red Bank, NJ 07701
Structures Unlimited
2740 Leonard Reid Ave., Sarasota, FL 33580
United Greenhouse Systems, Inc.
708 Washington St., Edgerton, WI 53534
Vaughan's Seed Co.
5300 Katrine Ave., Downers Grove, IL 60515-4095

Oil

American Horticultural Supply, Inc.
25603 West Ave. Stanford, Valencia, CA 91355
BFG Supply Co.
P.O. Box 479, Burton, OH 44021
CanaBurn Bioenergy Inc.
P.O. Box 2037, Windsor, ON N8Y 4R5
Caves Enterprises Inc.
2464 Pumpkin Center Rd., Hammond, LA 70401
Combustion Research
2516 Leach Rd., Pontiac, MI 48057
Conley's Greenhouse Mfg. and Sales
4344 Mission Blvd., Pomona, CA 91766
CropKing Inc.
P.O. Box 310, Medina, OH 44258
Dalsem Greenhouses USA Inc.
P.O. Box 54039, Jacksonville, FL 32245

Delta T Sales
3576 Empleo, Suite 2, San Luis Obispo, CA 93401
E.C. Geiger, Inc.
P.O. Box 285, Harleysville, PA 19438
Hydro-Gardens, Inc.
P.O. Box 9707, Colorado Springs, CO 80932
Keeler-Glasgow
P.O. Box 234, Hartford, MI 49057
Ludy Greenhouse Mfg. Corp.
143 West Washington St., New Madison, OH 45346
J.M. McConkey and Co., Inc.
P.O. Box 309, Sumner, WA 98390
Modine Mfg. Co. - Heating Div.
1500 De Koven Ave., Racine, WI 53401
Nepco International
P.O. Box 33918, Seattle, WA 98188
Packer Greenhouses
9308 CTH H, Cuba City, WI 53807
Reznor
McKinley Ave., Mercer, PA 16137
Sharp and Son
19219 62nd Ave. S., Kent, WA 98032
Siebring Mfg. Co.
303 South Main St., Box 658, George, IA 51237
X.S. Smith Inc.
P.O. Drawer X, Red Bank, NJ 07701
Structures Unlimited
2740 Leonard Reid Ave., Sarasota, FL 33580
Sunderman Mfg. Co.
Rt. 1, Box 14, Baltic, SD 57003
Van Wingerden Greenhouse Co.
4078 Haywood Rd., Horse Shoe, NC 28742
Vaughan's Seed Co.
5300 Katrine Ave., Downers Grove, IL 60515-4095
Waldo & Associates, Inc.
28214 Glenwood Rd., Perrysburg, OH 43551
Wetsel Seed Co. Inc.
P.O. Box 791, Harrisonburg, VA 22801
Winandy Greenhouse Co., Inc.
2211 Peacock Rd., Richmond, IN 47374

Root zone systems

American Horticultural Supply, Inc.
25603 West Ave. Stanford, Valencia, CA 91355
Ball Seed Co.
250 Town Rd., West Chicago, IL 60185
BFG Supply Co.
P.O. Box 479, Burton, OH 44021
Bio-Energy Systems Co.
221 Canal St., Ellenville, NY 12428
CropKing Inc.
P.O. Box 310, Medina, OH 44258
Dalsem Greenhouses USA Inc.
P.O. Box 54039, Jacksonville, FL 32245
Delta T Sales
3576 Empleo, Suite 2, San Luis Obispo, CA 93401
Florist Products, Inc.
2242 North Palmer Dr., Schaumburg, IL 60173

E.C. Geiger, Inc.
P.O. Box 285, Harleysville, PA 19438
Ken-Bar Inc.
24 Gould St., Reading, MA 01867
McCalif
2215 Ringwood Ave., San Jose, CA 95131
J.M. McConkey and Co., Inc.
P.O. Box 309, Sumner, WA 98390
Mee Industries Inc.
4443 North Rowland Ave., El Monte, CA 91731
Modine Mfg. Co. - Heating Div.
1500 De Koven Ave., Racine, WI 53401
Nepco International
P.O. Box 33918, Seattle, WA 98188
Penn State Seed Co.
Route 309, Box 390, Dallas, PA 18612
Reznor
McKinley Ave., Mercer, PA 16137
Sharp and Son
19219 62nd Ave. S., Kent, WA 98032
X.S. Smith Inc.
P.O. Drawer X, Red Bank, NJ 07701
Structures Unlimited
2740 Leonard Reid Ave., Sarasota, FL 33580
Sunderman Mfg. Co.
Rt. 1, Box 14, Baltic, SD 57003
United Greenhouse Systems, Inc.
708 Washington St., Edgerton, WI 53534
Jack Van Klaveren Ltd. (JVK)
P.O. Box 910, St. Catharines, ON L2R 6Z4
Vary Industries
P.O. Box 248, Lewiston, NY 14092
Waldo & Associates, Inc.
28214 Glenwood Rd., Perrysburg, OH 43551
Winandy Greenhouse Co., Inc.
2211 Peacock Rd., Richmond, IN 47374

Seed bed heaters

BFG Supply Co.
P.O. Box 479, Burton, OH 44021
Bio-Energy Systems Co.
221 Canal St., Ellenville, NY 12428
J.M. McConkey and Co., Inc.
P.O. Box 309, Sumner, WA 98390
Nepco International
P.O. Box 33918, Seattle, WA 98188
Sharp and Son
19219 62nd Ave. S., Kent, WA 98032
Sunderman Mfg. Co.
Rt. 1, Box 14, Baltic, SD 57003
Waldo & Associates, Inc.
28214 Glenwood Rd., Perrysburg, OH 43551
Winandy Greenhouse Co., Inc.
2211 Peacock Rd., Richmond, IN 47374

Steam

Aluminum Sun-Fin Radiation
4302 Woodland Ave., Kansas City, MO 64110
American Horticultural Supply, Inc.
25603 West Ave. Stanford, Valencia, CA 91355
BFG Supply Co.
P.O. Box 479, Burton, OH 44021

Conley's Greenhouse Mfg. and Sales
4344 Mission Blvd., Pomona, CA 91766
CropKing Inc.
P.O. Box 310, Medina, OH 44258
Delta T Sales
3576 Empleo, Suite 2, San Luis Obispo, CA 93401
Eshland Enterprises Inc.
P.O. Box 8A, Greencastle, PA 17225
McCalif
2215 Ringwood Ave., San Jose, CA 95131
J.M. McConkey and Co., Inc.
P.O. Box 309, Sumner, WA 98390
Modine Mfg. Co. - Heating Div.
1500 De Koven Ave., Racine, WI 53401
Nepco International
P.O. Box 33918, Seattle, WA 98188
Reznor
McKinley Ave., Mercer, PA 16137
Sharp and Son
19219 62nd Ave. S., Kent, WA 98032
Simburg Co.
2646 Pacific Park Dr., Whittier, CA 90601
X.S. Smith Inc.
P.O. Drawer X, Red Bank, NJ 07701
Structures Unlimited
2740 Leonard Reid Ave., Sarasota, FL 33580
United Greenhouse Systems, Inc.
708 Washington St., Edgerton, WI 53534
Van Wingerden Greenhouse Co.
4078 Haywood Rd., Horse Shoe, NC 28742
Winandy Greenhouse Co., Inc.
2211 Peacock Rd., Richmond, IN 47374

HYDROPONIC EQUIPMENT AND SUPPLIES

Agro-Dynamics Inc., Eastern Div.
Building #3, Navy Yard, Brooklyn, NY 11205
Agro-Dynamics Inc., Western Div.
6492 South Heritage Place E., Englewood, CO 80111
CropKing Inc.
P.O. Box 310, Medina, OH 44258
Engineered Systems and Designs
3 South Tatnall St., Wilmington, DE 19801
ENP
200 North Main St., Mendota, IL 61342
Fibrex, Inc.
P.O. Box 1148, Aurora, IL 60507
Hydro-Gardens, Inc.
P.O. Box 9707, Colorado Springs, CO 80932
Rambridge Structure & Design Ltd.
1316 Centre St., NE
Calgary, Alberta T2E 2A7

HYDROPONIC SUBSTRATES

Agro-Dynamics Inc., Eastern Div.
Building #3, Navy Yard, Brooklyn, NY 11205
Agro-Dynamics Inc., Western Div.
6492 South Heritage Place E., Englewood, CO 80111

ASB Greenworld Inc.
  82 Cherrywood Dr., Somerset, NJ 08873
CropKing Inc.
  P.O. Box 310, Medina, OH 44258
Fibrex, Inc.
  P.O. Box 1148, Aurora, IL 60507
Grow-Tech, Inc. of California
  56 Peckham Rd., Watsonville, CA 95076
Hydro-Gardens, Inc.
  P.O. Box 9707, Colorado Springs, CO 80932
Harold J. Schmidt, Inc.
  1409 Joliet Rd., Lemont, IL 60439
Smithers-Oasis
  P.O. Box 118, Kent, OH 44240

IRRIGATION SYSTEMS

Drip

Agro-Dynamics Inc., Eastern Div.
  Building #3, Navy Yard, Brooklyn, NY 11205
Agro-Dynamics Inc., Western Div.
  6492 South Heritage Place E., Englewood, CO
  80111
Ball Seed Co.
  250 Town Rd., West Chicago, IL 60185
BFG Supply Co.
  P.O. Box 479, Burton, OH 44021
BrushKing Div. of Loos & Co., Inc.
  924 Industrial Blvd., Naples, FL 33942
CropKing Inc.
  P.O. Box 310, Medina, OH 44258
Dalsem Greenhouses USA Inc.
  P.O. Box 54039, Jacksonville, FL 32245
Dramm International Inc.
  P.O. Box 528, Manitowoc, WI 54220
Florist Products, Inc.
  2242 North Palmer Dr., Schaumburg, IL 60173
E.C. Geiger, Inc.
  P.O. Box 285, Harleysville, PA 19438
Growers Technical Services Ltd.
  2245 Dunwin Dr., Mississauga, ON L5L 1A3
Harnois Industries Inc.
  1044 Principale, Saint-Thomas-of-Joliette, PQ
  J0K 3L0
Hydro-Gardens, Inc.
  P.O. Box 9707, Colorado Springs, CO 80932
International Irrigation Systems
  LPO 160, 1555 3rd Ave., Niagara Falls, NY
  14304
McCalif
  2215 Ringwood Ave., San Jose, CA 95131
Morton's Horticultural Products
  P.O. Box 24, McMinnville, TN 37110
Netafim Irrigation, Inc.
  104 South Central Ave., Valley Stream, NY
  11580
Packer Greenhouses
  9308 CTH H, Cuba City, WI 53807
Penn State Seed Co.
  Route 309, Box 390, Dallas, PA 18612
Roberts Irrigation Products, Inc.
  700 Rancheros Dr., San Marcos, CA 92069

Sharp and Son
  19219 62nd Ave. S., Kent, WA 98032
Simburg Co.
  2646 Pacific Park Dr., Whittier, CA 90601
Jack Van Klaveren Ltd. (JVK)
  P.O. Box 910, St. Catharines, ON L2R 6Z4
Van Wingerden Greenhouse Co.
  4078 Haywood Rd., Horse Shoe, NC 28742
Vary Industries
  P.O. Box 248, Lewiston, NY 14092
Westbrook Greenhouse Systems Ltd.
  270 Hunter Rd., Grimsby, ON L3M 4G1
Western Farm Service, Inc.
  1015 Linda Vista Dr., Bldg. B, San Marcos, CA
  92069

Filters

Agro-Dynamics Inc., Eastern Div.
  Building #3, Navy Yard, Brooklyn, NY 11205
Agro-Dynamics Inc., Western Div.
  6492 South Heritage Place E., Englewood, CO
  80111
American Horticultural Supply, Inc.
  25603 West Ave. Stanford, Valencia, CA 91355
CropKing Inc.
  P.O. Box 310, Medina, OH 44258
E.C. Geiger, Inc.
  P.O. Box 285, Harleysville, PA 19438
Harnois Industries Inc.
  1044 Principale, Saint-Thomas-of-Joliette, PQ
  J0K 3L0
Netafim Irrigation, Inc.
  104 South Central Ave., Valley Stream, NY
  11580
Sharp and Son
  19219 62nd Ave. S., Kent, WA 98032
Jack Van Klaveren Ltd. (JVK)
  P.O. Box 910, St. Catharines, ON L2R 6Z4
Westbrook Greenhouse Systems Ltd.
  270 Hunter Rd., Grimsby, ON L3M 4G1
Western Farm Service, Inc.
  1015 Linda Vista Dr., Bldg. B, San Marcos, CA
  92069

Overhead

Agro-Dynamics Inc., Eastern Div.
  Building #3, Navy Yard, Brooklyn, NY 11205
Agro-Dynamics Inc., Western Div.
  6492 South Heritage Place E., Englewood, CO
  80111
Andpro Ltd.
  R.R. 4, Waterford, ON N0E 1Y0
DACE
  1937 High St., Longwood, FL 32750
Dalsem Greenhouses USA Inc.
  P.O. Box 54039, Jacksonville, FL 32245
Dramm International Inc.
  P.O. Box 528, Manitowoc, WI 54220
Florist Products, Inc.
  2242 North Palmer Dr., Schaumburg, IL 60173
Harnois Industries Inc.
  1044 Principale, Saint-Thomas-of-Joliette, PQ
  J0K 3L0

Maxijet
P.O. Box 1849, Dundee, FL 33838
Morton's Horticultural Products
P.O. Box 24, McMinnville, TN 37110
Penn State Seed Co.
Route 309, Box 390, Dallas, PA 18612
Sharp and Son
19219 62nd Ave. S., Kent, WA 98032
Simburg Co.
2646 Pacific Park Dr., Whittier, CA 90601
Vary Industries
P.O. Box 248, Lewiston, NY 14092
Vaughan's Seed Co.
5300 Katrine Ave., Downers Grove, IL 60515-4095
Westbrook Greenhouse Systems Ltd.
270 Hunter Rd., Grimsby, ON L3M 4G1

Sub-irrigation

Agro-Dynamics Inc., Eastern Div.
Building #3, Navy Yard, Brooklyn, NY 11205
Agro-Dynamics Inc., Western Div.
6492 South Heritage Place E., Englewood, CO 80111
Mantis Mfg. Co.
1458 County Line Rd., Huntingdon Valley, PA 19006
Roberts Irrigation Products, Inc.
700 Rancheros Dr., San Marcos, CA 92069

Traveling sprinkler

Andpro Ltd.
R.R. 4, Waterford, ON N0E 1Y0
Growing Systems, Inc.
2950 North Weil St., Milwaukee, WI 53212
Integrated Tech. Systems Inc.
P.O. Box 1406, Hightstown, NJ 08520
Morton's Horticultural Products
P.O. Box 24, McMinnville, TN 37110
Sharp and Son
19219 62nd Ave. S., Kent, WA 98032
Siebring Mfg. Co.
303 South Main St., Box 658, George, IA 51237
Vary Industries
P.O. Box 248, Lewiston, NY 14092
Waldo & Associates, Inc.
28214 Glenwood Rd., Perrysburg, OH 43551
Westbrook Greenhouse Systems Ltd.
270 Hunter Rd., Grimsby, ON L3M 4G1

LIGHTS

Fluorescent plant growth

Agro-Dynamics Inc., Eastern Div.
Building #3, Navy Yard, Brooklyn, NY 11205
Agro-Dynamics Inc., Western Div.
6492 South Heritage Place E., Englewood, CO 80111
CropKing Inc.
P.O. Box 310, Medina, OH 44258
GTE Sylvania Lighting
Sylvania Lighting Center, Danvers, MA 01923

P.L. Light Systems
P.O. Box 206, Grimsby, ON L3M 4G3
Rambridge Structure & Design Ltd.
1316 Centre St., NE
Calgary, Alberta T2E 2A7
Van Wingerden Greenhouse Co.
4078 Haywood Rd., Horse Shoe, NC 28742

High intensity discharge

Agro-Dynamics Inc., Eastern Div.
Building #3, Navy Yard, Brooklyn, NY 11205
Agro-Dynamics Inc., Western Div.
6492 South Heritage Place E., Englewood, CO 80111
BFG Supply Co.
P.O. Box 479, Burton, OH 44021
CropKing Inc.
P.O. Box 310, Medina, OH 44258
Energy Technics
P.O. Box 3424, York, PA 17402
GTE Sylvania Lighting
Sylvania Lighting Center, Danvers, MA 01923
Hydro-Gardens, Inc.
P.O. Box 9707, Colorado Springs, CO 80932
P.L. Light Systems
P.O. Box 206, Grimsby, ON L3M 4G3
Sharp and Son
19219 62nd Ave. S., Kent, WA 98032
Jack Van Klaveren Ltd. (JVK)
P.O. Box 910, St. Catharines, ON L2R 6Z4
Van Wingerden Greenhouse Co.
4078 Haywood Rd., Horse Shoe, NC 28742
Vary Industries
P.O. Box 248, Lewiston, NY 14092
Vaughan's Seed Co.
5300 Katrine Ave., Downers Grove, IL 60515-4095

High pressure sodium

Agro-Dynamics Inc., Eastern Div.
Building #3, Navy Yard, Brooklyn, NY 11205
Agro-Dynamics Inc., Western Div.
6492 South Heritage Place E., Englewood, CO 80111
BFG Supply Co.
P.O. Box 479, Burton, OH 44021
CropKing Inc.
P.O. Box 310, Medina, OH 44258
Dalsem Greenhouses USA Inc.
P.O. Box 54039, Jacksonville, FL 32245
Energy Technics
P.O. Box 3424, York, PA 17402
GTE Sylvania Lighting
Sylvania Lighting Center, Danvers, MA 01923
Harnois Industries Inc.
1044 Principale, Saint-Thomas-of-Joliette, PQ J0K 3L0
P.L. Light Systems
P.O. Box 206, Grimsby, ON L3M 4G3
Sharp and Son
19219 62nd Ave. S., Kent, WA 98032
Jack Van Klaveren Ltd. (JVK)
P.O. Box 910, St. Catharines, ON L2R 6Z4

Van Rijn Enterprises Ltd.
429 Dewitt Rd., Unit 6, Stoney Creek, ON L8E 4C3

Van Wingerden Greenhouse Co.
4078 Haywood Rd., Horse Shoe, NC 28742

Vary Industries
P.O. Box 248, Lewiston, NY 14092

Vaughan's Seed Co.
5300 Katrine Ave., Downers Grove, IL 60515-4095

Waldo & Associates, Inc.
28214 Glenwood Rd., Perrysburg, OH 43551

Westbrook Greenhouse Systems Ltd.
270 Hunter Rd., Grimsby, ON L3M 4G1

MISTING SYSTEMS AND EQUIPMENT

AAA Associates Inc.
1445 South 3rd St., Niles, MI 49120

Andpro Ltd.
R.R. 4, Waterford, ON N0E 1Y0

Atomizing Systems Inc.
1 Hollywood Ave., Hohokus, NJ 07423

BFG Supply Co.
P.O. Box 479, Burton, OH 44021

CASSCO
P.O. Box 3508, Montgomery, AL 36193

Dalsem Greenhouses USA Inc.
P.O. Box 54039, Jacksonville, FL 32245

Davis Engineering
8217 Corbin Ave., Canoga Park, CA 91306

Delta T Sales
3576 Empleo, Suite 2, San Luis Obispo, CA 93401

Florist Products, Inc.
2242 North Palmer Dr., Schaumburg, IL 60173

Growing Systems, Inc.
2950 North Weil St., Milwaukee, WI 53212

Harnois Industries Inc.
1044 Principale, Saint-Thomas-of-Joliette, PQ J0K 3L0

Hydro-Gardens, Inc.
P.O. Box 9707, Colorado Springs, CO 80932

Maxijet
P.O. Box 1849, Dundee, FL 33838

McCalif
2215 Ringwood Ave., San Jose, CA 95131

Netafim Irrigation, Inc.
104 South Central Ave., Valley Stream, NY 11580

Oglevee Computer Systems
151 Oglevee Lane, Connellsville, PA 15425

Park Seed Co., Wholesale Div.
Cokesbury Rd., Greenwood, SC 29647-0001

Sharp and Son
19219 62nd Ave. S., Kent, WA 98032

Siebring Mfg. Co.
303 South Main St., Box 658, George, IA 51237

Simburg Co.
2646 Pacific Park Dr., Whittier, CA 90601

Stuppy Inc.
1212 Clay St., North Kansas City, MO 64116

Vaughan's Seed Co.
5300 Katrine Ave., Downers Grove, IL 60515-4095

Waldo & Associates, Inc.
28214 Glenwood Rd., Perrysburg, OH 43551

Westbrook Greenhouse Systems Ltd.
270 Hunter Rd., Grimsby, ON L3M 4G1

NFT TROUGHS (PVC AND ALUMINUM)

Agro-Dynamics Inc., Eastern Div.
Building #3, Navy Yard, Brooklyn, NY 11205

Agro-Dynamics Inc., Western Div.
6492 South Heritage Place E., Englewood, CO 80111

CropKing Inc.
P.O. Box 310, Medina, OH 44258

Harnois Industries Inc.
1044 Principale, Saint-Thomas-of-Joliette, PQ J0K 3L0

Hydro-Gardens, Inc.
P.O. Box 9707, Colorado Springs, CO 80932

Westbrook Greenhouse Systems Ltd.
270 Hunter Rd., Grimsby, ON L3M 4G1

PEAT-LITE MIXES

American Horticultural Supply, Inc.
25603 West Ave. Stanford, Valencia, CA 91355

ASB Greenworld Inc.
82 Cherrywood Dr., Somerset, NJ 08873

Ball Seed Co.
250 Town Rd., West Chicago, IL 60185

BFG Supply Co.
P.O. Box 479, Burton, OH 44021

CASSCO
P.O. Box 3508, Montgomery, AL 36193

Conrad Fafard Inc.
P.O. Box 3190, Springfield, MA 01101

ENP
200 North Main St., Mendota, IL 61342

Fisons Western Corp.
120-1100 31st St., Downers Grove, IL 60515

Florist Products, Inc.
2242 North Palmer Dr., Schaumburg, IL 60173

E.C. Geiger, Inc.
P.O. Box 285, Harleysville, PA 19438

W.R. Grace & Co.
62 Whittemore Ave., Cambridge, MA 02140

The Heflin Co.
P.O. Box 1485, Rockville, MD 20850

Hydro-Gardens, Inc.
P.O. Box 9707, Colorado Springs, CO 80932

Jiffy Products of America, Inc.
P.O. Box 338, West Chicago, IL 60185

J-M Trading Corp.
241 Frontage Rd., Suite 31, Burr Ridge, IL 60521

McCalif
2215 Ringwood Ave., San Jose, CA 95131
J.M. McConkey and Co., Inc.
P.O. Box 309, Sumner, WA 98390
Michigan Peat Co.
P.O. Box 980129, Houston, TX 77098-0129
Midwest Growers Supply, Inc.
2613 Kaneville Court, Geneva, IL 60134
Morton's Horticultural Products
P.O. Box 24, McMinnville, TN 37110
Mr. Mulch Soils, Inc.
Rt. 2, Box 381, Effingham, SC 29541
Park Seed Co., Wholesale Div.
Cokesbury Rd., Greenwood, SC 29647-0001
Penn State Seed Co.
Route 309, Box 390, Dallas, PA 18612
Premier Brands, Inc.
145 Huguenot St., New Rochelle, NY 10801
Sharp and Son
19219 62nd Ave. S., Kent, WA 98032
Sogevex
326 Main St., Red Hill, PA 18076
Southern Importers, Inc.
P.O. Box 8579, Greensboro, NC 27419
Jack Van Klaveren Ltd. (JVK)
P.O. Box 910, St. Catharines, ON L2R 6Z4
Vaughan's Seed Co.
5300 Katrine Ave., Downers Grove, IL 60515-4095
Waldo & Associates, Inc.
28214 Glenwood Rd., Perrysburg, OH 43551
Wetsel Seed Co. Inc.
P.O. Box 791, Harrisonburg, VA 22801

PEAT MOSS

American Horticultural Supply, Inc.
25603 West Ave. Stanford, Valencia, CA 91355
ASB Greenworld Inc.
82 Cherrywood Dr., Somerset, NJ 08873
CASSCO
P.O. Box 3508, Montgomery, AL 36193
Conrad Fafard Inc.
P.O. Box 3190, Springfield, MA 01101
Fisons Western Corp.
120-1100 31st St., Downers Grove, IL 60515
Hydro-Gardens, Inc.
P.O. Box 9707, Colorado Springs, CO 80932
J-M Trading Corp.
241 Frontage Rd., Suite 31, Burr Ridge, IL 60521
Keeler-Glasgow
P.O. Box 234, Hartford, MI 49057
McCalif
2215 Ringwood Ave., San Jose, CA 95131
Michigan Peat Co.
P.O. Box 980129, Houston, TX 77098-0129
Midwest Growers Supply, Inc.
2613 Kaneville Court, Geneva, IL 60134
Morton's Horticultural Products
P.O. Box 24, McMinnville, TN 37110
Mr. Mulch Soils, Inc.
Rt. 2, Box 381, Effingham, SC 29541

Park Seed Co., Wholesale Div.
Cokesbury Rd., Greenwood, SC 29647-0001
Penn State Seed Co.
Route 309, Box 390, Dallas, PA 18612
Premier Brands, Inc.
145 Huguenot St., New Rochelle, NY 10801
Sharp and Son
19219 62nd Ave. S., Kent, WA 98032
Sogevex
326 Main St., Red Hill, PA 18076
Southern Importers, Inc.
P.O. Box 8579, Greensboro, NC 27419
Jack Van Klaveren Ltd. (JVK)
P.O. Box 910, St. Catharines, ON L2R 6Z4
Vaughan's Seed Co.
5300 Katrine Ave., Downers Grove, IL 60515-4095
Waldo & Associates, Inc.
28214 Glenwood Rd., Perrysburg, OH 43551
Wetsel Seed Co. Inc.
P.O. Box 791, Harrisonburg, VA 22801

PERLITE

American Horticultural Supply, Inc.
25603 West Ave. Stanford, Valencia, CA 91355
Ball Seed Co.
250 Town Rd., West Chicago, IL 60185
BFG Supply Co.
P.O. Box 479, Burton, OH 44021
CASSCO
P.O. Box 3508, Montgomery, AL 36193
ENP
200 North Main St., Mendota, IL 61342
E.C. Geiger, Inc.
P.O. Box 285, Harleysville, PA 19438
W.R. Grace & Co.
62 Whittemore Ave., Cambridge, MA 02140
J-M Trading Corp.
241 Frontage Rd., Suite 31, Burr Ridge, IL 60521
McCalif
2215 Ringwood Ave., San Jose, CA 95131
J.M. McConkey and Co., Inc.
P.O. Box 309, Sumner, WA 98390
Midwest Growers Supply, Inc.
2613 Kaneville Court, Geneva, IL 60134
Morton's Horticultural Products
P.O. Box 24, McMinnville, TN 37110
Penn State Seed Co.
Route 309, Box 390, Dallas, PA 18612
Premier Brands, Inc.
145 Huguenot St., New Rochelle, NY 10801
Sharp and Son
19219 62nd Ave. S., Kent, WA 98032
Silbrico Corp.
6300 River Rd., Hodgkins, IL 60525
Touchstone Corp.
Route 2, Box 158, Columbia, MO 65201
Jack Van Klaveren Ltd. (JVK)
P.O. Box 910, St. Catharines, ON L2R 6Z4
Vaughan's Seed Co.
5300 Katrine Ave., Downers Grove, IL 60515-4095

Vermiculite Ltd. Inc.
  1078 Rte. 46, Clifton, NJ 07013
Waldo & Associates, Inc.
  28214 Glenwood Rd., Perrysburg, OH 43551
Wetsel Seed Co. Inc.
  P.O. Box 791, Harrisonburg, VA 22801

POLY CONVECTION TUBING

American Horticultural Supply, Inc.
  25603 West Ave. Stanford, Valencia, CA 91355
BFG Supply Co.
  P.O. Box 479, Burton, OH 44021
CASSCO
  P.O. Box 3508, Montgomery, AL 36193
Caves Enterprises Inc.
  2464 Pumpkin Center Rd., Hammond, LA 70401
Conley's Greenhouse Mfg. and Sales
  4344 Mission Blvd., Pomona, CA 91766
CropKing Inc.
  P.O. Box 310, Medina, OH 44258
Florist Products, Inc.
  2242 North Palmer Dr., Schaumburg, IL 60173
E.C. Geiger, Inc.
  P.O. Box 285, Harleysville, PA 19438
Hydro-Gardens, Inc.
  P.O. Box 9707, Colorado Springs, CO 80932
Ken-Bar Inc.
  24 Gould St., Reading, MA 01867
McCalif
  2215 Ringwood Ave., San Jose, CA 95131
J.M. McConkey and Co., Inc.
  P.O. Box 309, Sumner, WA 98390
Midwest Growers Supply, Inc.
  2613 Kaneville Court, Geneva, IL 60134
Morton's Horticultural Products
  P.O. Box 24, McMinnville, TN 37110
Packer Greenhouses
  9308 CTH H, Cuba City, WI 53807
Sharp and Son
  19219 62nd Ave. S., Kent, WA 98032
X.S. Smith Inc.
  P.O. Drawer X, Red Bank, NJ 07701
Structures Unlimited
  2740 Leonard Reid Ave., Sarasota, FL 33580
Stuppy Inc.
  1212 Clay St., North Kansas City, MO 64116
Van Wingerden Greenhouse Co.
  4078 Haywood Rd., Horse Shoe, NC 28742
Vary Industries
  P.O. Box 248, Lewiston, NY 14092
Vent-Tech U.S.A.
  Drawer Q, Richmond, IL 60071
Waldo & Associates, Inc.
  28214 Glenwood Rd., Perrysburg, OH 43551
Westbrook Greenhouse Systems Ltd.
  270 Hunter Rd., Grimsby, ON L3M 4G1
Winandy Greenhouse Co., Inc.
  2211 Peacock Rd., Richmond, IN 47374

ROCKWOOL

Agro-Dynamics Inc., Eastern Div.
  Building #3, Navy Yard, Brooklyn, NY 11205
Agro-Dynamics Inc., Western Div.
  6492 South Heritage Place E., Englewood, CO 80111
CropKing Inc.
  P.O. Box 310, Medina, OH 44258
Fibrex, Inc.
  P.O. Box 1148, Aurora, IL 60507
Gro-Prod, Inc.
  1078 Rte. 46, Clifton, NJ 07013
Hydro-Gardens, Inc.
  P.O. Box 9707, Colorado Springs, CO 80932
McCalif
  2215 Ringwood Ave., San Jose, CA 95131
Sharp and Son
  19219 62nd Ave. S., Kent, WA 98032

SOILLESS MIXES

Agro-Dynamics Inc., Eastern Div.
  Building #3, Navy Yard, Brooklyn, NY 11205
Agro-Dynamics Inc., Western Div.
  6492 South Heritage Place E., Englewood, CO 80111
American Horticultural Supply, Inc.
  25603 West Ave. Stanford, Valencia, CA 91355
ASB Greenworld Inc.
  82 Cherrywood Dr., Somerset, NJ 08873
BFG Supply Co.
  P.O. Box 479, Burton, OH 44021
Conrad Fafard Inc.
  P.O. Box 3190, Springfield, MA 01101
ENP
  200 North Main St., Mendota, IL 61342
Fibrex, Inc.
  P.O. Box 1148, Aurora, IL 60507
Fisons Western Corp.
  120-1100 31st St., Downers Grove, IL 60515
Florist Products, Inc.
  2242 North Palmer Dr., Schaumburg, IL 60173
E.C. Geiger, Inc.
  P.O. Box 285, Harleysville, PA 19438
W.R. Grace & Co.
  62 Whittemore Ave., Cambridge, MA 02140
Gro-Prod, Inc.
  1078 Rte. 46, Clifton, NJ 07013
Grow-Tech, Inc. of California
  56 Peckham Rd., Watsonville, CA 95076
The Heflin Co.
  P.O. Box 1485, Rockville, MD 20850
Hydro-Gardens, Inc.
  P.O. Box 9707, Colorado Springs, CO 80932
J-M Trading Corp.
  241 Frontage Rd., Suite 31, Burr Ridge, IL 60521
Keeler-Glasgow
  P.O. Box 234, Hartford, MI 49057
McCalif
  2215 Ringwood Ave., San Jose, CA 95131

J.M. McConkey and Co., Inc.
P.O. Box 309, Sumner, WA 98390
Michigan Peat Co.
P.O. Box 980129, Houston, TX 77098-0129
Midwest Growers Supply, Inc.
2613 Kaneville Court, Geneva, IL 60134
Morton's Horticultural Products
P.O. Box 24, McMinnville, TN 37110
Park Seed Co., Wholesale Div.
Cokesbury Rd., Greenwood, SC 29647-0001
Penn State Seed Co.
Route 309, Box 390, Dallas, PA 18612
Premier Brands, Inc.
145 Huguenot St., New Rochelle, NY 10801
Sharp and Son
19219 62nd Ave. S., Kent, WA 98032
Sogevex
326 Main St., Red Hill, PA 18076
Southern Importers, Inc.
P.O. Box 8579, Greensboro, NC 27419
Jack Van Klaveren Ltd. (JVK)
P.O. Box 910, St. Catharines, ON L2R 6Z4
Vaughan's Seed Co.
5300 Katrine Ave., Downers Grove, IL 60515-4095
Wetsel Seed Co. Inc.
P.O. Box 791, Harrisonburg, VA 22801

SOIL METERS, pH

Agro-Dynamics Inc., Eastern Div.
Building #3, Navy Yard, Brooklyn, NY 11205
Agro-Dynamics Inc., Western Div.
6492 South Heritage Place E., Englewood, CO 80111
American Horticultural Supply, Inc.
25603 West Ave. Stanford, Valencia, CA 91355
Ball Seed Co.
250 Town Rd., West Chicago, IL 60185
BFG Supply Co.
P.O. Box 479, Burton, OH 44021
CropKing Inc.
P.O. Box 310, Medina, OH 44258
Engineered Systems and Designs
3 South Tatnall St., Wilmington, DE 19801
ENP
200 North Main St., Mendota, IL 61342
Florist Products, Inc.
2242 North Palmer Dr., Schaumburg, IL 60173
E.C. Geiger, Inc.
P.O. Box 285, Harleysville, PA 19438
Hydro-Gardens, Inc.
P.O. Box 9707, Colorado Springs, CO 80932
J-M Trading Corp.
241 Frontage Rd., Suite 31, Burr Ridge, IL 60521
McCalif
2215 Ringwood Ave., San Jose, CA 95131
J.M. McConkey and Co., Inc.
P.O. Box 309, Sumner, WA 98390
Midwest Growers Supply, Inc.
2613 Kaneville Court, Geneva, IL 60134

Myron L Co.
6231 C Yarrow Dr., Carlsbad, CA 92009
Park Seed Co., Wholesale Div.
Cokesbury Rd., Greenwood, SC 29647-0001
Sharp and Son
19219 62nd Ave. S., Kent, WA 98032
Jack Van Klaveren Ltd. (JVK)
P.O. Box 910, St. Catharines, ON L2R 6Z4

SEEDS, GREENHOUSE VEGETABLE

Ball Seed Co.
250 Town Rd., West Chicago, IL 60185
Bruinsma Seed Co.
P.O. Box 1463, High River, AB T0L 1B0
CropKing Inc.
P.O. Box 310, Medina, OH 44258
Ferry-Morse Seed Co.
P.O. Box 4938, Modesto, CA 95352
H.G. German Seeds
201 West Main St., Smethport, PA 16749
Harris Moran Seed Co.
3670 Buffalo Rd., Rochester, NY 14624
Harris Moran Seed Co.
1155 Harkins Rd., Salinas, CA 93901
Hydro-Gardens, Inc.
P.O. Box 9707, Colorado Springs, CO 80932
Northrup King Co.
P.O. Box 959, Minneapolis, MN 55440
Park Seed Co., Wholesale Div.
Cokesbury Rd., Greenwood, SC 29647-0001
Penn State Seed Co.
Route 309, Box 390, Dallas, PA 18612
Jack Van Klaveren Ltd. (JVK)
P.O. Box 910, St. Catharines, ON L2R 6Z4

European cucumber

Bruinsma Seed Co.
P.O. Box 1463, High River, AB T0L 1B0
H.G. German Seeds
201 West Main St., Smethport, PA 16749
Northrup King Co.
P.O. Box 959, Minneapolis, MN 55440
Stokes Seeds Inc.
P.O. Box 548, Buffalo, NY 14240

Hybrid lettuce

Bruinsma Seed Co.
P.O. Box 1463, High River, AB T0L 1B0
H.G. German Seeds
201 West Main St., Smethport, PA 16749
Stokes Seeds Inc.
P.O. Box 548, Buffalo, NY 14240

Spinach

H.G. German Seeds
201 West Main St., Smethport, PA 16749
Stokes Seeds Inc.
P.O. Box 548, Buffalo, NY 14240

Tomato

Bruinsma Seed Co.
P.O. Box 1463, High River, AB T0L 1B0
Ferry-Morse Seed Co.
P.O. Box 4938, Modesto, CA 95352
Stokes Seeds Inc.
P.O. Box 548, Buffalo, NY 14240

SPHAGNUM PEAT

ASB Greenworld Inc.
82 Cherrywood Dr., Somerset, NJ 08873
BFG Supply Co.
P.O. Box 479, Burton, OH 44021
Conrad Fafard Inc.
P.O. Box 3190, Springfield, MA 01101
ENP
200 North Main St., Mendota, IL 61342
Fisons Western Corp.
120-1100 31st St., Downers Grove, IL 60515
Hydro-Gardens, Inc.
P.O. Box 9707, Colorado Springs, CO 80932
J-M Trading Corp.
241 Frontage Rd., Suite 31, Burr Ridge, IL 60521
Keeler-Glasgow
P.O. Box 234, Hartford, MI 49057
McCalif
2215 Ringwood Ave., San Jose, CA 95131
Michigan Peat Co.
P.O. Box 980129, Houston, TX 77098-0129
Morton's Horticultural Products
P.O. Box 24, McMinnville, TN 37110
Mr. Mulch Soils, Inc.
Rt. 2, Box 381, Effingham, SC 29541
Penn State Seed Co.
Route 309, Box 390, Dallas, PA 18612
Premier Brands, Inc.
145 Huguenot St., New Rochelle, NY 10801
Sharp and Son
19219 62nd Ave. S., Kent, WA 98032
Sogevex
326 Main St., Red Hill, PA 18076
Southern Importers, Inc.
P.O. Box 8579, Greensboro, NC 27419
Touchstone Corp.
Route 2, Box 158, Columbia, MO 65201
Vaughan's Seed Co.
5300 Katrine Ave., Downers Grove, IL 60515-4095

Wetsel Seed Co. Inc.
P.O. Box 791, Harrisonburg, VA 22801

VERMICULITE

American Horticultural Supply, Inc.
25603 West Ave. Stanford, Valencia, CA 91355
Ball Seed Co.
250 Town Rd., West Chicago, IL 60185
BFG Supply Co.
P.O. Box 479, Burton, OH 44021
CASSCO
P.O. Box 3508, Montgomery, AL 36193
ENP
200 North Main St., Mendota, IL 61342
E.C. Geiger, Inc.
P.O. Box 285, Harleysville, PA 19438
W.R. Grace & Co.
62 Whittemore Ave., Cambridge, MA 02140
McCalif
2215 Ringwood Ave., San Jose, CA 95131
J.M. McConkey and Co., Inc.
P.O. Box 309, Sumner, WA 98390
Midwest Growers Supply, Inc.
2613 Kaneville Court, Geneva, IL 60134
Morton's Horticultural Products
P.O. Box 24, McMinnville, TN 37110
Mr. Mulch Soils, Inc.
Rt. 2, Box 381, Effingham, SC 29541
Penn State Seed Co.
Route 309, Box 390, Dallas, PA 18612
Premier Brands, Inc.
145 Huguenot St., New Rochelle, NY 10801
Sharp and Son
19219 62nd Ave. S., Kent, WA 98032
Touchstone Corp.
Route 2, Box 158, Columbia, MO 65201
Jack Van Klaveren Ltd. (JVK)
P.O. Box 910, St. Catharines, ON L2R 6Z4
Vaughan's Seed Co.
5300 Katrine Ave., Downers Grove, IL 60515-4095
Vermiculite Ltd. Inc.
1078 Rte. 46, Clifton, NJ 07013
Waldo & Associates, Inc.
28214 Gienwood Rd., Perrysburg, OH 43551
Wetsel Seed Co. Inc.
P.O. Box 791, Harrisonburg, VA 22801

Bibliography

Crops

1. Flowers

A. General Texts

Baker, K. F., ed. 1957. *The U. C. system for producing healthy container-grown plants.* Manual 23. Berkeley: Agric. Publications, Univ. of Calif.

Ball, George J. Inc. Staff. 1976. *The Ball red book.* Ed. Vic Ball. 13th ed. West Chicago: Geo. J. Ball.

Eaton, Jerome A. 1973. *Gardening under glass.* New York: MacMillan.

Furuta, Tokuji. 1970. *Nursery management handbook.* Berkeley: Agric. Publications, Univ. of Calif.

Hanan, J. J., W. D. Holley and K. L. Goldsberry. 1978. *Greenhouse management.*

Hartmann, H. T. and D. E. Kester. 1975. *Plant propagation principles and practices.* 3rd ed. Englewood Cliffs, N.J.: Prentice-Hall.

Laurie, A., D. C. Kiplinger, and K. S. Nelson. 1969. *Commercial flower forcing.* 7th ed. New York: McGraw-Hill.

Mastalerz, John W., 1977. *The greenhouse environment.* New York: John Wiley.

McDonald, E. 1971. *Handbook for greenhouse gardeners.* 3rd ed. Irvington-on-Hudson, N.Y.: Lord and Burnham, Div. of Burnham Corp.

Nelson, K. S. *Flower and plant production in the greenhouse.* Danville, Ill.: Interstate Printers and Publishers.

―――. 1973. *Greenhouse management for flower and plant production.* Danville, Ill.: Interstate Printers and Publishers.

―――. 1980. *Greenhouse management for flower and plant production.*

Nelson, Paul V. 1978. *Greenhouse operation and management.* Reston, Virginia: Reston Publ. Co.

B. Publications

Carnations

Cornell University. 1961. *A manual of the culture, insects and diseases, and economics of carnations.* Available from: Dr. R. W. Langhans, Dept. of Floriculture, Cornell Univ., Ithaca, NY 14850.

Holley, W. D. and R. Baker. 1963. *Carnation production.* Dubuque, Iowa: Wm. C. Brown Co.

Nelson, K. S. and C. C. Kiplinger. 1957. *Carnation crop control.* Wooster, Ohio: Ohio Agr. Exp. Sta. Res. Bul. 786.

Chrysanthemums

Langhans, R. W. 1964. *Chrysanthemums: A manual of the culture, disease and insects, and economics of chrysanthemums.* Ithaca, N.Y.: Dept. of Floriculture, New York State College of Agric., Cornell Univ.

Waters, W. E. and C. A. Conover. 1969. *Chrysanthemum production in Florida.* Ag. Exp. Sta. Bull. 730. Available from: Bulletin Room, G 044 McCarty Hall, Univ. of Florida, Gainesville, FL 32601.

437

Geraniums

Mastalerz, J. W. 1971. *Geraniums: A manual on the culture, diseases, insects, economics, taxonomy and breeding of geraniums.* Pennsylvania Flower Growers, 103 Tyson Building, Univ. Park, PA 16802.

Gladiolus

Jenkins, Aycock and Haasis. *Commercial production of gladiolus in North Carolina.* Ext. Cir. 448. Raleigh: N.C. Agric. Ext. Ser.

North American Gladiolus Council. 1972. *The world of the gladiolus.* The North American Gladiolus Council, Box A, Edgewood, MD 21040.

Lilies

Kiplinger, D. C. and R. W. Langhans. 1967. *Easter Lilies: The culture, diseases, insects and economics of Easter Lilies.* Available from: Dept. of Floriculture, Cornell Univ., Ithaca, NY 14850.

Orchids

Dekle, G. W. and L. C. Kuitert. 1968. *Orchid insects, related pests and control.* Div. of Plant Industry, Florida Dept. of Agric., P.O. Box 1269, Gainesville, FL 32601.

Noble, Mary. 1964. *You can grow orchids.* Available from: Miss Mary Noble, 3003 Riverside Ave., Jacksonville, FL 32205.

———. *You can grow cattleya orchids.* Available from: Miss Mary Noble, 3003 Riverside Ave., Jacksonville, FL 32205.

———. *You can grow phalaenopsis orchids.* Available from: Miss Mary Noble, 3003 Riverside Ave., Jacksonville, FL 32205.

Northern, Rebecca. 1970. *Home orchid growing.* 3rd ed. New York: Van Nostrand Reinhold.

Withner, C.L. 1959. *The orchids, a scientific survey.* New York: The Ronald Press.

Poinsettias

Ecke, Paul, Jr. and O. A. Matkin. 1976. *The poinsettia manual.* Available from: Paul Ecke Poinsettias, Encinitas, CA 92024.

Miller and D. C. Kiplinger. 1963. *Poinsettias.* Ext. Bull. SB15. Office of Extension Information, The Ohio State Univ., 2120 Fyffe Rd., Columbus, Ohio.

Roses

Mastalerz, J. W. and R. W. Langhans. 1969. *Roses: A manual on the culture, management, diseases, insects, economics and breeding of greenhouse roses.* Available from: John W. Mastalerz, 207 Tyson Bldg., Pennsylvania State Univ., Univ. Park, PA 16802.

Snapdragons

Langhans, R. W. 1962. *Snapdragons: A manual on the culture, insects, diseases and economics of snapdragons.* Available from: Robert W. Langhans, Dept. of Floriculture, Cornell Univ., Ithaca, NY 14850.

2. Foliage Plants

Bailey, L. H. 1942. *Standard cyclopedia of horticulture.* New York: Mac-Millan.
———. 1949. *Manual of cultivated plants.* New York: MacMillan.
Bailey, L. H. and E. Z. Bailey. 1976. *Hortus Third.* New York: MacMillan.
Chidamian, C. 1958. *The book of cacti and other succulents.* New York: Doubleday.
Conover, C. A., Sheehan, T. J. and D. B. McConnell. 1971. *Using Florida grown foliage plants.* Fla. Ag. Exp. Sta. Bull. 746.
Crockett, J. 1971. *Flowering house plants.* New York: Time-Life Books.
———. 1972. *Foliage house plants.* New York: Time-Life Books.
Graf, A. B. 1966. *Exotic plants illustrated.* Rutherford, N.J.: Roehrs Co.
———. 1970. *Exotic plant manual.* Rutherford, N.J.: Roehrs Co.
———. 1970. *Exotica 3.* Rutherford, N.J.: Roehrs Co.
Kramer, Jack. 1965. *Bromeliads, the colorful house plants.* Princeton: D. van Nostrand.
———. 1967. *Begonias – Indoors and out.* New York: E. P. Dutton.
Lamb, E. and B. Lamb. 1969. *The pocket encyclopedia of cacti and succulents in color.* New York: MacMillan.
McDonald, E. 1963. *The world book of house plants.* New York: World Publishing.
Menninger, E. A. 1970. *Flowering vines of the world.* New York: Hearthside Press.
Nicolaisen, A. 1970. *The pocket encyclopedia of indoor plants in color.* New York: MacMillan.
Noble, M. and J. L. Merkel. *Plants indoors.* Avail. from: Miss Mary Noble, 3003 Riverside Ave., Jacksonville, FL 32205.
Watkins, J. V. 1969. *Florida landscape plants, native and exotic.* Gainsville: Univ. of Florida Press.
Wilson, H. van Pelt. 1970. *African violet book.* New York: Hawthorn Books.

3. Vegetables
A. Cucumbers

Jensen, M. H. *European cucumber varieties for greenhouse production in the United States.* Research Bulletin, Environmental Research Laboratory. Tucson: Univ. of Arizona.
———. 1971. Take a look at seedless cukes. *Am. Veg. Grower* 19(11):20-22, 58, 60.
Johnson, H. Jr. 1975. *Greenhouse cucumber production.* Cooperative Extension Service, Leaflet 2775. Berkeley: Univ. of Calif.
Loughton, A. 1971. *Growing long seedless cucumbers in plant-raising greenhouses.* Ontario Dept. of Agric. and Food, Factsheet, AGDEX 292/20, Horticultural Research Institute, Vineland Station, Ontario, Canada.
Loughton, A. 1975. The "how to" of European cucumbers. *Am. Veg. Grower* 23(11): 16, 18, 58, 60.
Ministry of Agriculture, Fisheries and Food. 1969. *Manual of cucumber production.* Bulletin 205. London: Her Majesty's Stationery Office.

B. Lettuce:

Hafen, L. 1961. *Bibb and leaf lettuce in plastic greenhouses.* Bulletin HO-61-1 (mimeo). Lafayette, Ind: Purdue Univ. Agric. Ext. Service.

Wittwer, S. H., S. Honma and W. Robb. 1964. *Practices for increasing yields of greenhouse lettuce.* Research Rept. No. 22. East Lansing: Michigan State Univ. Agric. Exp. Station.

C. Tomatoes

Banadyga, A. A. 1962. *Growing tomatoes in plastic greenhouses.* Hort. Inform. Leaflet 105. Raleigh: Dept. of Hort., North Carolina State College of Agric.

Brooks, W. M. 1969. *Growing greenhouse tomatoes in Ohio.* Publ. SB-19. Columbus: Ohio State Univ. Cooperative Extension Service.

Corgan, J. N. et al. 1967. *Greenhouse tomatoes: Structures, production, marketing.* Circ. 387. University Park: Cooperative Ext. Service, New Mexico State Univ.

Cotter, D. J. and J. N. Corgan. 1974. *Media, varieties, and cropping systems for greenhouse tomatoes.* Bulletin 617. Las Cruces: Agric. Expt. Stn., New Mexico State Univ.

Courter, J. S. and M. H. Jensen. *Greenhouse tomato production.* Vegetable Crops, Hort. and Forestry Dept., New Brunswick, N.J.: Rutgers—The State Univ.

Dhillon, P. S. and P. J. Kirschling. 1971. *Profitability of tomato production under plastic greenhouses.* A. E. 335. New Brunswick, N. J.: College of Agric. and Environ. Science, Rutgers Univ.

Hafen, L. and M. O. Thomas. 1961. *Tomato production in plastic greenhouses.* Circ. 493. Lafayette, Ind.: Purdue Univ., Agric. Ext. Service.

Johnson, H. Jr. 1973. *Greenhouse vegetable varieties – tomato and cucumber.* Riverside: Univ. of Calif. Ext. Service.

———. 1973. *Cultural practices for tomatoes.* Riverside: Univ. of Calif. Ext. Service.

———. 1975. *Greenhouse tomato production.* Leaflet No. 2806. Berkeley: Univ. of Calif. Cooperative Ext. Service.

Johnson, H. Jr. and R. C. Rock. 1975. *Sample costs for producing greenhouse tomatoes and cucumbers in Calif.* Riverside: Univ. of Calif. Ext. Service.

Larsen, J. E. 1970. *Growing tomatoes in plastic greenhouses.* College Station: Texas Agri. Ext. Service, Texas A&M Univ.

———. *Guide for commercial production of greenhouse tomatoes.* (mimeo) College Station: Texas A&M Univ.

Larsen, J. E., C. D. Welch and C. Gray. *A new approach to fertilizing greenhouse tomatoes.* Dept. Inform. Rep. #16. College Station: Texas Agric. Ext. Service, Texas A&M Univ.

Liner, H. L. and A. A. Banadyga. 1974. *Cost and returns from producing greenhouse tomatoes in North Carolina.* Circ. 558. Raleigh: Agric. Ext. Service, North Carolina State Univ., State University Station.

New, L. and R. E. Roberts. 1973. *Automatic drip irrigation for greenhouse tomato production.* MP-1082. Lubbock: Texas A&M Univ. Res. and Ext. Center.

Schales, F. D. and P. H. Massey, Jr. 1968. *Tomato production in plastic greenhouses.* Publ. 154. Blacksburg: Cooperative Ext. Service, Virginia Polytechnic Institute.

Sheldrake, Raymond, Jr. and S. Dallyn. 1969. *Production of greenhouse tomatoes in ring culture or in trough culture.* Cornell Veg. Crops Mimeo No. 149. Ithaca, N.Y.: Cornell Univ.

———. *The ring culture method for production of greenhouse tomatoes.* Veg. Crops Mimeo No. 128. Ithaca, N.Y.: Cornell Univ.

Spivey, C. D. 1962. *Growing winter tomatoes under plastic.* Bull. 621. Athens: Univ. of Georgia Cooperative Ext. Service.

Stoner, A. K. 1971. *Commercial production of greenhouse tomatoes.* U.S.D.A. Agric. Handbook No. AH 382. Washington D.C.: Government Printing Office.

Sullivan, G. H. and J. L. Robertson. 1974. *Production, marketing and economic trends in the greenhouse tomato industry.* Res. Bull. No. 908. West Lafayette, Ind.: Purdue Univ. Agric. Expt. Station.

Taylor, G. A. and R. L. Flannery. 1970. *Growing greenhouse tomatoes in a peat-vermiculite media.* Veg. Crops Offset Series #33. New Brunswick, N.J.: College of Agric. and Environ. Science, Rutgers Univ.

Vincent, C. L. 1961. *Growing tomatoes in greenhouses.* Station Circular 276. Pullman: Washington State Univ. Agric. Expt. Station.

Ward, G. M. 1965. *Fertilizer schedule for greenhouse tomatoes in southwestern Ontario.* Publ. No. 1237. Harrow: Canada Dept. of Agric., Research Station.

Wittwer, S. H. 1960. *Practices for increasing the yields of greenhouse tomatoes.* Cir. 228. East Lansing: Michigan State Univ. Agric. Expt. Station.

Wittwer, S. H. and S. Honma. 1972. *Greenhouse tomatoes: Guidelines for successful production.* East Lansing: Michigan State Univ. Press.

———. 1979. *Greenhouse tomatoes, lettuce and cucumbers.*

D. General

Boodley, J. W. and R. Sheldrake, Jr. 1963. *Artificial soils for commercial plant growing.* Bull. 1104. Ithaca, N.Y.: Cornell Univ. Agric. Ext.

Courter, J. W. and J. S. Vandemark. 1964. *Growing vegetable transplants.* Circ. 884. Urbana: Univ. of Illinois Agric. Ext. Service.

Johnson, H. Jr. 1973. *Peat-Lite: An artificial soil mix.* Mimeo. Riverside: Univ. of Calif.

———. 1973. *Transplant growing.* Mimeo. Riverside: Univ. of Calif.

Schales, F. D. and P. H. Massey Jr. 1969. *Starting early plants.* Publ. 226. Blacksburg: Ext. Div., Virginia Polytechnic Institute.

Sheldrake, Raymond Jr. and J. W. Boodley. 1961. *Commercial production of vegetables and flower plants.* Bull. 1056. Ithaca, N.Y.: Cornell Univ. Agric. Ext. Service.

Tiessen, H., J. Wiebe and C. Fisher. 1976. *Greenhouse vegetable production in Ontario.* Publ. 526, Ontario Ministry of Agric. and Food.

Insect and Disease Control

Hussey, N. W. and N. Scopes. *Biological pest control, the glasshouse experience.* New York: Sterling.

Linn, M. B. and W. H. Luckmann. 1965. *Tomato diseases and insect pests, identification and control.* Circ. 912. Urbana: Univ. of Illinois Agric. Ext. Service.

McKenn, C. D. 1974. *Tomato diseases.* Canada Dept. of Agric. Publ. 1479, Agric. Canada, Ottawa, Ontario.

Neiswander, R. B. and R. P. Holdsworth. 1964. *The control of insects and mites on greenhouse vegetables.* Columbus: Ohio State Univ. Cooperative Ext. Service.

Ohio State University. 1974. *Insect control on greenhouse vegetables.* Bull. 517. Wooster: Cooperative Ext. Service, Ohio State Univ., Ohio Agric. Res. and Develop. Center.

Ontario Dept. of Agriculture and Food. 1975. *Greenhouse vegetable production recommendations.* Publ. 365. Ontario Dept. of Agric. and Food, Parliament Buildings, Toronto, Ontario, Canada.

Osborne, L. S. and L. E. Ehler. *Biological control of greenhouse whitefly in California greenhouses.* (Leaflet 21260). Cooperative Extension, U.S. Dept. of Agric., Univ. of Calif., Berkeley, California 94720.

Osborne, L. S. and L. E. Ehler. *Biological control of two-spotted spider mite.* (Leaflet 21271). Cooperative Extension, U.S. Dept. of Agric., Univ. of Calif., Berkeley, California 94720.

Partyka, R. E. and L. J. Alexander. 1973. *Greenhouse tomatoes – disease control.* Bull. SB-16. Columbus: Ohio State Univ. Cooperative Ext. Service.

Shurtleff, M. C., D. P. Taylor, J. W. Courter and R. Randell. 1969. *Soil disinfestation – methods and materials.* Circ. 893. Champaign: College of Agric., Univ. of Illinois at Urbana.

Steiner, M.Y. and D. P. Elliott. 1983. *Biological pest management for interior plantscapes.* 30 pp. The Publications Office, Min. of Agric. and Food, Victoria, B.C., Canada.

Greenhouse Construction and Environmental Control

Augsburger, N. D., H. R. Bohanon and J. L. Calhoun. 1970. *The greenhouse climate control handbook.* Acme Engineering and Manufacturing Co., Muskogee, OK 74401.

Allen, W. S. 1971. *Design and operation of greenhouse cooling system.* Bull. AENG 1. College Station: Agric. Engineering Dept., Texas A&M Univ.

Cotter, D. J. and J. N. Walker. 1960. *An automatic system for environmental control in plastic greenhouses.* Misc. 275-A. Lexington: Univ. of Kentucky.

Courter, J. W. 1965. *Plastic greenhouses.* Circ. 905. Urbana: Univ. of Illinois, Cooperative Ext. Service.

Duncan, G. A. and J. N. Walker. 1973. *Greenhouse coverings.* AEN-10. Lexington: Dept. of Agric. Eng., Univ. of Kentucky.

———. 1973. *Poly-tube heating-ventilation systems and equipment.* AEN-7 Lexington: Dept. of Agric. Eng., Univ. of Kentucky.

————. 1973. *Preservative treatment of greenhouse wood.* AEN-6. Lexington: Dept. of Agric. Engineering, Univ. of Kentucky.

————. 1975. *Hotbeds for transplant production.* ID-16. Lexington: Dept. of Agric. Eng., Univ. of Kentucky.

Gray, R. W., M. Marshall and P. H. Massey Jr. 1966. *V.P.I. Gothic greenhouse.* Circ. 760B. Blacksburg: Cooperative Ext. Service, Virginia Polytechnic Institute.

Parsons, R. A. 1975. *Small plastic greenhouses.* Leaflet 2387. Berkeley: Cooperative Ext. Service, Univ. of Calif.

Roberts, W. J. 1965. *Slant-leg rigid frame plastic covered greenhouses.* Paper No. NA65-204. New Brunswick, N.J.: Agric. Eng. Dept., Rutgers — The State Univ.

————. 1968. *Double covering a film greenhouse using air to separate the layers.* Paper presented at the 8th Annual Meeting, National Agric. Plastics Conference. New Brunswick, N.J.: Agric. Eng. Dept., Rutgers — The State Univ.

————. 1969. *Heating and ventilating greenhouses.* New Brunswick, N.J.: Rutgers Univ.

Sheldrake, R. Jr. 1971. *Air makes the difference.* Bull. G-101. Ithaca, N.Y.: Dept. of Veg. Crops, Cornell Univ.

Sheldrake, R. Jr. and R. M. Sayles. 1964. *The Cornell "Twenty-One" plastic greenhouse.* Bull. 3. Ithaca, N.Y.: Dept. of Veg. Crops, Cornell Univ.

————. 1973. *Plastic greenhouse manual – planning, construction, and operation.* Ithaca, N.Y.: Dept. of Veg. Crops, Cornell Univ.

Walker, J. N. and G. A. Duncan. 1973. *Air circulation in greenhouses.* AEN-18. Dept. of Agric. Eng., Univ. of Kentucky, Lexington, Kentucky 40506.

————. 1973. *Estimating greenhouse heating requirements and fuel costs.* AEN-8. Dept. of Agric. Eng., Univ. of Kentucky, Lexington, Kentucky 40506.

————. 1973. *Estimating greenhouse ventilation requirements.* AEN-9. Dept. of Agric. Eng., Univ. of Kentucky, Lexington, Kentucky 40506.

————. 1973. *Greenhouse benches.* AEN-13. Dept. of Agric. Eng., Univ. of Kentucky, Lexington, Kentucky 40506.

————. 1973. *Greenhouse humidity control.* AEN-19. Lexington: Dept. of Agric. Eng., Univ. of Kentucky.

————. 1973. *Greenhouse structures.* AEN-12. Dept. of Agric. Eng., Univ. of Kentucky, Lexington, Kentucky 40506.

————. 1973. *Rigid-frame greenhouse construction.* AEN-15. Dept. of Agric. Eng., Univ. of Kentucky, Lexington, Kentucky 40506.

————. 1974. *Cooling greenhouses.* AEN-28. Lexington: Dept. of Agric. Eng., Univ. of Kentucky.

————. 1974. *Greenhouse heating systems.* AEN-31. Lexington: Dept. of Agric. Eng., Univ. of Kentucky.

————. 1974. *Greenhouse location and orientation.* AEN-32. Lexington: Dept. of Agric. Eng., Univ of Kentucky.

————. 1974. *Greenhouse ventilation systems.* AEN-30. Lexington: Dept. of Agric. Eng., Univ. of Kentucky.

————. 1975. *An automatic sidewall system for greenhouse environmental control.* AEN-37. Lexington: Dept. of Agric. Eng., Univ. of Kentucky.

──────. 1975. *Mist propagation systems.* AEN-36. Lexington: Dept. of Agric. Eng., Univ. of Kentucky.

USDA. 1973. *Building hobby greenhouses.* USDA Agric. Inform. Bull. No. 357. Washington, D.C.: Government Printing Office.

──────. *Lights and plants.* USDA Misc. Publ. No. 879. Washington, D.C.: Government Printing Office.

Wiebe, J. 1963. *Plastic greenhouses.* Publ. 40. Ontario Dept. of Agric., Parliament Buildings, Toronto, Canada.

Hydroponics
A. General

Bentley, M. 1959. *Commercial hydroponics, facts and figures.* Johannesburg: Benton Books.

Berry, W. L. 1974. Hydroponics — principles and guidelines. *Lasca Leaves*, December 1974, pp. 123-28.

Biebel, J. P. 1960. *Hydroponics – the science of growing crops without soil.* Fla. Dept. Agr. Bull. 130.

Bridwell, R. 1974. *Hydroponic gardening.* Santa Barbara, Calif.: Woodbridge Press.

Butler, J. D. and N. F. Oebker. 1970. *Hydroponics as a hobby – growing plants without soil.* Leaflet 423. New Brunswick, N.J.: College of Agric. and Environ. Science, Rutgers Univ.

Douglas, J. S. 1973. *Beginner's guide to hydroponics.* New York: Drake.

──────. 1976. *Advanced guide to hydroponics.* London: Pelham Books.

Dutt, J. O. and E. L. Bergman. *Nutrient solution culture of plants.* University Park: The Pennsylvania State Univ. College of Agric., Ext. Service.

Ellis, C. and M. W. Swaney. 1947. *Soilless growth of plants.* New York: Reinhold.

Ellis, N. K., M. Jensen, J. Larsen and N. Oebker. 1974. *Nutriculture systems – growing plants without soil.* Bull. No. 44. West Lafayette, Ind.: Purdue Univ.

Gericke, W. F. 1940. *The complete guide to soilless gardening.* New York: Prentice-Hall.

Hanan, J. J. and W. D. Holley. 1970. Introduction of hydroponics in Colorado. Technique and implications in a semiarid region. *Agric. Meteor.* 7:29-38.

──────. 1974. *Hydroponics.* Fort Collins: Dept. of Hort., Colorado State Univ. Expt. Station.

Harris, D. 1974. *Hydroponics: The gardening without soil.* 4th ed. Capetown: Purnell.

Hewitt, E. J. 1966. *Sand and water culture methods in plant nutrition.* Bucks, England: Commonwealth Agric. Bur.

Hilyer, C. I. 1940. *Hydroponics.* London: Penguin Books.

Hoagland, D. R. and D. I. Arnon. 1950. *The water-culture method for growing plants without soil.* Circ. 347. Berkeley: Calif. Agric. Exp. Station, Univ. of Calif.

Hollis, H. F. 1964. *Profitable growing without soil.* London: The English Univ. Press.

Hudson, J. 1975. *Hydroponic greenhouse gardening.* Garden Grove, Calif.: National Graphics.

International Working Group on Soilless Culture (IWOSC). 1973. *Proceedings of the 3rd International Congress on Soilless Culture, Sassari.* The Secretariat of IWOSC, P.O. Box 52, Wageningen, The Netherlands.

————. 1977. *Proceedings of the 4th International Congress on Soilless Culture, Las Palmas.* The Secretariat of IWOSC, P.O. Box 52, Wageningen, The Netherlands.

International Society for Soilless Culture (ISOSC). 1984. *Proceedings of the 6th International Congress on Soilless Culture, Lunteren.* The Secretariat of ISOSC, P.O. Box 52, Wageningen, The Netherlands.

Kenyon, Stewart. 1979. *Hydroponics for the home gardener.* Toronto: Van Nostrand Reinhold Ltd.

Larsen, J. E. 1971. *Formulas for growing tomatoes by nutriculture methods (Hydroponics).* (Mimeo) College Station: Texas A&M Univ.

Laurie, A. 1940. *Soilless culture simplified.* New York: McGraw-Hill.

Marlin, D. R. 1940. *Growing plants without soil.* New York: Chemical Publ.

Maynard, D. N. and A. V. Baker. 1970. *Nutriculture – A guide to the soilless culture of plants.* Publ. No. 41. Amherst: Univ. of Massachusetts.

Mittleider, Jacob R. 1975. *More food from your Garden.* Santa Barbara, Calif.: Woodbridge Press.

Phillips, A. H. 1940. *Gardening without soil.* New York: Chemical Publ.

Robbins, S. R. 1958. Commercial experiences in soilless culture. *Int. Hort. Cong. Proc.* 15(1):112-17.

Robbins, W. R. 1946. Growing plants in sand cultures for experimental work. *Soil Sci.* 62:3-22.

Sangster, D. M. 1974. *Soilless culture of tomatoes with slow-release fertilizers.* Ont. Min. of Agric. and Food Factsheet, Agdex 291/518.

Saunby, T. 1974. *Soilless culture.* 3rd printing. Levittown, N.Y.: Transatlantic Arts.

Schales, J. E. *Soilless culture of greenhouse tomatoes.* (Mimeo) Blacksburg: Virginia Polytechnic Institute.

Schwarz, M. 1963. The use of brackish water in hydroponic systems. *Plant and Soil* 19(2):166–172.

Schwarz, M. 1968. *Guide to commercial hydroponics.* Jerusalem: Israel Univ. Press.

Shive, J. W. and W. R. Robbins. 1938. *Methods of growing plants in solution and sand cultures.* New Jersey Agr. Expt. Sta. Bull. 636.

Steiner, A. A. 1961. The future of soilless culture: its possibilities and restrictions under various conditions all over the world. *Int. Hort. Cong. Proc.* 15(1):112-17.

————. 1961. A universal method for preparing nutrient solutions of a certain desired composition. *Plant and Soil* 15(2):134-54.

————. 1968. Soilless culture. *Proc. of the 6th Colloquium of the Int. Potash Instit.*, Florence, pp. 324-41.

Stoughton, R. H. 1969. *Soilless cultivation and its application to commercial horticultural crop production.* Document No. Ml/95768. Admin. Unit, Distribution and Sales Section, Food and Agric. Organization of the United Nations, Via delle Terme de Caracalla, Rome 00100, Italy.

Stout, J. G. and M. E. Marvel. 1966. *Hydroponic culture of vegetable crops.* Gainsville: Circ. 192-A. Florida Agric. Ext. Service.

Ticquet, C. E. 1956. *Successful gardening without soil.* New York: N.Y. Publ.

Turner, W. I. and V. M. Henry. 1939. *Growing plants in nutrient solutions, or scientifically controlled growth.* New York: Wiley.

Wallace, T. 1961. *The diagnosis of mineral deficiencies in plants.* 3rd ed. New York: Chemical Publ.

Wells, D. A. and R. Soffe. 1962. A bench method for the automatic watering by capillary of plants grown in pots. *J. Agr. Engin. Res.* 7(1):42-46.

Withrow, R. B. and J. P. Biebel. 1938. *Nutrient solution methods of greenhouse crop production.* Circ. 232. Purdue Univ. Agric. Expt. Sta.

Withrow, R. B., J. B. Biebel and T. M. Eastwood. 1943. *Nutrient solution culture of greenhouse crops.* Circ. 277. Purdue Univ. Agric. Ext. Sta.

Withrow, R. B. and A. P. Withrow. 1948. *Nutriculture.* Circ. 328. Purdue Univ. Agric. Expt. Sta.

B. Gravel Culture

Barker, A. V. and R. Bradfield. 1963. An outdoor gravel culture set-up for plant growth studies. *Agron. Journal* 55(5):420-25.

Greene, R. E., J. S. Bullock and R. H. Maier. 1962. Plastic beds as a supporting medium in nutriculture systems. *Agron. Journal* 54(4):363.

Kiplinger, D. C. 1956. *Growing ornamental greenhouse crops in gravel culture.* Ohio Agric. Extp. Sta. Spec. Circ. 92.

Kiplinger, D. C. and A. Laurie. 1942. *Growing ornamental greenhouse crops in gravel culture.* Ohio Agric. Expt. Sta. Bull. 634.

Templeman, W. G. 1947. *The culture of plants in sand and in aggregate.* Imperial Chemical Industries.

C. Nutrient Film Technique (NFT)

"Blueprint" is needed for real viability. *The Grower,* Sept. 2, 1976.

Charlesworth, R. 1977. Soil and nutritional problems; NFT problems. *The Grower,* Jan. 13, 1977, p. 65.

Cooper, A. J. 1973. Rapid turn-round is possible with experimental nutrient film technique. *The Grower,* May 5, 1973.

———. 1974. Improved film technique speeds growth. *The Grower,* March 2, 1974.

———. 1974. Hardy nursery stock production in nutrient film. *The Grower,* May 4, 1974.

———. 1974. Soil? Who needs it? Part I. *Am. Veg. Grower* 22(8): 18, 20.

———. 1974. Soil? Who needs it? Part II. *Am. Veg. Grower* 22(9): 13, 64.

———. 1975. Rapid progress through 1974 with nutrient film trials. *The Grower,* Jan. 25, 1975.

———. 1975. Nutrient film technique — early fears about nutrition unfounded. *The Grower,* Aug. 23, 1975, pp. 326-27.

———. 1975. Crop production in recirculating nutrient solution. *Scientia Horticulturae* 3:251-58.

———. 1975. Comparing a nutrient film tomato crop with one grown in the soil. *The Grower,* Dec. 12, 1975.

———. 1977. Crop production with nutrient film technique. *Proc. of 4th International Congr. on Soilless Culture,* Las Palmas, Oct. 25-Nov. 1, 1976, pp. 121-36.

———. 1979. *The ABC of NFT.* London: Grower Books.

Douglas, J. Shalto. 1976. Hydroponic layflats. *World Crops,* March/April 1976, pp. 82-87.

Guernsey cautions on NFT crops. When you fail, you lose the lot, warns adviser. *The Grower*, Feb. 24, 1977, p. 397.

How NFT compares. *The Grower*, Oct. 7, 1976.

Lauder, K. 1976. GCRI hope to make low cost crops worth growing by NFT. *The Grower*, July 15, 1976.

———. 1977. Lettuce on concrete. Supplement to *The Grower*, Feb. 24, 1977, pp. 40-46.

Lovelidge, B. 1976. Kent grower to go the whole hog with NFT tomato crops. *The Grower*, Aug. 19, 1976.

———. 1976. Better working life is extra benefit, says Sussex grower. *The Grower*, Nov. 4, 1976.

Maher, M. J. 1977. The use of hydroponics for the production of greenhouse tomatoes in Ireland. *Proc. of 4th International Congr. on Soilless Culture*, Las Palmas, Oct. 25-Nov. 1, 1976, pp. 161-69.

Making NFT commercial. *World Crops*, May/June 1977, pp. 125-26.

Miliev, K. 1977. Nutrient film experiments in Bulgaria. *Proc. of 4th International Congr. on Soilless Culture*, Las Palmas, Oct. 25-Nov. 1, 1976, pp. 149-59.

New twist for hydroponics. *Am. Veg. Grower* 24(11):21-23.

NFT package deal should be on offer next year, say ICI. *The Grower*, Nov. 4, 1976.

Nutrient film technique: Cropping with the Hydrocanal commercial system. *World Crops*, September/October 1976, pp. 212-18.

Nutrient film techniques; PP's seven factors for success. *The Grower*, April 21, 1977, p. 907.

Research is lagging behind NFT's development — Cooper. *The Grower*, March 31, 1977, pp. 735-36.

Rheinberg, P. and D. S. Shaw. 1977. The microbial ecology of a nutrient film hydroponic system. *Proc. of 4th International Congr. on Soilless Culture*, Las Palmas, Oct. 25-Nov. 1, 1976, pp. 137-48.

Schippers, P. A. 1977. Construction and operation of the nutrient flow technique for growing plants. (Mimeo 187). Ithaca, N.Y.: Dept. of Veg. Crops, N.Y. State College of Agric., Cornell Univ.

———. 1977. *Annotated bibliography on nutrient film technique.* Veg. Crops Mimeo 186. Cornell Univ., Ithaca, N.Y.

———. 1977 *Construction and operation of the nutrient flow technique for growing plants.* Veg. Crops Mimeo 187. Cornell Univ., Ithaca, N.Y.

———. 1979. *The nutrient flow technique.* Veg. Crops Mimeo 212. Cornell Univ., Ithaca, N.Y.

———. 1979. *The nutrient flow technique — a versatile and efficient hydroponic growing method.* Proc. 1st Ann. Conf. of the Hydroponic Society of America, Brentwood, Calif. Oct. 20, 1979.

Sparkes, B. 1977. Variation on NFT theme. *The Grower*, April 21, 1977, pp. 905-6.

Verwer, F. L. J. A. W. 1977. Growing horticultural crops in rockwood and nutrient film. *Proc. of 4th International Congr. on Soilless Culture*, Las Palmas, Oct. 25-Nov. 1, 1976, pp. 107-19.

D. Sand Culture

Alafifi, M. A. 1977. The use of the sea coastal areas in Abu Dhabi as a growing medium for vegetables. *Proc. of 4th International Congr. on Soilless Culture*, Las Palmas, Oct. 25-Nov. 1, 1976, pp. 377-84.

Cain, J. C. 1963. Automatic sub-irrigation equipment for sand culture. *Amer. Soc. Hort. Sci. Proc.* 82:631-36.

Eaton, F. M. 1936. Automatically operated sand culture equipment. *Jour. Agric. Research* 53(6):433-43.

Fontes, M. R. 1973. Controlled-environment horticulture in the Arabian Desert at Abu Dhabi. *Hort. Science* 8(1): 13-16.

Hodges, C. N. and C. O. Hodge. 1971. An integrated system for providing power, water and food for desert coasts. *HortScience* 6(1):10-16.

Jensen, M. H. 1971. *The use of polyethylene barriers between soil and growing medium in greenhouse vegetable production.* Tucson: Environ. Research Laboratory, Univ. of Arizona.

Jensen, M. H. and M. A. Teran. 1971. Use of controlled environment for vegetable production in desert regions of the world. *HortScience* 6:33-36.

Jensen, M. H. and N. G. Hicks. 1973. Exciting future for sand culture. *Am. Veg. Grower*, Nov. 1973, pp. 33, 34, 72, 74.

University of Arizona. 1973. Annual Report, Environ. Res. Lab., Univ. of Arizona, Arid Lands Res. Center, Abu Dhabi. Tucson, Ariz.: Environ. Research Laboratory.

E. Other Cultures

Apel, A. and S. Levi. 1966. Growing vegetables on straw bales. *N.Z. Gardener* 22:577.

Boodley, J. W. and R. Sheldrake Jr. 1973. *Cornell peat-lite mixes for commercial plant growing.* Inform. Bull. 43. Ithaca, N.Y.: Cornell Univ.

Currie, R. 1961. A successful formula for quick-growing plants. *Commercial Grower*, Sept. 8, 1961, p. 460.

Edson, S. N. 1958. Florida sawdust for home hydroponics. *Florida State Hort. Soc. Proc.* 71:63-67.

Harris, D. A. 1977. A modified drop-culture method for the commercial production of tomatoes in vermiculite. *Proc. of 4th Int. Congr. on Soilless Culture*, Las Palmas, Oct. 25-Nov. 1, 1976, pp. 85-90.

Larsen, J. E. 1971. *A peat-vermiculite mix for growing transplants and vegetables in trough culture.* College Station: Texas A&M Univ.

Maas, E. F. and R. M. Adamson. 1971. *Soilless culture of commercial greenhouse tomatoes.* Publ. 1460. Information Div., Canada Dept. of Agric., Ottawa, Ontario, Canada.

Massantini, F. 1977. Floating hydroponics; a new method of soilless culture. *Proc. 4th Int. Congr. on Soilless Culture*, Las Palmas, Oct. 25-Nov. 1, 1976, pp. 91-98.

Namioka, H. 1977. Kuntan as a substrate for soilless culture. *Proc. 4th Int. Congr. on Soilless Culture*, Las Palmas, Oct. 25-Nov. 1, 1976, pp. 289-302.

Penningsfeld, F. 1977. Soilless culture, using in-exchange resins. *Proc. 4th Int. Congr. on Soilless Culture*, Las Palmas, Oct. 25-Nov. 1, 1976, pp. 247-59.

Ter Hoeven, Th. and L. A. J. Lamers. 1977. Hydroponic gardens in offices. *Proc. 4th Int. Congr. on Soilless Culture*, Las Palmas, Oct. 25-Nov. 1, 1976, pp. 57-60.

Taylor, G. A. and R. L. Flannery. 1970. *Growing greenhouse tomatoes in a peat-vermiculite media.* Veg. Crops Offsets Series #33. New Brunswick, N.J.: College of Agric. and Environ. Sci., Rutgers Univ.

Tropea, M. 1977. The controlled nutrition of plants II — A new system of "vertical hydroponics." *Proc. 4th Int. Congr. on Soilless Culture,* Las Palmas, Oct. 25-Nov. 1, 1976, pp. 75-83.

Vincenzoni, A. 1977. "Colonna de coltura," a contribution to the development of hydroponics. *Proc. 4th Int. Congr. on Soilless Culture,* Las Palmas, Oct. 25-Nov. 1, 1976, pp. 99-105.

Irrigation

Cornell University. 1965. *Fertilizer proportioners in floricultural crop production management programs.* Ithaca, N.Y.: Dept. of Floriculture and Ornamental Hort, Plt. Sc. Bldg, Cornell Univ.

Harrison, D. 1968. *Injection of liquid fertilizer materials into irrigation systems.* Circ. 276A. Gainsville: Univ. of Florida.

Harrison, D. S. and R. E. Choate. 1968. *Selection of pumps and power units for irrigation systems in Florida.* Circ. 330. Gainsville: Univ. of Florida.

Karmeli, D. and J. Keller. 1975. *Trickle irrigation design.* Glendora, Calif.: Rainbird Sprinkler Manuf. Corp.

Mason, E. B. B. and R. M. Adamson. 1973. *Trickle watering and liquid feeding system for greenhouse crops.* Publ. 1510. Inform. Div., Canada Dept. of Agric., Ottawa, Ontario, Canada.

New, L. and R. E. Roberts. 1973. *Automatic drip irrigation for greenhouse tomato production.* HORT 4-7. Lubbock: Texas A&M Univ. Research and Ext. Center.

Extension Service Newsletters

Alabama Flower Growers *Newsletter.* Ed. R. L. Shumack, Extension Floriculturist, Auburn Univ., Auburn, AL 36830.

Bulletin of the Colorado Flower Growers Association, Inc. Ed. W. D. Holley, Colorado State Univ., Fort Collins, CO 80521.

California Florists. Publ. Calif. State Florists Assn., 16 California St., San Francisco, CA 94111.

California Plant Pathology. Ed. A. H. McCain, Extension Plant Pathologist, Univ. of Calif., Davis, Calif.

Connecticut Greenhouse *Newsletter.* Cooperative Extension Service, College of Agric. and Natural Resources, Univ. of Connecticut, Storrs, CT 06268.

Florida Flower Grower. Ed. Extension Floriculture Specialist, Dept. of Hort., IFAS, Univ. of Florida, Gainsville, FL 32601.

Florida Foliage Grower. Ed. R. W. Henley, ARC-Apopka, Apopka, FL 32703.

Florogram. Ed. F. J. Campbell, Floriculture Suburban Expt. Sta., 240 Beaver St., Waltham, MA 02154.

Flower and Nursery Report for Commercial Growers. Calif. Cooperative Ext. Service, Dept. of Environ. Hort., Univ. of California, Davis, CA 95616.

Flower Marketing Information. Prep. A. Voight, Marketing Specialist, Cooperative Ext. Service, The Pennsylvania State Univ., University Park, PA 16802.

Flower Notes. Ed. W. Carlson, Horticulture Dept., Coop. Ext. Service, Michigan State Univ., East Lansing, Mich.

Focus on Floriculture. Cooperative Ext. Service, Hort. Dept., Purdue Univ., West Lafayette, IN 47907.

Gladiograms. Ed. R. O. Magie, Commercial Growers Div. of the North American Gladiolas Council, 5007 60th St. East, Bradenton, FL 33505.

Greenhouse Notes. Ed. J. K. Rathmell Jr., Floriculture and Nursery Agent, Pennsylvania Coop. Ext. Ser., 400 Markley St., Norristown, Pa.

Horticulture Digest. Ed. F. D. Rauch, Dept. of Hort., Univ. of Hawaii, Honolulu, HI 96822.

Illinois State Florists Association *Bulletin.* ISFA, 1011 W. Healey St., Champaign, IL 61820.

Kentucky Florist Assn. *Newsletter.* Ed. B. Tjia, Dept. of Horticulture, Univ. of Kentucky, Lexington, KY 40506.

Minnesota State Florists *Bulletin.* Ed. R. E. Widmer and H. F. Wilkins, Dept. of Hort. Science, Univ. of Minn., Institute of Agric., St. Paul, MN 55101.

New York State Flower Industries (NYSFI), Inc., *Bulletin.* Executive Sec/ Treas: F. M. Fitzgerald, 900 Jefferson Rd., Rochester, NY 14623.

North Carolina Flower Growers *Bulletin.* N.C. Commercial Flower Growers Assoc. Ed. J.W. Love, Dept. of Hort., N.C. State Univ., Raleigh, NC 27607.

Ohio Florists Association *Bulletin.* Ed. D. C. Kiplinger, 2001 Fyffe Court, Columbus, OH 43210.

Oklahoma Greenhouse Growers *Newsletter.* Hort. Dept., Oklahoma State Univ., Stillwater, OK 74075.

Ornamentals Northwest. Cooperative Ext. Services, Wash. State Univ., Univ. of Idaho, and Oregon State Univ. Ed. by J. L. Green, Ornamentals Specialists, Hort. Dept. O.S.U., Corvallis, OR 97331.

Pennsylvania Flower Growers. Ed. J. W. Mastalerz, Pa. Flower Growers Assn., 50 N. Main St., Chalfont, Pa.

The Green Mountain Grower. Ed. N. L. Pellet, Dept. of Plant and Soil Science, Univ. of Vermont, Burlington, VT 05401.

The Maryland Florist. Ed. C. B. Link, Dept. of Hort., Univ. of Maryland, College Park, MD 20742.

The Potting Bench. Ed. A. C. Botacchi, Area Floriculture and Nursery Agent, Pennsylvania Coop. Ext. Ser., P.O. Box 1608, Butler, PA 16001.

U.R.I. *Floriculture Notes.* Ed. R. J. Shaw, Dept. of Plant and Soil Science, Univ. of Rhode Island, Kingston, RI 02881.

Washington Floricultural Association *Washline.* WFA, 12602-145th St. E., Puyallup, WA 98371.

Professional Publications and Research Journals

Horticultural Research. Scottish Academic Press, 33 Montgomery St., Edinburgh.

Hort Science. Publ. bimonthly by the American Society for Horticultural Science, 914 Main St., St. Joseph, MI 49085.

Journal of the American Society for Horticultural Science. Publ. bimonthly for ASHS. American Society for Horticultural Science, 914 Main St., St. Joseph, MI 49085.

The Journal of Horticultural Science. Headley Bros. Ltd., The Invicta Press, Ashford, Kent, England.

Proceedings of the Florida State Horticultural Society. Dr. H. J. Reitz, Secretary, Florida State Hort. Soc., P.O. Box 552, Lake Alfred, FL 33850.

Trade Magazines and Periodicals

American Horticulturist. Publ. by the American Horticultural Society, 7931 East Boulevard Dr., Alexandria, VA 22308.

American Nurseryman. 310 South Michigan Ave., Chicago, IL 60604.

American Vegetable Grower. Publ. by Meister Publ. Co., Willoughby, OH 44094.

Canadian Florist, Greenhouse and Nursery. 287 Queen St. South, Streetsville, Ont., Canada.

Florist, An FTD Publication. FTDA, 900 West Lafayette, Detroit, MI 48226.

Flower News, the Florists' National Weekly Newspaper. 549 West Randolph St., Chicago, IL 60606.

Grower Talks. Geo. J. Ball, Inc., W. Chicago, Ill.

Greenhouse Grower. Publ. by Meister Publ. Co., Willoughby, OH 44094.

Horticulture. Horticulture Subscription Service, 125 Garden St., Marion, OH 43302.

Seed World. 434 S. Wabash Ave., Chicago, IL 60605.

The Florists Review. Florist's Publ. Co., 343 S. Dearborn St., Chicago, Ill.

The Grower. 49 Doughty St., London, WCIN 2BR, England.

The Packer. Circulation Manager, One Gateway Center, Kansas City, KS 66101. Publ. by Vance Publ. Co., 300 W. Adams St., Chicago, IL 60606.

Yoder Grower Circle News. Yoder Bros., Inc., Barberton, Ohio.

General Subject Index

452